Mathcad

User's Guide

with Reference Manual

Mathcad 2001 Professional

Mathcad

User's Guide
with Reference Manual
Mathcad 2001 Professional

US and Canada

MathSoft, Inc.
101 Main Street
Cambridge, MA 02142

Phone: 617-577-1017
Fax: 617-577-8829

http://www.mathsoft.com/

All other countries

MathSoft International
Knightway House
Park Street
Bagshot, Surrey
GUI19 5AQ
United Kingdom

Phone: +44 1276 452299
Fax: +44 1276 451224

MathSoft
Σ + √ − = × ∫ ÷ δ

Contents

Computational Features

How to Use the *User's Guide with Reference Manual*

The Mathcad 2001 *User's Guide with Reference Manual* is organized as follows:

♦ **The Basics**

This section contains a quick introduction to Mathcad's features and workspace, including resources available in the product and on the Internet for getting more out of Mathcad. Be sure to read this section first if you are a new Mathcad user.

♦ **Creating Mathcad Worksheets**

This section describes in more detail how to create and edit Mathcad worksheets. It leads you through editing and formatting equations, text, and graphics, as well as opening, editing, saving, and printing Mathcad worksheets and templates.

♦ **Computational Features**

This section describes how Mathcad interprets equations and explains Mathcad's computational features: units of measurement, complex numbers, matrices, built-in functions, solving equations, programming, and so on. This section also describes how to do symbolic calculations and how to use Mathcad's two- and three-dimensional plotting features.

♦ **Reference Manual**

This section lists and describes in detail all built-in functions, operators, and symbolic keywords, emphasizing their mathematical and statistical aspects.

As much as possible, the topics in this guide are described independently of each other. This means that once you are familiar with the basic workings of Mathcad, you can simply select a topic of interest and read about it.

Online Resources

The Mathcad Resource Center (choose **Resource Center** from the **Help** menu in Mathcad) provides step by step tutorials, examples, and application files that you can use directly in your own Mathcad worksheets. Mathcad QuickSheets are templates available in the Resource Center that provide live examples that you can manipulate.

The Author's Reference (choose **Author's Reference** from the **Help** menu in Mathcad) provides information about creating Electronic Books in Mathcad. An Electronic Book is a browsable set of hyperlinked Mathcad worksheets that has its own Table of Contents and index.

The Developer's Reference (choose **Developer's Reference** from the **Help** menu in Mathcad) provides information about developing customized Mathcad components, specialized OLE objects in a Mathcad worksheet that allow you to access functions from other applications and data from remote sources.

The Developer's Reference also documents Mathcad's Object Model, which allows you to access Mathcad's functionality from another application or an OLE container (see "Online Resources" on page 21 for more details).

Notations and Conventions

This guide uses the following notations and conventions:

Italics represent scalar variable names, function names, and error messages.

Bold Courier represents keys you should type.

Bold represents a menu command. It is also used to denote vector and matrix valued variables.

An arrow such as that in "**Graph⇒X-Y Plot**" indicates a submenu command.

Function keys and other special keys are enclosed in brackets. For example, [↑], [↓], [←], and [→] are the arrow keys on the keyboard. [**F1**], [**F2**], etc., are function keys; [**BkSp**] is the Backspace key for backspacing over characters; [**Del**] is the Delete key for deleting characters to the right; [**Ins**] is the Insert key for inserting characters to the left of the insertion point; [**Tab**] is the Tab key; and [**Space**] is the space bar.

[**Ctrl**], [**Shift**], and [**Alt**] are the Control, Shift, and Alt keys. When two keys are shown together, for example, [**Ctrl**]**V**, press and hold down the first key, and then press the second key.

The symbol [↵] and [**Enter**] refer to the same key.

Additionally, in the *Reference Manual* portion of this book, the following specific notation is used whenever possible:

- x and y represent real numbers.
- z and w represent either real or complex numbers.
- m, n, i, j, and k represent integers.
- S and any names beginning with S represent string expressions.
- **u**, **v**, and any names beginning with **v** represent vectors.
- **A** and **B** represent matrices or vectors.
- **M** and **N** represent square matrices.
- f represents a scalar-valued function.
- **F** represents a vector-valued function.
- *file* is a string variable that corresponds to a filename or path.
- X and Y represent variables or expressions of any type.

In this guide, when spaces are shown in an equation, you need not type the spaces. Mathcad automatically spaces equations correctly.

This guide describes a few product features that are available only in add-on packages for Mathcad. For example, some numerical solving features and functions are provided only in the *Solving and Optimization Extension Pack*.

Chapter 1
Welcome to Mathcad

- ◆ What Is Mathcad?
- ◆ Highlights of the Mathcad 2001 Release
- ◆ System Requirements
- ◆ Installation
- ◆ Contacting MathSoft

What Is Mathcad?

Mathcad is the industry standard technical calculation tool for professionals, educators, and college students worldwide. Mathcad is as versatile and powerful as a programming language, yet it's as easy to learn as a spreadsheet. Plus, it is fully wired to take advantage of the Internet and other applications you use every day.

Mathcad lets you type equations as you're used to seeing them, expanded fully on your screen. In a programming language, equations look something like this:

$$\texttt{x=(-B+SQRT(B**2-4*A*C))/(2*A)}$$

In a spreadsheet, equations go into cells looking something like this:

$$\texttt{+(B1+SQRT(B1*B1-4*A1*C1))/(2*A1)}$$

And that's assuming you can see them. Usually all you see is a number.

In Mathcad, the same equation looks the way you might see it on a blackboard or in a reference book. And there is no difficult syntax to learn; you simply point and click and your equations appear.

$$x := \frac{-b + \sqrt{b^2 - 4 \cdot a \cdot c}}{2 \cdot a}$$

But Mathcad equations do much more than look good. You can use them to solve just about any math problem you can think of, symbolically or numerically. You can place text anywhere around them to document your work. You can show how they look with Mathcad's two- and three-dimensional plots. You can even illustrate your work with graphics taken from another Windows application. Plus, Mathcad takes full advantage of Microsoft's OLE 2 object linking and embedding standard to work with other applications, supporting drag and drop and in-place activation as both client and server.

Mathcad comes with its own online reference system called the Resource Center. It gives you access to basic and advanced tutorials as well as many useful formulas, "quicksheet" recipes for using Mathcad functions, example worksheets, and reference materials at the click of a button.

Mathcad simplifies and streamlines documentation, critical to communicating and to meeting business and quality assurance standards. By combining equations, text, and graphics in a single worksheet, Mathcad makes it easy to keep track of the most complex calculations. By printing the worksheet exactly as it appears on the screen, Mathcad lets you make a permanent and accurate record of your work.

Highlights of the Mathcad 2001 Release

Faster Performance in the Computational Engine

Mathcad 2001 Professional contains an improved computational engine that delivers faster performance. Additionally, there are other document-specific options that let you further customize your mode of calculation, like strict matrix singularity checking and backward compatibility.

New Components and Add-ins

Several new components, add-ins, and functions help you interface with other applications, data sources, and file types within your Mathcad worksheet.

- **ODBC Read component**. Enable streamlined connectivity to your databases. The ODBC Read component allows you read and filter data from any ODBC compliant database that supports SQL.

- **Data Acquisition component**. Get data from or send data to supported measurement devices. The Data Acquisition component allows you to acquire and send single point and waveform analog data in "real time."

- **MathSoft Controls components**. Create custom forms controls such as buttons and text boxes. MathSoft Controls allow you to customize interactivity in your worksheets.

- **New component SDK**. Build custom Mathcad components quickly and easily using the new Mathcad Component Wizard for Visual Studio, which generates the shell of a component, including documentation and sample source code.

- **WAV file support**. Read, write, and get format information from pulse code modulated (PCM) Microsoft WAV file using Mathcad's new WAV funtions.

- **Customization and redistribution of components**. Customize and distribute Scriptable Object components built in Mathcad using the new Save as Component feature. Once you have customized a component to your liking, you can share or reuse your component quickly and easily

- **New Add-ins**. Extend Mathcad's feature set to other applications. Visit the Dowload area of the Mathcad web site at **http://www.mathcad.com/** to get a complete list of current Mathcad Add-ins and information about how to download them. Other new Add-ins will be posted from time to time.

Improved Web Integration

With Mathcad 2001 Professional, you can save your Mathcad worksheets as HTML documents with embedded Mathematical Markup Language (MathML) and display them in the browser. Using IBM's techexplorer™ Hypermedia Browser, a plug-in application that comes with Mathcad, you can display any Mathcad worksheet saved in HTML/MathML format. Then, you can read those documents back into Mathcad with no loss of computational information.

Authoring Tools

Create Electronic Books faster and more easily with new and improved authoring tools. These tools include:

* Region-to-region hyperlinking
* An automatic index creation mechanism that allows you to tag regions with keywords
* An HBK debugging tool that allows you to check your electronic book for errors

Other Features

Other new features include:

* **New capabilities in embedded pictures**. You can import images to your Mathcad worksheet from a variety of new formats including JPEG, GIF, and PCX. Once in your worksheet, these images can be manipulated using the new picture toolbar, which includes tools for zooming, cropping, and changing orientation, brightness, contrast, and grayscale mapping of a picture.
* **More new functions**. There are several new ease-of-use functions including coordinate system transforms to convert between coordinate systems and lookup functions to streamline searching for values in large matrices.

System Requirements

In order to install and run Mathcad 2001 Professional, the following are recommended or required:

* Pentium 133MHz or compatible CPU.
* CD-ROM drive.
* Windows 95 or higher or Windows NT 4.0 or higher.
* At least 32 megabytes of memory. 64 MB is recommended.
* For improved appearance and full functionality of online Help, installation of Internet Explorer 4.0, Service Pack 2, or higher is recommended. IE does not need to be your default browser.

Installation

To install Mathcad:

1. Insert the CD into your CD-ROM drive. The first time you do this, the CD will automatically start the installation program. If the installation program does not start automatically, you can start it by choosing Run from the Start menu and typing D:\SETUP (where "D:" is your CD-ROM drive). Click "OK."

2. Click the Mathcad icon on main installation page.

3. When prompted, enter your product serial number, which is located on the back of the CD envelope.

4. Follow the remaining on-screen instructions.

To install other items such as SmartSketch LE, VoloView, or online documentation, click the icon for the item you want to install on the install startup screen.

Contacting MathSoft

Technical Support

MathSoft provides free technical support for individual users of Mathcad. Please visit the Support area of the Mathcad web site at `http://www.mathcad.com/`.

If you reside outside the U.S. and Canada, please refer to the technical support card in your Mathcad package to find details for your local support center. You may also contact:

- Automated solution center and fax-back system: +44 1276 475350
- Fax: +44 1276 451224 (Attn: Tech Support)
- Email: *help@mathsoft.co.uk*

Contact MathSoft or your local distributor for information about technical support plans for site licenses.

Chapter 2
Getting Started with Mathcad

- ♦ The Mathcad Workspace
- ♦ Regions
- ♦ A Simple Calculation
- ♦ Definitions and Variables
- ♦ Entering Text
- ♦ Iterative Calculations
- ♦ Graphs
- ♦ Saving, Printing, and Exiting

The Mathcad Workspace

For information on system requirements and how to install Mathcad on your computer, refer to Chapter 1, "Welcome to Mathcad."

When you start Mathcad, you'll see a window like that shown in Figure 2-1. By default the worksheet area is white. To select a different color, choose **Color⇒Background** from the **Format** menu.

Figure 2-1: Mathcad with various toolbars displayed.

Each button in the **Math toolbar**, shown in Figure 2-1, opens another toolbar of operators or symbols. You can insert many operators, Greek letters, and plots by clicking the buttons found on these toolbars:

Button   Opens math toolbar...

Calculator—Common arithmetic operators.

Graph—Various two- and three-dimensional plot types and graph tools.

Matrix—Matrix and vector operators.

Evaluation—Equal signs for evaluation and definition.

Calculus—Derivatives, integrals, limits, and iterated sums and products.

Boolean—Comparative and logical operators for Boolean expression.

Programming—Programming constructs.

Greek—Greek letters.

Symbolic—Symbolic keywords.

The **Standard toolbar** is the strip of buttons shown just below the main menus in Figure 2-1:

Many menu commands can be accessed more quickly by clicking a button on the Standard toolbar.

The **Formatting toolbar** is shown immediately below the Standard toolbar in Figure 2-1. This contains scrolling lists and buttons used to specify font characteristics in equations and text.

Tip   To learn what a button on any toolbar does, let the mouse pointer rest on the button momentarily. You'll see a tooltip beside the pointer giving a brief description.

To conserve screen space, you can show or hide each toolbar individually by choosing the appropriate command from the **View** menu. You can also detach and drag a toolbar around your window. To do so, place the mouse pointer anywhere other than on a button or a text box. Then press and hold down the mouse button and drag. You'll find that the toolbars rearrange themselves appropriately depending on where you drag them. And Mathcad remembers where you left your toolbars the next time you open the application.

Tip   You can customize the Standard, Formatting, and Math toolbars. To add and remove buttons from one of these toolbars, right-click on the toolbar and choose **Customize** from the pop-up menu to bring up the Customize Toolbar dialog box.

The **worksheet ruler** is shown towards the top of the screen in Figure 2-1. To hide or show the ruler, choose **Ruler** from the **View** menu. To change the measurement system used in the ruler, right-click on the ruler, and choose **Inches**, **Centimeters**, **Points**, or **Picas** from the pop-up menu. For more information on using the ruler to format your worksheet, refer to "Using the worksheet ruler" on page 86.

Working with Windows

When you start Mathcad, you open up a window on a Mathcad *worksheet*. You can have as many worksheets open as your available system resources allow. This allows you to work on several worksheets at once by simply clicking the mouse in whichever document window you want to work in.

There are times when a Mathcad worksheet cannot be displayed in its entirety because the window is too small. To bring unseen portions of a worksheet into view, you can:

*   Make the window larger as you do in other Windows applications.

*   Choose **Zoom** from the **View** menu or click 100% on the Standard toolbar and choose a number smaller than 100%.

You can also use the scroll bars, mouse, and keystrokes to move around the Mathcad window, as you can in your other Windows applications. When you move the mouse pointer and click the mouse button, for example, the cursor jumps from wherever it was to wherever you clicked.

Tip   Mathcad supports the Microsoft IntelliMouse and compatible pointing devices. Turning the wheel scrolls the window one line vertically for each click of the wheel. When you press [**Shift**] and turn the wheel, the window scrolls horizontally.

See "Arrow and Movement Keys" on page 499 in the Appendices for keystrokes to move the cursor in the worksheet. If you are working with a longer worksheet, choose **Go to Page** from the **Edit** menu and enter the page number you want to go to in the dialog box. When you click "OK," Mathcad places the top of the page you specify at the top of the window.

Tip   Mathcad supports standard Windows keystrokes for operations such as file opening, [**Ctrl**]**O**, saving, [**Ctrl**]**S**, printing, [**Ctrl**]**P**, copying, [**Ctrl**]**C**, and pasting, [**Ctrl**]**V**. Choose **Preferences** from the **View** menu and check "Standard Windows shortcut keys" in the Keyboard Options section of the General tab to enable all Windows shortcuts. Remove the check to use shortcut keys supported in earlier versions of Mathcad.

Regions

Mathcad lets you enter equations, text, and plots anywhere in the worksheet. Each equation, piece of text, or other element is a *region*. Mathcad creates an invisible rectangle to hold each region. A Mathcad worksheet is a collection of such regions. To start a new region in Mathcad:

1. Click anywhere in a blank area of the worksheet. You see a small crosshair. Anything you type appears at the crosshair.

2. If the region you want to create is a math region, just start typing anywhere you put the crosshair. By default Mathcad understands what you type as mathematics. See "A Simple Calculation" on page 12 for an example.

3. To create a text region, first choose **Text Region** from the **Insert** menu and then start typing. See "Entering Text" on page 14 for an example.

In addition to equations and text, Mathcad supports a variety of plot regions. See "Graphs" on page 18 for an example of inserting a two-dimensional plot.

Tip   Mathcad displays a box around any region you are currently working in. When you click outside the region, the surrounding box disappears. To put a permanent box around a region, click on it with the right mouse button and choose **Properties** from the pop-up menu. Click on the Display tab and click the box next to "Show Border."

Selecting Regions

To select a single region, simply click it. Mathcad shows a rectangle around the region.

To select multiple regions:

1. Press and hold down the left mouse button to anchor one corner of the selection rectangle.

2. Without letting go of the mouse button, move the mouse to enclose everything you want to select inside the selection rectangle.

3. Release the mouse button. Mathcad shows dashed rectangles around regions you have selected.

Tip   You can also select multiple regions anywhere in the worksheet by holding down the [**Ctrl**] key while clicking. If you click one region and [**Shift**]-click another, you select both regions and all regions in between.

Moving and Copying Regions

Once the regions are selected, you can move or copy them.

Moving regions

You can move regions by dragging with the mouse or by using **Cut** and **Paste**.

To drag regions with the mouse:

1. Select the regions as described in the previous section.

2. Place the pointer on the border of any selected region. The pointer turns into a small hand.

3. Press and hold down the mouse button.

4. Without letting go of the button, move the mouse. The rectangular outlines of the selected regions follow the mouse pointer.

At this point, you can either drag the selected regions to another spot in the worksheet, or you can drag them to another worksheet. To move the selected regions into another worksheet, press and hold down the mouse button, drag the rectangular outlines into the destination worksheet, and release the mouse button.

To move the selected regions by using **Cut** and **Paste**:

1. Select the regions as described in the previous section.

2. Choose **Cut** from the **Edit** menu (keystroke: [**Ctrl**] **X**), or click ![scissors icon] on the Standard toolbar. This deletes the selected regions and puts them on the Clipboard.

3. Click the mouse wherever you want the regions moved to. Make sure you've clicked in an empty space. You can click either someplace else in your worksheet or in a different worksheet altogether. You should see the crosshair.

4. Choose **Paste** from the **Edit** menu (keystroke: [**Ctrl**] **V**), or click ![paste icon] on the Standard toolbar.

Note You can move one region on top of another. To move a particular region to the top or bottom, right-click on it and choose **Bring to Front** or **Send to Back** from the pop-up menu.

Copying Regions

To copy regions by using the **Copy** and **Paste** commands:

1. Select the regions as described in "Selecting Regions" on page 10.

2. Choose **Copy** from the **Edit** menu (keystroke: [**Ctrl**] **C**), or click ![copy icon] on the Standard toolbar to copy the selected regions to the Clipboard.

3. Click the mouse wherever you want to place a copy of the regions. You can click either in your worksheet or in a different worksheet altogether. Make sure you've clicked in an empty space and that you see the crosshair.

4. Choose **Paste** from the **Edit** menu (keystroke: [**Ctrl**] **V**), or click ![paste icon] on the Standard toolbar.

Tip If the regions you want to copy are coming from a locked area (see "Safeguarding an Area of the Worksheet" on page 91) or an Electronic Book, you can copy them simply by dragging them with the mouse into your worksheet.

Deleting Regions

To delete one or more regions:

1. Select the regions.

2. Choose **Cut** from the **Edit** menu (keystroke: **[Ctrl] X**), or click ✂ on the Standard toolbar.

Choosing **Cut** removes the selected regions from your worksheet and puts them on the Clipboard. If you don't want to disturb the contents of your Clipboard, or if you don't want to save the selected regions, choose **Delete** from the **Edit** menu (Keystroke: **[Ctrl] D**) instead.

A Simple Calculation

Although Mathcad can perform sophisticated mathematics, you can just as easily use it as a simple calculator. To try your first calculation, follow these steps:

1. Click anywhere in the worksheet. You see a small crosshair. Anything you type appears at the crosshair.

2. Type **15-8/104.5=**. When you type the equal sign or click **=** on the Evaluation toolbar, Mathcad computes and shows the result.

$$15 - \frac{8}{104.5} = 14.923$$

This calculation demonstrates the way Mathcad works:

- Mathcad shows equations as you might see them in a book or on a blackboard. Mathcad sizes fraction bars, brackets, and other symbols to display equations the same way you would write them on paper.

- Mathcad understands which operation to perform first. In this example, Mathcad knew to perform the division before the subtraction and displayed the equation accordingly.

- As soon as you type the equal sign or click **=** on the Evaluation toolbar, Mathcad returns the result. Unless you specify otherwise, Mathcad processes each equation as you enter it. See the section "Controlling Calculation" in Chapter 8 to learn how to change this.

- As you type each operator (in this case, – and **/**), Mathcad shows a small rectangle called a *placeholder*. Placeholders hold spaces open for numbers or expressions not yet typed. As soon as you type a number, it replaces the placeholder in the expression. The placeholder that appears at the end of the expression is used for unit conversions. Its use is discussed in "Displaying Units of Results" on page 118.

Once an equation is on the screen, you can edit it by clicking in the appropriate spot and typing new letters, numbers, or operators. You can type many operators and Greek letters by clicking in the Math toolbars introduced in "The Mathcad Workspace" on page 7. Chapter 4, "Working with Math," details how to edit Mathcad equations.

Definitions and Variables

Mathcad's power and versatility quickly become apparent once you begin using *variables* and *functions*. By defining variables and functions, you can link equations together and use intermediate results in further calculations.

The following examples show how to define and use several variables.

Defining Variables

To define a variable t, follow these steps:

1. Type **t** followed by a colon **:** or click [:=] on the Calculator toolbar. Mathcad shows the colon as the definition symbol **:=**.

$$t := \blacksquare$$

2. Type **10** in the empty placeholder to complete the definition for t.

$$t := 10$$

If you make a mistake, click on the equation and press [**Space**] until the entire expression is between the two editing lines, just as you did earlier. Then delete it by choosing **Cut** from the **Edit** menu (keystroke: [**Ctrl**] **X**). See Chapter 4, "Working with Math," for other ways to correct or edit an expression.

These steps show the form for typing any definition:

1. Type the variable name to be defined.

2. Type the colon key **:** or click [:=] on the Calculator toolbar to insert the definition symbol. The examples that follow encourage you to use the colon key, since that is usually faster.

3. Type the value to be assigned to the variable. The value can be a single number, as in the example shown here, or a more complicated combination of numbers and previously defined variables.

Mathcad worksheets read from top to bottom and left to right. Once you have defined a variable like t, you can compute with it anywhere *below and to the right* of the equation that defines it.

Now enter another definition.

1. Press [↵]. This moves the crosshair below the first equation.

2. To define *acc* as –9.8, type: **acc:-9.8**. Then press [↵] again. Mathcad shows the crosshair cursor below the last equation you entered.

$$t := 10$$

$$acc := -9.8$$

$+$

Calculating Results

Now that the variables *acc* and *t* are defined, you can use them in other expressions.

1. Click the mouse a few lines below the two definitions.

2. Type **acc/2[Space]*t^2**. The caret symbol (^) represents raising to a power, the asterisk (*) is multiplication, and the slash (/) represents division.

3. Press the equal sign (=).

$$t := 10$$

$$acc := -9.8$$

$$\frac{acc}{2} \cdot t^2 = -490 \quad \blacksquare$$

This equation calculates the distance traveled by a falling body in time *t* with acceleration *acc*. When you enter the equation and press the equal sign (=), or click

= on the Evaluation toolbar, Mathcad returns the result.

Mathcad updates results as soon as you make changes. For example, if you click on the 10 on your screen and change it to some other number, Mathcad changes the result as soon as you press [↵] or click outside of the equation.

Entering Text

Mathcad handles text as easily as it does equations, so you can make notes about the calculations you are doing.

Here's how to enter some text:

1. Click in the blank space to the right of the equations you entered. You'll see a small crosshair.

$+$

2. Choose **Text Region** from the **Insert** menu, or press **"** (the double-quote key), to tell Mathcad that you're about to enter some text. Mathcad changes the crosshair into a vertical line called the insertion point. Characters you type appear behind this line. A box surrounds the insertion point, indicating you are now in a text region. This box is called a text box. It grows as you enter text.

3. Type **Equations of motion**. Mathcad shows the text in the worksheet, next to the equations.

> | Equations of motion‖ |

Note If **Ruler** under the **View** menu is checked when the cursor is inside a text region, the ruler resizes to indicate the size of your text region. For more information on using the ruler to set tab stops and indents in a text region, see "Changing Paragraph Properties" on page 61.

Tip If you click in blank space in the worksheet and start typing, which creates a math region, Mathcad automatically converts the math region to a text region when you press [**Space**].

To enter a second line of text, just press [↵] and continue typing:

1. Press [↵].

2. Then type **for falling body under gravity.**

3. Click in a different spot in the worksheet or press [**Ctrl**][**Shift**][↵] to move out of the text region. The text box disappears and the cursor appears as a small crosshair.

> | Equations of motion |
> | for falling body under gravity. |
> | + |

Note Use [**Ctrl**][**Shift**][↵] to move out of the text region to a blank space in your worksheet. If you press [↵], Mathcad inserts a line break in the *current* text region instead.

You can set the width of a text region and change the font, size, and style of the text in it. For more information, see Chapter 5, "Working with Text."

Iterative Calculations

Mathcad can do repeated or iterative calculations as easily as individual calculations. Mathcad uses a special variable called a *range variable* to perform iteration.

Range variables take on a range of values, such as all the integers from 0 to 10. Whenever a range variable appears in a Mathcad equation, Mathcad calculates the equation not just once, but once for each value of the range variable.

This section describes how to use range variables to do iterative calculations.

Creating a Range Variable

To compute equations for a range of values, first create a range variable. In the problem shown in "Calculating Results" on page 14, for example, you can compute results for a range of values of t from 10 to 20 in steps of 1.

To do so, follow these steps:

1. First, change t into a range variable by editing its definition. Click on the **10** in the equation **t:=10**. The insertion point should be next to the 10 as shown on the right.

$$t := 10|$$

2. Type **, 11**. This tells Mathcad that the next number in the range will be 11.

$$t := 10,\ 11|$$

3. Type **;** for the range variable operator, or click [m..n] on the Calculator toolbar, and then type the last number, **20**. This tells Mathcad that the last number in the range will be 20. Mathcad shows the range variable operator as a pair of dots.

$$t := 10,\ 11\ ..\ 20|$$

4. Now click outside the equation for t. Mathcad begins to compute with t defined as a range variable. Since t now takes on eleven different values, there must also be eleven different answers. These are displayed in an *output table* as shown at right. You may have to resize your window or scroll down to see the whole table.

$$\frac{acc}{2} \cdot t^2 =$$

-490
-592.9
-705.6
-828.1
-960.4
$-1.103 \cdot 10^3$
$-1.254 \cdot 10^3$
$-1.416 \cdot 10^3$
$-1.588 \cdot 10^3$
$-1.769 \cdot 10^3$
$-1.96 \cdot 10^3$

Defining a Function

You can gain additional flexibility by defining functions. Here's how to add a function definition to your worksheet:

1. First delete the table. To do so, drag-select the entire region until you've enclosed everything between the two editing lines. Then choose **Cut** from the **Edit** menu (keystroke: **[Ctrl] X**) or click [✂] on the Standard toolbar.

2. Now define the function $d(t)$ by typing **d(t):**

$$d(t) := \blacksquare|$$

3. Complete the definition by typing this expression:
   1600+acc/2[Space]*t^2[↵]

$$d(t) := 1600 + \frac{acc}{2} \cdot t^2$$

The definition you just typed defines a function. The function name is d, and the argument of the function is t. You can use this function to evaluate the above expression for different values of t. To do so, simply replace t with an appropriate number. For example:

1. To evaluate the function at a particular value, such as 3.5, type **d(3.5)=**. Mathcad returns the correct value as shown at right.

$$d(3.5) = 1.54 \times 10^3$$

2. To evaluate the function once for each value of the range variable *t* you defined earlier, click below the other equations and type **d(t)=**. As before, Mathcad shows a table of values, as shown at right.

$$d(t) =$$

$1.11 \cdot 10^3$
$1.007 \cdot 10^3$
894.4
771.9
639.6
497.5
345.6
183.9
12.4
-168.9
-360

Formatting a Result

You can set the display format for any number Mathcad calculates and displays. This means changing the number of decimal places shown, changing exponential notation to ordinary decimal notation, and so on.

For example, in the example above, the first two values, $1.11 \cdot 10^3$ and $1.007 \cdot 10^3$, are in exponential (powers of 10) notation. Here's how to change the table produced above so that none of the numbers in it are displayed in exponential notation:

1. Click anywhere on the table with the mouse.

2. Choose **Result** from the **Format** menu. You see the Result Format dialog box. This box contains settings that affect how results are displayed, including the number of decimal places, the use of exponential notation, the radix, and so on.

3. The default format scheme is General which has Exponential Threshold set to 3. This means that only numbers greater than or equal to 10^3 are displayed in exponential notation. Click the arrows to the right of the 3 to increase the Exponential Threshold to 6.

$$d(t) =$$

1110
1007.1
894.4
771.9
639.6
497.5
345.6
183.9
12.4
-168.9
-360

4. Click "OK." The table changes to reflect the new result format.

For more information on formatting results, refer to "Formatting Results" on page 115.

Note When you format a result, only the display of the result is affected. Mathcad maintains full precision internally (up to 15 digits).

Graphs

Mathcad can show both two-dimensional Cartesian and polar graphs, contour plots, surface plots, and a variety of other three-dimensional graphs. These are all examples of *graph regions*.

This section describes how to create a simple two-dimensional graph showing the points calculated in the previous section.

Creating a Graph

To create an X-Y plot in Mathcad, click in blank space where you want the graph to appear and choose **Graph**⇒**X-Y Plot** from the **Insert** menu or click on the Graph toolbar. An empty graph appears with placeholders on the *x*-axis and *y*-axis for the expressions to be graphed. X-Y and polar plots are ordinarily driven by range variables you define: Mathcad graphs one point for each value of the range variable used in the graph. In most cases you enter the range variable, or an expression depending on the range variable, on the *x*-axis of the plot. For example, here's how to create a plot of the function *d*(*t*) defined in the previous section:

1. Position the crosshair in a blank spot and type **d(t)**. Make sure the editing lines remain displayed on the expression.

2. Now choose **Graph**⇒**X-Y Plot** from the **Insert** menu, or click on the Graph toolbar. Mathcad displays the frame of the graph.

3. Type **t** in the bottom middle placeholder on the graph.

4. Click anywhere outside the graph. Mathcad calculates and graphs the points. A sample line appears under the "*d*(*t*)." This helps you identify the different curves when you plot more than one function. Unless you specify otherwise, Mathcad draws straight lines between the points and fills in the axis limits.

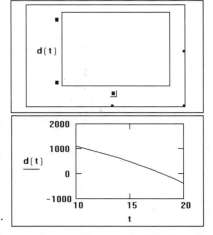

For detailed information on creating and formatting graphs, see Chapter 12, "2D Plots." In particular, refer to Chapter 12 for information about the *QuickPlot* feature in Mathcad which lets you plot expressions even when you don't specify the range variable directly in the plot.

Resizing a graph

To resize a plot, click in the plot to select it. Then move the cursor to a handle along the edge of the plot until the cursor changes to a double-headed arrow. Hold the mouse button down and drag the mouse in the direction that you want the plot's dimension to change.

Formatting a Graph

When you first create a graph it has *default* characteristics: numbered linear axes, no grid lines, and points connected with solid lines. You can change these characteristics by *formatting* the graph. To format the graph created previously:

5. Click on the graph and choose **Graph⇒X-Y Plot** from the **Format** menu, or double-click the graph to bring up the formatting dialog box. This box contains settings for all available plot format options. To learn more about these settings, see Chapter 12, "2D Plots."

6. Click the Traces tab.

7. Click "trace 1" in the scrolling list under "Legend Label." Mathcad places the current settings for trace 1 in the boxes under the corresponding columns of the scrolling list.

8. Click the arrow under the "Type" column to see a drop-down list of trace types. Select "bar" from this drop-down list.

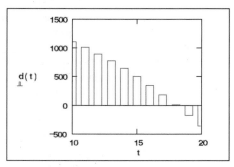

9. Click "OK" to show the result of changing the setting. Mathcad shows the graph as a bar chart instead of connecting the points with lines. Note that the sample line under the *d(t)* now has a bar on top of it.

10. Click outside the graph to deselect it.

Saving, Printing, and Exiting

Once you've created a worksheet, you will probably want to save or print it.

Saving a Worksheet

To save a worksheet:

1. Choose **Save** from the **File** menu (keystroke: **[Ctrl] S**) or click 📁 on the Standard toolbar. If the file has never been saved before, the **Save As** dialog box appears. Otherwise, Mathcad saves the file with no further prompting.

2. Type the name of the file in the text box provided. To save to another folder, locate the folder using the Save As dialog box.

By default Mathcad saves the file in Mathcad (MCD) format, but you have the option of saving in other formats, such as RTF and HTML, as a template for future Mathcad worksheets, or in a format compatible with earlier Mathcad versions. For more information, see Chapter 7, "Worksheet Management."

Printing

To print, choose **Print** from the **File** menu or click 🖨 on the Standard toolbar. To preview the printed page, choose **Print Preview** from the **File** menu or click 🔍 on the Standard toolbar.

For more information on printing, see Chapter 7, "Worksheet Management."

Exiting Mathcad

When you're done using Mathcad, choose **Exit** from the **File** menu. Mathcad closes down all its windows and returns you to the Desktop. If you've made any changes in your worksheets since the last time you saved, a dialog box appears asking if you want to discard or save your changes. If you have moved any toolbars, Mathcad remembers their locations for the next time you open the application.

Note To close a particular worksheet while keeping Mathcad open, choose **Close** from the **File** menu.

Chapter 3
Online Resources

- Resource Center and Electronic Books
- Help
- Internet Access in Mathcad
- The Collaboratory
- Other Resources

Resource Center and Electronic Books

An electronic book is a hyperlinked collection of Mathcad worksheets. If you learn best from examples, want information you can put to work immediately in your Mathcad worksheets, or wish to access any page on the Web from within Mathcad, choose

Resource Center from the **Help** menu or click ![icon] on the Standard toolbar. The Resource Center is a *Mathcad Electronic Book* that appears in a custom window with its own menus and toolbar, as shown in Figure 3-1.

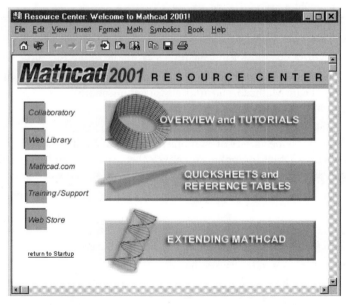

Figure 3-1: Resource Center in Mathcad 2001 Professional.

Note A number of Electronic Books are available on the MathSoft Web Library which you can access through the Resource Center. In addition, a variety of Mathcad Electronic Books are available from MathSoft or your local distributor or software reseller. To open an Electronic Book you have installed, choose **Open Book** from the **Help** menu and browse to find the location of the appropriate Electronic Book (HBK) file.

The Resource Center offers:

- A comprehensive Mathcad Electronic Book containing a collection of tutorials, QuickSheet templates, examples, reference tables, and samples of Mathcad add-on products. Simply drag and drop information from the Resource Center into your own Mathcad worksheets.

- Immediate access to Mathcad worksheets and Electronic Books on MathSoft's Web site and other Internet sites.

- Access to the full Web-browsing functionality of Microsoft Internet Explorer from within the Mathcad environment.

- Access to the Collaboratory where you can exchange messages with other Mathcad users.

Tip To prevent the Resource Center from opening automatically every time you start Mathcad, choose **Preferences** from the **View** menu, and uncheck "Open Resource Center at startup" on the general tab.

Note You can make your own Mathcad Electronic Book. See "Creating an Electronic Book" on page 97 for more information.

Content in the Resource Center

Here are brief descriptions of the topics available in the Resource Center.

- **Overview and Tutorials**. A description of Mathcad's features, tutorials for getting started with Mathcad, and tutorials for getting more out of Mathcad's data analysis, graphing, and worksheet creation features.

- **QuickSheets and Reference Tables**. Over 300 QuickSheets – "recipes" take you through a wide variety of common mathematical tasks that you can modify for your own use. Tables for looking up physical constants, chemical and physical data, and mathematical formulas you can use in your Mathcad worksheets.

- **Extending Mathcad**. Samples showing the use of MathCad components and Add-ins.

- **Collaboratory**. A connection to MathSoft's free Internet forum lets you consult with the world-wide community of Mathcad users.

- **Web Library**. A built-in connection to regularly updated content and resources for Mathcad users.

- **Mathcad.com**. MathSoft's Web page with access to Mathcad and mathematical resources and the latest information from MathSoft.

- **Training/Support**. Information on Mathcad training and support available from MathSoft.

- **Web Store**. MathSoft's Web store where you can get information on and purchase Mathcad add-on products and the latest educational and technical professional software products from MathSoft and other choice vendors.

Finding Information in an Electronic Book

The Resource Center is a *Mathcad Electronic Book*. As in other hypertext systems, you move around a Mathcad Electronic Book simply by clicking on icons or underlined text. The mouse pointer automatically changes into the shape of a hand when it hovers over a hypertext link, and a message in the status bar tells you what will happen when you click the link. Depending on how the book is organized, the activated link automatically opens the appropriate section or displays information in a pop-up window.

You can also use the buttons on the toolbar at the top of the Electronic Book window to navigate and use content within the Electronic Book:

Button	Function
	Links to the Table of Contents or home page, the page that appears when you first open the Electronic Book.
	Opens a toolbar for entering a Web address.
	Backtracks to whatever document was last viewed.
	Reverses the last backtrack.
	Goes backward one section in the Electronic Book.
	Goes forward one section in the Electronic Book.
	Displays a list of documents most recently viewed.
	Searches the Electronic Book for a particular term.
	Copies selected regions to the Clipboard.
	Saves current section of the Electronic Book.
	Prints current section of the Electronic Book.

Mathcad keeps a record of where you've been in the Electronic Book. When you click

, Mathcad backtracks through your navigation history in the Electronic Book. Backtracking is especially useful when you have left the main navigation sequence of a worksheet to look at a hyperlinked cross-reference. Use this button to return to a prior worksheet.

If you don't want to go back one section at a time, click . This opens a History window from which you can jump to any section you viewed since you first opened the Electronic Book.

Full-text search

In addition to using hypertext links to find topics in the Electronic Book, you can search for topics or phrases. To do so:

1. Click to open the Search dialog box.

2. Type a word or phrase in the "Search for" text box. Select a word or phrase and click "Search" to see a list of topics containing that entry and the number of times it occurs in each topic.

3. Choose a topic and click "Go To." Mathcad opens the Electronic Book section containing the entry you want to search for. Click "Next" or

"Previous" to bring the next or previous occurrence of the entry into the window.

Annotating an Electronic Book

A Mathcad Electronic Book is made up of fully interactive Mathcad worksheets. You can freely edit any math region in an Electronic Book to see the effects of changing a parameter or modifying an equation. You can also enter text, math, or graphics as *annotations* in any section of your Electronic Book, using the menu commands on the Electronic Book window and the Mathcad toolbars.

Tip　By default any changes or annotations you make to the Electronic Book are displayed in an annotation highlight color. To change this color, choose **Color⇒Annotation** from the **Format** menu. To suppress the highlighting of Electronic Book annotations, remove the check from **Highlight Changes** on the Electronic Book's **Book** menu.

Saving annotations

Changes you make to an Electronic Book are temporary by default: your edits disappear when you close the Electronic Book, and the Electronic Book is restored to its original appearance the next time you open it. You can choose to save annotations in an Electronic Book by checking **Annotate Book** on the **Book** menu or on the pop-up menu that appears when you right-click. Once you do so, you have the following annotation options:

- Choose **Save Section** from the **Book** menu to save annotations you made in the current section of the Electronic Book, or choose **Save All Changes** to save all changes made since you last opened the Electronic Book.

- Choose **View Original Section** to see the Electronic Book section in its original form. Choose **View Edited Section** to see your annotations again.

- Choose **Restore Section** to revert to the original section, or choose **Restore All** to delete all annotations and edits you have made to the Electronic Book.

Copying Information from an Electronic Book

There are two ways to copy information from an Electronic Book into your Mathcad worksheet:

- You can use the Clipboard. Select text or equations in the Electronic Book using one of the methods described in "Selecting Regions" on page 10, click on the Electronic Book toolbar or choose **Copy** from the **Edit** menu, click on the appropriate spot in your worksheet, and choose **Paste** from the **Edit** menu.

- You can drag regions from the Book window and drop them into your worksheet. Select the regions as above, then click and hold down the mouse button over one of the regions while you drag the selected regions into your worksheet. The regions are copied into the worksheet when you release the mouse button.

Web Browsing

If you have Internet access, the Web Library button in the Resource Center connects you to a collection of Mathcad worksheets and Electronic Books on the Web. You can also use the Resource Center window to browse to any location on the Web and open standard Hypertext Markup Language (HTML) and other Web pages, in addition to Mathcad worksheets. You have the convenience of accessing all of the Internet's rich information resources right in the Mathcad environment.

Note When the Resource Center window is in Web-browsing mode, Mathcad is using a Web-browsing OLE control provided by Microsoft Internet Explorer. Web browsing in Mathcad requires Microsoft Internet Explorer version 4.0 or higher to be installed on your system, but it does not need to be your default browser. Although Microsoft Internet Explorer is available for installation when you install Mathcad, refer to Microsoft Corporation's Web site at **http://www.microsoft.com/** for licensing and support information about Microsoft Internet Explorer and to download the latest version.

To browse to any Web page from within the Resource Center window:

1. Click ![icon] on the Resource Center toolbar. As shown below, an additional toolbar with an "Address" box appears below the Resource Center toolbar to indicate that you are now in a Web-browsing mode:

2. In the "Address" box type a Uniform Resource Locator (URL) for a document on the Web. To visit the MathSoft home page, for example, type `http://www.mathsoft.com/` and press [**Enter**]. If you have Internet access and the server is available, the requested page is loaded in your Resource Center window. If you do not have a supported version of Microsoft Internet Explorer installed, you must launch a Web browser.

The remaining buttons on the Web Toolbar have the following functions:

Button	Function
![icon]	Bookmarks current page.
![icon]	Reloads the current page.
![icon]	Interrupts the current file transfer.

Note When you are in Web-browsing mode and right-click on the Resource Center window, Mathcad displays a pop-up menu with commands appropriate for viewing Web pages. Many of the buttons on the Resource Center toolbar remain active when you are in Web-browsing mode, so that you can copy, save, or print material you locate on the Web, or backtrack to pages you previously viewed. When you click ![icon], you return to the Table of Contents for the Resource Center and disconnect from the Web.

Tip You can use the Resource Center in Web-browsing mode to open Mathcad worksheets anywhere on the Web. Simply type the URL of a Mathcad worksheet in the "Address" box in the Web toolbar.

Help

Mathcad provides several ways to get support on product features through an extensive online Help system. To see Mathcad's online Help at any time, choose **Mathcad Help** from the **Help** menu, click on the Standard toolbar, or press [**F1**]. Mathcad's Help system is delivered in Microsoft's HTML Help environment, as shown in Figure 3-2. You can browse the Explorer view in the Contents tab, look up terms or phrases on the Index tab, or search the entire Help system for a keyword or phrase on the Search tab.

Figure 3-2: Mathcad online Help is delivered in HTML Help.

Note To run the Help, you must have Internet Explorer 3.02 or higher installed, but not necessarily set as your default browser.

You can get context-sensitive help while using Mathcad. For Mathcad menu commands, click on the command and read the status bar at the bottom of your window. For toolbar buttons, hold the pointer over the button momentarily to see a tool tip.

Note The status bar in Mathcad is displayed by default. You can hide the status bar by removing the check from **Status Bar** on the **View** menu.

You can also get more detailed help on menu commands or on many operators and error messages. To do so:

1. Click an error message, a built-in function or variable, or an operator.

2. Press [**F1**] to bring up the relevant Help screen.

To get help on menu commands or on any of the toolbar buttons:

1. Press [**Shift**][**F1**]. Mathcad changes the pointer into a question mark.
2. Choose a command from the menu. Mathcad shows the relevant Help screen.
3. Click any toolbar button. Mathcad displays the operator's name and a keyboard shortcut in the status bar.

To resume editing, press [**Esc**]. The pointer turns back into an arrow.

Tip   Choose **Tip of the Day** from the **Help** menu for a series of helpful hints on using Mathcad. Mathcad automatically displays one of these tips whenever you launch the application if "Show Tips at Startup" is checked.

Special reference areas

There are two special reference areas accessible under the Help menu in Mathcad: **Author's Reference** and **Developer's Reference**.

- The **Author's Reference** contains all the information needed to create a Mathcad Electronic Book. Electronic Books created with Mathcad's authoring tools are browsable through the Resource Center window and, therefore, take advantage of all its navigation tools.

- The **Developer's Reference** provides information about all the properties and methods associated with each of the MathSoft custom Scriptable Object components, including MathSoft Control components and the Data Acquisition component. See Chapter 16, "Advanced Computational Features," for details. It also guides advanced Mathcad users through Mathcad's Object Model, which explains the tools needed to access Mathcad's feature set from within another application. Also included are instructions for using C or C++ to create your own functions in Mathcad in the form of DLLs.

Internet Access in Mathcad

Many of the online Mathcad resources described in this chapter are located not on your own computer or on a local network but on the Internet.

To access these resources on the Internet you need:

- Networking software to support a 32-bit Internet (TCP/IP) application. Such software is usually part of the networking services of your operating system; see your operating system documentation for details.

- A direct or dial-up connection to the Internet, with appropriate hardware and communications software. Consult your system administrator or Internet access provider for more information about your Internet connection.

Before accessing the Internet through Mathcad, you also need to know whether you use a *proxy server* to access the Internet. If you use a proxy, ask your system administrator for the proxy machine's name or Internet Protocol (IP) address, as well as the port number (socket) you use to connect to it. You may specify separate proxy servers for each of the three Internet protocols understood by Mathcad: HTTP, for the Web; FTP, a file transfer protocol; and GOPHER, an older protocol for access to information archives.

Once you have this information, choose **Preferences** from the **View** menu, and click the Internet tab. Then enter the information in the dialog box.

The Collaboratory

If you have a dial-up or direct Internet connection, you can access the MathSoft Collaboratory server from the Resource Center home page. The Collaboratory is an interactive Web service that puts you in contact with a community of Mathcad users. The Collaboratory consists of a group of forums that allow you to contribute Mathcad or other files, post messages, and download files and read messages contributed by other Mathcad users. You can also search the Collaboratory for messages containing a key word or phrase, be notified of new messages in forums that interest you, and view only the messages you haven't read yet. You'll find that the Collaboratory combines some of the best features of a computer bulletin board or an online news group with the convenience of sharing worksheets and other files created using Mathcad.

Logging in

To open the Collaboratory, choose **Resource Center** from the **Help** menu and click on the Collaboratory icon. Alternatively, you can open an Internet browser and go to the Collaboratory home page:

http://collab.mathsoft.com/~mathcad2000/

You'll see the Collaboratory login screen in a browser window:

Welcome!

To participate in the Mathcad Collaboratory, you can log in as an Existing User, a New User, or a Guest.

Name:

Password:

LOG IN

☐ Remember my password

Forgot your password?

NEW USER   New users click here to create a personalized profile.

GUEST   Guests entering conferences are limited to read-only access.

The first time you come to the login screen of the Collaboratory, click "New User." This brings you to a form that you can fill out with your name and other required and optional information about yourself.

Note　MathSoft does not use this information for any purposes other than for your participation in the Collaboratory.

Click "Create" when you are finished filling out the form. In a short while, check your email box for an email message with your login name and password. Go back to the Collaboratory, enter your login name and password given in the email message and click "Log In." You see the main page of the Collaboratory:

Figure 3-3: Opening the Collaboratory from the Resource Center. Available forums change over time.

A list of forums and messages appears on the left side of the screen. The toolbar at the top of the window gives you access to features such as search and online Help.

Tip　After logging in, you may want to change your password to one you will remember. To do so, click **More Options** on the toolbar at the top of the window, click Edit User Profile and enter a new password in the password fields. Then click "Save."

Note　MathSoft maintains the Collaboratory server as a free service, open to all in the Mathcad community. Be sure to read the Agreement posted in the top level of the Collaboratory for important information and disclaimers.

Reading Messages

When you enter the Collaboratory, you will see how many messages are new and how many are addressed to your attention. Click these links to see these messages or examine the list of messages in the left part of the screen. To read any message in any forum of the Collaboratory:

1. Click on the ⊞ next to the forum name or click on the forum name.

2. Click on a message to read it. Click the ⊞ to the left of a message to see replies underneath it.

3. The message shows in the right side of the window.

Messages that you have not yet read are shown in italics. You may also see a "new" icon next to the messages.

Posting Messages

After you enter the Collaboratory, you can go to any forum and post a message or a reply to a message. To post a new message or a reply to an existing one:

1. Click on the forum name to show the messages under it. If you want to reply to a message, click on the message.

2. Choose **Post** from the toolbar at the top of the Collaboratory window to post a new message. Or, to reply to a message, click **Reply** at the top of the message in the right side of the window. You'll see the post/reply page in the right side of the window. For example, if you post a new topic message in the Biology forum, you see:

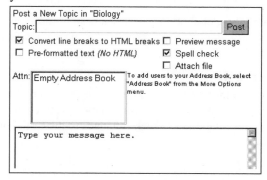

3. Enter the title of your message in the Topic field.

4. Click on any of the boxes below the title to specify whether you want to, for example, preview a message, spell check a message, or attach a file.

5. Type your text in the message field.

Tip   You can include hyperlinks in your message by entering an entire URL such as http://www.myserver.com/main.html.

6. Click "Post" after you finish typing. Depending on the options you selected, the Collaboratory either posts your message immediately or allows you to preview it. It might also display possible misspellings in red with links to suggested spellings.

7. If you preview the message and the text looks correct, click "Post."

8. If you are attaching a file, a new page appears. Specify the file type and file on the next page and click "Upload Now."

Note   For more information on reading, posting messages, and other features of the Collaboratory, click **Help** on the Collaboratory toolbar.

To delete a message that you posted, click on it to open it and click Delete in the small toolbar just above the message on the right side of the window.

Searching

To search the Collaboratory, click **Search** on the Collaboratory toolbar. You can search for messages containing specific words or phrases, messages within a certain date range, or messages posted by specific Collaboratory users.

You can also search the Collaboratory user database for users who are in a particular country or have a particular email address, etc. To do so, click Search Users at the top of the Search page.

Changing Your User Information

When you first logged into the Collaboratory, you filled out a New User Information form with your name, address, etc. This information is stored as your user profile. To change any of this information or to make changes to the Collaboratory defaults, you need to edit your profile.

To do so:

1. Click **More Options** on the toolbar at the top of the window.

2. Click Edit Your Profile.

3. Make changes to the information in the form and click "Save."

You can change information such as your login name and password. You can also hide your email address.

Other Features

The Collaboratory has other features which make it easy to find and provide information to the Mathcad community. To perform activities such as creating an address book, marking messages as read, viewing certain messages, and requesting automatic email announcements when specific forums have new messages, choose **More Options** from the Collaboratory toolbar.

The Collaboratory also supports participation via email or a news group. For more information on these and other features available in the Collaboratory, click Collaboratory **Help** on the toolbar.

Other Resources

Online Documentation

The following piece of Mathcad documentation is available in PDF form on the Mathcad CD in the DOC folder:

- *Mathcad User's Guide with Reference Manual*. This guide with the latest information, including updates since the printed edition was created.

You can read this PDF file by installing Adobe Acrobat Reader which is also available on the Mathcad CD in the DOC folder. See the readme file in the DOC folder for more information about the online documentation.

Samples Folder

The SAMPLES folder, located in your Mathcad folder, contains sample Mathcad and application files which demonstrate components such as the Axum, Excel, and Smart-Sketch components. There are also sample Visual Basic applications designed to work with Mathcad files. Refer to Chapter 16, "Advanced Computational Features," for more information on components and other features demonstrated in the samples.

Release Notes

Release notes are located in the DOC folder located in your Mathcad folder. It contains the latest information on Mathcad, updates to the documentation, and troubleshooting instructions.

Chapter 4
Working with Math

- ♦ Inserting Math
- ♦ Building Expressions
- ♦ Editing Expressions
- ♦ Math Styles

Inserting Math

You can place math equations and expressions anywhere you want in a Mathcad worksheet. All you have to do is click in the worksheet and start typing.

1. Click anywhere in the worksheet. You see a small crosshair. Anything you type appears at the crosshair.

2. Type numbers, letters, and math operators, or insert them by clicking buttons on Mathcad's math toolbars, to create a *math region*.

$$15 - \frac{8}{104.5} = 14.923$$

You'll notice that unlike a word processor, Mathcad by default understands anything you type at the crosshair cursor as math. If you want to create a *text region* instead, follow the procedures described in Chapter 5, "Working with Text."

You can also type math expressions in any math *placeholder*, which appears when you insert certain operators. See Chapter 9, "Operators," for more on Mathcad's mathematical operators and the placeholders that appear when you insert them.

The rest of this chapter introduces the elements of math expressions in Mathcad and describes the techniques you use to build and edit them.

Numbers and Complex Numbers

This section describes the various types of numbers that Mathcad uses and how to enter them into math expressions. A single number in Mathcad is called a *scalar*. For information on entering groups of numbers in *arrays*, see "Vectors and Matrices" on page 37.

Types of numbers

In math regions, Mathcad interprets anything beginning with one of the digits 0–9 as a number. A digit can be followed by:

- other digits
- a decimal point
- digits after the decimal point
- or appended as a suffix, one of the letters **b**, **h**, or **o**, for binary, hexadecimal, and octal numbers, or **i** or **j** for imaginary numbers. These are discussed in more detail below. See "Suffixes for Numbers" on page 497 in the Appendices for additional suffixes.

Note Mathcad uses the period (**.**) to signify the decimal point. The comma (**,**) is used to separate values in a range variable definition, as described in "Range Variables" on page 106. So when you enter numbers greater than 999, do not use either a comma or a period to separate digits into groups of three. Simply type the digits one after another. For example, to enter ten thousand, type "**10000**".

Imaginary and complex numbers

To enter an imaginary number, follow it with i or j, as in **1i** or **2.5j**.

Note You cannot use i or j alone to represent the imaginary unit. You must always type **1i** or **1j**. If you don't, Mathcad thinks you are referring to a variable named either i or j. When the cursor is outside an equation that contains $1i$ or $1j$, however, Mathcad hides the (superfluous) 1.

Although you can enter imaginary numbers followed by either i or j, Mathcad normally displays them followed by i. To have Mathcad display imaginary numbers with j, choose **Result** from the **Format** menu, click on the Display Options tab, and set "Imaginary value" to "j(J)." See "Formatting Results" on page 115 for a full description of the result formatting options.

Mathcad accepts complex numbers of the form $a + bi$ (or $a + bj$), where a and b are ordinary numbers.

Binary numbers

To enter a number in binary, follow it with the lowercase letter **b**. For example, **11110000b** represents 240 in decimal. Binary numbers must be less than 2^{31} .

Octal numbers

To enter a number in octal, follow it with the lowercase letter **o**. For example, **25636o** represents 11166 in decimal. Octal numbers must be less than 2^{31} .

Hexadecimal numbers

To enter a number in hexadecimal, follow it with the lowercase letter **h**. For example, **2b9eh** represents 11166 in decimal. To represent digits above 9, use the upper or lowercase letters **A** through **F**. To enter a hexadecimal number that begins with a letter, you must begin it with a leading zero. If you don't, Mathcad will think it's a variable name. For example, use **0a3h** (delete the implied multiplication symbol between **0** and **a**) rather than **a3h** to represent the decimal number 163 in hexadecimal.

Hexadecimal numbers must be less than 2^{31}.

Exponential notation

To enter very large or very small numbers in exponential notation, just multiply a number by a power of 10. For example, to represent the number $3 \cdot 10^8$, type **3*10^8**.

Vectors and Matrices

A column of numbers is a *vector*, and a rectangular array of numbers is called a *matrix*. The general term for a vector or matrix is an *array*.

There are a number of ways to create an array in Mathcad. One of the simplest is by filling in an array of empty placeholders as discussed in this section. This technique is useful for arrays that are not too large. See Chapter 11, "Vectors, Matrices, and Data Arrays," for additional techniques for creating arrays of arbitrary size.

Tip You may wish to distinguish between the names of matrices, vectors, and scalars by font. For example, in many math and engineering books, names of vectors are set in bold while those of scalars are set in italic. See "Math Styles" on page 54 for a description of how to do this.

Creating a vector or matrix

To create a vector or matrix in Mathcad, follow these steps:

1. Choose **Matrix** from the **Insert** menu or click on the Matrix toolbar. The dialog box shown on the right appears.

2. Enter a number of rows and a number of columns in the appropriate boxes. In this example, there are two rows and three columns. Then click "OK." Mathcad inserts a matrix of placeholders.

3. Fill in the placeholders to complete the matrix. Press [**Tab**] to move from placeholder to placeholder.

You can use this matrix in equations, just as you would a number.

$$\begin{pmatrix} 2 & 5 & 17 \\ 3.5 & 3.9 & -12.9 \end{pmatrix}$$

Tip The **Insert Matrix** dialog box also allows you to insert or delete a specified number of rows or columns from an array you have already created. See"Changing the size of a vector or matrix" on page 204.

Note Throughout this *User's Guide*, the term "vector" refers to a *column vector*. A column vector is simply a matrix with one column. You can also create a *row vector* by creating a matrix with one row and many columns.

Strings

Although in most cases the math expressions or variables you work with in Mathcad are numbers or arrays, you can also work with *strings* (also called *string literals* or *string variables*). Strings can include any character you can type at the keyboard, including letters, numbers, punctuation, and spacing, as well as a variety of special symbols as listed in "ASCII codes" on page 501. Strings differ from variable names or numbers because Mathcad always displays them between double quotes. You can assign a string to a variable name, use a string as an element of a vector or matrix, or use a string as the argument to a function.

To create a string:

1. Click on an empty math placeholder in a math expression, usually on the right-hand side of a variable definition.

2. Type the double-quote (**"**) key. Mathcad displays a pair of quotes and an insertion line between them.

3. Type any combination of letters, numbers, punctuation, or spaces. Click outside the expression or press the right arrow key ($\rightarrow$) twice when you are finished.

To enter a special character corresponding to one of the ASCII codes, do the following:

1. Click to position the insertion point in the string.

2. Hold down the [**Alt**] key, and type the number "0" followed immediately by the number of the ASCII code *using the numeric keypad at the right of the keyboard* in number-entry mode.

3. Release the [**Alt**] key to see the symbol in the string.

For example, to enter the degree symbol (**°**) in a string, press [**Alt**] and type "0176" using the numeric keypad.

Note The double-quote key (**"**) has a variety of meanings in Mathcad, depending on the exact location of the cursor in your worksheet. When you want to enter a string, you must *always* have a blank placeholder selected.

Valid strings include expressions such as "The Rain in Spain Falls Mainly on the Plain," "Invalid input: try a number less than -5," and "Meets stress requirements." A string in Mathcad, while not limited in size, always appears as a single line of text in your worksheet. Note that a string such as "123," created in the way described above, is understood by Mathcad to be a string of characters rather than the number 123.

Tip Strings are especially useful for generating custom error messages in programs, as described in Chapter 15, "Programming." Other string handling functions are listed in "String Functions" on page 198. Use strings also to specify system paths for arguments to some Mathcad built-in functions; see "File Access Functions" on page 199.

Names

A *name* in Mathcad is simply a sequence of characters you type or insert in a math region. A name usually refers to a variable or function that you use in your computations. Mathcad distinguishes between two kinds of names:

- Built-in names, which are the names of variables and functions that are always available in Mathcad and which you can use freely in building up math expressions.
- User-defined names, which are the names of variables and functions you create in your Mathcad worksheets.

Built-in names

Because Mathcad is an environment for numerical and symbolic computation, a large number of names are built into the product for use in math expressions. These built-in names include built-in *variables* and built-in *functions*.

- Mathcad includes several variables that, unlike ordinary variables, are already defined when you start Mathcad. These *predefined* or *built-in* variables either have a conventional value, like π (3.14159...) or e (2.71828...), or are used as system variables to control how Mathcad performs calculations. See "Built-in Variables" on page 102 for more information.

- In addition to these predefined variables, Mathcad treats the names of all built-in *units* as predefined variables. For example, Mathcad recognizes the name "A" as the ampere, "m" as the meter, "s" as the second, and so on. Choose **Unit** from the

  Insert menu or click on the Standard toolbar to insert one of Mathcad's predefined units. See "Units and Dimensions" on page 112 for more on built-in units in Mathcad.

- Mathcad includes a large number of built-in functions that handle a range of computational chores ranging from basic calculation to sophisticated curve fitting, matrix manipulation, and statistics. To access one of these built-in functions, you can simply type its name in a math region. For example, Mathcad recognizes the name "mean" as the name of the built-in *mean* function, which calculates the arithmetic mean of the elements of an array, and the name "eigenvals" as the name of the built-in *eigenvals* function, which returns a vector of eigenvalues for a matrix.

You can also choose **Function** from the **Insert** menu or click ![fx] on the Standard toolbar to insert one of Mathcad's built-in functions. See Chapter 10, "Built-in Functions," for a broad overview of Mathcad's built-in functions.

User-defined variable and function names

Mathcad lets you use a wide variety of expressions as variable or function names.

Names in Mathcad can contain any of the following characters:

- Uppercase and lowercase letters.
- The digits 0 through 9.
- The underscore (_).
- The prime symbol ('). Note that this is not the same as an apostrophe. You'll find the prime symbol on the same key as the tilde (~) or press [**Ctrl**][**F7**] to insert it.
- The percent symbol (**%**).
- Greek letters. To insert a Greek letter, click a button on the Greek toolbar or type the equivalent roman letter and press [**Ctrl**]**G**. The section "Greek letters" on page 41 gives more details.
- The infinity symbol ∞ that you insert by clicking ![∞] on the Calculus toolbar or by typing [**Ctrl**][**Shift**]**Z**.

The following are examples of valid names:

`alpha`	`b`
`xyz700`	`A1_B2_C3_D4%%%`
`F1'`	`a%%`

The following restrictions apply to variable names:

- A name cannot start with one of the digits 0 through 9. Mathcad interprets anything beginning with a digit as either an imaginary number ($2i$ or $3j$), a binary, octal, or hexadecimal number (e.g., 5o, 7h), or as a number *times* a variable ($3 \cdot x$).
- The infinity symbol ∞ can only appear as the first character in a name.
- Any characters you type after a period (.) appear as a subscript. This is discussed in "Literal subscripts" on page 41.
- All characters in a name must be in the same font, have the same point size, and be in the same style (italic, bold, etc.). Greek letters can, however, appear in any variable name. See "Math Styles" on page 54.
- Mathcad does not distinguish between variable names and function names. Thus, if you define $f(x)$, and later on you define the variable f, you will find that you cannot use $f(x)$ anywhere below the definition for f.

- Although you can redefine Mathcad's names for built-in functions, constants, and units, keep in mind that their built-in meanings will no longer exist after the definition. For example, if you define a variable *mean*, Mathcad's built-in function *mean*(**v**) can no longer be used.

Note Mathcad distinguishes between uppercase and lowercase letters. For example, *diam* is a different variable from *DIAM*. Mathcad also distinguishes between names in different fonts, as discussed in "Math Styles" on page 54. Thus, *Diam* is also a different variable from **Diam**.

Tip To type symbols such as $ in a name, press [**Ctrl**][**Shift**]**K**, type the symbol(s), and type [**Ctrl**][**Shift**]**K** again.

Greek letters

There are two ways to enter a Greek variable name in Mathcad:

- Click on the appropriate letter on the Greek toolbar. To see this toolbar, click on the Math toolbar or choose **Toolbars**⇒**Greek** from the **View** menu.

- Type the *Roman equivalent* of the Greek symbol and then press [**Ctrl**]**G**. For example, to enter φ, press **f**[**Ctrl**]**G**. See "Greek Letters" on page 498 in the Appendices for a table of Greek letters and their Roman equivalents.

Note Although many of the uppercase Greek letters look like ordinary capital letters, they are *not* the same. Mathcad distinguishes between Greek and Roman letters, even if they appear visually equivalent.

Tip Because it is used so frequently, the Greek letter π can also be typed by pressing [**Ctrl**][**Shift**]**P**.

Literal subscripts

If you include a period in a variable name, Mathcad displays whatever follows the period as a subscript. You can use these *literal subscripts* to create variables with names like vel_{init} and u_{air}.

To create a literal subscript, follow these steps:

1. Type the portion of the name that appears before the subscript.

2. Type a period (**.**) followed by the portion of the name that is to become the subscript.

Note Do not confuse literal subscripts with *array* subscripts, which are generated with the left bracket key ([) or by clicking on the Calculator toolbar. Although they appear similar—a literal subscript appears below the line, like an array subscript, but with a slight space before the subscript—they behave quite differently in computations. A literal subscript is simply a cosmetic part of a variable name. An array subscript represents a reference to an array element. See Chapter 11, "Vectors, Matrices, and Data Arrays," for a description of how to use subscripts with arrays.

Operators

As described in the previous section, certain characters, like letters and digits, make up parts of names and numbers. Other characters, like * and +, represent "operators."

Operators are symbols like "+" and "−" that link variables and numbers together to form *expressions*. The variables and numbers linked together by operators are called *operands*. For example, in an expression like:

$$a^{x+y}$$

the operands for the "+" are x and y. The operands for the *exponent* operator are a and the expression $x + y$.

You type the common arithmetic operators using the standard keystrokes, like * and +, used in your spreadsheet and other applications. But all of Mathcad's operators can be entered with keystrokes or by clicking buttons in the Math toolbars. For example,

you insert Mathcad's derivative operator by typing **?** or by clicking $\boxed{\frac{d}{dx}}$ on the Calculus toolbar. Mathcad's operators are discussed in Chapter 9, "Operators." See also "Operators" on page 447 in the Reference Manual section of this book for a complete list of operators.

Building Expressions

You can create many mathematical expressions by simply typing in a stream of characters or by inserting appropriate operators from the Math toolbars.

For example, if you type the characters

3/4+5^2=

you get the result shown at the right.

$$\frac{3}{4 + 5^2} = 0.103$$

On the surface, Mathcad's equation editor seems very much like a simple text editor, but there's more to it than this. Mathematical expressions have a well-defined structure and Mathcad's equation editor is designed specifically to work within that structure. In Mathcad, mathematical expressions are not so much typed-in as they are built.

Mathcad automatically assembles the various parts that make up an expression using the rules of precedence and some additional rules that simplify entering denominators, exponents, and expressions in radicals. For example, when you type **/** or click $\boxed{/}$ on the Calculator toolbar to create a fraction, Mathcad stays in the denominator until you press [**Space**] to select the entire expression.

Typing in Names and Numbers

When you type in names or numbers, Mathcad behaves very much like a standard word processor. As you type, you see the characters you type appear behind a vertical *editing line*. The left and right arrow keys move this vertical editing line to the left or to the right a character at a time, just as they would in a word processor. There are, however, two important differences:

- As it moves to the right, the vertical editing line leaves behind a trail. This trail is a "horizontal editing line." Its importance becomes apparent when you begin working with operators.

- Unless the equation you've clicked in already has an operator in it, pressing [**Space**] turns the math region into a text region. It is not possible to turn a text region back into a math region.

Typing in Operators

The key to working with operators is learning to specify what variable or expression is to become an *operand*. There are two ways to do this:

- You can type the operator first and fill in the placeholders with operands, or
- You can use the editing lines to specify what variable or expression you want to turn into an operand.

The first method feels more like you're building a skeleton and filling in the details later. This method may be easier to use when you're building very complicated expressions, or when you're working with operators like summation that require many operands but don't have a natural typing order.

The second method feels more like straight typing and can be much faster when expressions are simple. In practice, you may find yourself switching back and forth as the need arises.

Here's how to create the expression a^{x+y} using the first method:

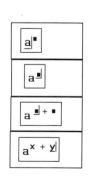

1. Press ^ to create the exponent operator, or click on the Calculator toolbar. You see two placeholders. The editing lines "hold" the exponent placeholder.

2. Click in the lower placeholder and type **a**.

3. Click in the upper placeholder.

4. Type **+**.

5. Click in the remaining placeholders and type **x** and **y**.

To use the editing lines to create the expression a^{x+y} proceed as follows:

1. Type **a**. The editing lines hold the a indicating that a becomes the first operand of whatever operator you type next.

2. Press **^** to create the exponent operator. As promised, a becomes the first operand of the exponent. The editing lines now hold another placeholder.

3. Type **x+y** in this placeholder to complete the expression.

Note that in this example, you could type the expression the same way you'd say it out loud. However, even this simple example already contains an ambiguity. When you say "a to the x plus y" there's no way to tell if you mean a^{x+y} or $a^x + y$. For more complicated expressions, the number of ambiguities increases dramatically.

Although you can always resolve ambiguities by using parentheses, doing so can quickly become cumbersome. A better way is to use the editing lines to specify the operands of whatever operator you type. The following example illustrates this by describing how to create the expression $a^x + y$ instead of a^{x+y}.

1. Enter **a^x** as you did in the previous example. Note how the editing lines hold the x between them. If you were to type **+** at this point, the x would become the first operand of the plus.

2. Press [**Space**]. The editing lines now hold the entire expression a^x.

3. Now type **+**. Whatever was held between the editing lines now becomes the first operand of the plus.

4. In the remaining placeholder, type **y**.

Multiplication

A common way to show multiplication between two variables on a piece of paper is to place them next to each other. For example, expressions like ax or $a(x+y)$ are easily understood to mean "a times x" and "a times the quantity x plus y," respectively.

This cannot be done with Mathcad variables for the simple reason that when you type **ax**, Mathcad has no way of knowing whether you mean "a times x" or "the variable named ax." Similarly, when you type **a(x+y)**, Mathcad cannot tell if you mean "a times the quantity x plus y" or whether you mean "the function a applied to the argument $x+y$."

To avoid ambiguity in your everyday work, we recommend that you always press ***** explicitly to indicate multiplication, as shown in the following example:

1. Type **a** followed by *****. Mathcad inserts a small dot after the "*a*" to indicate multiplication.

2. In the placeholder, type the second factor, **x**.

Note In the special case when you type a numerical constant followed immediately by a variable name, such as **4x**, Mathcad interprets the expression to mean the constant multiplied by the variable: $4 \cdot x$. Mathcad displays a space between the constant and the variable to indicate that the multiplication is implied. In this way, you can produce math notation that closely approximates the notation you see in textbooks and reference books. However, Mathcad reserves certain letters, such as "*i*" for the imaginary unit and "*o*" for octal, as suffixes for numbers, and in these cases does not attempt to multiply the number by a variable name but rather treats the expression as a single number with a suffix.

Tip You can change the display of the multiplication operator to an X, a thin space, or a large dot. To do so, click on the multiplication operator with the right mouse button and choose **View Multiplication As...** Or to change all the multiplication operators in a worksheet, choose **Options** from the **Math** menu, click on the Display tab, and choose from the selections next to "Multiplication." See "Changing the Display of an Operator" on page 130 for additional information.

An Annotated Example

When it comes to editing equations, knowing how to use the editing lines assumes an importance similar to knowing where to put the flashing vertical bar (insertion point) you see in most word processors. A word processor can use a simple vertical bar because text is inherently one-dimensional, like a line. New letters go either to the left or to the right of old ones. An equation, on the other hand, is really *two-dimensional*, with a structure more like a tree with branches than like a line of text. As a result, Mathcad has to use a *two-dimensional* version of that same vertical bar. That's why there are two editing lines: a vertical line and a horizontal line.

Suppose, for example, that you want to type the slightly more complicated expression

$$\frac{x - 3 \cdot a^2}{-4 + \sqrt{y+1} + \pi}$$

Watch what happens to the editing lines in the following steps:

1. Type **x-3*a^2**. Since the editing lines contain just the "2," only the "2" becomes the numerator when you press the **/**.

   Since we want the whole expression, $x - 3 \cdot a^2$, to be the numerator, we must make the editing lines hold that entire expression.

2. To do so, press [**Space**]. Each time you press [**Space**], the editing lines hold more of the expression. You need to press [**Space**] three times to enclose the entire expression.

3. Now press **/** to create a division bar. Note that the numerator is whatever was enclosed between the editing lines when you pressed **/**.

4. Now type **-4+** and click on the Calculator toolbar. Then type **y+1** under the radical to complete the denominator.

5. To add something *outside* the radical sign, press [**Space**] twice to make the editing lines hold the radical. For example, to add the number π to the denominator, press [**Space**] twice.

6. Press **+**. Since the editing lines are holding the entire radical, it is the entire radical that becomes the first operand when you press **+**.

7. Click on the Calculator toolbar or press [**Ctrl**][**Shift**]**P**. This is one of Mathcad's built-in variables.

Editing Expressions

This section describes how to make changes to an existing expression.

Changing a Name or Number

To edit a name or number:

1. Click on it with the mouse. This places the vertical editing line where you clicked the mouse.

2. Move the vertical editing line if necessary by pressing the [→] and [←] keys.

3. If you type a character, it appears just to the left of the vertical editing line. Pressing [**Bksp**] removes the character to the left of the vertical editing line. Pressing [**Delete**] removes the character to the right of the vertical editing line.

If you need to change several occurrences of the same name or number, you may find it useful to choose **Replace** from the **Edit** menu. To search for a sequence of characters, choose **Find** from the **Edit** menu. These commands are discussed further in "Text Tools" on page 67.

Inserting an Operator

The easiest place to insert an operator is between two characters in a name or two numbers in a constant. For example, here's how to insert a plus sign between two characters:

1. Place the editing lines where you want the plus sign to be.

2. Press the **+** key, or click **+** on the Calculator toolbar.

Note You never need to insert a space when typing an equation. Mathcad inserts spaces automatically around operators wherever doing so is appropriate. If you do try to insert a space, Mathcad assumes you meant to type text rather than math and converts your math region into a text region accordingly.

Operators such as division and exponentiation result in more dramatic formatting changes. For example, when you insert a divide sign, Mathcad moves everything that comes after the divide sign into the denominator. Here's how you insert a divide sign:

1. Place the editing lines where you want the divide sign to be.

2. Press the **/** key or click **/** on the Calculator toolbar. Mathcad reformats the expression to accommodate the division.

Some operators require only one operand. Examples are the square root, absolute value, and complex conjugate operators. To insert one of these, place the editing lines on either side of the operand and press the appropriate keystroke. Many of these operators are available on the Calculator toolbar as well. For example, to turn x into $\sqrt{x}$ do the following:

1. Place the editing lines around the "x," either preceding or following the character.

2. Press \ to insert the square root operator, or click **√** on the Calculator toolbar.

Applying an Operator to an Expression

The methods described in the previous section work most predictably when you want to apply an operator to a variable or a number. If, however, you want to apply an operator to an *entire expression,* there are two ways to proceed:

* Surround that expression in parentheses and proceed as described in the previous section, or

* Use the editing lines to specify the expression to which you want to apply the operator.

Although the first method may be more intuitive, it is slower since you need to type a pair of parentheses. The more efficient, second method is the subject of this section. The sections "Inserting Parentheses" on page 51 and "Deleting Parentheses" on page 52 describe ways to work with parentheses more efficiently.

The editing lines consist of a horizontal line and a vertical line that moves left to right along the horizontal line. To make an operator apply to an expression, select the expression by placing it between the two editing lines. The following examples show how typing *c results in completely different expressions depending on what was selected.

- Here, the two editing lines hold only the numerator. This means any operator you type will apply only to the numerator.

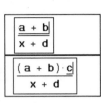

- Typing *c results in this expression. Note how the expression held between the editing lines became the first operand of the multiplication.

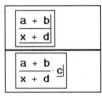

- Here, the editing lines hold the entire fraction. This means any operator you type will apply to the entire fraction.

- Typing *c results in this expression. Note how everything between the editing lines became the first operand of the multiplication.

- Here, the editing lines hold the entire fraction as they did in the previous example. However, this time the vertical editing line is on the *left* side instead of on the right side.

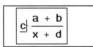

- Typing *c results in this expression. Note how the expression enclosed by the editing lines became the *second* rather than the first operand of the multiplication. This happened because the vertical editing line was on the *left* side rather than the right side.

Controlling the editing lines

You use the following techniques to control what's between the editing lines:

- Click on an operator. Depending on where on the operator you click, you'll find the vertical editing line either on the left or on the right of the operator, with the horizontal line selecting an operand of the operator. If you want to move the vertical editing line from one side to the other of the currently selected expression, press [**Insert**].

- Use the left and right arrow keys to move the vertical editing line one character at a time. The horizontal editing line selects an operand of the nearest operator. If your expression contains built-up fractions, you can also use the up and down arrow keys to move the editing lines.

- Press [**Space**] to select progressively larger parts of the expression with the editing lines. Each time you press [**Space**], the editing lines enclose more and more of the expression, until eventually they enclose the entire expression. Pressing [**Space**] one more time brings the editing lines back to where they were when you started.

Tip You can also *drag-select* parts of an expression to hold it between the editing lines. When you do this, the selected expression is highlighted in reverse video. Note that whatever you type next overwrites the highlighted expression.

The following example walks you through a short cycle of using [**Space**]:

1. This is the starting position. The two editing lines hold just the single variable "*d*."

$$\frac{a + b}{x + d}$$

2. Pressing [**Space**] makes the editing lines grow so that they now hold the entire denominator.

$$\frac{a + b}{x + d}$$

3. Pressing [**Space**] once makes the editing lines grow again so that they now hold the entire expression.

$$\frac{a + b}{x + d}$$

4. At this point, the editing lines can't become any longer. Pressing [**Space**] brings the editing lines back to the starting point of the cycle.

$$\frac{a + b}{x + d}$$

You'll notice that in stepping through the previous cycle there was never an intermediate step in which the editing lines held just the numerator. Nor was there ever a step in which the editing lines held just the *a* or just the *b* in the numerator. That's because the sequence of steps the editing lines go through as you press [**Space**] depends on the starting point of the cycle.

To set the starting point of the cycle, either click on the appropriate part of the expression as described earlier, or use the arrow keys to move around the expression. The arrow keys walk the editing lines through the expression in the indicated direction. Keep in mind, however, that the idea of "up" and "down" or "left" and "right" may not always be obvious, particularly when the expression becomes very complicated or if it involves summations, integrals, and other advanced operators.

Note Editing of strings differs from editing of other math expressions because you must use the arrow keys or click outside the string to move out of a string. Pressing [**Space**], which can be used in other expressions to change the position of the editing lines, is interpreted as just another character in a string.

Deleting an Operator

To delete an operator connecting two variable names or constants:

1. Place the vertical editing line after the operator.

2. Press [**BkSp**].

Now you can easily insert a new operator to replace the one you deleted just by typing it in.

Tip You can also delete an operator by placing the editing lines *before* it and pressing [**Delete**].

In the above examples, it is easy to see what "before" and "after" mean because the expressions involved naturally flow from left to right, the same way we read. Fractions behave the same way. Since we naturally say "*a* over *b*," putting the editing lines "after" the division bar means putting them just before the *b*. Similarly, putting the editing lines "before" the division bar means putting them immediately after the *a*. The following example illustrates this:

1. Place the vertical editing lines *after* the division bar.

2. Press [**BkSp**].

To delete an operator having only one operand (for example, $\sqrt{x}$, $|x|$ or $x!$):

1. Position the editing lines just after the operator.

2. Press [**BkSp**].

For certain operators, it may not be clear where to put the editing lines.
For example, it is not clear when looking at $|x|$ or $\bar{x}$ what "before" and "after" mean. When this happens, Mathcad resolves the ambiguity by referring to the spoken form of the expression. For example, since you read $\bar{x}$ as "x conjugate," the bar is treated as being *after* the x.

Replacing an Operator

To replace an operator after deleting it between two variables or constants or on a single variable, as shown in the steps above, simply type the new operator after pressing [**BkSp**].

To replace an operator between two expressions:

1. Position the editing lines just after the operator.

2. Press [**BkSp**]. An operator placeholder appears.

3. Type the new operator.

Inserting a Minus Sign

The minus sign that means "negation" uses the same keystroke as the one that means "subtract." To determine which one to insert, Mathcad looks at where the vertical editing line is. If it's on the left, Mathcad inserts the "negation" minus sign. If it's on the right, Mathcad inserts the "subtract" minus sign. To move the vertical editing line from one side to the other, use [**Insert**].

The following example shows how to insert a minus sign in front of "sin(*a*)."

1. Click on the sin(*a*). If necessary, press [**Space**] to select the entire expression.

    $$\boxed{\mathsf{sin}(\,\mathsf{a}\,)|}$$

2. If necessary, press [**Insert**] to move the vertical editing line all the way to the left.

    $$\boxed{|\mathsf{sin}(\,\mathsf{a}\,)}$$

3. Type –, or click on the Calculator toolbar, to insert a minus sign.

    $$\boxed{|\text{-}\,\mathsf{sin}(\,\mathsf{a}\,)}$$

If what you really want to do is turn $\sin(a)$ into $1 - \sin(a)$, insert another operator (say, "+") as described in the section "Inserting an Operator" on page 47. Then replace the operator with a minus sign as described in the section "Deleting an Operator" on page 50. Notice that in Mathcad the unary negation symbol in the expression $-\sin(a)$ appears smaller than the minus sign in expressions such as $1 - \sin(a)$.

Note When you are replacing an operator and the operator placeholder is showing, select an expression, rather than a single variable, to the right of the operator placeholder and type – in order to put a subtraction minus sign in the placeholder. Otherwise Mathcad inserts a negation sign.

Inserting Parentheses

Mathcad places parentheses automatically as needed to maintain the precedence of operations. There may be instances, however, when you want to place parentheses to clarify an expression or to change the overall structure of the expression. You can either insert a matched pair of parentheses all at once or insert the parentheses one at a time. We recommend you insert a matched pair since this avoids the possibility of unmatched parentheses.

To enclose an expression with a matched pair of parentheses:

1. Select the expression by placing it between the editing lines. Do this by clicking on the expression and pressing [**Space**] one or more times.

    $$\boxed{\dfrac{\mathsf{a + b}}{\mathsf{a - b}} \cdot \mathsf{c}}$$

2. Type the single-quote key ('), or click ( ) on the Calculator toolbar. The selected expression is now enclosed by parentheses.

    $$\boxed{\left(\dfrac{\mathsf{a + b}}{\mathsf{a - b}}\right) \cdot \mathsf{c}}$$

It is sometimes necessary to insert parentheses one at a time using the **(** and **)** keys. For example, to change $a - b + c$ to $a - (b + c)$ do the following:

1. Move the editing lines just to the left of the b. Make sure the vertical editing line is on the left as shown. Press [**Insert**] if necessary to move it over.

2. Type **(** and click to the right of the c. Make sure the vertical editing line is to the right as shown. Press [**Insert**] if necessary to move it over.

3. Type **)**.

Deleting Parentheses

You cannot delete one parenthesis at a time. Whenever you delete one parenthesis, Mathcad deletes the matched parenthesis as well. This prevents you from inadvertently creating an expression having unmatched parentheses.

To delete a matched pair of parentheses:

1. Move the editing lines to the right of the "(".

2. Press [**BkSp**]. Note that you could also begin with the editing lines to the left of the ")"and press [**Delete**] instead.

Applying a Function to an Expression

To turn an expression into the argument of a function, follow these steps:

1. Click in the expression and press [**Space**] until the entire expression, $w \cdot t - k \cdot z$, is held between the editing lines.

2. Type the single-quote key (**'**), or click on the Calculator toolbar. The selected expression is enclosed by parentheses.

3. Press [**Space**]. The editing lines now hold the parentheses as well.

4. If necessary, press the [**Insert**] key so that the vertical editing line switches to the left side. If the vertical editing line is already on the left side, skip this step.

5. Now type the name of the function. If the function you wish to use is a built-in function, you can also choose **Function**

from the **Insert** menu or click on the Standard toolbar and double-click the name of the function.

Moving Parts of an Expression

The menu commands **Cut**, **Copy**, and **Paste** from the **Edit** menu are useful for editing complicated expressions. They function as follows:

- **Cut** (✄ on the Standard toolbar or [**Ctrl**]**X** on the keyboard) deletes whatever is between the editing lines and copies it to the Clipboard.

- **Copy** (📄 on the Standard toolbar or [**Ctrl**]**C** on the keyboard) takes whatever is between the editing lines and copies it to the Clipboard.

- **Paste** (📋 on the Standard toolbar or [**Ctrl**]**V** on the keyboard) takes whatever is on the Clipboard and places it into your worksheet, either into a placeholder or into the blank space between other regions.

The **Copy** and **Paste** commands use the Clipboard to move expressions from one place to another. You can, however, bypass the Clipboard by using Mathcad's *equation drag and drop* feature.

Suppose you want to build the expression

$$\cos(wt + x) + \sin(wt + x)$$

1. Drag-select the argument to the cosine function so that it is highlighted in reverse video.

   $$\cos(\; \boxed{w \cdot t \; + \; x}\;) \; + \; \sin(\;\blacksquare\;)$$

2. Press and hold down [**Ctrl**] and the mouse button. The pointer changes to indicate that it carries the selected expression with it. It

   $$\cos(\; w \cdot t + x\;) \; + \; \sin(\;\blacksquare\;)$$

   continues to carry the selected expression until you release the mouse button.

3. With the mouse button still held down, drag the pointer over the placeholder.

   $$\cos(\; w \cdot t \; + \; x\;) \; + \; \sin(\;\blacksquare\;)$$

4. Release the mouse button. The pointer drops the expression into the placeholder. It then recovers its original form.

   $$\cos(\; w \cdot t \; + \; x\;) \; + \; \sin(\; w \cdot t \; + \; x\;)$$

Deleting Parts of an Expression

You can delete part of an expression by using either the [**Delete**] key or the [**BkSp**] key. If you use this method, whatever you delete is *not* placed on the Clipboard. This is useful when you intend to replace whatever you delete with whatever is currently on the Clipboard.

To delete part of an expression *without* placing it on the Clipboard:

1. Drag-select the part of the expression (in this case, the numerator) so that it is highlighted in reverse video.

2. Press [**Delete**] or [**BkSp**]. This removes the numerator and leaves behind a placeholder.

Note   If you select an expression with the editing lines instead of drag-selecting as shown above, you must press [**Bksp**] or [**Delete**] *twice* to remove it. In this case, [**Bksp**] removes the expression to the left of the editing lines, and [**Delete**] removes to the right.

Math Styles

You may already have encountered *styles* in your other applications to determine the appearance of text or other elements. By making changes to text styles rather than to individual text elements in a word processing document, you can make sweeping and strikingly uniform changes in the way that documents looks. (See Chapter 5, "Working with Text," for an explanation of Mathcad's text styles) You can get this same kind of leverage by using *math styles* to assign particular fonts, font sizes, font styles and effects, and colors to the elements of your math expressions.

Mathcad has predefined math styles that govern the default appearance of all the math in your worksheet, but you can define and apply additional styles to enhance the appearance of your equations.

Mathcad's predefined math styles are:

- **Variables**, which governs the default appearance of all variables.
- **Constants**, which governs the default appearance of all numbers you type in math regions as well as all numbers that appear in results.

Whenever you type a variable name, Mathcad:

- Assigns to it a math style named "Variables."
- Displays the variable name using the characteristics associated with the style named "Variables."

Similarly, when you type a number or when a result is calculated, Mathcad:

- Assigns to it a math style named "Constants."
- Displays the number using the characteristics associated with the style named "Constants."

Editing Math Styles

To change Mathcad's default style for all variables and plots:

1. Click on a variable name in your worksheet.

2. Choose **Equation** from the **Format** menu. The style name "Variables" is selected.

3. Click "Modify" to change the font associated with the "Variables" style. You'll see a dialog box for changing fonts.

4. Make any changes using the dialog box and click "OK." Mathcad changes the font of all variables in the worksheet.

If you change the Variables style, you may also want to change the style used for numbers so that the two look good together. To do so:

1. Click on a number.

2. Choose **Equation** from the **Format** menu to see the Equation Format dialog box. The style name "Constants" is now selected.

3. Follow the procedure given above for modifying the Variables style.

You can also use the Formatting toolbar to change the font, font size, or font style associated with a math style. For example, to use the Formatting toolbar to modify some of the settings for the Variables math style, click on a variable, then click on the appropriate Formatting toolbar button to make variables bold, italic, or underlined or to specify the font or point size in the drop-down lists.

Note Mathcad's line-and-character grid does not respond automatically to changes in the font sizes used in text and math. Changing font characteristics, particularly font sizes, may cause regions to overlap. You can separate these regions by choosing **Separate Regions** from the **Format** menu.

You may wish to have your equations display in a different color than your default text regions to avoid confusing the two. To change the default color of all equations in your worksheet,

1. Choose **Equation** from the **Format** menu.

2. Select a color in the "Default Equation Color" drop-down list.

3. Click "OK."

Applying Math Styles

The "Variables" and "Constants" styles govern the default appearance of all math in your worksheet. These two style names cannot be changed. You may, however, create and apply additional math styles, named as you choose, in your worksheets and templates.

To see what math style is currently assigned to a name or number, simply click in the name or number, and look at the style window on the Formatting toolbar.

Alternatively, click the name or number and choose **Equation** from the **Format** menu. The math style associated with whatever you clicked on appears in the drop-down list in the Equation Format dialog box.

If you click on the button to the right of "Variables" in either the Formatting toolbar or the Equation Format dialog box, you'll see a drop-down list of available math styles. If you now choose "User 1" and click "OK," a new math style is applied to the selected element and its appearance changes accordingly.

In this way you can apply any of a variety of math styles to:

- individual variable names in an expression, or
- individual numbers in a math expression (but not in computed results, which always display in the "Constants" style).

For example, many math books show vectors in a bold, underlined font. If you want to use this convention, do the following:

1. Choose **Equation** from the **Format** menu.
2. Click the down arrow beside the name of the current math styles to see a drop-down list of available math styles.
3. Click on an unused math style name like "User 1" to select it. The name "User 1" should now appear in the "New Style Name" text box. Click in this text box and change the name to something like "Vectors."
4. Click "Modify" to change this style to a bold, underlined font.

This creates a math style called "Vectors" with the desired appearance. When you're done defining the style, click "OK."

Now rather than individually changing the font, font size, and font style for names of vectors, you can simply change their math styles.

Note All names, whether function names or variable names, are font sensitive. This means that x and x refer to different variables, and $\mathbf{f}(x)$ and $f(x)$ refer to different functions. In deciding whether two variable names are the same, Mathcad actually checks *math styles* rather than fonts. To avoid having distinct variables that look identical, don't create a math style with exactly the same font, size, and other characteristics as another math style.

Saving Math Styles

Once you've completed a set of math styles that you like, you need not repeat the process for other worksheets. You can save math style information by saving a worksheet as a template. Choose **Save As** from the **File** menu and select Mathcad Template (*.mct) as the file type in the Save As dialog box.

To apply math style information to another worksheet, open your template from the **File** menu and copy the contents of the worksheet to the template. For more information about worksheet templates, see Chapter 7, "Worksheet Management."

Chapter 5
Working with Text

♦ Inserting Text

♦ Text and Paragraph Properties

♦ Text Styles

♦ Equations in Text

♦ Text Tools

Inserting Text

This section describes how to create text regions in Mathcad. Text regions are useful for inserting any kind of text into your worksheets and templates: comments around the equations and plots in your worksheet, blocks of explanatory text, background information, instructions for the use of the worksheet, and so on. Mathcad ignores text when it performs calculations, but you can insert working math equations into text regions as described in "Equations in Text" on page 65.

Creating a Text Region

To create a text region, follow these steps. First, click in a blank space in your worksheet to position the crosshair where you want the text region to begin. Then:

1. Choose **Text Region** from the **Insert** menu, or press the double-quote (**"**) key. Mathcad begins a text region. The crosshair changes into an insertion point and a text box appears.

2. Now begin typing some text. Mathcad displays the text and surrounds it with a text box. As you type, the insertion point moves and the text box grows.

3. When you finish typing the text, click outside the text region. The text box disappears.

Note   You cannot leave a text region simply by pressing [↵]. You must leave the text region by clicking outside the region, by pressing [**Ctrl**][**Shift**][↵], or by repeatedly pressing one of the arrow keys until the cursor leaves the region.

To insert text into an existing text region:

- Click anywhere in a text region. A text box now surrounds your text. Anything you type gets inserted at the insertion point.

To delete text from an existing text region, click in the text region and:

1. Press [**BkSp**] to delete the character to the left of the insertion point, or

2. Press [**Delete**] to delete the character to the right of the insertion point.

To overtype text:

1. Place the insertion point to the left of the first character you want to overtype.

2. Press [**Insert**] to begin typing in *overtype* mode. To return to the default *insert* mode, press [**Insert**] again.

You can also overtype text by first selecting it (see "Selecting Text" on page 59). Whatever you type next replaces your selection.

Tip To break a line or start a new line in a text region, press [↵]. Mathcad inserts a hard return and moves the insertion point down to the next line. Press [Shift][↵] to start a new line in the same paragraph. When you rewrap the text by changing the width of the text region, Mathcad maintains line breaks at these spots in the text.

Moving the Insertion Point

In general, you move the insertion point within text regions by clicking with the mouse wherever you want to put the insertion point. However, you can also use the arrow keys to move the insertion point.

The arrow keys move the insertion point character by character or line by line within text. Pressing [**Ctrl**] and an arrow key moves the insertion point word by word or line by line. These and other ways of moving the insertion point are summarized below.

Key	Action
[→]	Move right one character.
[←]	Move left one character.
[↑]	Move up to the previous line.
[↓]	Move down to the next line.
[**Ctrl**][→]	Move to the end of the current word. If the insertion point is already there, move to the end of the next word.
[**Ctrl**][←]	Move to the beginning of the current word. If the insertion point is already there, move to the beginning of the previous word.
[**Ctrl**][↑]	Move to the beginning of the current line. If the insertion point is already there, move to the beginning of the previous line.
[**Ctrl**][↓]	Move to the end of the current line. If the insertion point is already there, move to the end of the next line.
[**Home**]	Move to the beginning of the current line.
[**End**]	Move to the end of the current line.

Selecting Text

One way to select text within a text region is:

1. Click in the text region so that the text box appears.

2. Drag across the text holding the mouse button down.

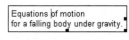

Mathcad highlights the selected text, including any full lines between the first and last characters you selected.

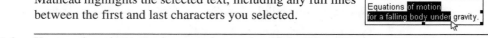

On-line Help You can also select text using arrow keys and multiple clicks of the mouse button, just as you can in most word processing applications. For more information, refer to the topic "Selecting text" in the on-line Help.

Once text is selected, you can delete it, copy it, cut it, check the spelling, or change its font, size, style, or color.

Tip Once you've cut or copied text to the Clipboard, you can paste it back into any text region or into an empty space to create a new text region.

To select and move an entire text region or group of regions, follow the same steps that you would use with math regions, described on "Moving and Copying Regions" on page 10. To perform other editing actions, select the regions, and then choose **Cut**, **Delete**, **Paste**, or **Copy** from the **Edit** menu, or click the corresponding buttons on the Standard toolbar.

Greek Letters in Text

To type a Greek letter in a text region, use one of these two methods:

- Click on the appropriate letter on the Greek toolbar. To see this toolbar, click on the Math toolbar, or choose **Toolbars⇒Greek** from the **View** menu, or

- Type the *Roman equivalent* of the Greek symbol and then press [**Ctrl**]**G**. For example, to enter ϕ, press **f**[**Ctrl**]**G**. See "Greek Letters" on page 498 in the Appendices for a table of Greek letters and their Roman equivalents.

Tip As discussed in the section "Inserting Math" in Chapter 4, typing [**Ctrl**]**G** after a letter in a math region also converts it to its Greek equivalent. In addition, [**Ctrl**]**G** converts a non alphabetic character to its Greek symbol equivalent. For example, typing [**Shift**]**2**[**Ctrl**]**G** in a text region produces the "≅" character.

To change a text *selection* into its Greek equivalent, select the text and then:

1. Choose **Text** from the **Format** menu.

2. From the Font list select the Symbol font.

You can also change the font of a text selection by using the Formatting toolbar.

Changing the Width of a Text Region

When you start typing in a text region, the region grows as you type, wrapping only when you reach the right margin or page boundary. (The location of the right margin is determined by the settings in the Page Setup dialog box, which you can modify by choosing **Page Setup** from the **File** menu.) Press [↵] whenever you want to start a new line. To set a width for your whole text region and have lines wrap to stay within that width as you type. To do this:

1. Type normally until the first line reaches the width you want.

2. Type a space and press [**Ctrl**][↵].

All other lines break to stay within this width. When you add to or edit the text, Mathcad rewraps the text according to the width set by the line at the end of which you pressed [**Ctrl**][↵].

To change the width of an existing text region, do the following:

1. Click anywhere in the text region. A selection box encloses the text region.

2. Move the pointer to the middle of the right edge of the text region until it hovers over the "handle" on the selection rectangle. The pointer changes to a double-headed arrow. You can now change the size of the text region the same way you change the size of any window—by dragging the mouse.

Tip   You can specify that a text region occupies the full page width by clicking on the region and choosing **Properties** from the **Format** menu. Click the Text tab and check "Occupy Page Width." As you enter more lines of text into a full-width text region, any regions that are below are automatically pushed down in the worksheet.

Text and Paragraph Properties

This section describes changing various font properties and changing the alignment and indenting of *paragraphs* within a text region.

Changing Text Properties

To change the font, size, style, position, or color of a portion of the text within a text region, first select the text. (See "Selecting Text" on page 59.) Then choose **Text** from the **Format** menu to access the Text Format dialog box. The Text Format dialog box also appears when you click with the right mouse button on selected text and choose **Font** from the pop-up menu.

Many of the options of the Text Format dialog box are also available via the buttons and drop-down lists on the Formatting toolbar:

When you first insert text, its properties are determined by the worksheet or template defaults for the style called "Normal." See "Text Styles" on page 63 to find out about applying and modifying existing text styles and creating new ones for governing the default appearance of entire text paragraphs or regions. Any properties that you change for selected text as described here *override* the properties associated with the style for that text region.

Tip   If you simply place the insertion point in text and then change the text properties through the Text Format dialog box or the Formatting toolbar, any text you now type at that insertion point will have the new properties you selected.

You can change the following properties of selected text:

- Font
- Font style
- Font size
- Effects such as subscripts and superscripts
- Color

Font sizes are in points. Note that some fonts are available in many sizes and others aren't. Remember that if you choose a bigger font, the text region you're in may grow and overlap nearby regions. Choose **Separate Regions** from the **Format** menu if necessary.

Tip   You can specify that a text region automatically pushes following regions down as it grows by clicking on the region and choosing **Properties** from the **Format** menu. Click the "Text" tab and select "Push Regions Down As You Type."

Tip   As a shortcut for creating subscripts and superscripts in text, use the **Subscript** and **Superscript** commands on the pop-up menu that appears when you click with the right mouse button on selected text.

Changing Paragraph Properties

A paragraph in a text region is any stream of characters followed by a hard return, which is created when you type [↵]. You can assign distinct properties to each paragraph in a text region, including *alignment, indenting* for either the first or all lines in the paragraph, *tab stops*, and *bullets* or *sequential numbering* to begin the paragraph.

When you first create a text region, its paragraph properties are determined by the worksheet or template defaults for the style called "Normal." See "Text Styles" on page 63 to find out about text styles for governing the default appearance of entire text regions or paragraphs. Any paragraph properties that you change as described here *override* the paragraph properties associated with the style for that text region.

Note When you type [Shift][↵] Mathcad inserts a new line within the current paragraph; it does not create a new paragraph.

You can change the properties for a paragraph within a text region by doing the following:

1. Select the paragraph by clicking in it to place the insertion point, by drag-selecting it, or by triple-clicking it.

2. Choose **Paragraph** from the **Format** menu, or click with the right mouse button and choose **Paragraph** from the pop-up menu. Mathcad displays the Paragraph Format dialog box.

3. Change the appropriate properties in the dialog box and click "OK."

You can change the following paragraph properties:

Indent

To indent every line in the paragraph the same amount, enter numbers in the "Left" and "Right" text boxes. To indent the *first* line of the paragraph a different amount than the rest of the lines, as for a conventional or hanging indent, select "First Line" or "Hanging" from the "Special" drop-down list and enter a value below.

You can also set indents using the text ruler. Click in a paragraph and choose **Ruler** from the **View** menu. Move the top or bottom arrow in the ruler to set a different indent for the first line, or move both arrows to indent all the lines in the paragraph.

Bullets and numbered lists

To begin the paragraph with a bullet, select "Bullets" from the "Bullets" drop-down list. Select "Numbers" from the drop-down list to have Mathcad number successive paragraphs in the region automatically. Alternatively, click or on the Formatting toolbar.

Alignment

To align the paragraph at either the left or right edge of the text region, or to center the text within the text region, use the three alignment buttons in the dialog box. Alternatively, click one of the three alignment buttons on the Formatting toolbar: , , or .

Tab stops

To specify tabs, click the "Tabs" button in the Paragraph Format dialog box to open the Tabs dialog box. Enter numbers into the "Tab stop position" text box. Click "Set" for each tab stop then click "OK."

Alternatively, you can set tab stops using the text ruler. Click in a paragraph and choose **Ruler** from the **View** menu. Click in the ruler where you want a tab stop to be. A tab stop symbol appears. To remove a tab stop, click on the tab stop symbol, hold the mouse button down, and drag the cursor away from the ruler.

Tip   To change the measurement system used in the Paragraph Format dialog box or in the text ruler, choose **Ruler** from the **View** menu to show the text ruler if it is not already showing, click on the ruler with the right mouse button, and choose **Inches**, **Centimeters**, **Points**, or **Picas** from the pop-up menu.

Text Styles

Mathcad uses *text styles* to assign default text and paragraph properties to text regions. Text styles give you an easy way to create a consistent appearance in your worksheets. Rather than choosing particular text and paragraph properties for each individual region, you can apply an available text style, setting a range of text and paragraph properties at once.

Every worksheet has a default "normal" text style with a particular choice of text and paragraph properties. Depending on your worksheet and the template from which the worksheet is derived, you may have other predefined text styles to which you can apply to existing or new text regions. You can also modify existing text styles, create new ones of your own, and delete ones you no longer need.

This section describes the procedures for applying, modifying, creating, and deleting text styles. See the previous section, "Text and Paragraph Properties," for details on the available text and paragraph properties.

Applying a Text Style to a Paragraph in a Text Region

When you create a text region in your worksheet, the region is tagged by default with the "Normal" style. You can, however, apply a different style to each paragraph—each stream of characters followed by a hard return—within the text region:

1. Click in the text region on the paragraph where you want to change the style.

2. Choose **Style** from the **Format** menu, or click with the right mouse button and choose **Style** from the pop-up menu, to see a list of the available text styles. Available text styles depend on the worksheet template used.

3. Select one of the available text styles and click "Apply." The default text in your paragraph acquires the text and paragraph properties associated with that style.

Tip   As an alternative to choosing **Style** from the **Format** menu, you can apply a text style to a text paragraph simply by clicking in the paragraph and choosing a style from the left-most drop-down list in the Formatting toolbar. To apply a text style to an entire text region, first select all the text in the region. For information on selecting text, refer to "Selecting Text" on page 59.

Modifying an Existing Text Style

You can change the definition of a text style—its text and paragraph properties—at any time.

To modify a text style:

1. Choose **Style** from the **Format** menu. Mathcad brings up the Text Styles dialog box showing the currently available text styles.

2. Select the name of the text style you want to modify and click "Modify."

3. The Define Style dialog box displays the definitions of that text style.

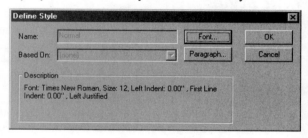

4. Click "Font" to modify text formats such as the font, font size, font styling, special effects, and color. Click "Paragraph" to modify the indenting and alignment and other properties for paragraphs. See "Text and Paragraph Properties" on page 60 for details about the available text and paragraph formatting options.

5. Click "OK" to save your changes.

Any new text regions to which you apply the modified text style will reflect the new definition for that text style. In addition, any text regions previously created with the text style will be modified accordingly.

Creating and Deleting Text Styles

You can modify the list of available text styles in your worksheet by creating new ones and deleting ones you no longer use; any text style changes are saved with your worksheet. You can base a new text style on an existing text style, such that it inherits text or paragraph properties, or you can create an entirely new style. For example, you may want to base a new "Subheading" style on an existing "Heading" style, but choose a smaller font size, keeping other text and paragraph properties the same.

Creating a text style

To create a new text style:

1. Choose **Style** from the **Format** menu. Mathcad brings up the Text Styles dialog box showing the currently available text styles.

2. Click "New" to bring up the Define Style dialog box.

3. Enter a name for the new style in the "Name" text box. If you want to base the new style on one of the existing styles in the current worksheet or template select a style from the "Based on" drop-down list.

4. Click the "Font" button to make your choices for text formats for the new style. Click the "Paragraph" button to choose paragraph formats for the new style.

5. Click "OK" when you have finished defining the new style.

Your new style now appears in the Text Styles dialog box and can be applied to any text region as described in "Applying a Text Style to a Paragraph in a Text Region" on page 63. When you save the worksheet, the new text style is saved with it. If you want to use the new text style in your future worksheets, save your worksheet as a template as described in Chapter 7, "Worksheet Management." You may also copy the text style into another worksheet simply by copying and pasting a styled region into the new worksheet.

Note If you base a new text style on an existing text style, any changes you later make to the original text style will be reflected in the new text style as well.

Deleting a text style

You may delete a text style at any time. To do so:

1. Choose **Style** from the **Format** menu. Mathcad brings up the Text Styles dialog box showing the currently available text styles.

2. Select one of the available text styles from the list.

3. Click "Delete."

The text style is removed from the list of available text styles. However, any text regions in your worksheet whose text and paragraph properties were defined in terms of that text style will continue to display the properties of that style.

Equations in Text

This section describes how to insert equations into your text regions. Equations inserted into text have the same properties as those in the rest of your worksheet. You can edit them using the methods described in Chapter 4, "Working with Math."

Inserting an Equation into Text

Place an equation into text either by creating a new equation inside a text region or by pasting an existing equation into a text region.

To add a new equation into a text region or a paragraph, follow these steps:

1. Click in the text region or paragraph to place the insertion point where you want the equation to start.

> The universal gravitational constant, G, has the value | and can be used to determine the acceleration of a less massive object toward a more massive object.

2. Choose **Math Region** from the **Insert** menu. A placeholder appears.

> The universal gravitational constant, G, has the value |▪ and can be used to determine the acceleration of a less massive object toward a more massive object.

3. Type in the equation just as you would in a math region.

4. When you've finished typing in the equation, click on any text to return to the text region. Mathcad adjusts the line spacing in the text region to accommodate the embedded math region.

> The universal gravitational constant, G, has the value $G := 6.67259 \cdot 10^{-11} \cdot \dfrac{m^3}{kg \cdot s^2}$ and can be used to determine the acceleration of a less massive object toward a more massive object.

To paste an existing equation into a text region, follow these steps:

1. Select the equation you want to paste into the text.

2. Choose **Copy** from the **Edit** menu, or click 📋 on the Standard toolbar.

3. Click in the text region to place the insertion point where you want the equation to start.

4. Choose **Paste** from the **Edit** menu, or click 📋 on the Standard toolbar.

Disabling Embedded Equations

When you first insert an equation into text, it behaves just like an equation in a math region; it affects calculations throughout the worksheet. If you want the equation to be purely cosmetic, you can disable it so that it no longer calculates. To do so:

1. Click on the equation you want to disable.

2. Choose **Properties** from the **Format** menu. Click on the Calculation tab.

3. Click the "Disable Evaluation" check box.

4. Click "OK."

Once you have done so, the equation can neither affect nor be affected by other equations in the worksheet. To turn it back on, remove the check next to "Disable Evaluation" in the Properties dialog box.

For a more general discussion of disabling and locking equations, see "Disabling Equations" on page 124.

Text Tools

Mathcad has tools for finding and replacing text as well as checking the spelling of text.

Find and Replace

Mathcad's **Find** and **Replace** commands on the **Edit** menu are capable of working in both text and math regions. By default, however, Mathcad finds and replaces text in text regions only.

Searching for text

To find a sequence of characters:

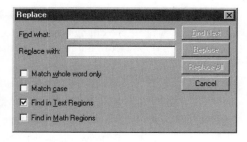

1. Choose **Find** from the **Edit** menu. Mathcad brings up the Find dialog box.

2. Enter the sequence of characters you want to find.

3. Click "Find Next" to find the occurrence of the character sequence immediately after the current insertion point location. Use the available options in the dialog box to search upward or downward in the worksheet, to match whole words only, to match the case exactly of the characters you entered, and to specify whether Mathcad should search in text or math regions or both.

On-line Help The Help topic "Characters You Can Find and Replace" details the characters you can find in math and text regions, including Greek symbols. Many special characters, including punctuation and spaces, can be located only in text or math strings.

Replacing characters

To search and replace text:

1. Choose **Replace** from the **Edit** menu to bring up the Replace dialog box.

2. Enter the string you want to find (the target string) in the "Find what" box.

3. Enter the string you want to replace it with in the "Replace with" box. Check the appropriate boxes to match whole words only, to match the case exactly of the characters you entered, and to specify whether Mathcad should search in text or math regions or both.

You now have the following options:

- Click "Find Next" to find and select the next instance of your target string.
- Click "Replace" to replace the currently selected instance of the string.
- Click "Replace All" to replace all instances of the string.

Spell-Checking

After creating text, Mathcad can search the text for misspelled words and suggest replacements. You can also add commonly used words to your personal dictionary.

Note Mathcad spell-checks text regions only, not math or graphics regions.

To begin spell-checking, specify the portion of the worksheet to spell-check:

- Click at the beginning of wherever you want to spell-check. Mathcad spell-checks starting from this point and continues to the end of the worksheet. You can then either continue the spell-check from the beginning of the worksheet or quit.

- Alternatively, select the text you want to spell-check.

Once you've defined a range over which to check spelling:

1. Choose **Check Spelling** from the **Edit** menu, or click 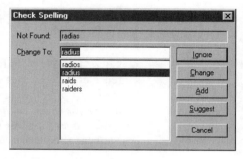 on the Standard toolbar.

2. When Mathcad finds a misspelled word, it opens the Check Spelling dialog box. The misspelled word is shown along with a suggested replacement or a list of possible replacements. If Mathcad has no immediate suggestions, it shows only the misspelled word.

Tip To determine whether a word is misspelled, Mathcad compares it with the words in two dictionaries: a general dictionary of common English words supplemented by mathematical terms and a personal dictionary. If Mathcad detects correctly spelled words throughout your worksheet you can add them to your personal dictionary.

After the Check Spelling dialog box appears, you have several options:

- To change the word to the suggested replacement, or to another word you select from the list of possible replacements, click "Change."

- Click "Suggest" to see additional but less likely replacements. If Mathcad can offer no additional suggestions, "Suggest" is grayed.

- To change the word to one not listed, type the replacement into the "Change to" box and click "Change."

- To leave the word as is, click "Ignore" or "Add." If you click "Ignore," Mathcad leaves the word alone, continues spell-checking, and ignores all future occurrences of the word. If you click "Add," the word is added to your personal dictionary.

Note To choose a dialect associated with the English dictionary, choose **Preferences** from the **View** menu, click on the General tab, and choose an option below "Spell Check Dialect."

Chapter 6
Working with Graphics
and Other Objects

◆   Overview

◆   Inserting Pictures

◆   Inserting Objects

◆   Inserting Graphics Computationally Linked to Your Worksheet

Overview

To illustrate your Mathcad calculations visually, it is often useful to add graphs, pictures, or other objects. You can include the following in your Mathcad worksheet:

- 2D graphs, including X-Y and polar plots
- 3D graphs, including surface plots, contour plots, three-dimensional scatter plots, and others
- Pictures based on values in a matrix, copied and pasted from another application, or based on an image file
- Objects created by another application (.AVI files, .DOC files, .MDI files, etc.)
- Graphics computationally linked to your calculations

For information on creating two-dimensional graphs, see Chapter 12, "2D Plots." Refer to Chapter 13, "3D Plots," for information on creating three-dimensional graphs.

The sections in this chapter describe how to insert pictures and objects into a Mathcad worksheet and format them. The last section of this chapter introduces the process of inserting a graphic that is computationally linked to your calculations. For a more detailed discussion of computationally linked applications, see Chapter 16, "Advanced Computational Features."

Inserting Pictures

This section describes techniques for creating and formatting *pictures*—static graphic images—in your Mathcad worksheet.

Creating a Picture

You can create a picture in a Mathcad worksheet in the following ways:

- By creating a *picture region* and supplying either the name of a Mathcad matrix (or matrices) or the name of an external image file.

- By importing an image from another application via the Clipboard.

Creating pictures from a matrices

You can view as a grayscale picture in Mathcad any single matrix by creating a picture region:

1. Click in a blank space in your Mathcad worksheet.

2. Choose **Picture** from the **Insert** menu or click [icon] on the Matrix toolbar.

3. Type the name of a matrix in the placeholder at the bottom of the picture region.

Mathcad creates a 256-shade grayscale representation of the data in the matrix, with each matrix element corresponding to a *pixel* in the picture.

Note Mathcad's picture region assumes a 256-color model with the value 0 represented as black and 255 as white. Numbers outside the range 0–255 are reduced modulo 256, and any noninteger value is treated as if its decimal part has been removed.

To create a color picture in Mathcad, you must define three matrices of the same size that describe, respectively, either:

- The red, green, and blue (RGB) components,

- The hue, saturation, and value (Smith's HSV color model) components, or

- The hue, lightness, and saturation (Otswald's HLS color model) components of each pixel in the picture.

To view as a color picture in Mathcad any three same-size matrices:

1. Click in a blank space in your worksheet, and choose **Picture** from the **Insert** menu.

2. Type the names of the three matrices, separated by commas, in the placeholder at the bottom of the picture region.

By default, Mathcad creates a 3-layer, 256-color, or RGB, representation of the data in the matrices. This setting can be changed, however, through the Properties dialog box and the Picture toolbar. See "Modifying a picture" on page 71 for details.

Since the matrices used in picture rendering are usually quite large, this technique of creating a picture is most useful when you import graphics files into Mathcad as matrices as described in "File Access Functions" on page 199. For example, you can use the READBMP function to read an external graphics file into a matrix, and then view it as a picture in Mathcad.

Creating a picture by reference to an image file

Mathcad can create a picture directly from an external image file in any one of a number of image file formats, including BMP, JPEG, GIF, TGA, PCX, and more. To do so, click in a blank space in your worksheet and then:

1. Choose **Picture** from the **Insert** menu, or click on the Matrix toolbar, to insert the picture operator.

2. In the placeholder, type a string containing the name of an image file in the current directory, or type a full path to an image file. You create a string in the placeholder by first typing the double-quote (**"**) key.

3. Click outside the picture region. The bitmap appears in your worksheet.

Each time you open the worksheet or calculate the worksheet, the image file is read into the picture region.

Note If you modify the source image file, you must recalculate your worksheet to see the modified image. If you move the source image file, Mathcad can no longer display the picture.

Modifying a picture

You can modify the orientation, view (zoom and pan factors), brightness, contrast, and grayscale mapping of a picture in Mathcad using the Picture toolbar. To do so:

1. Click on the picture so you see hash marks around the picture's border, as shown at the right.

2. The Picture toolbar will pop up. To find out what operation each tool performs, hover over it briefly to see its tooltip.

For example, to zoom in on the picture, click on the Picture toolbar and then repeatedly click the picture until you reach the desired resolution. To zoom out, zoom to window, or reset the zoom factor, click the toolbar buttons ![icon] , ![icon] , and ![icon] , respectively, to activate those commands.

Note If you have the Image Processing Extension Pack or the Communication System Design (CSD) Pack, then you already have an Image Viewer component that behaves in a manner similar to a picture region. Both the Image Viewer component and a picture region allow you to import image files and manipulate them with specialized toolbar options.

You can change your color model or select an output option under the Properties dialog box. To do so:

1. Right-click on the picture and select **Properties** from the pop-up menu.

2. Under the Input and Output tab of the Properties dialog box, make your adjustments in the Input and Output panels, and then click "OK."

For example, you can send the color map information for a selected rectangle of the picture to a variable in your Mathcad worksheet. You might do this if you want to create another picture that only captures part of the whole image. In the Properties dialog box, check "Output Selected Rectangle" in the output pane and select a color map option. Once you click "OK," you need to type a variable name in the placeholder at the left of the picture region.

Creating a picture by importing from the Clipboard

You can copy an image from another application to the Clipboard and paste it into Mathcad in one of the formats put on the Clipboard at the time of copying. This section describes using the **Paste Special** command on the **Edit** menu to paste a graphic image into a Mathcad worksheet from the Clipboard in a noneditable format: as a metafile or bitmap. A metafile, which is strictly a Windows graphic format, can be resized in Mathcad without undue loss of resolution, whereas a bitmap is usually viewed best only at its original size. A device-independent bitmap, or DIB, is stored in a bitmap format that is portable to other operating systems.

Note If you use the **Paste** command on Mathcad's **Edit** menu to paste in an image from the Clipboard (or use drag-and-drop from another application), you typically paste a linked OLE *object* into your Mathcad worksheet, as discussed in "Inserting Objects" on page 74. When you double-click a linked OLE object, you activate the application that created the object and are able to edit the object in your Mathcad worksheet.

To paste a graphics image from another application into Mathcad, do the following:

1. Open the application and place the graphics image on the Clipboard, usually via a **Copy** command on the **Edit** menu. Many Windows applications have this feature.

2. Click the mouse wherever you want the image in your Mathcad worksheet.

3. Choose **Paste Special** from the **Edit** menu, and choose "Picture (metafile)" or "Device Independent Bitmap."

4. Click "OK." Mathcad creates a picture region and puts into it the image stored on the clipboard.

Note The format choices in the Paste Special dialog box will vary, depending on the application from which you originally copied a picture.

Mathcad stores the color depth—the number of colors in the image—at the time you paste it into a worksheet. This means that you can safely resave any worksheets that contain color images on systems that have different color displays, either fewer or more colors. The images continue to display at the proper color depth on the systems that created the worksheets.

Note   When you import directly from the Clipboard, the picture information is stored as part of the Mathcad worksheet. This makes the file size larger. It also means that when you copy the worksheet, the picture information travels along with it.

Note   To avoid making your Mathcad file too large, paste bitmaps that have been saved in as few colors as possible such as 16 or 256 colors.

Formatting a Picture

This section describes your options for formatting a picture once you've created it.

Resizing a picture

To resize a picture region, do the following:

1. Click the mouse inside the picture region to select it.
2. Move the mouse pointer to one of the handles along the edge of region. The pointer changes to a double-headed arrow.
3. Press and hold down the left mouse button. With the button still held, drag the mouse in the direction you want the picture region to be stretched.

Tip   When you change the size of the picture region, the picture inside may be distorted. If you resize the picture by dragging diagonally on the handle in the lower right corner, you preserve the aspect ratio—the ratio of height to width—of the original picture. To restore a picture to its original size, click on the picture and choose **Properties** from the **Format** menu. On the display tab of the Properties dialog box, check "Display at Original Size."

Framing a picture

Mathcad allows you to place a border all the way around a picture region. To do so:

1. Double-click the picture itself, or choose **Properties** from the **Format** menu. This brings up the Properties dialog box.
2. Click "Show Border."
3. Click "OK." Mathcad draws a border around the picture region.

Controlling color palettes

If you are using a 256-color display and have color bitmaps in your Mathcad worksheets, Mathcad by default uses a single 256-color palette to display all the bitmaps in your worksheets. This is the same default color palette Mathcad uses for displaying the rest of the Mathcad screen and is suitable for most pictures.

This default color palette, however, may not be the exact one that any color bitmaps in a worksheet were designed to use. To improve the appearance of bitmaps in your worksheet, you can tell Mathcad to optimize its default color palette so that it chooses the best possible 256 colors to display bitmaps in the worksheet. To do so:

1. Choose **Color⇒Optimize Palette** from the **Format** menu. Mathcad surveys the pictures in the worksheet and generates an optimal 256-color palette to use for all of them.

2. Make sure that **Color⇒Use Default Palette** in the **Format** menu is checked. Then Mathcad uses the new default palette it generates.

Note If your display driver supports more than 256 colors, the palette-setting options on the **Format** menu are grayed.

Inserting Objects

This section describes techniques for inserting and editing *objects* created by other applications in your Mathcad worksheets. OLE (Object Linking and Embedding) technology in Microsoft Windows makes it possible not only to insert static pictures of such objects into your applications (or of Mathcad objects into other applications), but to insert the objects in such a way that they can be fully edited in their originating applications.

An object can be either *embedded* in or *linked* to a Mathcad worksheet. An object that is linked must exist in an external saved file. An object that you embed may be created at the time of insertion. When you edit a linked object, any changes you make to the object also update the original file containing the object. When you edit an embedded object, any changes you make to the object affect it only in the context of the Mathcad worksheet. The original object in the source application, if there is one, is unchanged.

Tip For information about using specialized objects called *components* to import and export data, as well as establish dynamic connections between Mathcad and other applications, see Chapter 11, "Vectors, Matrices, and Data Arrays," and Chapter 16, "Advanced Computational Features."

Inserting an Object into a Worksheet

You insert an object into Mathcad, which is an OLE 2–compatible application, by using the **Object** command from the **Insert** menu, by copying and pasting, or by dragging and dropping. The method you choose depends on whether you want to create the object on the fly, whether the object has already been created, or whether you want the object to be an entire file. You can edit objects in a Mathcad worksheet simply by double-clicking them, causing *in-place activation* of the originating application in most cases.

Tip In general, you use the same methods to insert a *Mathcad object* into another application and edit it inside that application as you do to insert objects into a Mathcad worksheet. However, the details depend on the extent to which the application receiving a Mathcad object supports OLE 2. Once you've inserted a Mathcad object into a compatible application, you can edit it by double-clicking it. If the application supports in-place activation, as current releases of Microsoft Office applications do, the menus and toolbars will change to Mathcad's.

Insert Object command

When you use the **Object** command from the **Insert** menu, you can insert an object that you create at the time you are inserting it, or you can insert an entire file you've already created.

To insert an object or a saved file:

1. First click in your worksheet where you want to insert the object. Make sure you see the crosshair.

2. Choose **Object** from the **Insert** menu to bring up the Insert Object dialog box. By default "Create New" is selected:

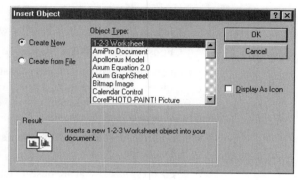

3. Check "Display As Icon" if you want an icon, rather than the actual object, to appear in your worksheet. The icon is typically the icon of the application that created the object.

To create a new object:

1. Select an application from the "Object Type" list. The available object types depend on the applications you have installed on your system.

2. Click "OK."

The source application opens so that you can create the object. When you are finished working to create the object, exit the source application. The object you created is then embedded in your Mathcad worksheet.

If you want to insert a previously created file:

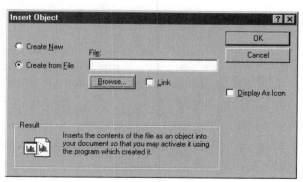

1. Click "Create from File" in the Insert Object dialog box. The dialog box then changes appearance.

2. Type the path to the object file or click "Browse" to locate it.

3. Check "Link" to insert a linked object. Otherwise, the object is embedded.

4. Click "OK."

Pasting an object into a worksheet

You can copy an object from a source application to the Clipboard and paste it directly into Mathcad. This method is particularly useful when you've already created the object in another application and you don't want to insert an entire file.

To insert an embedded or linked object into a worksheet via the Clipboard:

1. Open the source application containing the object.
2. Copy the object from the source application to the Clipboard. You typically do this by choosing **Copy** from the **Edit** menu or by pressing [**Ctrl**]**C**.
3. Click in the Mathcad worksheet where you'd like to place the object.
4. Choose **Paste** or **Paste Special** from Mathcad's **Edit** menu.

If you choose **Paste**, the object is pasted in your Mathcad worksheet in a format that depends on what the source application has placed on the Clipboard. The behavior differs depending on whether you have selected a math placeholder or are pasting into a blank space in the worksheet. Mathcad creates one of the following:

- A *matrix,* if you are pasting numeric data from the clipboard into an empty math placeholder.
- A *text region,* if you are pasting text that does not contain numeric data exclusively.
- A *bitmap* or *picture (metafile),* if the originating application generates graphics.
- An embedded object, if the originating application supports OLE.

If you choose **Paste Special**, you have the option of pasting the object in one of the available formats placed on the Clipboard. Typically you can choose to paste the object as an embedded or linked OLE object (if the object was stored in a saved file in an OLE-compatible source application), a picture (metafile), or a bitmap. See "Creating a picture by importing from the Clipboard" on page 72 for more information on pasting metafiles and bitmaps.

Dragging and dropping an object into a worksheet

A third way to insert an OLE object into a Mathcad worksheet is to drag it from the source application and drop it into the worksheet. This is very similar to copying and pasting, but does not allow you to create a link to an object. To do so, open both Mathcad and the source application and arrange the two windows side by side on the screen. Then select the object in the source application and drag it with the mouse into your Mathcad worksheet. The object appears when you release the mouse button.

Editing an Object

To edit an embedded object in a Mathcad worksheet, double-click the object. Mathcad's menus and toolbars change to those of the source application, and a hatched border surrounds the object so that you can edit it. This OLE editing mechanism is called *in-place activation*. For example, you can use in-place activation to edit objects created by Microsoft Office applications such as Excel and Word inside Mathcad.

If the source application does not support in-place activation inside Mathcad or the object is linked, the behavior is different. In the case of an embedded object, a copy of the object is placed into a window from the other application. If the object is linked, the source application opens the file containing the object.

Editing a Link

If you've inserted a linked object into a Mathcad worksheet, you can update the link, eliminate it, or change the source file to which the object is linked. To do so, choose **Links** from the **Edit** menu.

Choose the link you want to edit from the list of links. Then make changes using the available options.

On-line Help   See the on-line Help topic "Links dialog box" for information on each option in the dialog box.

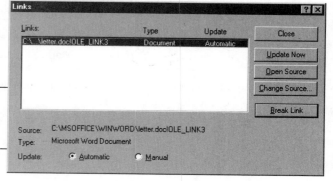

Inserting Graphics Computationally Linked to Your Worksheet

If you want to insert a drawing or other kind of graphic that is computationally linked to your Mathcad worksheet, you can insert a *component*. A component is a specialized OLE object. Unlike other kinds of OLE objects you can insert into a worksheet, as described in "Inserting Objects" on page 74, a component can receive data from Mathcad, return data to Mathcad, or both, linking the object dynamically to your Mathcad computations.

The SmartSketch component, for example, allows you to insert SmartSketch drawings whose dimensions are computationally linked to your Mathcad calculations.

Figure 6-1: The SmartSketch component inserted into a Mathcad worksheet.

An example using the SmartSketch component is shown in Figure 6-1. In addition to the SmartSketch component, Mathcad includes several components for exchanging data with applications such as Excel, MATLAB, and ODBC databases. For more information on these and other components, refer to Chapter 16, "Advanced Computational Features."

Chapter 7
Worksheet Management

♦ Worksheets and Templates

♦ Rearranging Your Worksheet

♦ Layout

♦ Safeguarding an Area of the Worksheet

♦ Worksheet References

♦ Hyperlinks

♦ Creating an Electronic Book

♦ Printing and Mailing

Worksheets and Templates

As you use Mathcad you typically create a *worksheet* that contains unique text, math, and graphic regions. Mathcad uses MCD as the file extension for worksheets.

When you create a new worksheet in Mathcad, you can start with Mathcad's default choices for formats and layout, or you can use a *template* that contains customized information for laying out and formatting the worksheet. When you create a worksheet based on a template, all of the formatting information and any text, math, and graphic regions from the template are copied to the new worksheet. Templates allow you to maintain consistency across multiple worksheets.

Mathcad comes with a variety of predefined templates for you to use as you create new worksheets. You can extend the collection of templates by saving any of your Mathcad worksheets as a template. Mathcad uses MCT as the file extension for templates.

Other saving options are available in Mathcad. You can save a worksheet in Hypertext Markup Language (HTML), so that the file can be viewed through a Web browser, or in rich-text format (RTF), so that it can be opened by most word processors. You can also save a worksheet in a format that can be read by earlier versions of Mathcad.

Creating a New Worksheet

When you first open Mathcad or click 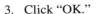 on the Standard toolbar, you see an empty worksheet based on a *worksheet template* (NORMAL.MCT). You can enter and format equations, graphs, text, and graphics in this space, as well as modify worksheet attributes such as the page margins, numerical format, headers and footers, and text and math styles. The normal template is only one of the built-in templates Mathcad provides. There is a template for Electronic Books, one for engineering reports, and one for specification forms.

To create a new worksheet based on a template:

1. Choose **New** from the **File** menu. Mathcad displays a list of available worksheet templates. The exact templates available differ depending on the templates you have developed.

2. Choose a template other than "Blank Worksheet." By default Mathcad displays worksheet templates saved in the TEMPLATE folder of the directory you used to install Mathcad. Click "Browse" to find a template in another directory or on another drive.

3. Click "OK."

Saving Your Worksheet

When you want to save the worksheet, choose either **Save** or **Save As...** from the **File** menu and enter a file name with the extension MCD. After the first time you save the worksheet, simply choose **Save** from the **File** menu or click ⊞ on the Standard toolbar to update the saved copy of the worksheet.

Tip   To work on a worksheet you saved before, choose **Open** from the **File** menu or click 📂 on the Standard toolbar. Mathcad prompts you for a name by displaying the Open dialog box. You can locate and open a Mathcad worksheet from other directories or drives just as you would in any other Windows application. At the bottom of the **File** menu, Mathcad maintains a list of the most recently used worksheets, from which you can choose directly, if you wish.

Saving your worksheet in HTML format

There are two ways to save a Mathcad worksheet in HTML format. One way creates a standard HTML document in which Mathcad text regions are saved as HTML and all other regions are saved as JPEG files linked to the document.

New to Mathcad 2001 is the ability to save your Mathcad worksheet as HTML with embedded Mathematical Markup Language (MathML). In order to view an HTML file that contains MathML, you must install IBM's techexplorer™ Hypermedia Browser, a MathML renderer that works as a plug-in for your browser application. Your Mathcad 2001 package includes a specialized version of techexplorer™ or you can download a free viewer-only version of techexplorer™ from IBM's web site.

Tip To download the free viewer-only version of IBM's techexplorer™ Hypermedia Browser, go to `http://www3.software.ibm.com/download/`, the downloads area of the IBM web site.

When you save your Mathcad worksheets in HTML/MathML format, you can read them back into Mathcad with no loss of information. All regions are displayed and calculate in Mathcad as they would if the document was saved in MCD format.

Note When you save a Mathcad worksheet in HTML or HTML/MathML format, an HTM file is created and a subdirectory with the name "(filename)_images" is also created to contain all the associated JPEG files. Another subdirectory with the name "(filename)_data" contains the information needed to perserve the functionality of Mathcad regions that cannot be rendered in HTML or MathML.

To save a worksheet in either HTML or HTML/MathML format:

1. Choose **Save As...** from the **File** menu.
2. In the Save As dialog box, choose "HTML File" or "HTML/MathML File" from the "Save as type" drop-down list.
3. Enter a file name and then click "Save." The document is saved with the HTM extension.

Figure 7-1 shows a Mathcad worksheet viewed in a browser enabled with IBM's techexplorer™ Hypermedia Browser.

Figure 7-1: Mathcad worksheet saved in HTML/MathML format, viewed in a browser enabled with IBM's techexplorer™ Hypermedia Browser.

Note Not all regions in Mathcad that contain numerical expressions or calculations can be rendered in MathML. For example, there are no markup tags that allow you to display a 2D or 3D graph. You may find that your HTML/MathML document still has many JPEG files associated with it, which display those regions that have no MathML equivalents. In Figure 7-1, the equations, range variable, and results are rendered in MathML, while the graph is displayed through a JPEG file.

Using Microsoft's Internet Explorer, you can activate Mathcad to edit worksheets that have been saved in HTML/MathML format.

To edit your Mathcad worksheets through an Internet Explorer browser:

1. Load your Mathcad worksheet that has been saved in HTML/MathML format into Internet Explorer.

2. Select **Edit with Mathcad Application** under the **File** menu.

Edit your file as usual and then save it using the Save button on Standard toolbar or with the **Save** command from the **File** menu. In either case, the file will be saved in HTML/MathML format.

Tip To publish your HTML files on the web, you can use Windows' Web Folders or the Web Publishing Wizard. These utilities help you establish a direct connection to your web server in order to publish or update your web files.

Saving your worksheet in RTF format

To save a worksheet so you can open it in a word processor capable of reading an RTF file with embedded graphics:

1. Scroll to the bottom of your worksheet to update all calculated results.

2. Choose **Save As** from the **File** menu.

3. In the Save As dialog box, choose "Rich Text Format File" from the "Save as type" drop-down list.

4. Enter a file name and then click "Save."

When you open an RTF file with a word processor such as Microsoft Word, you'll find all the Mathcad regions lined up one above the other at the left edge of the document. You may have to move regions in the word processor to make them look like your original Mathcad worksheet. Once the Mathcad regions have been loaded into a word processor, you will be able to edit the text. However, you'll no longer be able to edit math regions and graphs, which have become embedded graphics. To embed Mathcad worksheets or regions in a word processing document in a form that allows you to continue to edit the original Mathcad worksheets, see "Inserting Objects" on page 74.

Tip Mathcad's text supports Microsoft's "Rich Text Format" (RTF) specification. This means you can easily export text from Mathcad text regions to most word processing programs via the Clipboard. Simply select text in a Mathcad text regions, copy the text to the Clipboard by choosing **Copy** from the **Edit** menu or clicking [icon] on the Standard toolbar, and choose **Paste** from the **Edit** menu in your word processing application.

Saving your worksheet in an earlier format

In general, worksheets created in an earlier version of Mathcad open in the current version, but files created in the current version of Mathcad *do not* open in earlier versions. Mathcad 2001, however, allows you to save a worksheet as a Mathcad 2000, 8, 7, or 6 worksheet.

Note Features in your worksheet available only in Mathcad 2001 will not be recognized in earlier versions of Mathcad. Regions or features that won't work in an earlier version are rendered as bitmaps.

To save a worksheet in a form that can be read by an earlier version of Mathcad:

1. Choose **Save** or **Save As** from the **File** menu.
2. In the "Save as type" drop-down list, select "Mathcad 2000 Worksheet," or one of the earlier formats listed, and provide a file name.
3. Click "Save." A message appears warning you that certain features available only in Mathcad 2001 will not work in earlier versions.

Creating a New Template

You can extend the collection of templates by creating your own. A template you create can have equations, text, and graphics in places you determine, as well as customized information in the headers and footers (see "Layout" on page 89).

The template also specifies:

- Definitions of all math styles (Chapter 4).
- Definitions of all text styles (Chapter 5).
- Margins for printing (see "Layout" on page 89).
- Numerical result formats and values for Mathcad's built-in variables (Chapter 8).
- Names of Mathcad's basic units and the default unit system (Chapter 8).
- The default calculation mode (Chapter 8).
- Ruler visibility and measurement system (see "Aligning Regions" on page 85).

To create a new template, first create a new worksheet having the options listed above set the way you want. The worksheet can also contain any equations, text, and graphics that you want in the template. The next step is to save this worksheet as a template. To do so:

1. Choose **Save As** from the **File** menu.
2. Double-click the TEMPLATE folder in the Save As dialog.
3. In the "Save as type" drop-down list, select "Mathcad Templates (*.mct)."
4. Type a name for the template in the "File name" box.
5. Click "Save."

Your template is now added to the list of templates available in the dialog box that appears when you choose **New** from the **File** menu. To make a new worksheet based on a template you've created, simply choose **New** from the **File** menu and select your template from the list. If you did not save your template to the TEMPLATE folder, you need to browse to find the template.

Modifying a Template

To modify an existing worksheet template:

1. Choose **Open** from the **File** menu or click ⎙ on the Standard toolbar.
2. In the "Files of type" drop-down list, select "All Files."
3. Type the name of the template in the "File name" box, or browse to locate it in the dialog box. Worksheet templates are saved by default in the TEMPLATE folder.
4. Click "Open." The template opens in the Mathcad window.

You may now edit the template as you would modify any Mathcad worksheet. To save your changes under the current template name, choose **Save** from the **File** menu or click ⎙ on the Standard toolbar. If you want to give a new name to the modified template, choose **Save As** from the **File** menu and enter a new name for the template.

Tip To modify the default template for a blank worksheet, modify the template file NORMAL.MCT.

Note When you modify a template, your changes affect only new files created from the modified template. The changes do not affect any worksheets created with the template before the template was modified.

Rearranging Your Worksheet

This section describes how to rearrange math, graphics, and text in your worksheets. See the section "Regions" on page 10 for the basics on selecting, copying, moving, and deleting regions.

Note You can get an overall view of how your worksheet looks by choosing **Zoom** from the **View** menu or clicking ⎙ on the Standard toolbar and choosing a magnification. Choose a magnification less than 100% to zoom out of the worksheet, or use a magnification greater than 100% to zoom in. Alternatively, use the **Print Preview** command as described under "Print Preview" on page 99.

Aligning Regions

Once you've inserted regions into your worksheet, you can align them vertically or horizontally using menu commands or you can align them using the worksheet ruler.

Using commands

To align regions horizontally or vertically using commands:

1. Select regions as described on page 10.
2. Choose **Align Regions**⇒**Across** (to align horizontally) or **Align Regions**⇒**Down** (to align vertically) from the Format menu. Or choose these commands by clicking ⎙ and ⎙ on the Standard toolbar.

When you choose **Align Regions**⇒**Down** from the pull-right menu or click ▤ on the Standard toolbar, Mathcad does the following:

- Mathcad draws an invisible vertical line halfway between the right edge of the right-most selected region and the left edge of the left-most selected region.
- All selected regions to the right of this line are moved left until their left edges are aligned with this line.
- All selected regions to the left of this line are moved right until their left edges are aligned with this line.

Choosing **Align Regions**⇒**Across** or clicking ▤ on the Standard toolbar works in much the same way. Mathcad draws an invisible horizontal line halfway between the top edge of the uppermost region and the bottom edge of the lowest region. Selected regions below and above this line are moved up and down respectively until the midpoints of their left edges are on this line.

Note Aligning regions may inadvertently cause regions to overlap. Mathcad warns you when this will occur, but you can separate overlapping regions as described in "Separating Regions" below.

Using the worksheet ruler

When you choose **Ruler** from the **View** menu while the cursor is in a blank spot or in a math region, you see the worksheet ruler at the top of the window. You can use alignment guidelines on the ruler to align regions at particular measurements along the worksheet.

To set an alignment guideline on the ruler:

1. Click on the ruler wherever you want the alignment guideline to appear. A tab stop symbol appears on the ruler.
2. Click on the tab stop symbol with the right mouse button and choose **Show Guideline** from the pop-up menu. A check appears next to the command.

The alignment guideline appears as a green vertical line. Select and move regions to the guideline. Figure 7-2 shows how you can use an alignment guideline to align math regions.

Note The tab stops you insert on the ruler specify where the cursor should move when you press the [**TAB**] key. To remove a tab stop, click on its symbol, hold the mouse button down, and drag the cursor away from the ruler.

To remove an alignment guideline, click on the ruler with the right mouse button where the guideline is located and choose **Show Guideline** from the menu to uncheck it.

Tip You can change the measurement system used in the ruler by clicking on the ruler with the right mouse button, and choosing **Inches**, **Centimeters**, **Points**, or **Picas** from the pop-up menu. To change the ruler measurement for all documents, make this change to NORMAL.MCT.

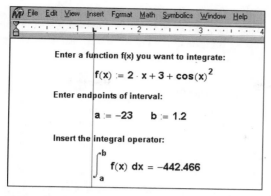

Figure 7-2: Using an alignment guideline to align regions vertically.

Inserting or Deleting Blank Lines

You can easily insert one or more blank lines into your worksheet:

1. Click on the blank line below which you want to insert one or more blank lines. Make sure the cursor looks like a crosshair.

2. Press [**Enter**] to insert a blank line and move the cursor to the left margin. Do this as many times as you want to insert lines.

To delete one or more blank lines from your worksheet:

1. Click above the blank lines you want to delete. Make sure the cursor looks like a crosshair and that there are no regions to the right or left of the cursor.

2. Press [**Delete**] as many times as there are lines you want to delete. Mathcad deletes blank lines below your cursor. Alternatively, press [**BkSp**] to remove blank lines *above* your cursor.

If you press either [**Delete**] or [**BkSp**] and nothing seems to be happening, check to make sure that the cursor is on a line all by itself. If any region in your worksheet extends into the line you are trying to delete, Mathcad won't be able to delete that line.

Tip   To quickly insert or delete a *specific number* of lines from your worksheet, right-click in a blank part of the worksheet, choose **Insert Lines** or **Delete Lines** from the pop-up menu, and enter the number of lines in the dialog box.

Separating Regions

As you move and edit the regions in a Mathcad worksheet, they may end up overlapping one another. Overlapping regions don't interfere with each other's calculations, but they may make your worksheet hard to read.

A good way to determine whether regions overlap is to choose **Regions** from the **View** menu. As shown at right, Mathcad displays blank space in gray and leaves the regions in your default background color. To return to the default background color, choose **Regions** from the **View** menu again.

To separate all overlapping regions, choose **Separate Regions** from the **Format** menu. Wherever regions overlap, this command moves the regions in such a way as to avoid overlaps.

Note Be careful with the **Separate Regions** command since not only can it have far-reaching effects, it also cannot be undone. Regions are moved around and the order of calculation can change. You can also drag regions individually, add lines by pressing [**Enter**], or cut and paste the regions so they don't overlap.

Highlighting Regions

Mathcad allows you to highlight regions so that they stand out from the rest of the equations and text in your worksheet:

To apply a background highlight color to a region:

1. Click in the region you want to highlight.

2. Choose **Properties** from the **Format** menu.

3. Click the Display tab.

4. Check "Highlight Region." Click "Choose Color" to choose a highlight color other than the default choice.

5. Click "OK."

Mathcad fills a box around the equation with either the default background highlight color or the color you chose. This is a purely cosmetic change with no effect on the equation other than making it more conspicuous.

Note The appearance of a highlighted region on printing depends on the capabilities of your printer and the choice of highlight color. Some black and white printers render a color as black, obscuring the equation or text. Others render just the right gray to highlight the equation without obscuring it. Still other printers will disregard the background highlight color entirely.

To change the default background color of highlighted regions:

1. Choose **Color** from the **Format** menu.

2. Pull right and choose **Highlight** to bring up a dialog box containing a palette of colors. Click the appropriate color.

3. Click "OK."

Changing the worksheet background color

To change the color of the background of your worksheet:

1. Choose **Color** from the **Format** menu.

2. Pull right and choose **Background** to bring up a dialog box containing a palette of colors. Click the appropriate color.

3. Click "OK."

Layout

Before printing a worksheet, you may need to adjust the margins, paper options, page breaks, and headers and footers so that pages of the worksheet are printed appropriately.

Setting Margins, Paper Size, Source, and Orientation

Mathcad worksheets have user-specifiable margins at the left, right, top, and bottom of the worksheet. To set these margins, choose **Page Setup** from the **File** menu.

Use the four text boxes in the lower right of the Page Setup to specify the distances from the margin to the corresponding edge of the actual sheet of paper on which you are printing.

You can also use settings in the Page Setup dialog box to change the size, source, or orientation of the paper on which you print your worksheet. See "Printing and Mailing" on page 98 for more about printing your Mathcad worksheets.

Tip   If you want the margin and other page setup settings in the current worksheet to be used in other worksheets, save the worksheet as a template as described in "Creating a New Template" on page 84.

Page Breaks

Mathcad provides two kinds of page breaks:

- **Soft page breaks**: Mathcad uses your default printer settings and your top and bottom margins to insert these page breaks automatically. These show up as dotted horizontal lines, which you see as you scroll down in your worksheet. You cannot add or remove soft page breaks.

- **Hard page breaks**: You can insert a hard page break by placing the cursor at a place in your worksheet and choosing **Page Break** from the **Insert** menu. Hard pagebreaks display as solid horizontal lines in your worksheets.

When Mathcad prints your worksheet, it begins printing on a new page whenever it encounters either a soft or a hard page break.

To delete a hard page break:

1. Drag-select the hard page break as you would select any other region in your Mathcad worksheet. A dashed selection box appears around the page break.

2. Choose **Delete** from the **Edit** menu.

Tip   Because Mathcad is a WYSIWYG environment, any region that overlaps a soft or hard page break prints by default in pieces on successive pages. To separate a region from a hard page break, choose **Separate Regions** from the **Format** menu. However, this command does not separate regions from any overlapping *soft* page breaks. Choose **Repaginate Now** from the **Format** menu to force Mathcad to insert a soft page break above any region that otherwise would print in pieces on successive pages.

Headers and Footers

To add a header or a footer to every printed page, to create a different header or footer for the first page of a worksheet, or to modify an existing header or footer, choose **Headers/Footers** from the **Format** menu. The Header/Footer dialog box appears:

To add or edit a header or footer:

1. Click the Header or Footer tab to modify the header or footer for the worksheet. To create a different header or footer for the first page of your worksheet, check the "Different header and footer on first page" option and click the Header–Page 1 or Footer–Page 1 tab.

2. Type the header or footer information into one or more of the text boxes. Whatever you type into the Left, Center, and Right text boxes will appear in these positions on the page. Click "Format" in the Tools group to change the header or footer font, font style, size, or alignment. Click "Use full width for each section" if you want text in any of the boxes to extend beyond the width of the text box.

3. Click one or more of the buttons in the Tools group to insert items such as the file name, page number, current date, or time automatically wherever the insertion point is. To insert an image, click "Image" in the Tools group and browse to locate a bitmap (.BMP format) file.

Tip Mathcad by default begins numbering at page 1. You can set a different starting page number in the Options group in the Header/Footer dialog box.

Safeguarding an Area of the Worksheet

The ease with which you can alter a Mathcad worksheet can present a problem. It is all too easy to alter a worksheet and to change things which are not meant to be changed. For example, if you've developed and thoroughly tested a set of equations, you may want to prevent readers of your worksheet from tampering with them. To avoid unintended edits to your worksheet, you can safeguard an area of your worksheet by locking it such that you can still edit it even though nobody else can.

To lock an area of your worksheet:

1. Create an *area* in your worksheet to contain the regions to be protected.

2. Place the regions that you want to safeguard into that area.

3. Lock the area. Optionally you can password protect and collapse the area.

Once a region is safely inside a locked area, nobody can edit it. Any math regions inside a locked area continue, however, to affect other equations in the document. For example, if you define a function inside a locked area, you can still use that function anywhere below and to the right of its definition. You cannot, however, change the function's definition itself unless you unlock the area first.

Inserting an Area

To insert a lockable area into your worksheet:

1. Choose **Area** from the **Insert** menu. Mathcad inserts a pair of lines into the worksheet. These mark the boundaries of the lockable area.

2. Select either of these boundary lines just as you'd select any region: by dragging the mouse across the line or by clicking the line itself.

3. Once you've selected the boundary line, drag it just as you'd drag any other region to move it.

You should position the boundaries so that there's enough space between them for whatever regions you want to lock. You can have any number of lockable areas in your worksheet. The only restriction is that you cannot have one lockable area inside another.

Tip To name an area in your worksheet, click on an area boundary, choose **Properties** from the **Format** menu, and enter a name on the Area tab. The Area tab also lets you modify other display attributes of an area, such as whether a border or icon appears.

Locking and Collapsing an Area

Once you've placed whatever regions you want inside an area, you can lock the area. You can choose to lock an area with a password to prevent unauthorized editing of the regions in it. You can also collapse the area, either with or without locking it, so that the regions are hidden from view.

To lock an area:

1. Click in the area.

2. Choose **Area⇒Lock** from the **Format** menu.

3. In the Lock Area dialog box, enter a password if you want to lock the area with a password. Type any combination of letters, numbers, and other characters. You must re-enter the password to confirm it.

4. Check "Collapse when locked" to hide the locked regions from view. Check "Show lock timestamp" to display the date and time the area was last locked above and below the boundary lines.

5. Click "OK."

The area is now locked and by default shows padlocks on the boundaries and a timestamp.

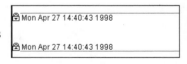

Note If you choose to password protect an area, make sure you remember your password. If you forget it, you will find yourself permanently locked out of that area. Keep in mind also that the password is case sensitive.

To collapse an area without locking it first:

1. Click in the area.

2. Choose **Area⇒Collapse** from the **Format** menu.

A collapsed area appears by default as a single line in your worksheet.

Unlocking and Expanding an Area

If you want to make changes to a region inside a locked area, you have to unlock it. If the area is collapsed, you must also expand it.

To unlock a locked area:

1. Click in the area you want to unlock.
2. Choose **Area**⇒**Unlock** from the **Format** menu.
3. If a password is required, you are prompted for the password.

To expand a collapsed area:

1. Click on the boundary line.
2. Choose **Area**⇒**Expand** from the **Format** menu.

Once an area is unlocked and expanded, you can make whatever changes you want to just as freely as you would elsewhere in your worksheet.

Tip When you lock an area without a password, anyone can unlock it by simply choosing **Area**⇒**Unlock** from the **Format** menu.

Deleting an Area

You can delete a lockable area just as you would any other region. To do so:

1. Make sure the area is unlocked. You cannot delete a locked area.
2. Select either of the two lines indicating the extent of the locked area by dragging the mouse across it.
3. Choose **Cut** from the **Edit** menu or click on the Standard toolbar.

Worksheet References

There may be times when you want to use formulas and calculations from one Mathcad worksheet inside another. You may also have calculations and definitions that you re-use frequently in your work. You can, of course, simply use **Copy** and **Paste** from the **Edit** menu to move whatever you need to move, or drag regions from one worksheet and drop them in another. However, when entire worksheets are involved, this method can be cumbersome or may obscure the main computations of your worksheet.

Mathcad therefore allows you to *reference* one worksheet from another—that is, to access the computations in the other worksheet without opening it or typing its equations or definitions directly in the current worksheet. When you insert a reference to a worksheet, you won't see the formulas of the referenced worksheet, but the current worksheet behaves as if you could.

Tip An alternative described in "Safeguarding an Area of the Worksheet" on page 91 is to create a collapsible *area* to hide calculations in your worksheet. This method, while it does not let you re-use calculations in the same way as a worksheet reference, does give you the option of password protecting or locking an area of calculations.

To insert a reference to a worksheet:

1. Click the mouse wherever you want to insert the reference. Make sure you click in empty space and not in an existing region. The cursor should look like a crosshair.

2. Choose **Reference** from the **Insert** menu.

3. Click "Browse" to locate and select a worksheet. Alternatively, enter the path to a worksheet. You can also enter an Internet address (URL) to insert a reference to a Mathcad file that is located on the World Wide Web.

4. Click "OK" to insert the reference into your worksheet.

To indicate that a reference has been inserted, Mathcad pastes a small icon wherever you had the crosshair. The path to the referenced worksheet is to the right of the icon. All definitions in the referenced worksheet are available below or to the right of this icon. If you double-click this icon, Mathcad opens the referenced worksheet in its own window for editing. You can move or delete this icon just as you would any other Mathcad region.

> ▣ **Reference:http://www.mathsoft.com/mcad60/ug/**

Note   By default, the location of the referenced file is stored in the worksheet as an absolute system path (or URL). This means that if you move the main worksheet and the referenced worksheet to a different file system with a different directory structure, Mathcad cannot locate the referenced file. If you want the location of the referenced file on a drive to be stored relative to the Mathcad worksheet containing the reference, click "Use relative path for reference" in the Insert Reference dialog box. The reference is then valid even if you move the referenced file and the main worksheet to a different drive but keep the *relative* directory structure intact. To use a relative path, you must first save the file containing the reference.

If you edit the contents of a referenced file so that any calculations change, you must re-open any worksheets that contain references to that file for calculations to update. The calculations in those worksheets do not update automatically.

Hyperlinks

Mathcad allows you to create *hyperlinks* in your Mathcad worksheets that, when double-clicked, open Mathcad worksheets, jump to other regions of a Mathcad worksheet, or link to other files.

Creating Hyperlinks Between Worksheets

You can create a hyperlink from any Mathcad region, such as a text region or a graphic element, to any other Mathcad region, either within the same worksheet or in another worksheet. When you double-click the hyperlink, Mathcad opens the worksheet designated by the hyperlink, and if a region is specified it jumps to that region. In this way you can connect groups of related worksheets in a form similar to Mathcad's Electronic Books, or simply cross-reference related areas of a worksheet or worksheets.

Creating hyperlinks from worksheet to worksheet

When you create a hyperlink from one worksheet to another you have two options for the appearance of the target worksheet:

- The target worksheet can open in a full-sized Mathcad worksheet window that overlays the current worksheet window and allows you to edit its contents.

- The target worksheet can open in a small *pop-up window* that displays the contents of the worksheet, but does not allow you to edit its contents.

Mathcad can follow a hyperlink to any worksheet, whether it is stored on a local drive, a network file system, or the World Wide Web.

To create a hyperlink from one worksheet to another, first specify the hyperlink by:

1. Selecting a piece of text, or

2. Clicking anywhere in an equation or graphics region, or

3. Placing the insertion point anywhere within an entire text region.

Tip There are two ways to link text to a target file or destination. You can select a word or phrase, or you can click an entire text region. When you use selected text, Mathcad underlines the word or phrase and the mouse pointer changes to a hand cursor when you hover over it. In general, either selected text or an embedded graphic works best as a hyperlink to another worksheet.

The next step is to specify the target worksheet. To do so:

1. Choose **Hyperlink** from the **Insert** menu. Mathcad opens the Insert Hyperlink dialog box.

2. Click "Browse" to locate and select the target worksheet. Alternatively, enter the complete path to a worksheet in the empty text box at the top of the dialog box, or enter an Internet

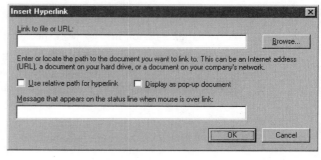

address (URL) to create a hyperlink to a file on the World Wide Web.

3. Check "Use relative path for hyperlink" to store the location of the target worksheet relative to the Mathcad worksheet containing the hyperlink. This allows the hyperlink to be valid even if you move the target file and the worksheet containing the hyperlink, but keep the relative directory structure between the two the same.

Note In order for "Use relative path for hyperlink" to be available, you must first save the worksheet in which you are inserting the hyperlink.

4. Check "Display as pop-up document" if you want the target worksheet to open in a small pop-up window.

5. If you want a message to appear on the status line at the bottom of the window when the mouse hovers over the hyperlink, type the message in the text box at the bottom of the dialog box.

6. Click "OK."

To change any aspects of a hyperlink—for example, if you move the target worksheet and still want the hyperlink to work—click the hyperlink and choose **Hyperlink** from the **Insert** menu. Make any changes you wish in the Edit Hyperlink dialog box.

To remove a hyperlink, click the hyperlink and choose **Hyperlink** from the **Insert** menu. Click "Remove Link" in the dialog box. Mathcad removes all traces of the link.

Creating hyperlinks from region to region

Before you can link to a specific region in a worksheet, you must mark it with a *tag*. A tag uniquely identifies a region in a worksheet, allowing you to jump directly to that region. A tag can be any collection of words, numbers, or spaces, but no symbols.

To create a region tag:

1. Right-click on any region in your worksheet for which you would like to create a region tag.

2. Select **Properties** from the pop-up menu.

3. In the Properties dialog box, under the Display tab, type a tag in the text box provided and click "OK."

Now, you will be able to link to that region from within the worksheet or from any other worksheet.

To create a hyperlink to a region that has been *tagged*:

1. Click a region in your worksheet, and choose **Hyperlink** from the **Insert** menu.

2. Click "Browse" to locate and select the target worksheet, or type the complete path to a worksheet, or enter an Internet address (URL). You must enter the name of the target worksheet even if you are creating a hyperlink to a region within the same worksheet.

3. At the end of the worksheet path type "#" followed by the region tag. The complete path for your target region will look something like this: **C:\filename#region tag**

4. Make further desired specifications in the Hyperlink dialog box and click "OK."

Note When you link from region to region within or between Mathcad worksheets, you cannot use the pop-up window option.

Creating Hyperlinks to Other Files

You can use the methods described in the previous section to create a hyperlink not only from one Mathcad worksheet to another, but also from a Mathcad worksheet to any other file type, either on a local or network file system or on the Web. Use this feature to create Electronic Books, as described in "Creating an Electronic Book," or compound documents that contain not only Mathcad worksheets but word processing files, animation files, web pages—any file type that you want.

Note When you double-click a hyperlink to a file other than a Mathcad worksheet, you launch either the application that created the file or an application associated with a file of that type in the Windows Registry. You cannot display such hyperlinked files within a pop-up window.

Creating an Electronic Book

As described in Chapter 3, "Online Resources," an Electronic Book is a hyperlinked collection of Mathcad worksheets. When you open an Electronic Book in Mathcad, it opens in its own window. The Electronic Book has a table of contents and an index as well as other browsing features which you can access using the buttons on the toolbar in the window. The worksheets in an Electronic Book are live so a reader can experiment directly within the book.

If you have several Mathcad worksheets that you want to collect together, you can create your own Electronic Book. There are several steps to creating an Electronic Book, and they include:

1. Creating individual Mathcad files

2. Preparing a Table of Contents

3. Adding hyperlinks between appropriate files

4. Creating an HBK file to specify the order of the files in the book

5. Developing an index (optional)

6. Checking the index, HBK file, and worksheets for errors

For more details about each step of this process, see the **Author's Reference** under the **Help** menu in Mathcad. There you will find tips and techniques for creating Electronic Books, as well as other details associated with turning a collection of worksheets into a navigable handbook of information.

It is recommended that you read all steps of the process before you undertake the project of creating an Electronic Book. After you have created an Electronic Book, you or others can open it in Mathcad and navigate through it using the toolbar buttons of the Electronic Book window. For more information on Electronic Books and the navigation tools, refer to Chapter 3, "Online Resources."

Printing and Mailing

To print a Mathcad worksheet, choose **Print** from the **File** menu. The Print dialog box lets you control whether to print the entire worksheet, selected pages, or selected regions; what printer to print on; and the number of copies to print. The particular dialog box you see depends on the printer you've selected. A typical dialog box is shown at right.

Printing Wide Worksheets

Mathcad worksheets can be wider than a sheet of paper, since you can scroll as far to the right as you like in a Mathcad worksheet and place equations, text, and graphics wherever you like. As you scroll horizontally, however, you see dashed vertical lines appearing to indicate the right margins of successive "pages" corresponding to the settings for your printer. The sections of the worksheet separated by the dashed vertical lines print on separate sheets of paper, yet the page number at the bottom of the Mathcad window does not change as you scroll to the right.

You can think of the worksheet as being divided into vertical strips. Mathcad begins printing at the top of each strip and continues until it reaches the last region in this strip. It prints successive strips left to right. Note that certain layouts will produce one or more blank pages.

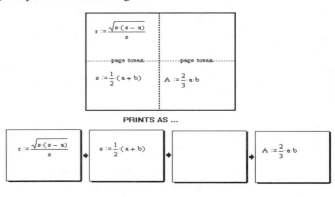

Tip You can control whether a wide worksheet is printed in its entirety or in a single page width. To do so, choose **Page Setup** from the **File** menu to open the Page Setup dialog box. Then, to suppress printing of anything to the right of the right margin, check "Print single page width."

You can ask Mathcad to print a range of pages in the worksheet by using the Print dialog box. The page numbers in the dialog box refer only to horizontal divisions. For example, if your worksheet looks like that shown above, and you ask Mathcad to print page 2, you will see two sheets of paper corresponding to the lower-left and lower-right quadrants.

Tip   Mathcad allows you to change the display of some operators including the **:=**, the bold equals, the derivative operator, and the multiplication operator. Before you print, you can choose **Options** from the **Math** menu and click on the Display tab to change the appearance of these operators. This can make your printout clearer to someone unfamiliar with Mathcad notation.

Print Preview

To check your worksheet's layout before printing, choose **Print Preview** from the **File** menu or click [icon] on the Standard toolbar. The Mathcad window shows the current section of your worksheet in miniature, as it will appear when printed, with a strip of buttons across the top of the window:

To print your worksheet from this screen, click "Print." Click "Close" to go back to the main worksheet screen. The remaining buttons give you more control over the preview.

Tip   Although you can use the "Zoom In" and "Zoom Out" buttons to magnify the worksheet, you can also magnify the worksheet by moving the cursor onto the previewed page so that the cursor changes to a magnifying glass. Then click the mouse. Click again to magnify your worksheet even more. Once you're at the maximum magnification, clicking on the page de-magnifies it.

Note   You cannot edit the current page or change its format in the Print Preview screen. To edit the page or change its format, return to the normal worksheet view by clicking "Close."

Mailing

If you're connected to a mail system that's compatible with Microsoft's Mail API (MAPI), you can use Mathcad to direct that system to send an electronic mail message and your current Mathcad worksheet. When you use Mathcad to send a worksheet by electronic mail, the recipient receives the worksheet as a file attached to an ordinary e-mail message, provided that the recipient's mail system uses the same encoding technique as yours.

Tip   The settings in your mail system determine how Mathcad worksheets are attached to or encoded in the mail message. We recommend that you use a compression or encoding method such as ZIP, MIME, or UUENCODE, if available, to attach Mathcad worksheets to mail messages.

To send a Mathcad worksheet by electronic mail:

1. Open the worksheet you want to send.
2. Choose **Send** from the **File** menu.

Once you do so, your mail system launches and creates a new message with your worksheet as an attachment. You should then enter the text of your mail message, the address of the recipient, and any other information allowed by your mail system.

Chapter 8
Calculating in Mathcad

♦ Defining and Evaluating Variables

♦ Defining and Evaluating Functions

♦ Units and Dimensions

♦ Working with Results

♦ Controlling Calculation

♦ Animation

♦ Error Messages

Defining and Evaluating Variables

When you type an expression into a worksheet, you are usually doing one of two things:

• You could be typing a variable or function name and assigning some value to it.

• You could be typing an equation and asking Mathcad to give you the answer.

We introduce these topics in this and the following section. See "Evaluating Expressions Numerically" on page 103 for details on numerical evaluation.

Defining a Variable

A variable definition defines the value of a variable everywhere below and to the right of the definition. To define a variable, follow these three steps:

1. Type the variable name to be defined. Chapter 4, "Working with Math," contains a description of valid variable names.

2. Press the colon (**:**) key, or click ▓ on the Calculator toolbar. The definition symbol (:=) appears with a blank placeholder to the right.

3. Type an expression to complete the definition. This expression can include numbers and any previously defined variables and functions.

The left-hand side of a ":=" can contain any of the following:

- A simple variable name like x.

- A subscripted variable name like v_i.

- A matrix whose elements are either of the above. For example, $\begin{bmatrix} x \\ y_1 \end{bmatrix}$. This technique allows you to define several variables at once: each element on the right-hand side is assigned simultaneously to the corresponding element on the left-hand side.

- A function name with an argument list of simple variable names. For example, $f(x, y, z)$. This is described further in the next section.

- A superscripted variable name like $\mathbf{M}^{\langle 1 \rangle}$.

Built-in Variables

Mathcad includes *predefined* or *built-in variables*. Predefined variables can have a conventional value, like π and e, or be used as system variables to control how Mathcad works. See "Predefined Variables" on page 496 in the Appendices for a list of built-in variables in Mathcad.

Note In addition to the built-in variables described here, Mathcad treats the names of all built-in *units* as predefined variables. See "Units and Dimensions" on page 112.

Although Mathcad's predefined variables already have values when you start Mathcad, you can still redefine them. For example, if you want to use a variable called e with a value other than the one Mathcad provides, enter a new definition, like $e := 2$. The variable e takes on the new value everywhere in the worksheet below and to the right of the new definition. Alternatively, create a global definition for the variable as described in "Global Definitions" on page 104.

Note Mathcad's predefined variables are defined for all fonts, sizes, and styles. This means that if you redefine e as described above, you can still use e, for example, as the base for natural logarithms. Note, however, that Greek letters are not included.

You can modify many of Mathcad's built-in variables without having to explicitly define them in your worksheet. To do so, choose **Options** from the **Math** menu, and click the Built-In Variables tab on the Math Options dialog box.

To set new starting values for any of these variables, enter a new value in the appropriate text box and click "OK." Then choose **Calculate Worksheet** from the **Math** menu to ensure that all existing equations take the new values into account.

The numbers in brackets to the right of the variable names represent the default values for those variables. To restore these default values for the built-in variables listed in the dialog box, click "Restore Defaults" and then click "OK."

Evaluating Expressions Numerically

To evaluate an expression numerically, follow these steps:

1. Type an expression containing any valid combination of numbers, variables, and functions. Any variables or functions in this expression should be defined earlier in the worksheet.

$$\frac{1}{2} \cdot m \cdot v^2|$$

2. Press the "=" key, or click = on the Calculator toolbar. Mathcad computes the value of the expression and shows it after the equal sign.

$$\frac{1}{2} \cdot m \cdot v^2| = 567.108 \quad \blacksquare$$

Tip   Whenever you evaluate an expression, Mathcad shows a final placeholder at the end of the equation. You can use this placeholder for unit conversions, as explained in "Working with Results" on page 115. As soon as you click outside the region, Mathcad hides the placeholder.

Figure 8-1 shows some results calculated from preceding variable definitions.

How Mathcad Scans a Worksheet

Mathcad scans a worksheet the same way you read it: left to right and top to bottom. This means that a variable or function definition involving a ":=" affects everything below and to the right of it.

To see the placement of regions more clearly in your worksheet, choose **Regions** from the **View** menu. Mathcad displays blank space in gray and leaves regions in your background color.

Figure 8-1: Calculations based on simple variable definitions.

Figure 8-2 shows examples of how placement of equations in a worksheet affects the evaluation of results. In the first evaluation, both x and y are highlighted (Mathcad shows them in red on screen) to indicate that they are undefined. This is because the definitions for x and y lie below where they are used. Because Mathcad scans from top to bottom, when it gets to the first equation, it doesn't know the values of x and y.

The second evaluation, on the other hand, is below the definitions of x and y. By the time Mathcad gets to this equation, it has already assigned values to both x and y.

Figure 8-2: Mathcad evaluates equations from top to bottom in a worksheet. Undefined variables are highlighted.

Note You can define a variable more than once in the same worksheet. Mathcad simply uses the first definition for all expressions below the first definition and above the second. For expressions below the second definition and above the third, Mathcad uses the second definition, and so on.

Global Definitions

Global definitions are exactly like local definitions except that they are evaluated before any local definitions. If you define a variable or function with a global definition, that variable or function is available to all local definitions in your worksheet, regardless of whether the local definition appears above or below the global definition.

To type a global definition, follow these steps:

1. Type a variable name or function to be defined.

2. Press the tilde (~) key, or click ▤ on the Evaluation toolbar. The global definition symbol appears.

3. Type an expression. The expression can involve numbers or other globally defined variables and functions.

You can use global definitions for functions, subscripted variables, and anything else that normally uses the definition symbol ":=".

This is the algorithm that Mathcad uses to evaluate all definitions, global and otherwise:

- First, Mathcad takes one pass through the entire worksheet from top to bottom. During this first pass, Mathcad evaluates global definitions only.

- Mathcad then makes a second pass through the worksheet from top to bottom. This time, Mathcad evaluates all definitions made with ":=" as well as all equations containing "=" and "≡". Note that during this pass, global definitions do not use any local definitions.

Note A global definition of a variable can be overridden by a local definition of the same variable name with the definition symbol ":=".

Figure 8-3 shows the results of a global definition for the variable *R* which appears at the bottom of the figure.

Start with these definitions and calculations . . .

$V := 1000 \qquad n := 3 \qquad T := 373$

$P := \dfrac{n \cdot R \cdot T}{V} \qquad\qquad P = 0.092$

Now change the definitions of V and T . . .

$V := 500 \qquad\qquad T := 323$

$P := \dfrac{n \cdot R \cdot T}{V} \qquad\qquad P = 0.159$

Since R is defined globally, its definition applies everywhere in the document . . .

$R \equiv .0820562$

Figure 8-3: Using the global definition symbol.

Although global definitions are evaluated before any local definitions, Mathcad evaluates global definitions the same way it evaluates local definitions: top to bottom and left to right. This means that whenever you use a variable to the right of a "≡":

- that variable must also have been defined with a "≡," *and*
- the variable must have been defined *above* the place where you are trying to use it.

Otherwise, the variable is marked in red to indicate that it is undefined.

Tip   It is good practice to allow only one definition for each global variable. Although you can do things like define a variable with two different global definitions or with one global and one local definition, this may make your worksheet difficult for others to understand.

Range Variables

Iterative processes in Mathcad worksheets depend on *range variables*. Except for the way it is defined, a range variable looks just like a conventional variable. The difference is that a conventional variable takes on only one value. A range variable, on the other hand, takes on a range of values separated by uniform steps. For example, you could define a range variable to go from –4 through 4 in steps of 2. If you now use this range variable in an expression, Mathcad evaluates that expression five times, once for each value taken by the range variable.

Range variables are crucial to exploiting Mathcad's capabilities to their fullest. This section shows how to define and use range variables to perform iteration. For a description of more advanced iterative operations made possible by the programming operators in Mathcad Professional, turn to Chapter 15, "Programming."

Defining and using range variables

To define a range variable, type the variable name followed by a colon and a range of values. For example, here's how to define the variable j ranging from 0 to 15 in steps of 1:

1. Type **j** and then press the colon key (**:**), or click ⬛ on the Calculator toolbar. The empty placeholder indicates that Mathcad expects a definition for j. At this point, Mathcad does not know whether j is to be a conventional variable or a range variable. $\boxed{j := \blacksquare}$

2. Type **0**. Then press the semicolon key (**;**), or click ⬛ on the Calculator toolbar. This tells Mathcad that you are defining a range variable. Mathcad displays the semicolon as two periods ".." to indicate a range. Complete the range variable definition by typing **15** in the remaining placeholder. $\boxed{j := 0 \,.. \, 15}$

This definition indicates that j now takes on the values $0, 1, 2 \ldots 15$. To define a range variable that changes in steps other than 1, see the section "Types of ranges" on page 108.

Once you define a range variable, it takes on its complete range of values *every time you use it*. If you use a range variable in an equation, for example, Mathcad evaluates that equation once for each value of the range variable.

You must define a range variable exactly as shown above. There must be:

- a variable name on the left,
- either a ":=" or a "≡" in the middle, and
- a valid range on the right.

Note   You *cannot* define a variable in terms of a range variable. For example, if after having defined j as shown you now define $i := j + 1$, Mathcad assumes you are trying to set a scalar variable equal to a range variable and marks the equation with an appropriate error message.

One application of range variables is to fill up the elements of a vector or matrix. You can define vector elements by using a range variable as a subscript. For example, to define x_j for each value of j:

- Type **x[j:j^2[Space]+1**.

$$x_j := j^2 + 1$$

Figure 8-4 shows the vector of values computed by this equation. Since j is a range variable, the entire equation is evaluated once for each value of j. This defines x_j for each value of j from 0 to 15.

$$j := 0 .. 15$$
$$x_j := j^2 + 1$$

x_j
1
2
5
10
17
26
37
50
65
82
101
122
145
170

$x_0 = 1$

$x_1 = 2$

$x_3 = 10$

$x_7 = 50$

$x_{11} = 122$

$x_{15} = 226$

Figure 8-4: Using a range variable to define the values of a vector.

To understand how Mathcad computes with range variables, keep in mind this fundamental principle:

If you use a range variable in an expression, Mathcad evaluates the expression once for each value of the range variable.

If you use two or more range variables in an equation, Mathcad evaluates the equation once for each value of each range variable.

<table>
<tr><td>**Tip**</td><td>Mathcad takes longer to compute equations with ranged expressions since there may be many computations for each equation. While Mathcad is computing, the mouse pointer changes its appearance. To learn how to interrupt a calculation in progress, see "Interrupting Calculations" on page 124.</td></tr>
</table>

Types of ranges

The definition of j in the previous section, ranging from 0 to 15, is an example of the simplest type of range definition. But Mathcad permits range variables with values ranging from any value to any other value, using any constant increment or decrement.

To define a range variable with a step size other than 1, type an equation of this form:

$$\mathtt{k:1,1.1;2}$$

This appears in your worksheet window as:

$$k := 1, 1.1 .. 2$$

In this range definition:

- The variable k is the name of the range variable itself.
- The number 1 is the first value taken by the range variable k.
- The number 1.1 is the second value in the range. *Note that this is not the step size.* The step size in this example is 0.1, the difference between 1.1 and 1. If you omit the comma and the 1.1, Mathcad assumes a step size of one in whatever direction (up or down) is appropriate.
- The number 2 is the last value in the range. In this example, the range values are constantly increasing. If instead you had defined $k := 10 .. 1$, then k would count down from 10 to 1. If the third number in the range definition is not an even number of increments from the starting value, the range will not go beyond it. For example, if you define $k := 10, 20 .. 65$ then k takes values 10, 20, 30, . . ., 60.

<table>
<tr><td>**Note**</td><td>You can use arbitrary scalar expressions in range definitions. However, these values must always be *real* numbers. Also note that if you use a fractional increment for a range variable, you will not be able to use that range variable as a subscript because subscripts must be integers.</td></tr>
</table>

Defining and Evaluating Functions

As described in Chapter 10, "Built-in Functions," Mathcad has an extensive built-in function set. You can augment Mathcad's built-in function set by defining your own functions.

You define a function in much the same way you define a variable. The name goes on the left, a definition symbol goes in the middle, and an expression goes on the right. The main difference is that the name includes an *argument list*. The example below shows how to define a function called *dist(x, y)* that returns the distance between the point *(x, y)* and the origin.

To type such a function definition:

1. Type the function name.

2. Type a left parenthesis followed by one or more names separated by commas. Complete this argument list by typing a right parenthesis.

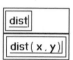

Note It makes no difference whether or not the names in the argument list have been defined or used elsewhere in the worksheet. What is important is that these arguments *must be names*. They cannot be more complicated expressions.

- Press the colon (**:**) key, or click $\boxed{:=}$ on the Calculator toolbar. You see the definition symbol (:=).

$$\text{dist}(x, y) := \blacksquare$$

- Type an expression to define the function. In this example, the expression involves only the names in the argument list. In general though, the expression can contain any previously defined functions and variables as well.

$$\text{dist}(x, y) := \sqrt{x^2 + y^2}$$

Once you have defined a function, you can use it anywhere below and to the right of the definition, just as you would use a variable.

When you evaluate an expression containing a function, as shown in Figure 8-5, Mathcad:

1. evaluates the arguments you place between the parentheses,

2. replaces the dummy arguments in the function definition with the actual arguments you place between the parentheses,

3. performs whatever arithmetic is specified by the function definition,

4. returns the result as the value of the function.

Note As shown in Figure 8-5, if you type only the name of a function without its arguments, Mathcad returns the word "function."

```
Computing distances between points

x1 := 0              y1 := 1.5

x2 := 3              y2 := 4

x3 := -1             y3 := 1          dist(x, y) := √(x² + y²)

Compute distance from origin:
                                      dist = function
dist(x1, y1) = 1.5

dist(x2, y2) = 5

dist(x3, y3) = 1.414
```

Figure 8-5: A user-defined function to compute the distance to the origin.

The arguments of a user-defined function can represent scalars, vectors, or matrices.

For example, you could define the distance function as $dist(v) := \sqrt{v_0^2 + v_1^2}$. This is an example of a function that accepts a vector as an argument and returns a scalar result. See Chapter 11, "Vectors, Matrices, and Data Arrays," for more information.

Note   User-defined function names are font and case sensitive. The function $\mathbf{f}(x)$ is different from the function $f(x)$ and $\mathrm{SIN}(x)$ is different from $\sin(x)$. Mathcad's built-in functions, however, are defined for all fonts (except the Symbol font), sizes, and styles. This means that $\mathbf{sin}(x)$, $sin(x)$, and $\mathtt{sin}(x)$ all refer to the same function.

Variables in User-Defined Functions

When you define a function, you don't have to define any of the names in the argument list since you are telling Mathcad *what to do* with the arguments, not what they are. When you define a function, Mathcad doesn't even have to know the types of the arguments—whether the arguments are scalars, vectors, matrices, and so on. It is only when Mathcad *evaluates* a function that it needs to know the argument types.

However, if in defining a function you use a variable name that *is not* in the argument list, you must define that variable name above the function definition. The value of that variable at the time you make the function definition then becomes a permanent part of the function. This is illustrated in Figure 8-6.

If you want a function to depend on the value of a variable, you must include that variable as an argument. If not, Mathcad just uses that variable's fixed value at the point in the worksheet where the function is defined.

Figure 8-6: The value of a user function depends on its arguments.

Recursive Function Definitions

Mathcad supports *recursive* function definitions—you may define the value of a function in terms of a previous value of the function. As shown in Figure 8-7, recursive functions are useful for defining arbitrary periodic functions, as well as elegantly implementing numerical functions like the factorial function

Note that a recursive function definition should always have at least two parts:

- An initial condition that prevents the recursion from going forever.

- A definition of the function in terms of some previous value(s) of the function.

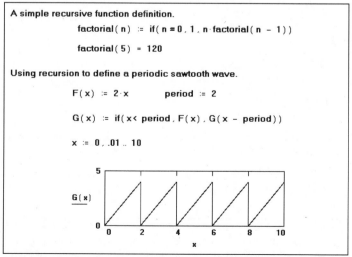

Figure 8-7: Mathcad allows recursive function definitions.

If you do not specify an initial condition that stops the recursion, Mathcad generates a "stack overflow" error message when you try to evaluate the function.

The programming operators in Mathcad Professional also support recursion. See the section "Programs Within Programs" in Chapter 15 for examples.

Units and Dimensions

When you first start Mathcad, a complete set of units is available for your calculations. You can treat these units just like built-in variables. To assign units to a number or expression, just multiply it by the name of the unit.

Mathcad recognizes most units by their common abbreviations. Lists of all of Mathcad's built-in units in several systems of units are in the Appendices. By default Mathcad uses units from the SI unit system (also known as the International System of Units) in the *results* of any calculations, but you may use any supported units you wish in creating your expressions. See "Displaying Units of Results" on page 118 for more information about selecting a unit system for results.

For example, type expressions like the following:

```
mass:75*kg
acc:100*m/s^2
acc_g:9.8*m/s^2
F:mass*(acc + acc_g)
```

Figure 8-8 shows how these equations appear in a worksheet.

$$mass := 75 \cdot kg$$

$$acc := 100 \cdot \frac{m}{s^2}$$

$$acc\_g := 9.8 \cdot \frac{m}{s^2}$$

$$F := mass \cdot (acc + acc\_g)$$

$$F = 8.235 \times 10^3 \, N$$

$$mass := 75kg$$ <--Mathcad treats the multiplication as implied when you type
an expression like **mass:75kg**

$$mass = 75 \, kg$$

Figure 8-8: Equations using units.

Tip If you define a variable which consists of a number followed immediately by a unit name, you can omit the multiplication symbol; Mathcad inserts a very small space and treats the multiplication as implied. See the definition of mass at the bottom of Figure 8-8.

You can also use the Insert Unit dialog box to insert one of Mathcad's built-in units into any placeholder.

To use the Insert Unit dialog box:

1. Click in the empty placeholder and choose **Unit** from the **Insert** menu, or click on the Standard toolbar. Mathcad opens the Insert Unit dialog box.

2. The list at the bottom shows built-in units, along with their Mathcad names, corresponding to whatever physical quantity is selected in the top scrolling list. When "Dimensionless" is selected at the top, a list of all available built-in units shows on the bottom.

3. If necessary, use the top scrolling list to display only those units corresponding to a particular physical quantity. This makes it easier to find a particular unit or to see what choices are appropriate.

4. In the bottom list, double-click the unit you want to insert, or click the unit you want and then click "Insert." Mathcad inserts that unit into the empty placeholder.

Note Mathcad performs some dimensional analysis by trying to match the dimensions of your selected result with one of the common physical quantities in the top scrolling list. If it finds a match, you'll see all the built-in units corresponding to the highlighted physical quantity in the bottom scrolling list. If nothing matches, Mathcad simply lists all available built-in units on the bottom.

Dimensional Checking

Whenever you enter an expression involving units, Mathcad checks it for dimensional consistency. If you add or subtract values with incompatible units, or violate other principles of dimensional analysis, Mathcad displays an appropriate error message.

For example, suppose you had defined *acc* as $100 \cdot m/s$ instead of $100 \cdot m/s^2$ as shown at right. Since *acc* is in units of velocity and *acc_g* is in units of acceleration, it is inappropriate to add them together. When you attempt to do so, Mathcad displays an error message.

$$mass := 75 \cdot kg$$

$$acc := 100 \cdot \frac{m}{s}$$

$$acc\_g := 9.8 \cdot \frac{m}{s^2}$$

$$F := mass \cdot (acc + acc\_g)$$

The units in this expression do not match.

Other unit errors are usually caused by one of the following:

- An incorrect unit conversion.
- A variable with the wrong units.
- Units in exponents or subscripts (for example $v_{3 \cdot acre}$ or $2^{3 \cdot ft}$).
- Units as arguments to inappropriate functions (for example, $\sin(0 \cdot henry)$).

Tip   If you want to temporarily remove units from an argument, x, divide x by $UnitsOf(x)$. For example, if p is defined as $2\,ft$ then $\sin(p)$ gives an error but $\sin\left(\dfrac{p}{UnitsOf(p)}\right) = 0.573$.

Defining Your Own Units

Although Mathcad recognizes many common units, you may need to define your own unit if that unit isn't one of Mathcad's built-in units or if you prefer to use your own abbreviation instead of Mathcad's abbreviation.

Note   Although absolute temperature units are built into Mathcad, the Fahrenheit and Celsius temperature units are not. See the QuickSheet "Temperature Conversions" in the on-line Resource Center for samples of defining these temperature scales and converting between them.

You define your own units in terms of existing units in exactly the same way you would define a variable in terms of an existing variable. Figure 8-9 shows how to define new units as well as how to redefine existing units.

$$\text{Å} := 10^{-10}\,m \qquad \text{µs} := 10^{-6} \cdot s$$

$$\text{week} := 7 \cdot day \qquad \text{kilo} := 1 \cdot kg$$

Results are displayed by default in terms of the base units of the current unit system, but you can type other units into the units placeholder to see the result in different units.

$$\text{Å} = 1 \times 10^{-10}\,m \qquad\qquad \text{week} = 6.048 \times 10^{5}\,s$$

$$\text{week} = 0.019\,yr \qquad\qquad \text{µs} = 1.667 \times 10^{-8}\,min$$

$$\text{kilo} = 1\,kg$$

Figure 8-9: Defining your own units.

Note   Since units behave just like variables, you may run into unexpected conflicts. For example, if you define the variable m in your worksheet, you won't be able to use the built-in unit m for meters anywhere below that definition. However, Mathcad automatically displays the unit m in any results involving meters, as described in "Displaying Units of Results" on page 118.

Working with Results

Formatting Results

The way that Mathcad displays numbers (the number of decimal places, whether to use *i* or *j* for imaginary numbers, and so on) is called the *result format*. You can set the result format for a single calculated result or for an entire worksheet.

Setting the format of a single result

When you evaluate expressions numerically in Mathcad, results are formatted in the worksheet according to the worksheet default result format. You can modify the format for a single result as follows:

1. Click anywhere in the equation whose result you want to format.

2. Choose **Result** from the **Format** menu. Alternatively, double-click the equation itself. The Result Format dialog box appears.

3. Change the desired settings. See below to learn about the various settings in the dialog box. To display a result with six decimal places, you would increase "Number of decimal places" from 3 to 6.

4. Click "OK." Mathcad redisplays the result using the new format.

To redisplay a result using the worksheet default result format settings, click on the result to enclose the result between the editing lines, delete the equal sign, and press **=** to replace the equal sign. The result is now restored to the default worksheet settings.

Note When the format of a result is changed, only the *appearance* of the result changes in the worksheet. Mathcad continues to maintain full precision internally for that result. To see a number as it is stored internally, click on the result, press [**Ctrl**][**Shift**]N, and look at the message line at the bottom of the Mathcad window. If you copy a result, however, Mathcad copies the number only to the precision displayed.

Setting worksheet default format

To change the default display of numerical results in your worksheet:

1. Click in a blank part of your worksheet.

2. Choose **Result** from the **Format** menu.

---

3. Change the desired settings in the Result Format dialog box.

4. Click "OK."

Mathcad changes the display of all results whose formats have not been explicitly specified.

Alternatively, you can change the worksheet default by clicking on a particular result, choosing Result from the Format menu, changing the settings in the Result Format dialog box, and clicking "Set as Default."

The Result Format dialog box

The tabs in the Result Format dialog box lead to pages containing options for formatting various aspects of a result.

The **Number Format** page lets you control the number of decimal places, trailing zeros, and other options. Depending on the format scheme you choose under the Format section, you see different options.

- Choosing **General** lets you control the number of digits to the right of the decimal point, trailing zeros, and exponential threshold. A result is displayed in exponential notation when the exponential threshold is exceeded. You can use E-notation for the exponents by choosing "Show exponents as ± E 000." You can display trailing zeros to the right of the decimal until you exceed 15 digits total.

- Choosing **Decimal** lets you control the number of digits to the right of the decimal point and never display the results in exponential notation. You can display trailing zeros to the right of the decimal point beyond 15 digits total, but only the first 15 digits are accurate.

- Choosing **Scientific** or **Engineering** lets you control the number of digits to the right of the decimal point and always display results in exponential notation. For Engineering, the exponents are displayed in multiples of three. You can use E-notation for the exponents by choosing "Show exponents as ± E 000." You can display trailing zeros to the right of the decimal point beyond 15 digits total, but only the first 15 digits are accurate.

- Choosing **Fractional** lets you display results as fractions or mixed numbers. Use the level of accuracy setting to control the number of decimal places of accuracy of the fraction displayed. You can display a fraction that is accurate to up to 15 decimal places.

The **Display Options** page lets you control whether arrays are displayed as tables or matrices, whether nested arrays are expanded, and whether i or j is used to indicated imaginary. You can also specify another radix such as Binary or Octal.

The **Unit Display** page gives you options to format units (as fractions) or simplify the units to derived units.

The **Tolerance** page allows you to specify when to hide a real or imaginary part of a result and how small a number has to be for it to display as zero.

On-line Help   For more details and examples of the options available on a particular page in the Result Format dialog box, click the Help button at the bottom of the dialog box.

Figure 8-10 shows some examples of formatting options.

$x := 5.2574 \quad y := \pi \cdot 10^4$	Definitions
$x = 5.26$	General format, Exponential threshold = 15, Number of decimal places = 2
$x = 5.2574$	Decimal format, Number of decimal places = 4
$x = 5.25740$	Decimal format, Number of decimal places = 5 Show trailing zeros ☑
$y = 3.142 \times 10^4$	Scientific format
$y = 31.416 \times 10^3$	Engineering format
$x = 5.257 \, E+000$	Engineering format, Show exponents as E±000 ☑

Figure 8-10: Several ways to format the same number.

Complex Results

Complex numbers can arise in results if you enter an expression that contains a complex number. Even a Mathcad expression that involves only real numbers can have a complex value. For example, if you evaluate $\sqrt{-1}$, Mathcad returns i. See Figure 8-11 for examples.

Note   When complex numbers are available, many functions and operators we think of as returning unique results become multivalued. In general, when a function or operator is multivalued, Mathcad returns the *principal value:* the value making the smallest positive angle relative to the positive real axis in the complex plane. For example, when it evaluates $(-1)^{1/3}$, Mathcad returns $.5 + .866i$ despite the fact that we commonly think of the cube root of -1 as being -1. This is because the number $.5 + .866i$ makes an angle of only 60 degrees from the positive real axis. The number -1, on the other hand, is 180 degrees from the positive real axis. Mathcad's nth root operator returns -1 in this case, however.

Figure 8-11: Examples of complex results.

Displaying Units of Results

Mathcad by default displays results in terms of the fundamental units of the unit system you're working with. Mathcad offers the following unit system choices: SI, CGS, MKS, U.S. customary units, or no unit system (see below).

Tip   Check "Simplify units when possible" in the Result Format dialog box (see page 115) to see units in a result expressed in terms of derived units rather than in base units. Check "Format units" to see units in a result displayed as a built-up fraction containing terms with positive exponents only rather than as a product of units with positive and negative exponents.

You can have Mathcad redisplay a particular result in terms of any of Mathcad's built-in units. To do so:

1. Click in the result. You'll see an empty placeholder to its right. This is the *units placeholder.*

2. Click the units placeholder and choose **Unit** from the **Insert** menu, or click ▧ on the Standard toolbar. Mathcad opens the Insert Unit dialog box. This is described in "Units and Dimensions" on page 112.

3. Double-click the unit in which you want to display the result. Mathcad inserts this unit in the units placeholder.

Note   For some engineering units—such as *hp*, *cal*, *BTU*, and *Hz*—Mathcad adopts one common definition for the unit name but allows you to insert one of several alternative unit names, corresponding to alternative definitions of that unit, in your results. In the case of horsepower, for example, Mathcad uses the U.K. definition of the unit *hp* but gives you several variants, such as water horsepower, metric horsepower, boiler horsepower, and electric horsepower.

Another way to insert a unit is to type its name directly into the units placeholder. This method is more general since it works not only for built-in units but also for units you've defined yourself and for combinations of units.

Unit systems

When you start Mathcad, the SI system of units is loaded by default. This means that when you use the equal sign to display a result having units, Mathcad automatically displays the units in the result in terms of base or derived SI units.

You can have Mathcad display results in terms of the units of any of the other built-in unit systems in Mathcad: CGS, US customary, MKS, or no unit system at all. To do so, choose **Options** from the **Math** menu and click the Unit System tab.

Select the default unit system in which you want to display results. The SI unit system, widely used by scientists and engineers in many countries, provides two additional base units over the other systems, one for luminosity (*candela*) and one for substance (*mole*), and the base SI electrical unit (*ampere*) differs from the base electrical unit in the other systems (*coulomb*).

The following table summarizes the base units available in Mathcad's unit systems:

Unit System	Base Units
SI	*m, kg, s, A, K, cd*, and *mole*
MKS	*m, kg, sec, coul*, and *K*
CGS	*cm, gm, sec, coul*, and *K*
U.S.	*ft, lb, sec, coul*, and *K*
None	Displays results in terms of fundamental dimensions of length, mass, time, charge, and absolute temperature. All built-in units are disabled.

The standard SI unit names—such as *A* for *ampere*, *L* for *liter*, *s* for *second*, and *S* for *siemens*—are generally available only in the SI unit system. Many other unit names are available in all the available systems of units. For a listing of which units are available in each system, see the Appendices. Mathcad includes most units common to scientific and engineering practice. Where conventional unit prefixes such as *m-* for *milli-*, *n-* for *nano-*, etc. are not understood by Mathcad, you can easily define custom units such as μm as described in "Defining Your Own Units" on page 114.

Tip   For examples of units with prefixes not already built into Mathcad, see the QuickSheets in the on-line Resource Center.

If you click "None" in the Unit System tab of the Math Options dialog box, Mathcad doesn't understand any built-in units and displays answers in terms of the fundamental dimensions of *length*, *mass*, *time*, *charge*, and *temperature*. However, even if you are working in one of Mathcad's built-in unit systems, you can always choose to see results in your worksheet displayed in terms of fundamental dimension names rather than the base units of the unit system. To do so:

1. Choose **Options** from the **Math** menu.

2. Click the Dimensions tab.

3. Check "Display dimensions."

4. Click "OK."

Unit conversions

There are two ways to convert from one set of units to another:

- By using the Insert Unit dialog box, or
- By typing the new units in the units placeholder itself.

To convert units using the Insert Unit dialog box:

1. Click the unit you want to replace.

2. Choose **Unit** from the **Insert** menu, or click 🖽 on the Standard toolbar.

3. In the scrolling list of units, double-click the unit in which you want to display the result.

As a quick shortcut, or if you want to display the result in terms of a unit not available through the Insert Unit dialog box—for example, a unit you defined yourself or an algebraic combination of units—you can edit the units placeholder directly.

Figure 8-12 shows F displayed both in terms of fundamental SI units and in terms of several combinations of units.

When you enter an inappropriate unit in the units placeholder, Mathcad inserts a combination of base units that generate the correct units for the displayed result. For example, in the last equation in Figure 8-12, $kW \cdot s$ is not a unit of force. Mathcad therefore inserts m^{-1} to cancel the extra length dimension.

Whenever you enter units in the units placeholder, Mathcad divides the value to be displayed by whatever you enter in the units placeholder. This ensures that the complete displayed result—the number *times* the expression you entered for the placeholder—is a correct value for the equation.

Note   Conversions involving an offset in addition to a multiplication, for example gauge pressure to absolute pressure, or degrees Fahrenheit to Celsius, cannot be performed directly with Mathcad's unit conversion mechanism. You can, however, perform conversions of this type by defining suitable functions. See the QuickSheet "Temperature Conversions" in the on-line Resource Center for examples of temperature conversion functions.

$$\text{mass} := 75kg \qquad \text{acc} := 100 \cdot m \cdot s^{-2} \qquad \text{acc\_g} := 9.8 \cdot m \cdot s^{-2}$$

$$F := \text{mass} \cdot (\text{acc} + \text{acc\_g})$$

$F = 8.235 \times 10^3 \, kg\,m\,s^{-2}$ ⟵   Default display using fundamental SI units. Click on result to see the "units placeholder."

$F = 8.235 \times 10^3 \, N$

      ⟵   Type desired unit in the units placeholder.

$F = 8.235 \times 10^8 \, dyne$

$F = 82.35 \cdot \dfrac{J}{cm}$ ⟵   You can type combinations of units in the units placeholder.

$F = 8.235 \, m^{-1} \, kW \cdot s$ ⟵   Since kW s is not a force unit, Mathcad inserts an extra m^{-1} to make the units come out right.

Figure 8-12: A calculated result displayed with different units

You can enter *any* variable, constant, or expression in a units placeholder. Mathcad then redisplays the result in terms of the value contained in the units placeholder. For example, you can use the units placeholder to display a result as a multiple of π or in engineering notation (as a multiple of 10^3, 10^6, etc.).

Tip   You can also use the units placeholder for dimensionless units like degrees and radians. Mathcad treats the unit *rad* as a constant equal to 1, so if you have a number or an expression in radians, you can type *deg* into the units placeholder to convert the result from radians to degrees.

Copying and Pasting Numerical Results

You can copy a numerical result and paste it either elsewhere in your worksheet or into a new application.

To copy a single number appearing to the right of an equal sign:

4. Click on the result to the right of the equal sign. This puts the result between the editing lines.

5. Choose **Copy** from the **Edit** menu, or click 📋 on the Standard toolbar to place the result on the Clipboard.

6. Click wherever you want to paste the result. If you're pasting into another application, choose **Paste** from that application's **Edit** menu. If you're pasting into a Mathcad worksheet, choose **Paste** from Mathcad's **Edit** menu or click 📋 on the Standard toolbar.

When you paste a numerical result into a Mathcad worksheet, it appears as:

- A math region consisting of a number if you paste it into empty space.

- A number if you paste it into a placeholder in a math region.

- A number if you paste it directly into text or into a placeholder in text created using the **Math Region** command on the **Insert** menu.

To copy more than one number, follow the steps for copying from an array. See "Displaying Arrays" on page 210 for information on copying and pasting arrays.

Note The **Copy** command copies the numerical result only to the precision displayed. To copy the result in greater precision, double-click it and increase "Displayed Precision" on the Result Format dialog box. **Copy** does not copy units and dimensions from a numerical result.

Controlling Calculation

When you start Mathcad, you are in *automatic mode*. This means that Mathcad updates results in the worksheet window automatically. You can tell you're in automatic mode because the word "Auto" appears in the message line at the bottom of the window.

If you don't want to wait for Mathcad to make computations as you edit, you can disable automatic mode by choosing **Automatic Calculation** from the **Math** menu. The word "Auto" disappears from the message line and the check beside **Automatic Calculation** disappears to indicate that automatic mode is now off. You are now in *manual mode*.

Tip The calculation mode—either manual or automatic—is a property saved in your Mathcad worksheet. As described in Chapter 7, "Worksheet Management," the calculation mode is also a property saved in Mathcad template (MCT) files.

Calculating in Automatic Mode

Here is how Mathcad works in automatic mode:

- As soon as you press the equal sign, Mathcad displays a result.

- As soon as you click outside of an equation having a ":=" or a "≡," Mathcad performs all calculations necessary to make the assignment statement.

When you process a definition in automatic mode by clicking outside the equation region, this is what happens:

- Mathcad evaluates the expression on the right side of the definition and assigns it to the name on the left.

- Mathcad then takes note of all other equations in the worksheet that are in any way affected by the definition you just made.

- Finally, Mathcad updates any of the affected equations that are currently visible in the worksheet window.

Note Although the equation you altered may affect equations throughout your worksheet, Mathcad performs only those calculations necessary to guarantee that whatever you can see in the window is up-to-date. This optimization ensures you don't have to wait for Mathcad to evaluate expressions that are not visible. If you print or move to the end of the worksheet, however, Mathcad automatically updates the whole worksheet.

Whenever Mathcad needs time to complete computations, the mouse pointer changes its appearance and the word "WAIT" appears on the message line. This can occur when you enter or calculate an equation, when you scroll, during printing, or when you enlarge a window to reveal additional equations. In all these cases, Mathcad evaluates pending calculations from earlier changes.

As Mathcad evaluates an expression, it surrounds it with a green rectangle. This makes it easy to follow the progress of a calculation.

To force Mathcad to recalculate all equations throughout the worksheet, choose **Calculate Worksheet** from the **Math** menu.

Calculating in Manual Mode

In manual mode, Mathcad does not compute equations or display results until you specifically request it to recalculate. This means that you don't have to wait for Mathcad to calculate as you enter equations or scroll around a worksheet.

Mathcad keeps track of pending computations while you're in manual mode. As soon as you make a change that requires computation, the word "Calc" appears on the message line. This is to remind you that the results you see in the window are not up-to-date and that you must recalculate them before you can be sure they are updated.

You can update the screen by choosing **Calculate** from the **Math** menu or clicking ☰ on the Standard toolbar. Mathcad performs whatever computations are necessary to update all results visible in the worksheet window. When you move down to see more of the worksheet, the word "Calc" reappears on the message line to indicate that you must recalculate to see up-to-date results.

To process the whole worksheet, including those portions not visible in the worksheet window, choose **Calculate Worksheet** from the **Math** menu.

Note When you print a worksheet in manual calculation mode, the results on the printout are not necessarily up-to-date. In this case, make sure to choose **Calculate Worksheet** from the **Math** menu before you print.

Interrupting Calculations

To interrupt a computation in progress:

1. Press [**Esc**]. The dialog box shown at right appears.

2. Click "OK" to stop the calculations or "Cancel" to resume calculations.

If you click "OK," the equation that was being processed when you pressed [**Esc**] is marked with an error message (see "Error Messages" on page 126) indicating that calculation has been interrupted. To resume an interrupted calculation, first click in the equation having the error message, then choose **Calculate** from the **Math** menu or click ▣ on the Standard toolbar.

Tip If you find yourself frequently interrupting calculations to avoid having to wait for Mathcad to recalculate as you edit your worksheet, you can switch to manual mode as described above.

Disabling Equations

You can *disable* a single equation so that it no longer calculates along with other regions in your worksheet. Disabling an equation does not affect Mathcad's equation editing, formatting, and display capabilities.

To disable calculation for a single equation in your worksheet, follow these steps:

1. Click on the equation you want to disable.

2. Choose **Properties** from the **Format** menu, and click the Calculation tab.

3. Under "Calculation Options" check "Disable Evaluation."

4. Mathcad shows a small rectangle after the equation to indicate that it is disabled. An example is shown at right.

$$KE := \frac{1}{2} \cdot m \cdot v^2 \ \blacksquare$$

Tip An easy shortcut for disabling evaluation is to click with the right mouse button on an equation and select **Disable Evaluation** from the pop-up menu.

To re-enable calculation for a disabled equation:

1. Click on the equation to select it.

2. Choose **Properties** from the **Format** menu, and click the Calculation tab.

3. Remove the check from "Disable Evaluation."

Mathcad removes the small rectangle beside the equation, and calculation is re-enabled.

Animation

This section describes how to use Mathcad to create and play short animation clips by using the built-in variable FRAME. Anything that can be made to depend on this variable can be animated. This includes not only plots but numerical results as well. You can play back the animation clips at different speeds or save them for use by other applications.

Creating an Animation Clip

Mathcad comes with a predefined constant called FRAME whose sole purpose is to drive animations. The steps in creating any animation are as follows:

1. Create an expression or plot, or a group of expressions, whose appearance ultimately depends on the value of FRAME. This expression need not be a graph. It can be anything at all.

2. Choose **Animate** from the **View** menu to bring up the Animate dialog box.

3. Drag-select the portion of your worksheet you want to animate as shown in Figure 8-13. Draw a rectangle around as many regions as you want to appear in the animation.

4. Set the upper and lower limits for FRAME in the dialog box. When you record the animation, the FRAME variable increments by one as it proceeds from the lower limit to the upper limit.

5. Enter the playback speed in the Frames/Sec. box.

6. Click "Animate." You'll see a miniature rendition of your selection inside the dialog box. Mathcad redraws this once for each value of FRAME. This won't necessarily match the playback speed since at this point you're just *creating* the animation.

7. To save your animation clip as a Windows AVI file, suitable for viewing in other Windows applications, click "Save As" in the dialog box.

Figure 8-13: Selecting an area of a worksheet for animation.

Tip   Since animation clips can take considerable disk space, Mathcad saves them in compressed format. Before creating the animation, you can choose what compression method to use or whether to compress at all. To do so, click "Options" in the Animate dialog box.

Playing an Animation Clip

As soon as you've created an animation clip as described in the previous section, Mathcad opens a Playback window:

The first frame of the animation clip you just created is already in the window. To play back the animation clip, click the arrow at the lower left corner of the window. You can also play back the animation clip on a frame by frame basis, either forward or backward. To do so, drag the slider below the animated picture to the left or right.

Tip You can control the playback speed by clicking the button to the right of the play button, which then opens a pop-up menu. Choose **Speed** from the menu and adjust the slider control.

Playing a Previously Saved Animation

If you have an existing Windows AVI file on your disk, you can play it within Mathcad. To do so:

1. Choose **Playback** from the **View** menu to bring up the Playback dialog box. The window is collapsed since no animation clip has been opened.

2. Click on the button to the right of the play button and choose **Open** from the menu. Use the Open File dialog box to locate and open the AVI file you want to play.

Once you've loaded a Windows AVI file, proceed as described in the previous section.

Tip To launch an animation directly from your worksheet, you can insert a hyperlink to an AVI file by choosing **Hyperlink** from the **Insert** menu. You can also embed a shortcut to the AVI file in your worksheet by dragging the icon for the AVI file from the Windows Explorer and dropping it into your worksheet. Finally, you can embed or link an OLE animation object in your worksheet (see "Inserting Objects" on page 74).

Error Messages

If Mathcad encounters an error when evaluating an expression, it marks the expression with an error message and highlights the offending name or operator in red.

An error message is visible only when you *click on* the associated expression, as shown to the right.

$$g(x) := \frac{3}{x}$$

$$f(x) := g(x) \cdot 10$$

$$f(0) = \blacksquare$$

Found a singularity while evaluating this expression. You may be dividing by zero.

Mathcad cannot process an expression containing an error. If the expression is a definition, the variable or function it is supposed to define remains undefined. This can cause any expressions that reference that variable to be undefined as well.

Tip You can get on-line help about some error messages by clicking on them and pressing [**F1**].

Finding the Source of an Error

When a Mathcad worksheet contains an expression that is dependent on one or more definitions made earlier in the worksheet, an error on that expression may originate in an earlier definition.

For example, in the figure above, the error appears on the third region, *f(0)*. However, *f(x)* is based on the definition of *g(x)*. When x is zero, *g(x)* is the first region that exhibits the error.

You can try to find the source of an error yourself simply by examining your worksheet to see where the error began, or you can use Mathcad to trace the error back through your worksheet. To find the source of an error using Mathcad:

1. Click on the region showing the error with the right mouse button and choose Trace Error from the pop-up menu. The Trace Error dialog box appears:

2. Use the buttons in the dialog box to navigate among the regions associated with the region showing the error.

For example, click Back to step back to the previous dependent region.

Or click First to jump to the first region causing the error.

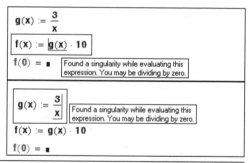

Tip If you anticipate time-consuming calculations, switch to manual mode as described in "Controlling Calculation" on page 122. When you are ready to recalculate, choose **Calculate** from the **Math** menu or click **=** on the Standard toolbar turn. Alternatively, turn on automatic mode again.

Fixing Errors

Once you have determined which expression caused the error, edit that expression to fix the error or change the variable definitions that led to the error. When you click in the expression and begin editing, Mathcad removes the error message. When you click outside the equation (or in manual calculation mode, when you recalculate), Mathcad recomputes the expression. Once you have fixed the error, Mathcad then recomputes the other expressions affected by the expression you changed.

Note When you define a function, Mathcad does not try to evaluate it until you subsequently use it in the worksheet. If there is an error, the use of the function is marked in error, even though the real problem may lie in the definition of the function itself, possibly much earlier in the worksheet.

Chapter 9
Operators

- ◆ Working with Operators
- ◆ Arithmetic and Boolean Operators
- ◆ Vector and Matrix Operators
- ◆ Summations and Products
- ◆ Derivatives
- ◆ Integrals
- ◆ Customizing Operators

Working with Operators

Inserting an Operator

You insert the common arithmetic operators into math expressions in Mathcad using the standard keystrokes, like ***** and **+**, that you use in spreadsheet and other applications. Additionally, all of Mathcad's operators can be inserted into math expressions by clicking buttons in the math toolbars. For example, you insert Mathcad's derivative

operator by clicking $\frac{d}{dx}$ on the Calculus toolbar, or by typing **?**. Choose **Toolbars** from the **View** menu to see any of the math toolbars. See "Operators" on page 447 for a complete list of operators, their keystrokes, and descriptions.

Note In general, you only insert operators into blank space in your worksheet or when you have already clicked in a math region. To use operators in text, first click in the text and choose **Math Region** from the **Insert** menu. This creates a math placeholder in the text into which you can insert operators.

Tip You can find the keyboard shortcut for inserting an operator by hovering the mouse pointer over an operator button in one of the Math toolbars and reading the tooltip that appears.

As introduced in Chapter 4, "Working with Math," when you insert a Mathcad operator into a blank space in your worksheet, a mathematical symbol with empty *placeholders* appears in the worksheet. The placeholders are for you to enter expressions that are the *operands* of the operator. The number of empty placeholders varies with the operator: some operators like the factorial operator have only a single placeholder, while others such as the definite integral have several. You must enter a valid math expression in each placeholder of an operator in order to calculate a result.

Here is a very simple example involving Mathcad's addition operator:

1. Click in a blank space in your worksheet and click $\boxed{+}$ on the Calculator toolbar, or simply type **+**. The addition operator with two placeholders appears.

   $\boxed{\blacksquare + \blacksquare}$

2. Enter **2** in the first placeholder.

   $\boxed{2 + \blacksquare}$

3. Click in the second placeholder, or press [**Tab**] to move the cursor, and enter **6**.

   $\boxed{2 + 6}$

4. Press =, or click $\boxed{=}$ on the Evaluation toolbar, to see the numerical result.

   $\boxed{2 + 6 = 8 \ \blacksquare}$

Tip   See Chapter 4, "Working with Math," for a discussion of how to build and edit more complex math expressions, including how to use the *editing lines* to specify what becomes the operand of the next operator you insert or delete.

Additional Operators

This chapter focuses on those Mathcad operators you can use to calculate numerical answers. Additional operators in Mathcad include:

- *Symbolic operators*, which can only be used to generate other math expressions or exact numerical answers. As described in Chapter 14, "Symbolic Calculation," Mathcad's symbolic processor understands virtually any Mathcad expression, but expressions that include the following operators on the Calculus toolbar can *only* be evaluated symbolically: indefinite integral $\boxed{\int}$, two-sided limit $\boxed{\lim_{\rightarrow a}}$, limit from above $\boxed{\lim_{\rightarrow a^+}}$, and limit from below $\boxed{\lim_{\rightarrow a^-}}$. To evaluate an expression symbolically, click $\boxed{\rightarrow}$ on the Evaluation toolbar.

- *Programming operators*, which you use to link multiple Mathcad expressions via conditional branching, looping constructs, local scoping of variables, and other attributes of traditional programming languages. These operators, available only in Mathcad Professional (click $\boxed{\ }$ on the Math toolbar), are introduced in Chapter 15, "Programming."

Changing the Display of an Operator

When you insert an operator into a worksheet, it has a certain default appearance. For example, when you type a colon **:** or click $\boxed{:=}$ on the Calculator toolbar, Mathcad shows the colon as the definition symbol **:=**. This is a special symbol used by Mathcad to indicate a variable or function definition.

There may be times when you want to control the appearance of a special symbol such as the definition symbol. For example you may want the definition symbol to look like an ordinary equal sign, but you still want to use it to define variables and functions in your worksheet. Mathcad therefore allows you to change the appearance of some operators, such as the definition symbol, so that they appear different but behave the same way.

To change the way an operator is displayed throughout a worksheet:

1. Choose **Options** from the **Math** menu.

2. Click the Display tab.

3. Use the drop-down options next to each operator to select a display option.

4. Click "OK."

For information on the options available for each operator, click the Help button at the bottom of the Display tab in the Math Options dialog box.

To change the appearance of an operator in one or more individual expressions, click with the right mouse button and use the pop-up menu. For example, to change the multiplication in an expression from a dot to an **X**:

1. Click on the multiplication with the right mouse button.

2. Choose **View Multiplication As... ⇒ X** from the pop-up menu.

Arithmetic and Boolean Operators

Arithmetic Operators

You can freely combine all types of numbers with arithmetic operators you access on the Calculator toolbar. Figure 9-1 shows examples.

Boolean Operators

Mathcad includes logical or *Boolean* operators on the Boolean toolbar. Unlike other operators, the Boolean operators can return only a zero or a one. Despite this, they can be very useful to perform tests on your expressions.

$a := \pi$ — Predefined variable — $a = 3.142$

$b := 123456789012$ — Large floating point number — $b = 1.235 \times 10^{11}$

$c := 5 - 7i$ — Complex number (could use 5-7j as well) — $c = 5 - 7i$

$e := 3.5m$ — Dimensional value (SI unit system) — $e = 3.5\,m$

$a + 4 \cdot 10^{-5} = 3.142$

$a \cdot \dfrac{d}{e} = 4.81 \times 10^3 \dfrac{1}{m}$ $a \cdot d \div e = 4.81 \times 10^3 \dfrac{1}{m}$

$b \cdot c = 6.173 \times 10^{11} - 8.642i \times 10^{11}$

Figure 9-1: Combining different types of numbers with arithmetic operators.

The following table lists the Boolean operators available on the Boolean toolbar and their meaning. Note that the "Equal to" operator (bold equal sign) is different from the evaluation equal sign you insert by typing **=**.

Appearance	Button	Description	Keystroke
$w = z$	=	Equal to; displays as bold equal sign.	[Ctrl] =
$x < y$	<	Less than	<
$x > y$	>	Greater than	>
$x \le y$	≤	Less than or equal to	[Ctrl] 9
$x \ge y$	≥	Greater than or equal to	[Ctrl] 0
$w \ne z$	≠	Not equal to	[Ctrl] 3
$\neg z$	¬	Not	[Ctrl] [Shift] 1
$w \wedge z$	∧	And	[Ctrl] [Shift] 7
$w \vee z$	∨	Or	[Ctrl] [Shift] 6
$w \oplus z$	⊕	Xor (Exclusive Or)	[Ctrl] [Shift] 5

Note The Boolean operators return 1 if the expression is true, 0 otherwise. The four operators $>, <, \le$, and $\ge$ cannot take complex numbers because the concepts of greater than and less than lose their meaning in the complex plane.

		Evaluation equals
$10 > 0 = 1$	$10 < 0 = 0$	$3 + 5 = 7 = 0$
$.5 = \dfrac{1}{2} = 1$	$14 \neq 10 = 1$	$12345 < 12345 = 0$
$\dfrac{1}{3} < \dfrac{1}{2} = 1$	$19^2 \geq 360 = 1$	$2000 \neq 2000 = 0$
$1 \vee 1 = 1$	$1 \wedge 0 = 0$	$\neg 1 = 0$
$1 \oplus 1 = 0$	$2 \wedge 0 = 0$	$\neg(1 - 1) = 1$

Figure 9-2: Using boolean operators.

Tip   The comparative boolean operators such as < and > can also be used to compare *strings*. Mathcad compares two strings character by character by determining the ASCII codes of the characters. For example, the string "Euler" precedes the string "Mach" in ASCII order and so the expression ("Euler"<"Mach") evaluates to 1. To determine the character ordering Mathcad uses in comparing strings, see "ASCII codes" on page 501 in the Appendices.

Complex Operators

Mathcad has the following arithmetic operators for working with complex numbers:

Appearance	Button	Description
$\bar{z}$		Complex conjugate of z. To apply the conjugate operator to an expression, select the expression, then press the double-quote key ("). The conjugate of the complex number $a + b \cdot i$ is $a - b \cdot i$.
$|z|$	$|\times|$	The magnitude of the number z.

Figure 9-3 shows some examples of how to use complex numbers in Mathcad.

Vector and Matrix Operators

Most of the operators on the Calculator toolbar also have meaning for vectors and matrices. For example, when you use the addition operator to add two arrays of the same size, Mathcad performs the standard element-by-element addition. Mathcad also uses the conventional arithmetic operators for matrix subtraction, matrix multiplication, integer powers, and determinants, among others.

Some of Mathcad's operators have special meanings for vectors and matrices, and many

of these are grouped on the Matrix toolbar (click ⊞ on the Math toolbar). For example, the multiplication symbol means multiplication when applied to two numbers, but it means dot product when applied to vectors, and matrix multiplication when applied to matrices.

$r := 2$ $\theta := \dfrac{3 \cdot \pi}{4}$ Type q [Ctrl] G for θ

Define complex variables z1 and z2

$z1 := \sqrt{-1}$ $z2 := r \cdot e^{(i \cdot \theta)}$ Type 1i for the complex variable i

$z1 = i$ $z2 = -1.414 + 1.414i$

Now compute with them

$z1 + z2 = -1.414 + 2.414i$ $Re(z2) = -1.414$

$z1 \cdot z2 = -1.414 - 1.414i$ $Im(z2) = 1.414$

$\overline{z2} = -1.414 - 1.414i$ $\sin(z2) = -2.152 + 0.302i$

$\dfrac{z2}{z1} = 1.414 + 1.414i$ $\sinh(z2) = -0.302 + 2.152i$

   $\ln(z2) = 0.693 + 2.356i$

Decompose z2 in polar form

$|z2| = 2$ $\arg(z2) = 2.356$

Figure 9-3: Complex numbers in Mathcad.

The table below describes Mathcad's vector and matrix operations. Operators not listed in this table do not work for vectors and matrices. You can, however, use the vectorize operator (click ⊞ on the Matrix toolbar) to perform any scalar operation or function element by element on a vector or matrix. See "Doing Calculations in Parallel" on page 213. Figure 9-4 shows some ways to use vector and matrix operators.

Matrix M . . .   **Vectors v and w . . .**

$M := \begin{pmatrix} 0 & 1 & 2 \\ 3 & 0 & 2 \\ 5 & 3 & 1 \end{pmatrix}$ $v := \begin{pmatrix} 3 + 10 \\ 1 - 4 \\ 5 \cdot 10 \end{pmatrix}$ $v = \begin{pmatrix} 13 \\ -3 \\ 50 \end{pmatrix}$ $w := 2 \cdot v$ $w = \begin{pmatrix} 26 \\ -6 \\ 100 \end{pmatrix}$

Sum . . .   **Determinant . . .**   **Dot and Cross Product . . .**

$\sum v = 60$ $|M| = 25$ $v \cdot w = 5.356 \cdot 10^3$ $v \times w = \begin{pmatrix} 0 \\ 0 \\ 0 \end{pmatrix}$

Inverse . . .

$M^{-1} = \begin{pmatrix} -0.24 & 0.2 & 0.08 \\ 0.28 & -0.4 & 0.24 \\ 0.36 & 0.2 & -0.12 \end{pmatrix}$ **Transpose . . .**

   $w^T = (26 \ -6 \ 100)$

   Solve linear system Mx=v with inverse . . .

   $x := M^{-1} \cdot v$

$M \cdot M^{-1} = \begin{pmatrix} 1 & 0 & 0 \\ 0 & 1 & 0 \\ 0 & 0 & 1 \end{pmatrix}$ $x = \begin{pmatrix} 0.28 \\ 16.84 \\ -1.92 \end{pmatrix}$ $M \cdot x = \begin{pmatrix} 13 \\ -3 \\ 50 \end{pmatrix}$

Figure 9-4: Vector and matrix operations.

In the following table,

- **A** and **B** represent arrays, either vector or matrix
- **u** and **v** represent vectors
- **M** represents a square matrix
- u_i and v_i represent the individual elements of vectors **u** and **v**
- z represents a scalar
- m and n represent integers

Appearance	Button	Description
$\mathbf{A} \cdot z$		Scalar multiplication. Multiplies each element of **A** by the scalar z.
$\mathbf{u} \cdot \mathbf{v}$		Dot product. Returns a scalar: $\Sigma \langle u_i \cdot v_i \rangle$. The vectors must have the same number of elements.
$\mathbf{A} \cdot \mathbf{B}$		Matrix multiplication. Returns the matrix product of **A** and **B**. The number of columns in **A** must match the number of rows in **B**.
$\mathbf{A} \cdot \mathbf{v}$		Vector/matrix multiplication. Returns the product of **A** and **v**. The number of columns in **A** must match the number of rows in **v**.
$\dfrac{\mathbf{A}}{z}$	/	Scalar division. Divides each element of the array **A** by the scalar z.
$A \div z$	÷	Scalar division. Divides each element of the array **A** by the scalar z. Type [**Ctrl**] / to insert.
$\mathbf{A} + \mathbf{B}$	+	Vector and matrix addition. Adds corresponding elements of **A** and **B**. The arrays **A** and **B** must have the same number of rows and columns.
$\mathbf{A} + z$	+	Scalar addition. Adds z to each element of **A**.
$\mathbf{A} - \mathbf{B}$	−	Vector and matrix subtraction. Subtracts corresponding elements of **A** and **B**. The arrays **A** and **B** must have the same number of rows and columns.
$\mathbf{A} - z$	−	Scalar subtraction. Subtracts z from each element of **A**.
$-\mathbf{A}$	−	Negative of vector or matrix. Returns an array whose elements are the negatives of the elements of **A**.

$\mathbf{M}^n$		nth power of square matrix $\mathbf{M}$ (using matrix multiplication). n must be an integer. $\mathbf{M}^{-1}$ represents the inverse of $\mathbf{M}$. Other negative powers are powers of the inverse. Returns a matrix.
$|\mathbf{v}|$		Magnitude of vector. Returns $\sqrt{\mathbf{v} \cdot \bar{\mathbf{v}}}$ where $\bar{\mathbf{v}}$ is the complex conjugate of $\mathbf{v}$.
$|\mathbf{M}|$		Determinant. $\mathbf{M}$ must be a square matrix.
$\mathbf{A}^{\mathsf{T}}$		Transpose. Interchanges row and columns of $\mathbf{A}$.
$\mathbf{u} \times \mathbf{v}$		Cross product. $\mathbf{u}$ and $\mathbf{v}$ must be three-element vectors; result is another three-element vector.
$\bar{\mathbf{A}}$		Complex conjugate. Takes complex conjugate of each element of $\mathbf{A}$. Insert in math with the double-quote key (").
$\Sigma \mathbf{v}$		Vector sum. Sum elements in $\mathbf{v}$.
$\vec{\mathbf{A}}$		Vectorize. Treat all operations in $\mathbf{A}$ element by element. See "Doing Calculations in Parallel" on page 213 for details.
$\mathbf{A}^{\langle n \rangle}$		Array superscript. nth column of array $\mathbf{A}$. Returns a vector.
v_n		Vector subscript. nth element of a vector.
$A_{m,n}$		Matrix subscript. m, nth element of a matrix.

Tip Operators and functions that expect vectors always expect column vectors. They do not apply to row vectors. To change a row vector into a column vector, use the transpose operator by clicking [M^{T}] on the Matrix toolbar.

Summations and Products

The summation operator sums an expression over all values of an index. The iterated product operator works much the same way. It takes the product of an expression over all values of an index.

To create a summation operator in your worksheet:

1. Click in a blank space. Then click on the Calculus toolbar. A summation sign with four placeholders appears.

2. Type a variable name in the placeholder to the left of the equal sign. This variable is the index of summation. It is defined only within the summation operator and therefore has no effect on, and is not influenced by, variable definitions outside the summation operator.

3. Type integers, or any expressions that evaluate to integers, in the placeholders to the right of the equal sign and above the sigma.

4. Type the expression you want to sum in the remaining placeholder. Usually, this expression involves the index of summation. If this expression has several terms, first type an apostrophe (') to create parentheses around the placeholder.

$$\sum_{\blacksquare=\blacksquare}^{\blacksquare} \blacksquare$$

$$\sum_{n=\blacksquare}^{\blacksquare} \blacksquare$$

$$\sum_{n=1}^{10} \blacksquare$$

$$\sum_{n=1}^{10} n^2$$

Iterated products are similar to summations. Just click $\prod_{n=1}^{m}$ on the Calculus toolbar and fill in the placeholders as described earlier.

Tip   Use the keyboard shortcut [**Ctrl**][**Shift**]4 to enter the iterated sum and the shortcut [**Ctrl**][**Shift**]3 to enter the iterated product operator.

Figure 9-5 shows some examples of how to use the summation and product operators.

To evaluate multiple summations, place another summation in the final placeholder of the first summation. An example appears at the bottom of Figure 9-5.

$$i := 0 .. 20 \qquad\qquad x_i := \sin(0.1 \cdot \pi\, i)$$

$$\sum_{n=0}^{20} n = 210 \qquad\qquad \prod_{n=0}^{20} (n+1) = 5.109 \times 10^{19}$$

$$\sum_{n=0}^{20} x_n = 0 \qquad\qquad \sum_{n=0}^{20} x_n \cdot n = -63.138$$

$$\sum_{n=0}^{20} \sum_{m=0}^{10} n^m = 2.554 \times 10^{13}$$

Figure 9-5: Summations and products.

When you use the summation operator shown in Figure 9-5, the summation must be carried out over subsequent integers and in steps of one. Mathcad provides more general versions of these operators that can use any range variable you define as an index of summation. To use these operators:

1. Define a range variable. For example, type **i:1,2;10**.

   $i := 1, 2 .. 10$

2. Click in a blank space. Then click $\sum_n$ on the Calculus toolbar. A summation sign with two placeholders appears.

3. Click on the bottom placeholder and type the name of a range variable.

4. Click on the placeholder to the right of the summation sign and type an expression involving the range variable. If this expression has several terms, first type an apostrophe (**'**) to create parentheses around the placeholder.

5. Press =, or click $=$ on the Evaluation toolbar, to get a result.

   $\sum_i i^{2\mid} = 385$

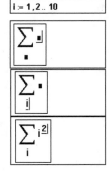

Tip   To enter the expression in the example above using fewer keystrokes and mouse clicks, type **i$i^2**.

A generalized version of the iterated product also exists. To use it, click $\prod_n$ on the Calculus toolbar. Then fill in the two placeholders.

Tip   The operation of summing the elements of a vector is so common that Mathcad provides a special operator for it. The vector sum operator (click Σv on the Matrix toolbar) sums the elements of a vector without needing a range variable.

Variable Upper Limit of Summation

Mathcad's range summation operator runs through each value of the range variable you place in the bottom placeholder. It is possible, by judicious use of Boolean expressions, to sum only up to a particular value. In Figure 9-6, the term $i \leq x$ returns the value 1 whenever it is true and 0 whenever it is false. Although the summation operator still sums over each value of the index of summation, those terms for which $i > x$ are multiplied by 0 and hence do not contribute to the summation.

You can also use the four-placeholder summation and product operators to compute sums and products with a variable upper limit, but note that the upper limit in these operators must be an integer.

Figure 9-6: A variable upper limit of summation.

Derivatives

You can use Mathcad's derivative operators to evaluate the first or higher order derivatives of a function at a particular point.

As an example, here's how to evaluate the first derivative of x^3 with respect to x at the point $x = 2$:

1. First define the point at which you want to evaluate the derivative. As a shortcut, type **x:2** .

2. Click below the definition of x. Then click $\frac{d}{dx}$ on the Calculus toolbar. A derivative operator appears with two placeholders.

3. Type **x** in the bottom placeholder. You are differentiating with respect to this variable. In the placeholder to the right of the $\frac{d}{dx}$, enter **x^3**. This is the expression to be differentiated.

4. Press =, or click = on the Evaluation toolbar, to get the result.

Figure 9-7 shows examples of differentiation in Mathcad.

$x := 2 \qquad y := 10 \qquad\qquad t := 0$

$g(t) := 5 \cdot t^4 \qquad v := \begin{bmatrix} 2 \\ 3 \\ -8 \end{bmatrix} \qquad z := v_2$

Derivative

$\dfrac{d}{dx} x^5 = 80 \qquad \dfrac{d}{dx} x^5 \cdot y = 800 \qquad \dfrac{d}{dy} x^5 \cdot y = 32$

$\dfrac{d}{dt} x^5 \cdot y = 0 \qquad$ **(Since expression does not involve t, derivative is zero)**

$\dfrac{d}{dz} z^5 = 2.048 \cdot 10^4 \qquad$ **(evaluating the derivative at a vector element)**

In the above examples, results may vary depending on settings for Displayed Precision in the Result Format dialog box.

Figure 9-7: Examples of Mathcad differentiation.

With Mathcad's derivative algorithm, you can expect the first derivative to be accurate within 7 or 8 significant digits, provided that the value at which you evaluate the derivative is not too close to a singularity of the function. The accuracy of this algorithm tends to decrease by one significant digit for each increase in the order of the derivative (see "Derivatives of Higher Order" on page 141).

Note Keep in mind that the result of numerical differentiation is not a function, but a single number: the computed derivative at the indicated value of the differentiation variable. In the previous example, the derivative of x^3 is not the expression $3x^2$ but $3x^2$ evaluated at $x = 2$. To evaluate derivatives symbolically, see Chapter 14, "Symbolic Calculation."

Although differentiation returns just one number, you can still define one function as the derivative of another. For example:

$$f(x) := \frac{d}{dx} g(x)$$

Evaluating $f(x)$ returns the numerically computed derivative of $g(x)$ at x.

You can use this technique to evaluate the derivative of a function at many points. An example of this is shown in Figure 9-8.

There are some important things to remember about differentiation in Mathcad:

- The expression to be differentiated can be either real or complex.

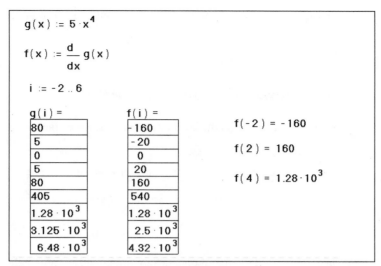

$$g(x) := 5 \cdot x^4$$

$$f(x) := \frac{d}{dx} g(x)$$

$$i := -2 .. 6$$

$g(i) =$	$f(i) =$
80	-160
5	-20
0	0
5	20
80	160
405	540
$1.28 \cdot 10^3$	$1.28 \cdot 10^3$
$3.125 \cdot 10^3$	$2.5 \cdot 10^3$
$6.48 \cdot 10^3$	$4.32 \cdot 10^3$

$$f(-2) = -160$$

$$f(2) = 160$$

$$f(4) = 1.28 \cdot 10^3$$

Figure 9-8: Evaluating the derivative of a function at several points.

- The differentiation variable must be a single variable name. If you want to evaluate the derivative at several different values stored in a vector, you must evaluate the derivative at each individual vector element (see Figure 9-8).

Tip   You can change the display of the derivative operator to partial derivative symbols. For example you can make $\frac{d}{dx}$ look like $\frac{\partial}{\partial x}$. To change the display of a derivative operator to partial derivative symbols, click on it with the mouse button and choose **View Derivative As...** $\Rightarrow$ **Partial.** Or to change the display of all the derivative operators in a worksheet, choose **Options** from the **Math** menu, click on the Display tab, and select "Partial Derivative" next to Derivative. See "Changing the Display of an Operator" on page 130 for additional information.

Derivatives of Higher Order

To evaluate a higher order derivative, insert the *n*th derivative operator using steps similar to those for inserting the derivative operator described above.

As an example, here's how to evaluate the third derivative of x^9 with respect to x at the point $x = 2$: After defining x as 2:

1. Click below the definition of x. Then click ⬛ on the Calculus toolbar. A derivative operator appears with four placeholders.

2. Click on the bottom-most placeholder and type **x**.

3. Click on the expression above and to the right of the previous placeholder and type **3**. This must be an integer

$$\frac{d^3}{dx^3}\blacksquare$$

between 0 and 5 inclusive. Note that the placeholder in the numerator automatically mirrors whatever you've typed.

4. Click on the placeholder to the right of the $\dfrac{d}{dx^3}$ and type $\dfrac{d^3}{dx^3}x^9$

   x^9. This is the expression to be differentiated.

5. Press =, or click ▣ on the Evaluation toolbar, to see the result. $\dfrac{d^3}{dx^3}x^9 = 3.226 \cdot 10^4$ ▪

Note For $n = 1$, the nth derivative operator gives the same answer as the first-derivative operator discussed on page 139.

Integrals

You can use Mathcad's integral operator to numerically evaluate the definite integral of a function over some interval.

As an example, here's how to evaluate the definite integral of $\sin^2(x)$ from 0 to $\pi/4$. (In Mathcad you enter $\sin^2(x)$ as $\sin(x)^2$.) Follow these steps:

1. Click in a blank space and click ▣ on the Calculus toolbar. An integral symbol appears, with placeholders for the integrand, limits of integration, and variable of integration. $\displaystyle\int_{\blacksquare}^{\blacksquare} \blacksquare \; d\blacksquare$

2. Click on the bottom placeholder and type **0**. Click on the top placeholder and type **p[Ctrl]G/4**. These are the upper and lower limits of integration. $\displaystyle\int_{0}^{\frac{\pi}{4}} \blacksquare \; d\blacksquare$

3. Click on the placeholder between the integral sign and the "d." Then type **sin(x)^2**. This is the expression to be integrated. $\displaystyle\int_{0}^{\frac{\pi}{4}} \sin(x)^2 \; d\blacksquare$

4. Click on the remaining placeholder and type **x**. This is the variable of integration. Then press =, or click ▣ on the Evaluation toolbar, to see the result. $\displaystyle\int_{0}^{\frac{\pi}{4}} \sin(x)^2 \; dx = 0.143$

Note Some points to keep in mind when you evaluate integrals in Mathcad: 1) The limits of integration must be real. The expression to be integrated can, however, be either real or complex. 2) Except for the integrating variable, all variables in the integrand must have been defined previously in the worksheet. 3) The integrating variable must be a single variable name. 4) If the integrating variable involves units, the upper and lower limits of integration must have the same units.

Integration Algorithms and AutoSelect

Mathcad has a number of numerical integration methods at its disposal to calculate the numerical approximation of an integral. When you evaluate an integral, by default

Mathcad uses an *AutoSelect* procedure to choose the most accurate integration method. You can override AutoSelect and choose from among the available integration algorithms yourself.

Here are the methods from which Mathcad chooses when you evaluate an integral numerically:

Romberg

Applies a Romberg integration method that divides the interval of integration into equally spaced subintervals.

Adaptive

Applies an adaptive quadrature algorithm in cases where the integrand varies considerably in magnitude over the interval of integration.

Infinite Limit

Applies an algorithm designed for improper integral evaluation in cases where either limit of integration is ∞ or $-\infty$.

Singular Endpoint

Applies a routine that avoids use of the interval endpoints in cases where the integrand is undefined at either limit of integration.

Note Although designed to handle a wide range of problems, Mathcad's integration algorithms—like all numerical methods—can have difficulty with ill-behaved integrands. For example, if the expression to be integrated has singularities or discontinuities the solution may still be inaccurate.

You can override Mathcad's integration AutoSelect as follows:

1. Evaluate the value of the integral as described on page 142, allowing Mathcad to AutoSelect an integration algorithm.

2. Click with the right mouse button on the integral.

3. Click one of the listed integration methods on the pop-up menu. Mathcad recalculates the integral using the method you selected.

Tip In some cases, you may be able to find an exact numerical value for your integral by using Mathcad's symbolic integration capability. You can also use this capability to evaluate *indefinite* integrals. See Chapter 14, "Symbolic Calculation."

Variable Limits of Integration

Although the result of an integration is a single number, you can always use an integral with a range variable to obtain results for many numbers at once. You might do this, for example, when you set up a variable limit of integration. Figure 9-9 shows how to do this.

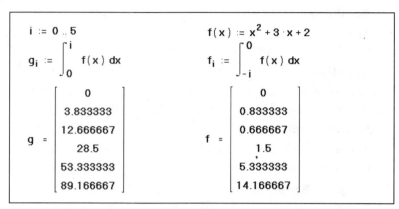

Figure 9-9: Variable limits of integration.

Keep in mind that calculations such as those shown in Figure 9-9 require repeatedly evaluating an integral. This may take considerable time depending on the complexity of the integrals, the length of the interval, and the value of the tolerance parameter TOL (see below).

Tolerance for Integrals

Mathcad's numerical integration algorithms make successive estimates of the value of the integral and return a value when the two most recent estimates differ by less than the value of the built-in variable TOL.

As described in "Built-in Variables" on page 102, you can change the value of the tolerance by including definitions for TOL directly in your worksheet. You can also change the tolerance by using the Built-In Variables tab when you choose **Options** from the **Math** menu. To see the effect of changing the tolerance, choose **Calculate Document** from the **Math** menu to recalculate all the equations in the worksheet.

If Mathcad's approximation to an integral fails to converge to an answer, Mathcad marks the integral with an error message. Failure to converge can occur when the function has singularities or "spikes" in the interval or when the interval is extremely long.

Note   When you change the tolerance, keep in mind the trade-off between accuracy and computation time. If you decrease (tighten) the tolerance, Mathcad computes integrals more accurately, but takes longer to return a result. Conversely, if you increase (loosen) the tolerance, Mathcad computes more quickly, but the answers are less accurate.

Contour Integrals

You can use Mathcad to evaluate complex contour integrals. To do so, first parametrize the contour and then integrate over the parameter. If the parameter is something other than arc length, you must also include the derivative of the parametrization as a correction factor (see Figure 9-10). Note that the imaginary unit i used in specifying the path must be typed as **1i**.

$$x(t) := 2 \cdot \cos(t) \qquad y(t) := 2 \cdot \sin(t)$$

Path: $\quad z(t) := x(t) + i \cdot y(t)$

Function to integrate: $\quad f(z) := \dfrac{1}{z}$

$$\int_0^\pi f(z(t)) \cdot \frac{d}{dt} z(t) \, dt = 3.142i$$

Figure 9-10: A complex contour integral in Mathcad.

Multiple integrals

You can also use Mathcad to evaluate double or multiple integrals. To set up a double integral, for example, click [⌠ᵇ⌡ₐ] on the Calculus toolbar twice. Fill in the integrand, the limits, and the integrating variable for each integral. Figure 9-11 shows an example.

Center of mass of triangle described
by: $0 < x < 1$ and $0 < y < x$
and mass density proportional to the
distance from the origin.

$$\delta(x, y) := \sqrt{x^2 + y^2}$$

$$\text{mass} := \int_0^1 \int_0^x \delta(x, y) \, dy \, dx \qquad\qquad \text{mass} = 0.383$$

$$\text{xctr} := \frac{1}{\text{mass}} \cdot \int_0^1 \int_0^x x \cdot \delta(x, y) \, dy \, dx \qquad\qquad \text{xctr} = 0.75$$

$$\text{yctr} := \frac{1}{\text{mass}} \cdot \int_0^1 \int_0^x y \cdot \delta(x, y) \, dy \, dx \qquad\qquad \text{yctr} = 0.398$$

Figure 9-11: Double integrals.

Customizing Operators

This section describes how to define and use your own customized operators.

You can think of operators and functions as being fundamentally very similar. A function takes "arguments" and returns a result. An operator, likewise, takes "operands" and returns a result. The differences are largely notational:

- Functions usually have names you can spell, like *tan* or *spline*; operators are generally math symbols like "+" or "×."

- Arguments to a function are enclosed by parentheses, they come after the function's name, and they're separated by commas. Operands, on the other hand, can appear elsewhere. For example, you'll often see $f(x, y)$ but you'll rarely see $x f y$. Similarly, you'll often find "$x + y$" but you rarely find "$+(x, y)$."

Defining a Custom Operator

You define a custom operator just as if you were defining a function that happens to have an unusual looking name:

1. Type the operator name followed by a pair of parentheses. Enter the operands (two at the most) between the parentheses.

2. Enter the definition symbol **:=**.

3. Type an expression describing what you want the operator to do with its operands on the other side of the definition symbol.

Tip Mathcad provides a collection of math symbols to define custom operators. To access these symbols, open the QuickSheets from the Resource Center (choose **Resource Center** on the **Help** menu) and then click on "Extra Math Symbols." You can drag any of these symbols to your worksheet for use in creating a new operator name.

For example, suppose you want to define a new union operator using the symbol "∪".

1. Drag the symbol into your worksheet from the "Extra Math Symbols" QuickSheet.

2. Type a left parenthesis followed by two names separated by a comma. Complete this argument list by typing a right parenthesis.

3. Press the colon (**:**) key, or click ▦ on the Calculator toolbar. You see the definition symbol followed by a placeholder.

4. Type the function definition in the placeholder.

$$\cup(x, y) := \mathbf{stack}(x, y)$$

Chapter 9 Operators

At this point, you've defined a function which behaves in every way like the user-defined functions described in Chapter 8, "Calculating in Mathcad." You could, if you wanted to, type " $\cup(1, 2) = $ " in your worksheet and see the result, a vector with the elements 1 and 2, on the other side of the equal sign.

Tip   Once you've defined the new operator, click on "Personal QuickSheets" in the QuickSheets of the Mathcad Resource Center. Then choose **Annotate Book** from the **Book** menu and drag or type the definition into the QuickSheet. Then choose **Save Section** from the **Book** menu. When you need to use this operator again, just open your Personal QuickSheet and drag it into a new worksheet.

Using a Custom Operator

Once you've defined a new operator, you can use it in your calculations just as you would use any of Mathcad's built-in operators. The procedure for using a custom operator depends on whether the operator has one operand (like "-1" or "5!") or two (like "$1 \div 2$").

To use an operator having two operands:

1. Define any variables you want to use as arguments.

$$v := \begin{pmatrix} 1 \\ 2 \\ 3 \end{pmatrix} \quad u := \begin{pmatrix} 2 \\ 4 \\ 6 \end{pmatrix}$$

2. Click $\boxed{x f y}$ on the Evaluation toolbar. You'll see three empty placeholders.

$$\boxed{\bullet \ \bullet \ \bullet}$$

3. In the middle placeholder, insert the name of the operator. Alternatively, copy the name from the operator definition and paste it into the placeholder.

$$\boxed{\bullet \cup \bullet}$$

4. In the remaining two placeholders, enter the two operands.

$$\boxed{v \cup u}$$

5. Press =, or click $\boxed{=}$ on the Evaluation toolbar, to get the result.

$$v \cup u = \begin{pmatrix} 1 \\ 2 \\ 3 \\ 2 \\ 4 \\ 6 \end{pmatrix}$$

Tip   An alternative way to display an operator having two operands is to click $\boxed{x \ f \ y}$ on the Evaluation toolbar. If you follow the preceding steps using this operator, you'll see a tree-shaped display.

To insert an operator having only one operand, decide first whether you want the operator to appear before the operand, as in "−1 ," or after the operand as in "5!." The former is called a *prefix* operator; the latter is a *postfix* operator. The example below shows how to use a postfix operator. The steps for creating a prefix operator are almost identical.

The following example shows how to define and use a new logical Not operator. First define an operator " $'(x)$ " . To do so, follow the steps for defining $\cup(x, y)$ in the previous section, substituting the symbol " ´ " for "$\cup$" and using only one argument instead of two.

$$' (\mathbf{x}) := \neg \mathbf{x}$$

Then, to evaluate with the new operator:

1. Click $\boxed{\mathbf{x\ f}}$ on the Evaluation toolbar to make a *postfix* operator. Otherwise, click $\boxed{\mathbf{f\ x}}$. In either case, you see two empty placeholders.

   $\boxed{\blacksquare\,\lrcorner}$

2. If you clicked $\boxed{\mathbf{x\ f}}$, put the operator name in the second placeholder. Otherwise put it in the first placeholder. In either case, you may find it more convenient to copy the name from the operator definition and paste it into the placeholder.

   $\boxed{\blacksquare\,\lceil}$

3. In the remaining placeholder, place the operand.

   $\boxed{\mathbf{0}\,\lceil}$

4. Press =, or click $\boxed{\mathbf{=}}$ on the Evaluation toolbar, to see the result.

   $\mathbf{0}\,{\lceil} = \mathbf{1}\,\blacksquare$

Tip   Just as Mathcad can display a custom operator as if it were a function, you can conversely display a function as if it were an operator. For example, many publishers prefer to omit parentheses around the arguments to certain functions such as trigonometric functions, i.e., *sin* x rather than $\sin(x)$. To create this notation, you can treat the *sin* function as an operator with one operand.

Chapter 10
Built-in Functions

+ Inserting Built-in Functions
+ Core Mathematical Functions
+ Discrete Transform Functions
+ Vector and Matrix Functions
+ Solving and Optimization Functions
+ Statistics, Probability, and Data Analysis Functions
+ Finance Functions
+ Differential Equation Functions
+ Miscellaneous Functions

Inserting Built-in Functions

Mathcad's set of built-in functions can change depending on whether you've installed additional Extension Packs or whether you've written your own built-in functions. These functions can come from the following sources:

Built-in Mathcad functions

This is the core set of functions that come with Mathcad. These functions are introduced in this chapter.

Mathcad Extension Packs

An Extension Pack consists of a collection of advanced functions geared to a particular area of application. Documentation for these functions comes with an Electronic Book accompanying the Extension Pack itself. The list of available Extension Packs currently includes collections for signal processing, image processing, steam tables, numerical analysis, solving and optimization, and wavelets. To find out more about these and other Extension Packs, contact MathSoft or your local distributor, or visit MathSoft's Web site at:

http://www.mathsoft.com/

After you purchase and install an Extension Pack, the additional functions appear in the Insert Function dialog box.

Built-in functions you write yourself in C

If you have a supported 32-bit C/C++ compiler, you can write your own built-in functions for Mathcad. For details see the Adobe Acrobat file CREATING A USER DLL.PDF included on your installation CD.

Insert Function Feature

To see a list of built-in functions available with your copy of Mathcad, arranged alphabetically or by category, or to insert a function together with placeholders for its arguments, use the Insert Function dialog box:

1. Click in a blank area of your worksheet or on a placeholder.

2. Choose **Function** from the

   Insert menu or click on the Standard toolbar. Mathcad opens the Insert Function dialog box.

3. Click a Function Category or click "All" to see all available functions sorted alphabetically.

4. Double-click the name of the function you want to insert from the right-hand scrolling list, or click "Insert." The function and placeholders for its arguments are inserted into the worksheet.

5. Fill in the placeholders.

$$\boxed{\mathbf{acos(.866|)}}$$

To apply a function to an expression you have already entered, place the expression between the two editing lines and follow the steps given above. See Chapter 4, "Working with Math," for information about using the editing lines.

You can also simply type the name of a built-in function directly into a math placeholder or in a math region.

Tip Although built-in function names are not font sensitive, they are case sensitive. If you do not use the Insert Function dialog box to insert a function name, you must enter the name of a built-in function in a math region exactly as it appears in the tables throughout this chapter: uppercase, lowercase, or mixed, as indicated.

Note Throughout this chapter and in the Insert Function dialog box, brackets, [ ], around an argument indicate that the argument is optional.

Assistance for Using Built-in Functions

Mathcad includes several sources of assistance for using built-in functions:

- The Insert Function dialog box gives you a convenient way to look up a function by category, to see the arguments required, and to see a brief function synopsis. When you click "Help" in the Insert Function dialog box, you immediately open the Help topic associated with the currently selected function.

- The online Help system (choose **Mathcad Help** from the **Help** menu, or click on the Standard toolbar) provides both overview and detailed help topics on functions and function categories.

- The *Mathcad Reference Manual*, which provides details on the syntax, arguments, algorithms, and behavior of all of Mathcad's built-in functions, operators, and keywords.

- The Resource Center (choose **Resource Center** from the **Help** menu, or click on the Standard toolbar) includes a range of Mathcad files to help you use built-in functions to solve problems including Tutorials and QuickSheet examples.

Core Mathematical Functions

Trigonometric Functions

angle(x, y) Returns the angle (in radians) from the positive x-axis to point (x, y) in the x-y plane. The result is between 0 and 2π.

cos(z) Returns the cosine of z. In a right triangle, this is the ratio of the length of the side *adjacent* to the angle over the length of the hypotenuse.

cot(z) Returns $1/\tan(z)$, the cotangent of z. z should not be a multiple of π.

csc(z) Returns $1/\sin(z)$, the cosecant of z. z should not be a multiple of π.

sec(z) Returns $1/\cos(z)$, the secant of z. z should not be an odd multiple of $\pi/2$.

sin(z) Returns the sine of z. In a right triangle, this is the ratio of the length of the side *opposite* the angle over the length of the hypotenuse.

tan(z) Returns $\sin(z)/\cos(z)$, the tangent of z. In a right triangle, this is the ratio of the length of the side *opposite* the angle over the length of the side *adjacent* to the angle. z should not be an odd multiple of $\pi/2$.

Mathcad's trig functions and their inverses accept any scalar argument: real, complex, or imaginary. They also return complex numbers wherever appropriate.

Note Trigonometric functions expect their arguments in *radians*. To pass an argument in degrees, use the built-in unit *deg*. For example, to evaluate the sine of 45 degrees, type **sin(45*deg)**.

Tip In Mathcad you enter powers of trig functions such $\sin^2(x)$ as $\sin(x)^2$. Alternatively, you can use the prefix operator described in "Customizing Operators" on page 146. For example, to type $\sin^2(x)$. Click $\boxed{\text{f x}}$ on the Evaluation toolbar, enter **sin²** in the left-hand placeholder, enter **(x)** in the right-hand placeholder.

Inverse Trigonometric Functions

acos(z)	Returns the angle (in radians) whose cosine is z.
acot(z)	Returns the angle (in radians) whose cotangent is z.
acsc(z)	Returns the angle (in radians) whose cosecant is z.
asec(z)	Returns the angle (in radians) whose secant is z.
asin(z)	Returns the angle (in radians) whose sine is z.
atan(z)	Returns the angle (in radians) whose tangent is z.
atan2(x, y)	Returns the angle (in radians) from the positive x-axis to point (x, y) in the x-y plane.

With the exception of *atan2* and *acot*, the inverse trigonometric functions can take either a real or complex argument and return an angle in radians between $-\pi/2$ and $\pi/2$, or the principal value in the case of a complex argument. *atan2* takes only real arguments and returns a result between $-\pi$ and π, *acot* returns an angle in radians between 0 and π for a real argument or the principal value in the case of a complex argument.

To convert a result into degrees, either divide the result by the built-in unit *deg* or type **deg** in the units placeholder as described in "Displaying Units of Results" on page 118.

Hyperbolic Functions

acosh(z)	Returns the number whose hyperbolic cosine is z.
acoth(z)	Returns the number whose hyperbolic cotangent is z.
acsch(z)	Returns the number whose hyperbolic cosecant is z.
asech(z)	Returns the number whose hyperbolic secant is z.
asinh(z)	Returns the number whose hyperbolic sine is z.
atanh(z)	Returns the number whose hyperbolic tangent is z.
cosh(z)	Returns the hyperbolic cosine of z.
coth(z)	Returns $1/\tanh(z)$, the hyperbolic cotangent of z.
csch(z)	Returns $1/\sinh(z)$, the hyperbolic cosecant of z.
sech(z)	Returns $1/\cosh(z)$, the hyperbolic secant of z.
sinh(z)	Returns the hyperbolic sine of z.
tanh(z)	Returns $\sinh(z)/\cosh(z)$, the hyperbolic tangent of z.

Log and Exponential Functions

exp(z)	Returns e raised to the power z.
ln(z)	Returns the natural log of z. ($z \neq 0$).
log(z, b)	Returns the base b logarithm of z. ($z \neq 0$, $b \neq 0$). If b is omitted, returns the base 10 logarithm.

Mathcad's exponential and logarithmic functions can accept and return complex arguments. *ln* returns the *principal branch* of the natural log function.

Bessel Functions

Ai(x)	Returns the value of the Airy function of the first kind. x must be real.
bei(n, x)	Returns the value of the imaginary Bessel Kelvin function of order n.
ber(n, x)	Returns the value of the real Bessel Kelvin function of order n.
Bi(x)	Returns the value of the Airy function of the second kind. x must be real.
I0(x)	Returns the value of the zeroth order modified Bessel function of the first kind. x must be real.
I1(x)	Returns the value of the first order modified Bessel function of the first kind. x must be real.

In(*m*, *x*)   Returns the value of the *m*th order modified Bessel function of the first kind. *x* must be real, *m* is an integer, $0 \le m \le 100$.

J0(*x*)   Returns the value of the zeroth order Bessel function of the first kind. *x* must be real.

J1(*x*)   Returns the value of the first order Bessel function of the first kind. *x* must be real.

Jn(*m*, *x*)   Returns the value of the *m*th order Bessel function of the first kind. *x* real, $0 \le m \le 100$.

js(*n*, *x*)   Returns the value of the spherical Bessel function of the first kind, of integer order *n*. $x > 0$, $n \ge -200$.

K0(*x*)   Returns the value of the zeroth order modified Bessel function of the second kind. *x* real, $x > 0$.

K1(*x*)   Returns the value of the first order modified Bessel function of the second kind. *x* real, $x > 0$.

Kn(*m*, *x*)   Returns the value of the *m*th order modified Bessel function of the second kind. $x > 0$, *m* is an integer, $0 \le m \le 100$.

Y0(*x*)   Returns the value of the zeroth order Bessel function of the second kind. *x* real, $x > 0$.

Y1(*x*)   Returns the value of the first order Bessel function of the second kind. *x* real, $x > 0$.

Yn(*m*, *x*)   Returns the value of the *m*th order Bessel function of the second kind. $x > 0$, *m* is an integer, $0 \le m \le 100$.

ys(*n*, *x*)   Returns the value of the spherical Bessel function of the second kind, of integer order *n*. *x* must be real. $x > 0$, $n \ge -200$.

Complex Numbers

arg(*z*)   Returns the angle in complex plane from real axis to *z*. The result is between $-\pi$ and π radians.

csgn(*z*)   Returns 0 if $z = 0$, 1 if $\mathrm{Re}(z) > 0$ or $(\mathrm{Re}(z) = 0$ and $\mathrm{Im}(z) > 0)$, -1 otherwise.

Im(*z*)   Returns the imaginary part of a number *z*.

Re(*z*)   Returns the real part of a number *z*.

signum(*z*)   Returns 1 if $z = 0$, $z/|z|$ otherwise.

Piecewise Continuous Functions

if(*cond, tvl, fvl*)   Returns *tvl* if *cond* is nonzero (true), *fvl* if *cond* is zero (false). *cond* is usually a Boolean expression.

$\delta(m, n)$ Kronecker's delta function. Returns 1 if $m = n$, 0 otherwise. Both arguments must be integers.

$\varepsilon(i, j, k)$ Completely antisymmetric tensor of rank 3. i, j, and k must be integers between 0 and 2 inclusive (or between ORIGIN and ORIGIN + 2 inclusive if ORIGIN≠0). Result is 0 if any two are the same, 1 for even permutations, −1 for odd permutations.

$\Phi(x)$ Heaviside step function. Returns 1 if $x \geq 0$, 0 otherwise. x must be real.

sign(*x*)   Returns 0 if $x = 0$, 1 if $x > 0$, and −1 otherwise. x must be real.

Note   The *if* function is useful for branching in calculation: choosing one of two values based on a condition. Although the first argument of the *if* function, *cond,* can be any expression at all, it is usually a Boolean expression that relates two math expressions with a Boolean operator. See "Arithmetic and Boolean Operators" on page 131.

Number Theory/Combinatorics

combin(*n, k*)   Returns the number of combinations: the number of subsets of size k that can be formed from n objects. n and k integers, $0 \leq k \leq n$.

gcd(**A, B, C, ...**)   Returns the greatest common divisor: the largest integer that evenly divides all the elements in arrays or scalars **A, B, C, ...** The elements of **A, B, C, ...** must be non-negative integers.

lcm(**A, B, C, ...**)   Returns the least common multiple: the smallest positive integer that is a multiple of all the elements in the arrays or scalars **A, B, C, ...** The elements of **A, B, C, ...** must be non-negative integers.

mod(*x, y*)   Remainder on dividing real number x by y ($y \neq 0$). Result has same sign as x.

permut(*n, k*)   Returns the number of permutations: the number of ways of ordering n distinct objects taken k at a time. n and k integers, $0 \leq k \leq n$.

Truncation and Round-Off Functions

ceil(x)	Least integer $\geq x$ (x real).
floor(x)	Greatest integer $\leq x$ (x real).
round(x, n)	Rounds real number x to n decimal places. If $n < 0$, x is rounded to the left of the decimal point. If n is omitted, returns x rounded to the nearest integer.
trunc(x)	Returns the integer part of a real number x by removing the fractional part.

Special Functions

erf(x)	Returns the value of the error function at x. x must be real.
erfc(x)	Returns the value of the complementary error function at x: $1 - \mathrm{erf}(x)$. x real.
fhyper(a, b, c, x)	Returns the value of the Gauss hypergeometric function at the point x given parameters a, b, c. $-1 < x < 1$.
$\Gamma(z)$	Returns the value of the classical Euler gamma function at z, a real or complex number. Undefined for $z = 0, -1, -2, \ldots$
$\Gamma(x, y)$	Returns the value of the extended Euler gamma function for real numbers $x > 0$, $y \geq 0$.
Her(n, x)	Returns the value of the Hermite polynomial of degree n at x.
ibeta(a, x, y)	Returns the value of the incomplete beta function of x and y with parameter a. $0 \leq a \leq 1$
Jac(n, a, b, x)	Returns the value of the Jacobi polynomial of degree n at x with parameters a and b.
Lag(n, x)	Returns the value of the Laguerre polynomial of degree n at x.
Leg(n, x)	Returns the value of the Legendre polynomial of degree n at x.
mhyper(a, b, x)	Returns the value of the confluent hypergeometric function at the point x given parameters a and b.
Tcheb(n, x)	Returns the value of the Chebyshev polynomial of degree n, of the first kind, at x.
Ucheb(n, x)	Returns the value of the Chebyshev polynomial of degree n, of the second kind, at x.

Discrete Transform Functions

Mathcad contains a variety of functions for performing discrete transforms. All of these functions require vectors as arguments.

> **Note** When you define a vector **v** for use with Fourier or wavelet transforms, Mathcad indexes the vector beginning at 0, by default, unless you have set the value of the built-in variable ORIGIN to a value other than 0 (see page 102). If you do not define v_0, Mathcad automatically sets it to zero. This can distort the results of the transform functions.

Fourier Transforms on Real and Complex Data

cfft($\mathbf{A}$)   Returns the fast Fourier transform of a vector or matrix of complex data representing equally spaced measurements in the time domain. The array returned is the same size as its argument.

icfft($\mathbf{A}$)   Returns the inverse Fourier transform of a vector or matrix of data corresponding to *cfft*. Returns an array of the same size as its argument.

fft($\mathbf{v}$)   Returns the fast discrete Fourier transform of a 2^m element vector of real data representing measurements at regular intervals in the time domain. $m > 2$.

ifft($\mathbf{v}$)   Returns the inverse Fourier transform of a vector of data corresponding to *fft*. Takes a vector of size $1 + 2^{n-1}$, and returns a real vector of size 2^n. $n > 2$.

CFFT($\mathbf{A}$)   Returns a transform identical to *cfft*, except using a different normalizing factor and sign convention.

ICFFT($\mathbf{A}$)   Returns the inverse Fourier transform of a vector or matrix of data corresponding to *CFFT*. Returns an array of the same size as its argument.

FFT($\mathbf{v}$)   Returns a transform identical to *fft*, except using a different normalizing factor and sign convention.

IFFT($\mathbf{v}$)   Returns the inverse Fourier transform of a vector of data corresponding to *FFT*. Takes a vector of size $1 + 2^{n-1}$, and returns a real vector of size 2^n.

Mathcad comes with two types of Fourier transform pairs: *fft* / *ifft* (or the alternative *FFT*/*IFFT*) and *cfft*/*icfft* (or the alternative *CFFT*/*ICFFT*). These functions are discrete: they apply to and return vectors and matrices only. You cannot use them with other functions.

Use the *fft* and *ifft* (or *FFT* / *IFFT*) functions if:

- the data values in the time domain are real, and
- the data vector has 2^m elements.

Use the *cfft* and *icfft* (or *CFFT* / *ICFFT*) functions in all other cases.

Be sure to use these functions in pairs. For example, if you used *CFFT* to go from the time domain to the frequency domain, you must use *ICFFT* to transform back to the time domain. See Figure 10-1 for an example.

Figure 10-1: Use of fast Fourier transforms in Mathcad. Since the random number generator gives different numbers every time, you may not be able to recreate this example exactly as you see it.

Note Different sources use different conventions concerning the initial factor of the Fourier transform and whether to conjugate the results of either the transform or the inverse transform. The functions *fft*, *ifft*, *cfft*, and *icfft* use $1/\sqrt{N}$ as a normalizing factor and a positive exponent in going from the time to the frequency domain. The functions *FFT*, *IFFT*, *CFFT*, and *ICFFT* use $1/N$ as a normalizing factor and a negative exponent in going from the time to the frequency domain.

Wavelet Transforms

wave(**v**)   Returns the discrete wavelet transform of **v**, a 2^m element vector containing real data, using the Daubechies four-coefficient wavelet filter. The vector returned is the same size as **v**.

iwave(**v**)   Returns the inverse discrete wavelet transform of **v**, a 2^m element vector containing real data. The vector returned is the same size as **v**.

Vector and Matrix Functions

Note that functions that expect vectors always expect column vectors rather than row vectors. To change a row vector into a column vector, use the transpose operator (click $\boxed{M^T}$ on the Matrix toolbar).

Size and Scope of an Array

cols(**A**)   Returns the number of columns in array **A**. If **A** is a scalar, returns 0.

last(**v**)   Returns the index of the last element in vector **v**.

length(**v**)   Returns the number of elements in vector **v**.

max(**A, B, C, ...**)   Returns the largest of the strings, arrays, or scalars **A, B, C, ...** If any value is complex, returns the largest real part plus i times the largest imaginary part.

min(**A, B, C, ...**)   Returns the smallest of the strings, arrays, or scalars **A, B, C, ...** If any value is complex, returns the smallest real part plus i times the smallest imaginary part.

rows(**A**)   Returns the number of rows in array **A**. If **A** is a scalar, returns 0.

Special Types of Matrices

diag(**v**)   Returns a diagonal matrix containing on its diagonal the elements of **v**.

geninv(**A**)   Returns the left inverse matrix **L** of **A**, such that $\mathbf{L} \cdot \mathbf{A} = \mathbf{I}$, where **I** is the identity matrix having the same number of columns as **A**. Matrix **A** is an $m \times n$ real-valued matrix, where $m \geq n$.

identity(n)   Returns an $n \times n$ matrix of 0's with 1's on the diagonal.

rref(**A**)   Returns the reduced-row echelon form of **A**.

$$\mathbf{v} := \begin{bmatrix} 2 \\ 8 \\ 9 \\ 7 \end{bmatrix} \qquad \text{diag}(\mathbf{v}) = \begin{bmatrix} 2 & 0 & 0 & 0 \\ 0 & 8 & 0 & 0 \\ 0 & 0 & 9 & 0 \\ 0 & 0 & 0 & 7 \end{bmatrix}$$ ← A diagonal matrix formed from a vector. (Mathcad Professional)

$$\mathbf{A} := \begin{pmatrix} 2 & 4 & 6 \\ 4 & 5 & 6 \\ 2 & 7 & 12 \end{pmatrix} \qquad \text{rref}(\mathbf{A}) = \begin{pmatrix} 1 & 0 & -1 \\ 0 & 1 & 2 \\ 0 & 0 & 0 \end{pmatrix}$$ ← The reduced-row echelon form of a matrix.

$$\mathbf{B} := \begin{bmatrix} 5 + 2i \\ 2.54 - 3i \\ 3 + (4 + .8) \cdot i \end{bmatrix} \qquad \text{Im}(\mathbf{B}) = \begin{pmatrix} 2 \\ -3 \\ 4.8 \end{pmatrix}$$ ← The imaginary part of a matrix.

Figure 10-2: Functions for transforming arrays.

Special Characteristics of a Matrix

cond1($\mathbf{M}$)   Returns the condition number of the matrix $\mathbf{M}$ based on the L_1 norm.

cond2($\mathbf{M}$)   Returns the condition number of the matrix $\mathbf{M}$ based on the L_2 norm.

conde($\mathbf{M}$)   Returns the condition number of the matrix $\mathbf{M}$ based on the Euclidean norm.

condi($\mathbf{M}$)   Returns the condition number of the matrix $\mathbf{M}$ based on the infinity norm.

norm1($\mathbf{M}$)   Returns the L_1 norm of the matrix $\mathbf{M}$.

norm2($\mathbf{M}$)   Returns the L_2 norm of the matrix $\mathbf{M}$.

norme($\mathbf{M}$)   Returns the Euclidean norm of the matrix $\mathbf{M}$.

normi($\mathbf{M}$)   Returns the infinity norm of the matrix $\mathbf{M}$.

rank($\mathbf{A}$)   Returns the rank of the real-valued matrix $\mathbf{A}$.

tr($\mathbf{M}$)   Returns the sum of the diagonal elements, known as the *trace*, of $\mathbf{M}$.

Chapter 10 Built-in Functions

Forming New Matrices

augment(**A**, **B**, **C**, ...) — Returns an array formed by placing **A**, **B**, **C**, ... left to right. **A**, **B**, **C**, ... are arrays having the same number of rows or they are scalars and single-row arrays.

CreateMesh(**F**, [[*s0*], [*s1*], [*t0*], [*t1*], [*sgrid*], [*tgrid*], [**fmap**]]) — Returns a nested array of three matrices representing the *x*-, *y*-, and *z*-coordinates of a parametric surface defined by the function, **F**. **F** is a three-element vector-valued function of two variables. *s0*, *s1*, *t0*, and *t1* are the variable limits, and *sgrid* and *tgrid* are the number of gridpoints. All must be real scalars. **fmap** is a three-element vector-valued mapping function. All arguments but the function argument are optional.

CreateSpace(**F**,[[*t0*], [*t1*], [*tgrid*], [**fmap**]]) — Returns a nested array of three vectors representing the *x*-, *y*-, and *z*-coordinates of a space curve defined by the function, **F**. **F** is a three-element vector-valued function of one variable. *t0* and *t1* are the variable limits, and *tgrid* is the number of gridpoints. All must be real scalars. **fmap** is a three-element vector-valued mapping function. All arguments but the function argument are optional.

matrix(*m*, *n*, *f*) — Creates a matrix in which the i,jth element contains $f(i, j)$ where $i = 0, 1, ..., m - 1$ and $j = 0, 1, ..., n - 1$. Function f must have been defined previously in the worksheet.

stack(**A**, **B**, **C**, ...) — Returns an array formed by placing **A**, **B**, **C**, ... top to bottom. **A**, **B**, **C**, ... are arrays having the same number of columns or they are scalars and vectors.

submatrix(**A**, *ir*, *jr*, *ic*, *jc*) — Returns a submatrix of **A** consisting of all elements contained in rows *ir* through *jr* and columns *ic* through *jc*. Make sure $ir \leq jr$ and $ic \leq jc$ or the order of rows or columns will be reversed.

Note For the functions *CreateMesh* and *CreateSpace*, instead of using a vector-valued function, **F**, you can use three functions, **f1**, **f2**, and **f3**, representing the *x*-, *y*-, and *z*-coordinates of the parametric surface or space curve. Your call to one of these functions might look something like this: $CreateMesh(f1, f2, f3)$.

Alternatively, for **CreateMesh**, you can use a single function of two variables such as $F(x, y) = \dfrac{\sin(x) + \cos(y)}{2}$.

Figure 10-3 shows examples of using *stack* and *augment*.

Figure 10-3: Joining matrices with the augment *and* stack *functions.*

Mapping Functions

cyl2xyz(r, θ, z)   Converts the cylindrical coordinates of a point in 3D space, represented by r, θ, and z, to rectangular coordinates. r, θ, and z must be real numbers.

pol2xy(r, θ)   Converts the polar coordinates of a point in 2D space, represented by r and θ, to rectangular coordinates. r and θ must be real numbers.

sph2xyz(r, θ, ϕ)   Converts the spherical coordinates of a point in 3D space, represented by r, θ, and ϕ, to rectangular coordinates. r, θ, and ϕ must be real numbers.

xy2pol(x, y)   Converts the rectangular coordinates of a point in 2D space, represented by x and y, to polar coordinates. x and y must be real numbers.

xyz2cyl(x, y, z)   Converts the rectangular coordinates of a point in 3D space, represented by x, y, and z, to cylindrical coordinates. x, y, and z must be real numbers.

xyz2sph(x, y, z)   Converts the rectangular coordinates of a point in 3D space, represented by x, y, and z, to spherical coordinates. x, y, and z must be real numbers.

Tip   Use any of the 3D mapping functions as the fmap argument for the CreateSpace and CreateMesh functions.

Lookup Functions

lookup(z, **A**, **B**) Looks in a vector or matrix, **A**, for a given value, z, and returns the value(s) in the same position(s) (i.e. with the same row and column numbers) in another matrix, **B**. z may be a real or complex number or a string. **A** and **B** must have the same dimensions and contain real, complex, or string values.

hlookup(z, **A**, r) Looks in the first row of a given matrix, **A**, for a given value, z, and returns the value(s) in the same column(s) in the row specified, r. z may be a real or complex number or a string. **A** must contain real, complex, or string values. r must be an integer.

vlookup(z, **A**, r) Looks in the first column of a given matrix, **A**, for a given value, z, and returns the value(s) in the same row(s) in the column specified, r. z may be a real or complex number or a string. **A** must contain real, complex, or string values. r must be an integer.

match(z, **A**) Looks in a vector or matrix, **A**, for a given value, z, and returns the index (indices) of its positions in **A**. z may be a real or complex number or a string. **A** must contain real, complex, or string values.

Eigenvalues and Eigenvectors

eigenvals(**M**) Returns a vector containing the eigenvalues of the square matrix **M**.

eigenvec(**M**, z) Returns a vector containing the normalized eigenvector corresponding to the eigenvalue z of the square matrix **M**.

eigenvecs(**M**) Returns a matrix containing normalized eigenvectors corresponding to the eigenvalues of the square matrix **M**. The nth column of the matrix returned is an eigenvector corresponding to the nth eigenvalue returned by *eigenvals*.

genvals(**M**, **N**) Returns a vector **v** of computed eigenvalues each of which satisfies the generalized eigenvalue problem $\mathbf{M} \cdot \mathbf{x} = v_i \cdot \mathbf{N} \cdot \mathbf{x}$. Vector **x** is the corresponding eigenvector. **M** and **N** are real square matrices having the same number of columns.

genvecs(**M**, **N**) Returns a matrix containing the normalized eigenvectors corresponding to the eigenvalues in **v**, the vector returned by *genvals*. The nth column of this matrix is the eigenvector **x** satisfying the generalized eigenvalue problem $\mathbf{M} \cdot \mathbf{x} = v_n \cdot \mathbf{N} \cdot \mathbf{x}$.

Matrices **M** and **N** are real-valued square matrices having the same number of columns.

Figure 10-4 shows how some of these functions are used.

Finding eigenvalues and eigenvectors of a real matrix . .

$$A := \begin{pmatrix} 1 & -2 & 6 \\ 3 & 0 & 10 \\ 2 & 5 & -1 \end{pmatrix} \quad c := \text{eigenvals}(A) \quad c = \begin{pmatrix} 0.105 \\ 7.497 \\ -7.602 \end{pmatrix}$$

To find **all** the corresponding eigenvectors at once:

$$v := \text{eigenvecs}(A) \quad v = \begin{pmatrix} 0.873 & 0.244 & -0.554 \\ -0.408 & 0.81 & -0.574 \\ -0.266 & 0.534 & 0.603 \end{pmatrix}$$

The first column of v is the eigenvector corresponding to 0.105, the first element of c. Similarly, the second column of v is the eigenvector corresponding to 7.497, the second element of c.

Figure 10-4: Eigenvalues and eigenvectors in Mathcad.

Solving a Linear System of Equations

lsolve($\mathbf{M}$, $\mathbf{v}$) Returns a solution vector $\mathbf{x}$ such that $\mathbf{M} \cdot \mathbf{x} = \mathbf{v}$. $\mathbf{v}$ is a vector having the same number of rows as the matrix $\mathbf{M}$.

Use the *lsolve* function to solve a linear system of equations whose coefficients are arranged in a matrix $\mathbf{M}$.

Note The argument $\mathbf{M}$ for *lsolve* must be a matrix that is neither singular nor nearly singular. An alternative to *lsolve* is to solve a linear system by using matrix inversion. See "Solving and Optimization Functions" on page 166 for additional solving functions.

Decomposition

cholesky(**M**)   Returns a lower triangular matrix **L** such that $\mathbf{L} \cdot \mathbf{L}^T = \mathbf{M}$. This uses only the upper triangular part of **M**. The upper triangular of **M**, when reflected about the diagonal, must form a positive definite matrix.

lu(**M**)   Returns a single matrix containing the three square matrices **P**, **L**, and **U**, all having the same size as **M** and joined together side by side, in that order. These three matrices satisfy the equation $\mathbf{P} \cdot \mathbf{M} = \mathbf{L} \cdot \mathbf{U}$, where **L** and **U** are lower and upper triangular respectively.

qr(**A**)   Returns a matrix whose first n columns contain the square, orthonormal matrix **Q**, and whose remaining columns contain the upper triangular matrix, **R**. Matrices **Q** and **R** satisfy the equation $\mathbf{A} = \mathbf{Q} \cdot \mathbf{R}$, where **A** is a real-valued array.

svd(**A**)   Returns a single matrix containing two stacked matrices **U** and **V**, where **U** is the upper $m \times n$ submatrix and **V** is the lower $n \times n$ submatrix. Matrices **U** and **V** satisfy the equation $\mathbf{A} = \mathbf{U} \cdot \mathrm{diag}(\mathbf{s}) \cdot \mathbf{V}^T$, where **s** is a vector returned by svds(**A**). **A** is an $m \times n$ array of real values, where $m \geq n$.

svds(**A**)   Returns a vector containing the singular values of the $m \times n$ real-valued array **A**, where $m \geq n$.

Sorting Functions

csort(**A**, n)   Returns an array formed by rearranging rows of the matrix **A** such that the elements in column n are in ascending order. The result has the same size as **A**.

reverse(**A**)   Returns an array in which the elements of a vector, or the rows of a matrix, are in reverse order.

rsort(**A**, n)   Returns an array formed by rearranging the columns of the matrix **A** such that the elements in row n are in ascending order. The result has the same size as **A**.

sort(**v**)   Returns the elements of the vector **v** sorted in ascending order.

Tip   Unless you change the value of ORIGIN, matrices are numbered by default starting with row zero and column zero. To sort on the first column of a matrix, for example, use *csort*(**A**, 0).

Solving and Optimization Functions

This section describes how to solve equations ranging from a single equation in one unknown to large systems with multiple unknowns. The techniques described here generate numeric solutions. Chapter 14, "Symbolic Calculation," describes a variety of techniques for solving equations symbolically.

Finding Roots

polyroots($\mathbf{v}$)   Returns the roots of an nth degree polynomial whose coefficients are in $\mathbf{v}$, a vector of length $n + 1$. Returns a vector of length n.

root($f(z)$, z)   Returns the value of z which the expression $f(z)$ is equal to 0. The arguments are a real- or complex-valued expression $f(z)$ and a real or complex scalar, z. Must be preceded in the worksheet by a guess value for z. Returns a scalar.

root($f(z)$, z, a, b)   Returns the value of z lying between a and b at which the expression $f(z)$ is equal to 0. The arguments to this function are a real-valued expression $f(z)$, a real scalar, z, and real endpoints $a<b$. No guess value for z is required. Returns a scalar.

Note When you specify the arguments a and b for the root function, Mathcad will only find a root for the function f if $f(a)$ is positive and $f(b)$ is negative or vice versa.

The *root* function solves a single equation in a single unknown. This function takes an arbitrary expression or function and one of the variables from the expression. *root* can also take a range in which the solution lies. It then varies that variable until the expression is equal to zero and lies in the specified range. Once this is done, the function returns the value that makes the expression equal zero and lies in the specified range.

Tip *root* makes successive estimates of the value of the root and returns a value when the two most recent estimates differ by less than the value of the tolerance parameter, TOL. As described in "Built-in Variables" on page 102, you can change the value of the tolerance, and hence the accuracy of the solution, by including definitions for TOL directly in your worksheet. You can also change the tolerance by using the Built-in Variables tab when you choose **Options** from the **Math** menu.

To find the roots of a polynomial or an expression having the form:

$$v_n x^n + \ldots + v_2 x^2 + v_1 x + v_0$$

you can use *polyroots* rather than *root*. *polyroots* does not require a guess value, and *polyroots* returns all roots at once, whether real or complex. Figure 10-5 shows examples.

Figure 10-5: Finding roots with root *and* polyroots.

By default, *polyroots* uses a LaGuerre method of finding roots. If you want to use the companion matrix method instead, click on the *polyroots* function with the right mouse button and choose **Companion Matrix** from the pop-up menu.

Note *root* and *polyroots* can solve only one equation in one unknown, and they always return numerical answers. To solve several equations simultaneously, use the techniques described in "Linear/Nonlinear System Solving and Optimization." To solve an equation symbolically, or to find an exact numerical answer in terms of elementary functions, choose **Solve for Variable** from the **Symbolic** menu or use the **solve** keyword. See Chapter 14, "Symbolic Calculation."

Linear/Nonlinear System Solving and Optimization

Mathcad includes numerical solving functions that solve problems such as:

- Linear systems of equations with constraints (equalities or inequalities).
- Nonlinear systems of equations with constraints.
- Optimization (maximization or minimization) of an objective function.
- Optimization (maximization or minimization) of an objective function with constraints.

- Linear programming, in which all constraints are either equalities or inequalities that compare linear functions to constants and the objective function is of the form:

$$c_0 x_0 + c_1 x_1 + \dots + c_n x_n$$

- Quadratic programming, in which all constraints are linear but the objective function contains linear terms and quadratic terms. Quadratic programming features are available in the *Solving and Optimization Extension Pack* (*Expert Solver*), available for separate sale from MathSoft or your local distributor or reseller.

Note Mathcad solves nonlinear systems of up to 200 variables and linear systems of up to 500 variables. With the *Solving and Optimization Extension Pack* (*Expert Solver*), you can solve nonlinear systems of up to 250 variables, linear systems of up to 1000 variables, and quadratic systems of up to 1000 variables.

Solve Blocks

The general form for using system solving functions in Mathcad is within the body of a *solve block*. There are four general steps to creating a solve block. These are:

1. Provide an initial guess (definition) for each of the unknowns you intend to solve for. Mathcad solves equations by making iterative calculations that ultimately converge on a valid solution. The initial guesses you provide give Mathcad a place to start searching for solutions. Guess values are usually required for all systems.

2. Type the word *Given* in a separate math region below the guess definitions. This tells Mathcad that what follows is a system of constraint equations. Be sure you don't type "Given" in a text region.

3. Now enter the constraints (equalities and inequalities) in any order below the word

   Given. Make sure you use the bold equal symbol (click **=** on the Boolean toolbar or press [**Ctrl**]=) for any equality. You can separate the left and right sides of an inequality with any of the symbols <, >, ≤, and ≥.

4. Enter any equation that involves one of the functions *Find*, *Maximize*, *Minimize*, or *Minerr* below the constraints.

Note Solve blocks cannot be nested inside each other—each solve block can have only one *Given* and one *Find* (or *Maximize*, *Minimize*, or *Minerr*). You can, however, define a function like $f(x) := \text{Find}(x)$ at the end of one solve block and refer to this function in another solve block.

Solve Blocks

Find($z0$, $z1$, ...)   Returns values of $z0$, $z1$, ... that satisfy the constraints in a solve block. $z0$, $z1$, ... are real or complex scalars, vectors, arrays, or individual elements of vectors equal in number to the number of unknowns in the system. Returns a scalar for a single unknown; otherwise returns a vector of solutions.

Maximize(f, $z0$, $z1$, ...)   Returns values of $z0$, $z1$, ... that make the function f take on its largest value. $z0$, $z1$, ... are real or complex scalars, vectors, arrays, or individual elements of vectors equal in number to the number of unknowns in the system. Returns a scalar for a single unknown; otherwise returns a vector of solutions. Solve block constraints are optional.

Minerr($z0$, $z1$, ...)   Returns values of $z0$, $z1$, ... that come closest to satisfying the constraints in a solve block. $z0$, $z1$, ... are real or complex scalars, vectors, arrays, or individual elements of vectors equal in number to the number of unknowns in the system. Returns a scalar for a single unknown; otherwise returns a vector of solutions.

Minimize(f, $z0$, $z1$, ...)   Returns values of $z0$, $z1$, ... that make the function f take on its smallest value. $z0$, $z1$, ... are real or complex scalars, vectors, arrays, or individual elements of vectors equal in number to the number of unknowns in the system. Returns a scalar for a single unknown; otherwise returns a vector of solutions. Solve block constraints are optional.

Tip   Unlike most Mathcad functions, the solving functions *Find*, *Maximize*, *Minerr*, and *Minimize* can be entered in math regions with either an initial lowercase or an initial capital letter.

Figure 10-6 shows a solve block with several kinds of constraints and ending with a call to the *Find* function. There are two unknowns. As a result, the *Find* function here takes two arguments, x and y, and returns a vector with two elements.

Constraints

The table below lists the kinds of constraints that can appear in a solve block between the keyword *Given* and one of the functions *Find*, *Maximize*, *Minerr*, and *Minimize*. In the table, x and y represent real-valued expressions, and z and w represent arbitrary expressions. The Boolean constraints are inserted using buttons on the Boolean toolbar. Constraints are often scalar expressions but can also be vector or array expressions.

Figure 10-6: A solve block with both equalities and inequalities.

Condition	Button	Description
$w = z$	$=$	Constrained to be equal.
$x > y$	$>$	Greater than.
$x < y$	$<$	Less than.
$x \geq y$	$\geq$	Greater than or equal to.
$x \leq y$	$\leq$	Less than or equal to.
$x \wedge y$	$\wedge$	And
$x \vee y$	$\vee$	Or
$x \otimes y$	$\oplus$	Xor (Exclusive Or)
$\neg x$	$\neg$	Not

Mathcad does not allow the following inside a solve block:

- Constraints with "$\neq$."
- Assignment statements (statements like **x:=1**).

You can, however, include compound statements such as $1 \leq x \leq 3$.

Note Mathcad returns only one solution for a solve block. There may, however, be multiple solutions to a set of equations. To find a different solution, try different guess values or enter an additional inequality constraint that the current solution does not satisfy.

Tolerances for solving

Mathcad's numerical solvers make use of two tolerance parameters in calculating solutions in solve blocks:

- **Convergence tolerance.** The solvers calculate successive estimates of the values of the solutions and return values when the two most recent estimates differ by less than the value of the built-in variable TOL. A smaller value of TOL often results in a more accurate solution, but the solution may take longer to calculate.

- **Constraint tolerance.** This parameter, determined by the value of the built-in variable CTOL, controls how closely a constraint must be met for a solution to be acceptable. For example, if the constraint tolerance were 0.0001, a constraint such as $x < 2$ would be considered satisfied if, in fact, the value of x satisfied $x < 2.0001$.

Procedures for modifying the values of these tolerances are described in "Built-in Variables" on page 102.

Tip   If you use *Minerr* in a solve block, you should always include additional checks on the reasonableness of the results. The built-in variable ERR returns the size of the error vector for the approximate solution returned by *Minerr*. There is no built-in variable for determining the size of the error for individual solutions to the unknowns.

Solving algorithms and AutoSelect

When you solve an equation, by default Mathcad uses an *AutoSelect* procedure to choose an appropriate solving algorithm. You can override Mathcad's choice of algorithm and select another available algorithm yourself.

Here are the available solving methods:

Linear

Applies a linear programming algorithm to the problem. Guess values for the unknowns are not required.

Nonlinear

Applies either a conjugate gradient, Levenberg-Marquardt, or quasi-Newton solving routine to the problem. Guess values for all unknowns must precede the solve block. Choose **Nonlinear⇒Advanced Options** from the pop-up menu to control settings for the conjugate gradient and quasi-Newton solvers.

Note   The Levenberg-Marquardt method is not available for the *Maximize* and *Minimize* functions.

Quadratic

Applies a quadratic programming algorithm to the problem. This option is available only if the *Solving and Optimization Extension Pack* (*Expert Solver*) is installed. Guess values for the unknowns are not required.

You can override Mathcad's default choice of solving algorithm as follows:

1. Create and evaluate a solve block, allowing Mathcad to AutoSelect an algorithm.

2. Click with the right mouse button on the name of the function that terminates the solve block, and remove the check from **AutoSelect** on the pop-up menu.

3. Check one of the available solving methods on the pop-up menu. Mathcad recalculates the solution using the method you selected.

Reports

If you have the *Solving and Optimization Extension Pack* (*Expert Solver*) installed, you can generate reports for a linear optimization problems. To generate a report, click on a solving function with the right mouse button and choose **Report** from the pop-up menu. For more information on reports, refer to the online Help.

Mixed integer programming

If you have *Solving and Optimization Extension Pack* (*Expert Solver*) installed, you can perform mixed integer programming. Using mixed integer programming you can force the solution for an unknown variable to be a binary number (1 or 0) or an integer. For more information mixed integer programming, refer to the online Help.

Statistics, Probability, and Data Analysis Functions

Statistics

corr(**A**, **B**)
: Returns the Pearson's r correlation coefficient for the $m \times n$ arrays **A** and **B**.

cvar(**A**, **B**)
: Returns the covariance of the elements in $m \times n$ arrays **A** and **B**.

gmean(**A**, **B**, **C**, ...)
: Returns the geometric mean of the elements of the arrays or scalars **A**, **B**, **C**, ... All elements must be real and greater than 0.

hist(**int**, **A**)
: Returns a vector representing the frequencies with which values in **A** fall in the intervals represented by **int**. When **int** is a vector of intervals in ascending order, the ith element of the returned vector is the number of points in data falling between the ith and $(i+1)$th element of **int**. When **int** is an integer, it represents the number of subintervals of equal length. Both **int** and **A** must be real.

histogram(**int**, **A**)
: Returns a matrix with two columns. When **int** is an integer, the first column contains the midpoints of **int** subintervals of the range $\min(\mathbf{A}) \le \text{value} \le \max(\mathbf{A})$ of equal length and the second column is identical to *hist*(**int**, **A**). When **int** is a vector of intervals in ascending order, the first column contains midpoints of the intervals represented by the **int** vector. Both **int** and **A** must be real.

Tip If you are interested in graphing the result of a frequency analysis in a 2D bar plot showing the distribution of data across the bins, use the function *histogram* rather than *hist*, and plot the first column of the result against the second column of the result.

---

hmean(**A**, **B**, **C**, ...)
: Returns the harmonic mean of the elements of the arrays or scalars **A**, **B**, **C**, ... All elements must be nonzero

kurt(**A**, **B**, **C**, ...)
: Returns the kurtosis of the elements of the arrays or scalars **A**, **B**, **C**, ...

mean(**A**, **B**, **C**, ...)
: Returns the arithmetic mean of the elements of the arrays or scalars **A**, **B**, **C**, ...

median(**A**, **B**, **C**, ...)
: Returns the median of the elements of the arrays or scalars **A**, **B**, **C**, ... the value above and below which there are an equal number of values. If there are an even number of elements, this is the arithmetic mean of the two central values.

mode(**A**, **B**, **C**, ...)
: Returns the element from the arrays or scalars **A**, **B**, **C**, ... that occurs most often.

skew(**A, B, C, ...**)	Returns the skewness of the elements of the arrays or scalars **A, B, C, ...**
stdev(**A, B, C, ...**)	Returns the population standard deviation (square root of the variance) of the elements of the arrays or scalars **A, B, C, ...**
Stdev(**A, B, C, ...**)	Returns the sample standard deviation (square root of the sample variance) of the elements of the arrays or scalars **A, B, C, ...**
var(**A, B, C, ...**)	Returns the population variance of the elements of the arrays or scalars **A, B, C, ...**
Var(**A, B, C, ...**)	Returns the sample variance of the elements of the arrays or scalars **A, B, C, ...**

Probability Distributions

Mathcad includes functions for working with several common probability densities. These functions fall into four classes:

- **Probability densities.** These functions, beginning with the letter "d," give the likelihood that a random variable will take on a particular value.

- **Cumulative probability distributions.** These functions, beginning with the letter "p," give the probability that a random variable will take on a value *less than or equal to* a specified value. These are obtained by simply integrating (or summing when appropriate) the corresponding probability density from $-\infty$ to a specified value.

- **Inverse cumulative probability distributions.** These functions, beginning with the letter "q," take a probability p between 0 and 1 as an argument and return a value such that the probability that a random variable will be *less than or equal to* that value is p.

- **Random number generators.** These functions, beginning with the letter "r," return a vector of m elements drawn from the corresponding probability distribution. Each time you recalculate an equation containing one of these functions, Mathcad generates new random numbers.

Tip   Mathcad's random number generators have a "seed value" associated with them. A given seed value always generates the same sequence of random numbers, and choosing **Calculate** from the **Math** menu advances Mathcad along this random number sequence. Changing the seed value, however, advances Mathcad along a different random number sequence. To change the seed value, choose **Options** from the **Math** menu and enter a value on the Built-in Variables tab.

Note   See comments above about the nomenclature, arguments, and returned values for the probability distribution functions in the following table.

Probability Distributions

$\text{dbeta}(x, s_1, s_2)$
$\text{pbeta}(x, s_1, s_2)$
$\text{qbeta}(p, s_1, s_2)$
$\text{rbeta}(m, s_1, s_2)$

Probability distribution functions for the beta distribution in which $(s_1, s_2 > 0)$ are the shape parameters. $0 < x < 1$. $0 \le p \le 1$.

$\text{dbinom}(k, n, p)$
$\text{pbinom}(k, n, p)$
$\text{qbinom}(p, n, r)$
$\text{rbinom}(m, n, p)$

Probability distribution functions for the binomial distribution in which n and k are integers satisfying $0 \le k \le n$. $0 \le p \le 1$. r is the probability of success on a single trial.

$\text{dcauchy}(x, l, s)$
$\text{pcauchy}(x, l, s)$
$\text{qcauchy}(p, l, s)$
$\text{rcauchy}(m, l, s)$

Probability distribution functions for the Cauchy distribution in which l is a location parameter and $s > 0$ is a scale parameter. $0 < p < 1$.

$\text{dchisq}(x, d)$
$\text{pchisq}(x, d)$
$\text{qchisq}(p, d)$
$\text{rchisq}(m, d)$

Probability distribution functions for the chi-squared distribution in which $d > 0$ are the degrees of freedom and $x \ge 0$. $0 \le p < 1$.

$\text{dexp}(x, r)$
$\text{pexp}(x, r)$
$\text{qexp}(p, r)$
$\text{exp}(m, r)$

Probability distribution functions for the exponential distribution in which $r > 0$ is the rate and $x \ge 0$. $0 \le p < 1$.

$\text{dF}(x, d_1, d_2)$
$\text{pF}(x, d_1, d_2)$
$\text{qF}(p, d_1, d_2)$
$\text{rF}(m, d_1, d_2)$

Probability distribution functions for the F distribution in which $(d_1, d_2 > 0)$ are the degrees of freedom and $x \ge 0$. $0 \le p < 1$.

$\text{dgamma}(x, s)$
$\text{pgamma}(x, s)$
$\text{qgamma}(p, s)$
$\text{rgamma}(m, s)$

Probability distribution functions for the gamma distribution in which $s > 0$ is the shape parameter and $x \ge 0$. $0 \le p < 1$.

$\text{dgeom}(k, p)$
$\text{pgeom}(k, p)$
$\text{qgeom}(p, r)$
$\text{rgeom}(m, p)$

Probability distribution functions for the geometric distribution in which $0 < p \le 1$ is the probability of success and k is a nonnegative integer. r is the probability of success on a single trial.

$\text{dhypergeom}(M, a, b, n)$
$\text{phypergeom}(M, a, b, n)$
$\text{qhypergeom}(p, a, b, n)$
$\text{rhypergeom}(M, a, b, n)$

Probability distribution functions for the hypergeometric distribution in which M, a, b, and n are integers with $0 \le M \le a$, $0 \le n - M \le b$, and $0 \le n \le a + b$. $0 \le p < 1$.

$\text{dlnorm}(x, \mu, \sigma)$
$\text{plnorm}(x, \mu, \sigma)$
$\text{qlnorm}(p, \mu, \sigma)$
$\text{rlnorm}(m, \mu, \sigma)$

Probability distribution functions for the lognormal distribution in which μ is the logmean and $\sigma > 0$ is the logdeviation. $x \ge 0$. $0 \le p < 1$.

dlogis(x, l, s) plogis(x, l, s) qlogis(p, l, s) rlogis(m, l, s)	Probability distribution functions for the logistic distribution in which l is the location parameter and $s > 0$ is the scale parameter. $0 < p < 1$.
dnbinom(k, n, p) pnbinom(k, n, p) qnbinom(p, n, r) rnbinom(m, n, p)	Probability distribution functions for the negative binomial distribution in which $0 < p \leq 1$ and n and k are integers, $n > 0$ and $k \geq 0$.
dnorm(x, μ, σ) pnorm(x, μ, σ) qnorm(p, μ, σ) rnorm(m, μ, σ)	Probability distribution functions for the normal distribution in which μ and σ are the mean and standard deviation. $\sigma > 0$.
dpois(k, λ) ppois(k, λ) qpois(p, λ) rpois(m, λ)	Probability distribution functions for the Poisson distribution in which $\lambda > 0$ and k is a nonnegative integer. $0 \leq p \leq 1$.
dt(x, d) pt(x, d) qt(p, d) t(m, d)	Probability distribution functions for Student's t distribution in which $d > 0$ are the degrees of freedom. $0 < p < 1$.
dunif(x, a, b) punif(x, a, b) qunif(p, a, b) runif(m, a, b)	Probability distribution functions for the uniform distribution in which b and a are the endpoints of the interval with $a \leq x \leq b$. $0 \leq p \leq 1$.
dweibull(x, s) pweibull(x, s) qweibull(p, s) rweibull(m, s)	Probability distribution functions for the Weibull distribution in which $s > 0$ is the shape parameter and $x \geq 0$. $0 < p < 1$.

Tip Two additional functions that are useful for common probability calculations are *rnd*(x), which is equivalent to *runif*(1, 0, x), and *cnorm*(x), which is equivalent to *pnorm*(x, 0, 1).

Interpolation and Prediction Functions

Note Whenever you use arrays in any of the functions described in this section, be sure that every element in the array contains a data value. Mathcad assigns 0 to any elements you have not explicitly assigned.

bspline(**vx**, **vy**, **u**, n) Returns a vector of coefficients of a B-spline of degree n, which is used in the *interp* function. The knot locations of the spline are specified in vector **u**. **vx** and **vy** must be real vectors of the same length. The values in **vx** must be in ascending order.

cspline(**vx**, **vy**) Returns a vector of coefficients of a cubic spline with cubic endpoints, which is used in the *interp* function. **vx** and **vy** must be real vectors of the same length. The values in **vx** must be in ascending order.

interp(**vs**, **vx**, **vy**, x) Returns the interpolated y value corresponding to the argument x. The vector **vs** is a vector of intermediate results obtained by evaluating *bspline*, *cspline*, *lspline*, or *pspline* or the regression routine *regress* or *loess* using the data vectors **vx** and **vy**. **vx** and **vy** must be real vectors of the same length. The vector **vx** must be in ascending order.

linterp(**vx**, **vy**, x) Uses the data vectors **vx** and **vy** to return a linearly interpolated y value corresponding to the argument x. **vx** and **vy** must be real vectors of the same length. The vector **vx** must be in ascending order.

lspline(**vx**, **vy**) Returns a vector of coefficients of a cubic spline with linear endpoints, which is used in the *interp* function. **vx** and **vy** must be real vectors of the same length. The values in **vx** must be in ascending order.

predict(**v**, m, n) Returns n predicted values based on m consecutive values from the data vector **v**. Elements in **v** should represent samples taken at equal intervals. m and n are integers

pspline(**vx**, **vy**) Returns a vector of coefficients of a cubic spline with parabolic endpoints, which is used in the *interp* function. **vx** and **vy** must be real vectors of the same length. The values in **vx** must be in ascending order.

Interpolation involves using existing data points to predict values between these data points. Mathcad allows you to connect the data points either with straight lines (linear interpolation) or with sections of a cubic polynomial (cubic spline interpolation). Unlike the regression functions discussed in the next section, these interpolation functions return a curve which must pass through the points you specify. If your data is noisy, you should consider using regression functions instead (see page 179).

Cubic spline interpolation passes a curve through a set of points in such a way that the first and second derivatives of the curve are continuous across each point. This curve is assembled by taking three adjacent points and constructing a cubic polynomial passing through those points. These cubic polynomials are then strung together to form the completed curve. In the case of "traditional" cubic splines, the data points to be interpolated define the "knots" where the polynomials are joined, but B-splines (implemented in the function *bspline*) join the polynomials at arbitrary points.

Linear prediction involves using existing data values to predict values beyond the existing ones.

The coefficients returned by the spline interpolation functions *bspline*, *cspline*, *lspline*, and *pspline* and the regression functions *regress* and *loess* described in the next section are designed to be passed to Mathcad's *interp* function. *interp* returns a single interpolated *y* value for a given *x* value, but as a practical matter you'll probably be evaluating *interp* for many different points, as shown in Figure 10-7. Store the coefficients returned by the spline or regression functions in a vector (such as **vs** in Figure 10-7) that can be passed to *interp* for evaluation, plotting, or further calculation.

Figure 10-7: Spline curve for the points stored in vx and vy. Since the random number generator gives different numbers every time, you may not be able to recreate this example exactly as you see it.

Tip	For best results with spline interpolation, do not use the *interp* function on values of x far from the fitted points. Splines are intended for interpolation, not extrapolation.

Note	Mathcad handles *two-dimensional* cubic spline interpolation in much the same way as the one-dimensional case illustrated: in this case the spline function takes two matrix arguments, **Mxy** and **Mz**. The first is an $n \times 2$ matrix specifying the points along the diagonal of a rectangular grid, and the second is an $n \times n$ matrix of z-values representing the surface to be interpolated. Mathcad passes a *surface* through the grid of points. This surface corresponds to a cubic polynomial in x and y in which the first and second partial derivatives are continuous in the corresponding direction across each grid point. For an example see the "Data Analysis" QuickSheets and in the Resource Center (choose **Resource Center** from the **Help** menu).

Regression and Smoothing Functions

Mathcad includes a number of functions for performing *regression*. Typically, these functions generate a curve or surface of a specified type in some sense minimizes the error between itself and the data you supply. The functions differ primarily in the type of curve or surface they use to fit the data. Unlike interpolation functions, these functions do not require that the fitted curve or surface pass through points you supply, and they are therefore less sensitive to spurious data.

Smoothing involves taking a set of y (and possibly x) values and returning a new set of y values that is smoother than the original set. Unlike the regression and interpolation functions, smoothing results in a new set of y values, not a function that can be evaluated between the data points you specify. Thus, if you are interested in y values *between* the y values you specify, you should use a regression or interpolation function.

Linear regression

intercept(**vx**, **vy**)	Returns a scalar: the y-intercept of the least-squares regression line for the data points in **vx** and **vy**.
slope(**vx**, **vy**)	Returns a scalar: the slope of the least-squares regression line for the data points in **vx** and **vy**.
stderr(**vx**, **vy**)	Returns the standard error associated with linear regression of the elements of **vy** on the elements of **vx**.
line(**vx**, **vy**)	Returns the y-intercept and slope of the line that best approximates the data in **vx** and **vy**.
medfit(**vx**, **vy**)	Returns the y-intercept and slope of the line that best approximates the data in **vx** and **vy** using median-median regression.

Polynomial regression

regress(**vx**, **vy**, *n*)   Returns a vector of coefficients for the *n*th degree least-squares polynomial fit for the data points specified in vectors **vx** and **vy**. This vector becomes the first argument of the *interp* function.

loess(**vx**, **vy**, *span*)   Returns a vector specifying a set of second order polynomials that best fit particular neighborhoods of data points specified in vectors **vx** and **vy**. This vector becomes the first argument of the *interp* function. The argument *span*, *span* > 0, specifies how large a neighborhood *loess* considers in performing this local regression.

These functions are useful when you have a set of measured *y* values corresponding to *x* values (or possibly multiple *x* values) and you want to fit a polynomial through those *y* values.

Use *regress* when you want to use a *single* polynomial to fit all your data values. The *regress* function lets you fit a polynomial of any order. However as a practical matter, you rarely should go beyond $n = 4$.

The *loess* function performs a more localized regression. Instead of generating a single polynomial the way *regress* does, *loess* generates a different second order polynomial depending on where you are on the curve. It does this by examining the data in a small neighborhood of a point you're interested in.

As in the case of Mathcad's spline interpolation functions, the coefficients returned by *regress* and *loess* are designed to be passed to Mathcad's *interp* function. *interp* returns a single interpolated *y* value for a given *x* value, but as a practical matter you'll probably be evaluating *interp* for many different points.

Note   Mathcad also allows *multivariate* polynomial regression with *regress* or *loess* to fit *y* values corresponding to two or more independent variables. In this case, the regression function's first two arguments are **Mx** and **vy**: the first is an $n \times m$ matrix specifying the *m* values of *n* predictor variables, and the second is a vector of response data corresponding to the factors in **Mx**. For an example see the "Data Analysis" QuickSheets in the Resource Center (choose **Resource Center** from the **Help** menu). You can add independent variables by simply adding columns to the **Mx** array and a corresponding number of rows to the vector you pass to the *interp* function.

Specialized regression

expfit(**vx**, **vy**, **vg**)   Returns the parameter values for the exponential curve $a \cdot e^{(b \cdot x)} + c$ that best approximates the data in **vx** and **vy**. Vector **vg** specifies guess values for the three unknown parameters *a*, *b*, and *c*. See Figure 10-8 for an example.

lgsfit(**vx**, **vy**, **vg**)   Returns the parameter values for the logistic curve $a/(1 + b \cdot e^{(-c \cdot x)})$ that best approximates the data in **vx** and **vy**. Vector **vg** specifies guess values for the three unknown parameters *a*, *b*, and *c*.

---

lnfit(**vx**, **vy**)   Returns the parameter values for the logarithmic curve
$a \cdot \ln(x) + b$ that best approximates the data in **vx** and **vy**. A vector
of guess values is not required.

logfit(**vx**, **vy**, **vg**)   Returns the parameter values for the logarithmic curve
$a \cdot \ln(x + b) + c$ that best approximates the data in **vx** and **vy**.
Vector **vg** specifies guess values for the three unknown parameters
a, b, and c.

pwrfit(**vx**, **vy**, **vg**)   Returns the parameter values for the power curve
$a \cdot x^b + c$ that best approximates the data in **vx** and **vy**. Vector **vg**
specifies guess values for the three unknown parameters a, b, and c.

sinfit(**vx**, **vy**, **vg**)   Returns the parameter values for the sine curve
$a \cdot \sin(x + b) + c$ that best approximates the data in **vx** and **vy**.
Vector **vg** specifies guess values for the four unknown parameters a,
b, and c.

Use these functions when you have a set of measured y values corresponding to x values
and you want to fit a special type of curve through those y values. Although you can
use the *genfit* function described on page 182 to perform a curve fit on any function,
the functions outlined above are designed for ease of use. Use them if they address the
particular function curve to which you are fitting your data.

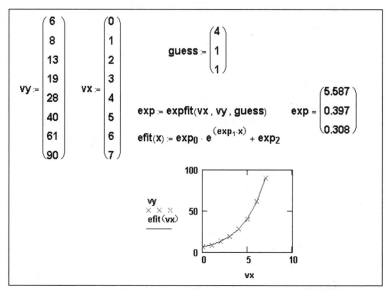

Figure 10-8: Using the specialized regression function expfit.

Generalized regression

linfit(**vx**, **vy**, **F**)   Returns a vector containing the coefficients used to create a linear combination of the functions in **F** that best approximates the data points in vectors **vx** and **vy**. **F** is a function which returns a vector consisting of the functions to be linearly combined. Elements of **vx** should be in ascending order.

genfit(**vx**, **vy**, **vg**, **F**)   Returns the parameters for the best fit by the (possibly nonlinear) function defined by f to the data points in the vectors **vx** and **vy**. **F** is a function that returns an $n + 1$ element vector containing f and its partial derivatives with respect to each of its n parameters. **vg** is an n-element vector of guess values for the n parameters.

linfit is designed to model your data by a linear combination of arbitrary functions:

$$y = a_0 \cdot f_0(x) + a_1 \cdot f_1(x) + \dots + a_n \cdot f_n(x)$$

genfit is designed to model your data by some arbitrary (possibly nonlinear) function whose parameters must be chosen. For example, if your data is to be modeled by the sum

$$f(x) = 2 \cdot \sin(a_1 x) + 3 \cdot \tanh(a_2 x)$$

and you wish to solve for the unknown parameters a_1 and a_2, you would use *genfit*. An example of using *genfit* is given in Figure 10-9.

Figure 10-9: Using genfit *for finding the parameters of a function so that it best fits the data.*

Anything you can do with *linfit* you can also do, albeit less conveniently, with *genfit*. The difference between these two functions is the difference between solving a system of linear equations and solving a system of nonlinear equations. The latter generally must be solved by iteration, which explains why *genfit* needs a vector of guess values as an argument and *linfit* does not.

Smoothing functions

medsmooth(**vy**, *n*) Returns an *m*-element vector created by smoothing **vy** with running medians. **vy** is an *m*-element vector of real numbers. *n* is the width of the window over which smoothing occurs. *n* must be an odd number less than the number of elements in **vy**.

ksmooth(**vx**,**vy**, *b*) Returns an *n*-element vector created by using a Gaussian kernel to return weighted averages of **vy**. **vy** and **vx** are *n*-element vectors of real numbers. The bandwidth *b* controls the smoothing window and should be set to a few times the spacing between your *x* data points. Elements in **vx** must be in ascending order.

supsmooth(**vx**,**vy**) Returns an *n*-element vector created by the piece wise use of a symmetric *k*-nearest neighbor linear least-squares fitting procedure in which *k* is adaptively chosen. **vy** and **vx** are *n*-element vectors of real numbers. The elements of **vx** must be in increasing order.

medsmooth is the most robust of the three smoothing functions since it is least likely to be affected by spurious data points. This function uses a running median smoother, computes the residuals, smooths the residuals the same way, and adds these two smoothed vectors together. Note that *medsmooth* leaves the first and last $(n-1)/2$ points unchanged. In practice, the length of the smoothing window, *n*, should be small compared to the length of the data set.

ksmooth uses a Gaussian kernel to compute local weighted averages of the input vector **vy**. This smoother is most useful when your data lies along a band of relatively constant width. If your data lies scattered along a band whose width fluctuates considerably, you should use an adaptive smoother like *supsmooth*. *supsmooth* uses a symmetric *k* nearest neighbor linear least-squares fitting procedure to make a series of line segments through your data. Unlike *ksmooth* which uses a fixed bandwidth for all your data, *supsmooth* adaptively chooses different bandwidths for different portions of your data.

Finance Functions

These personal finance functions perform a variety of calculations for making credit and investment decisions. All finance functions take only real values. Payments you make, such as deposits in a savings account or payments toward a loan, must be entered as negative numbers. Cash you receive, such as dividend checks, must be entered as positive numbers. If you want to specify the timing of a payment, use the optional timing variable, *type*, which can be equal to 0 for the end of the period and 1 for the beginning. If omitted, *type* is 0.

Rate and period

cnper(*rate*, *pv*, *fv*)

Returns the number of compounding periods required for an investment to yield a future value, *fv*, given a present value, *pv*, and an interest rate period, *rate*. *rate* > -1. *pv* > 0. *fv* > 0.

crate(*nper*, *pv*, *fv*)

Returns the fixed interest rate required for an investment at present value, *pv*, to yield a future value, *fv*, over a given number of compounding periods, *nper*. *nper* is a positive integer. *pv* > 0. *fv* > 0.

nper(*rate*, *pmt*, *pv*, [[*fv*], [*type*]])

Returns the number of compounding periods for an investment or loan based on periodic, constant payments, *pmt*, using a fixed interest rate, *rate*, and a present value, *pv*. If omitted, *fv* = 0 and *type* = 0. If *pmt* > 0, *rate* and *pv* must be opposite signs.

rate(*nper*, *pmt*, *pv*, [[*fv*], [*type*], [*guess*]])

Returns the interest rate per period of an investment or loan over a number of compounding periods, *nper*, given a periodic, constant payment, *pmt*, and a present value, *pv*. *nper* is a positive integer. If omitted, *fv* = 0, *type* = 0, and *guess* = 0.1 (10%).

Tip   If *rate* does not converge to within 1×10^{-7} after 20 iterations, *rate* returns an error. In such a case, try different values for *guess*. In most cases, *rate* converges if *guess* is between 0 and 1.

Cumulative interest and principal

cumint(*rate*, *nper*, *pv*, *start*, *end*, [*type*])

Returns the cumulative interest paid on a loan between a starting period, *start*, and an ending period, *end*, given a fixed interest rate, *rate*, the total number of compounding periods, *nper*, and the present value of the loan, *pv*. *rate* ≥ 0. *nper*, *start*, and *end* are positive integers. If omitted, *type* = 0.

cumprn(*rate*, *nper*, *pv*, *start*, *end*, [*type*])

Returns the cumulative principal paid on a loan between a starting period, *start*, and an ending period, *end*, given a fixed interest rate, *rate*, the total number of compounding periods, *nper*, and the present value of the loan, *pv*. *rate* ≥ 0. *nper*, *start*, and *end* are positive integers. If omitted, *type* = 0.

```
A home mortgage has the following terms:

    Interest rate:     9%   (annually)          Term:      30yrs
    Present value:   $125,000

Calculate the total (cumulative) interest paid in the
10th year of payments (payments 121 through 132):

    rate := 9%/12        nper := 30 · 12        pv := 125000

    start := 120       end := 132

    cumint(rate, nper, pv, start, end) = -10815.54
```

Figure 10-10: Using the cumint *function.*

Interest rate

eff(*rate, nper*)　　　Returns the effective annual interest rate (APR) given the nominal interest rate, *rate*, and the number of compounding periods per year, *nper. nper* is positive.

nom(*rate, nper*)　　Returns the nominal interest rate given the effective annual interest rate (APR), *rate*, and the number of compounding periods per year, *nper. rate* > -1. *nper* is positive.

Future value

fv(*rate, nper, pmt,* [[*pv*], [*type*]])　　Returns the future value of an investment or loan over a number of compounding periods, *nper*, given a periodic, constant payment, *pmt*, and a fixed interest rate, *rate. nper* is a positive integer. If omitted, present value *pv* = 0 and *type* = 0.

fvadj(*prin,* **v**)　　Returns the future value of an initial principal, *prin*, after applying a series of compound interest rates stored in **v**. **v** is a vector.

fvc(*rate,* **v**)　　Returns the future value of a list of cash flows occurring at regular intervals, **v**, earning an interest rate, *rate.* **v** is a vector.

Note　When using functions that require information about rates and periods, use the same unit of time for each. For example, if you make monthly payments on a four-year loan at an annual interest rate of 12%, use 1% as the interest rate per period (one month) and 48 months as the number of periods.

Payment

pmt(*rate, nper, pv,* [[*fv*], [*type*]])

Returns the payment for an investment or loan based on periodic constant payments over a given number of compounding periods, *nper*, using a fixed interest rate, *rate*, and a present value, *pv*. *nper* is a positive integer. If omitted, future value *fv* = 0 and *type* = 0.

ipmt(*rate, per, nper, pv,* [[*fv*], [*type*]])

Returns the interest payment of an investment or loan for a given period, *per*, based on periodic constant payments over a given number of compounding periods, *nper*, using a fixed interest rate, *rate*, and a present value, *pv*. *per* and *nper* are positive integers, *per* ≤ *nper*. If omitted, future value *fv* = 0 and *type* = 0.

ppmt(*rate, per, nper, pv,* [[*fv*], [*type*]])

Returns the payment on the principal, of a investment or loan, for a given period, *per*, based on periodic constant payments over a given number of compounding periods, *nper*, using a fixed interest rate, *rate*, and a present value, *pv*. *per* and *nper* are positive integers, *per* ≤ *nper*. If omitted, future value *fv* = 0 and *type* = 0.

The monthly payment for a $10,000 loan that accrues interest at an annual rate of 8% and that you must pay off in 10 months:

$$rate := \frac{8\%}{12} \quad nper := 10 \quad pv := 10000 \quad per := 5$$

pmt(rate , nper , pv) = −1037.03

The portion of the 5th payment that is interest:

ipmt(rate , per , nper , pv) = −40.53

The portion of the 5th payment that is principal:

ppmt(rate , per , nper , pv) = −996.50

Figure 10-11: Using the pmt, ipmt, *and* ppmt *functions.*

Internal rate of return

irr(**v**, [*guess*])

Returns the internal rate of return for a series of cash flows, **v**, occurring at regular intervals. **v** is a vector that must contain at least one positive value and one negative value. If omitted, *guess* = 0.1 (10%).

mirr(**v**, *fin_rate, rein_rate*)

Returns the modified internal rate of return for a series of cash flows occurring at regular intervals, **v**, given a finance rate payable on the cash flows you borrow, *fin_rate*, and a reinvestment rate earned on the cash flows as you reinvest them, *rein_rate*. **v** is a vector that must contain at least one positive value and one negative value.

Present value

pv(*rate, nper, pmt*, [[*fv*] [*type*]])

Returns the present value of an investment or loan based on periodic constant payments over a given number of compounding periods, *nper*, using a fixed interest rate, *rate*, and a payment, *pmt*. *nper* is a positive integer. If omitted, *fv* = 0 and *type* = 0.

npv(*rate*, **v**)

Returns the net present value of an investment given a discount rate, *rate*, and a series of cash flows occurring at regular intervals, **v**. **v** is a vector.

Differential Equation Functions

In a differential equation, you solve for an unknown function rather than just a variable. For ordinary differential equations, the unknown function is a function of one variable. Partial differential equations are differential equations in which the unknown is a function of two or more variables.

The easiest way to solve a single differential equation of any order is to use a solve block and the function *Odesolve*. To solve systems of equations or to have more control over the solving process, you can use the general-purpose differential equation solver *rkfixed*. Alternatively you can choose from additional, more specialized functions for solving differential equations.

Solving a Differential Equation Using a Solve Block

Odesolve(*x, b*, [*step*]) Returns a function of *x* which is the solution to a single ordinary differential equation. *b* is the terminal point of the integration interval. *step* (optional) is the number of steps.

To solve a single differential equation of any order, use a *solve block* and the function *Odesolve*. A solve block for solving a differential equation is similar to a solve block for solving a system of equations as described on page 168. There are three steps to creating a differential equation solve block:

1. Type the word *Given*. You can type *Given* or *given* in any style, but be sure not to type it in a text region.

2. Type the differential equation and constraints in any order below the word *Given*.

    Use the bold equal sign (click **=** on the Boolean toolbar or press [**Ctrl**]=) for an equality. The independent variable *x* must be explicitly indicated throughout. A typical initial value constraint might be *y(a)=c or y'(a)=d*; Mathcad does not allow more complicated constraints like *y(a)+y'(a)=e*. The differential equation can be written using the derivative operators d/dx, d^2/dx^2, d^3/dx^3, ... (press **?** or [**Ctrl**]**?** to insert the derivative or *n*th derivative operators), or using prime notation *y'(x)*, *y''(x)*, *y'''(x)*, ... (Press [**Ctrl**] [**F7**] for the prime symbol.)

3. Finally, type the *Odesolve* function. The terminal point *b* must be larger than the initial point *a*.

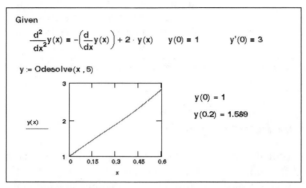

Figure 10-12: Solving a single differential equation.

Tip   Prime notation is only allowed inside a solve block. If you use it outside of a solve block, you see an error.

The output of *Odesolve* is a function of *x*, interpolated from a table of values computed using the fixed step method employed by the function *rkfixed*, described below. If you prefer to use an adaptive step method employed by the function *Rkadapt*:

1. Click on *Odesolve* with the right mouse button.

2. Choose **Adaptive** from the pop-up menu.

Note   Mathcad is very specific about the types of expressions that can appear between *Given* and *Odesolve*. The lower derivative terms can appear nonlinearly in the differential equation (e.g., they can be multiplied together or raised to powers), but the highest derivative term must appear linearly. Inequality constraints are not allowed. There must be *n* independent equality constraints for an *n*th order differential equation. For an initial value problem, the values for *y(x)* and its first *n−1* derivatives at a single initial point *a* are required. For a boundary value problem, the *n* equality constraints should prescribe values for *y(x)* and certain derivatives at exactly two points *a* and *b*.

General Purpose Differential Equation Solver: *rkfixed*

To solve systems of equations or to specify a starting point for the interval and the number of points at which to approximate a solution, you can use the differential equation solver *rkfixed*. Alternatively you can choose from additional, more specialized functions for solving differential equations, described in the following section "Specialized Differential Equation Solvers."

First order differential equations

A first order differential equation is one in which the highest order derivative of the unknown function is the first derivative. To solve a first order differential equation in Mathcad, you can use *Odesolve* as described in "Solving a Differential Equation Using a Solve Block" or you can use *rkfixed*. *rkfixed* uses the fourth order Runge-Kutta method to solve a first order differential equation and return a two-column matrix in which:

- The left-hand column contains the points at which the solution to the differential equation is evaluated.

- The right-hand column contains the corresponding values of the solution.

rkfixed($\mathbf{y}$, *x1*, *x2*, *npoints*, $\mathbf{D}$)

$\mathbf{y}$ = A vector of n initial values where n is the order of the differential equation or the size of the system of equations you're solving. For a first order differential equation, the vector degenerates to one point,
$y(0) = y(x1)$.

x1, *x2* = The endpoints of the interval on which the solution to the differential equations will be evaluated. The initial values in $\mathbf{y}$ are the values at *x1*.

npoints = The number of points beyond the initial point at which the solution is to be approximated. This controls the number of rows ($1 + npoints$) in the matrix returned by *rkfixed*.

$\mathbf{D}(x, \mathbf{y})$ = An n-element vector-valued function containing the first n derivatives of the unknown functions.

Figure 10-13 shows how to solve the differential equation $\dfrac{dy}{dx} + 3 \cdot y = 0$ subject to the initial condition $y(0) = 4$.

Figure 10-13: Solving a first order differential equation.

Note	The most difficult part of solving a differential equation using *rkfixed*, particularly with nonlinear differential equations, is solving for the first derivative so you can define the function $\mathbf{D}(x, \mathbf{y})$. In such cases, you can sometimes solve for $y'(x)$ symbolically and paste it into the definition for $\mathbf{D}(x, \mathbf{y})$. To do so, use the symbolic solving techniques discussed in the section "Examples of Symbolic Calculation" in Chapter 14.

Second and higher order differential equations

You can use *Odesolve* and a solve block, as described on page 187, or you can use *rkfixed* to solve higher order differential equations. Using *rkfixed* to solve a second order differential equation is similar to solving a first order differential equation. The key differences are:

- The vector of initial values **y** now has two elements: the value of the function and its first derivative at the starting value, *x1*.

- The function $\mathbf{D}(t, \mathbf{y})$ is now a vector with two elements:

$$\mathbf{D}(t, \mathbf{y}) = \begin{bmatrix} y'(t) \\ y''(t) \end{bmatrix}$$

- The solution matrix contains three columns: the left-hand one for the *t* values; the middle one for $y(t)$; and the right-hand one for $y'(t)$.

See Figure 10-14 for an example using *rkfixed*. See Figure 10-12 for an example using *Odesolve*.

Figure 10-14: Solving a second order differential equation.

Tip   The procedure for solving higher order differential equations is an extension of that used for second order differential equations. The main differences are that the vector of initial values **y** now has n elements for specifying initial conditions of $y, y', y'', \ldots, y^{(n-1)}$, the function **D** is now a vector with n elements corresponding to the first n derivatives of the unknown functions, and the solution matrix contains n columns: the left-hand one for the t values and the remaining columns for values of $y(t), y'(t), y''(t), \ldots, y^{(n-1)}(t)$.

Systems of differential equations

Solving a system of differential equations is similar to solving a higher order differential equation using *rkfixed*. To solve a system of first order differential equations:

1. Define a vector containing the initial values of each unknown function.

2. Define a vector-valued function containing the first derivatives of each of the unknown functions.

3. Decide at which points you want to evaluate the solutions.

4. Pass all this information into *rkfixed*.

rkfixed returns a matrix whose first column contains the points at which the solutions are evaluated and whose remaining columns contain the solution functions evaluated at the corresponding point. Figure 10-15 shows an example solving the equations:

$$x'_0(t) = \mu \cdot x_0(t) - x_1(t) - (x_0(t)^2 + x_1(t)^2) \cdot x_0(t)$$

$$x'_1(t) = \mu \cdot x_1(t) + x_0(t) - (x_0(t)^2 + x_1(t)^2) \cdot x_1(t)$$

with initial conditions $x_0(0) = 0$ and $x_1(0) = 1$.

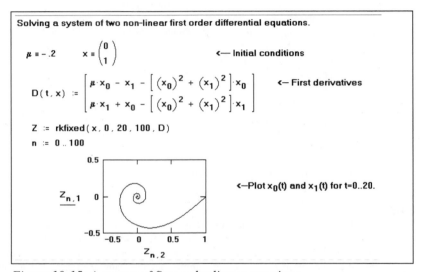

Figure 10-15: A system of first order linear equations.

Solving a system of nth order differential equations is similar to solving a system of first order differential equations. The main differences are:

- The vector of initial conditions must contain initial values for the $n-1$ derivatives of each unknown function in addition to initial values for the functions themselves.

- The vector-valued function must contain expressions for the $n-1$ derivatives of each unknown function in addition to the nth derivative.

rkfixed returns a matrix in which the first column contains the values at which the solutions and their derivatives are to be evaluated, and the remaining columns contain the solutions and their derivatives evaluated at the corresponding point in the first column. The order in which the solution and its derivatives appear matches the order in which you put them into the vector of initial conditions.

Chapter 10 Built-in Functions

Specialized Differential Equation Solvers

Mathcad includes several, specialized functions for solving differential equations, and there are cases in which you may want to use these rather than the general-purpose *rkfixed*. These cases fall into the three categories given below. Each of these functions solves differential equations numerically: you always get back a matrix containing the values of the function evaluated over a set of points.

Tip   When solving a differential equation it is a good idea to try more than one differential equation solver because one method might suit your differential equation better than another method.

Smooth systems

When you know the solution is smooth, use *Bulstoer*, which uses the Bulirsch-Stoer method rather than the Runge-Kutta method used by *rkfixed*.

Bulstoer(**y**, *x1*, *x2*, *npoints*, **D**)

The argument list and the matrix returned by *Bulstoer* are identical to that for *rkfixed*.

Slowly varying solutions

Given a fixed number of points, you can approximate a function more accurately if you evaluate it frequently wherever it's changing fast and infrequently wherever it's changing more slowly.

Rkadapt(**y**, *x1*, *x2*, *npoints*, **D**)

The argument list and the matrix returned by *Rkadapt* are identical in form to that for *rkfixed*.

If you know that the solution has this property, you may be better off using *Rkadapt*. Unlike *rkfixed*, *Rkadapt* examines how fast the solution is changing and adapts its step size accordingly.

Note   Although *Rkadapt* uses nonuniform step sizes internally when it solves the differential equation, it nevertheless returns the solution at equally spaced points.

Stiff systems

A system of differential equations expressed in the form $\mathbf{y} = \mathbf{A} \cdot \mathbf{x}$ is a *stiff system* if the matrix **A** is nearly singular. Under these conditions, the solution returned by *rkfixed* may oscillate or be unstable. When solving a stiff system, you should use one of the two differential equation solvers specifically designed for stiff systems, *Stiffb* and *Stiffr*, which use the Bulirsch-Stoer method and the Rosenbrock method, respectively. They take the same arguments as *rkfixed* as well as one additional argument.

Stiffb($\mathbf{y}$, $x1$, $x2$, $npoints$, $\mathbf{D}$, $\mathbf{J}$)
Stiffr($\mathbf{y}$, $x1$, $x2$, $npoints$, $\mathbf{D}$, $\mathbf{J}$)

$\mathbf{J}(x, \mathbf{y}) =$ A function you define that returns the $n \times (n + 1)$ matrix whose first column contains the derivatives $\partial \mathbf{D} / \partial x$ and whose remaining rows and columns form the Jacobian matrix $(\partial \mathbf{D} / \partial y_k)$ for the system of differential equations. For example, if:

$$\mathbf{D}(x, \mathbf{y}) = \begin{bmatrix} x \cdot y_1 \\ -2 \cdot y_1 \cdot y_0 \end{bmatrix} \quad \text{then} \quad \mathbf{J}(x, \mathbf{y}) = \begin{bmatrix} y_1 & 0 & x \\ 0 & -2 \cdot y_1 & -2 \cdot y_0 \end{bmatrix}$$

See *rkfixed* for a description of other parameters.

Evaluating Only the Final Value

If you care about only the value of the solution at the endpoint, $y(x2)$, rather than over a number of uniformly spaced x values in the integration interval bounded by $x1$ and $x2$, use the functions listed below. Each function corresponds to the capitalized versions already discussed. The properties of each of these functions are identical to those of the corresponding function in the previous sections, except for the arguments below:

bulstoer($\mathbf{y}$, $x1$, $x2$, acc, $\mathbf{D}$, $kmax$, $save$)
rkadapt($\mathbf{y}$, $x1$, $x2$, acc, $\mathbf{D}$, $kmax$, $save$)
stiffb($\mathbf{y}$, $x1$, $x2$, acc, $\mathbf{D}$, $\mathbf{J}$, $kmax$, $save$)
stiffr($\mathbf{y}$, $x1$, $x2$, acc, $\mathbf{D}$, $\mathbf{J}$, $kmax$, $save$)

$acc =$ Controls the accuracy of the solution. A small value of *acc* forces the algorithm to take smaller steps along the trajectory, thereby increasing the accuracy of the solution. Values of *acc* around 0.001 generally yield accurate solutions.

$kmax =$ The maximum number of intermediate points at which the solution will be approximated. The value of *kmax* places an upper bound on the number of rows of the matrix returned by these functions.

$save =$ The smallest allowable spacing between the values at which the solutions are to be approximated. This places a lower bound on the difference between any two numbers in the first column of the matrix returned by the function.

Boundary Value Problems

The specialized differential equation solvers discussed above are useful for solving *initial value problems*. In some cases, however, you may know the value taken by the solution at the *endpoints* of the interval of integration, which is a *boundary value problem*.

To solve boundary value problems in Mathcad, use *Odesolve*, described in "Solving a Differential Equation Using a Solve Block", or *sbval* or *bvalfit* as described here.

Two-point boundary value problems

Two-point boundary value problems are one-dimensional systems of differential equations in which the solution is a function of a single variable and the value of the solution is known at two points. You can use *sbval* in the following case:

- You have an nth order differential equation.

- You know some, but not all, of the values of the solution and its first $n - 1$ derivatives at the beginning of the interval of integration, $x1$, and at the end of the interval of integration, $x2$.

- Between what you know about the solution at $x1$ and at $x2$, you have n known values.

sbval returns a vector containing those initial values left unspecified at the first endpoint of the interval. Once you know the missing initial values at $x1$, you have an initial value problem that can be solved using any of the functions discussed earlier in this section.

sbval($\mathbf{v}$, $x1$, $x2$, $\mathbf{D}$, **load**, **score**)

$\mathbf{v}$ = Vector of guesses for initial values left unspecified at $x1$.

$x1$, $x2$ = The endpoints of the interval on which the solution to the differential equations will be evaluated.

$\mathbf{D}(x, \mathbf{y})$ = An n-element vector-valued function containing the first derivatives of the unknown functions.

load($x1$, $\mathbf{v}$) = A vector-valued function whose n elements correspond to the values of the n unknown functions at $x1$. Some of these values will be constants specified by your initial conditions. Others will be unknown at the outset but will be found by *sbval*. If a value is unknown, you should use the corresponding guess value from $\mathbf{v}$.

score($x2$, $\mathbf{y}$) = A vector-valued function having the same number of elements as $\mathbf{v}$. Each element is the difference between an initial condition at $x2$, as originally specified, and the corresponding estimate from the solution. The *score* vector measures how closely the proposed solution matches the initial conditions at $x2$. A value of 0 for any element indicates a perfect match between the corresponding initial condition and that returned by *sbval*.

Note As shown in Figure 10-16, *sbval* does not actually return a solution to a differential equation. It merely computes the initial values the solution must have in order for the solution to match the final values you specify. You must then take the initial values returned by *sbval* and solve the resulting initial value problem using a function such as *rkfixed*.

Figure 10-16: Using sbval *to obtain initial values corresponding to given final values of a solution to a differential equation.*

It's also possible that you don't have all the information you need to use *sbval* but you do know something about the solution and its first $n - 1$ derivatives at some intermediate value, *xf*. *bvalfit* solves a two-point boundary value problem of this type by shooting from the endpoints and matching the trajectories of the solution and its derivatives at the intermediate point. This method becomes especially useful when the derivative has a discontinuity somewhere in the integration interval.

bvalfit(**v1**, **v2**, *x1*, *x2*, *xf*, **D**, **load1**, **load2**, **score**)

v1, **v2** = Vector **v1** contains guesses for initial values left unspecified at *x1*. Vector **v2** contains guesses for initial values left unspecified at *x2*.

x1, *x2* = The endpoints of the interval on which the solution to the differential equations will be evaluated.

xf = A point between *x1* and *x2* at which the trajectories of the solutions beginning at *x1* and those beginning at *x2* are constrained to be equal.

D(*x*, **y**) = An *n*-element vector-valued function containing the first derivatives of the unknown functions.

load1(*x1*, **v1**) = A vector-valued function whose *n* elements correspond to the values of the *n* unknown functions at *x1*. Some of these values will be constants specified by your initial conditions. If a value is unknown, you should use the corresponding guess value from **v1**.

load2(*x2*, **v2**) = Analogous to *load1* but for values taken by the *n* unknown functions at *x2*.

score(*xf*, **y**) = An *n* element vector valued function that specifies how the solutions match at *xf*. You'll usually want to define *score*(*xf*, **y**) := **y** to make the solutions to all unknown functions match up at *xf*.

Partial differential equations

A second type of boundary value problem arises when you are solving a partial differential equation. Rather than being fixed at two points, the solution is fixed at a whole continuum of points representing some boundary.

Two partial differential equations that arise often in the analysis of physical systems are Poisson's equation:

$$\frac{\partial^2 u}{\partial x^2} + \frac{\partial^2 u}{\partial y^2} = \rho(x, y)$$

and its homogeneous form, Laplace's equation.

Tip   To type a partial differential equation symbol such as $\frac{\partial}{\partial x}$, insert the derivative operator $\frac{d}{dx}$ by typing **?**, click on the derivative operator with the right mouse button, and choose **View Derivative As** ⟹ **Partial Derivative** from the pop-up menu.

Mathcad has two functions for solving these equations over a square boundary. You should use *relax* if you know the value taken by the unknown function $u(x, y)$ on all four sides of a square region.

If $u(x, y)$ is zero on all four sides of the square, you can use *multigrid*, which often solves the problem faster than *relax*. Note that if the boundary condition is the same on all four sides, you can simply transform the equation to an equivalent one in which the value is zero on all four sides.

relax returns a square matrix in which:

- An element's location in the matrix corresponds to its location within the square region, and

- Its value approximates the value of the solution at that point.

This function uses the relaxation method to converge to the solution. Poisson's equation on a square domain is represented by:

$$a_{j, k} u_{j + 1, k} + b_{j, k} u_{j - 1, k} + c_{j, k} u_{j, k + 1} + d_{j, k} u_{j, k - 1} + e_{j, k} u_{j, k} = f_{j, k}$$

---

relax(**a**, **b**, **c**, **d**, **e**, **f**, **u**, *rjac*)

a . . . **e** = Square matrices all of the same size containing coefficients of the above equation.

f = Square matrix containing the source term at each point in the region in which the solution is sought.

u = Square matrix containing boundary values along the edges of the region and initial guesses for the solution inside the region.

rjac = Spectral radius of the Jacobi iteration. This number between 0 and 1 controls the convergence of the relaxation algorithm. Its optimal value depends on the details of your problem.

multigrid(**M**, *ncycle*)

M = $(1 + 2^n)$ row square matrix whose elements correspond to the source term at the corresponding point in the square domain.

ncycle = The number of cycles at each level of the *multigrid* iteration. A value of 2 generally gives a good approximation of the solution.

Miscellaneous Functions

Expression Type

IsArray(x)   Returns 1 if x is a matrix or vector, 0 otherwise.

IsScalar(x)   Returns 1 if x is a real or complex number, 0 otherwise.

IsString(x)   Returns 1 if x is a string, 0 otherwise.

UnitsOf(x)   Returns the units of x, 1 otherwise.

String Functions

concat(*S1, S2, S3, ...*)   Returns a string formed by appending string *S2* to the end of string *S1*, *S3* to the end of *S2*, and so on.

error(*S*)   Returns the string *S* as an error tip. When Mathcad evaluates the *error* function, the expression is highlighted in red and further numerical evaluation is suspended. When you click on the expression, the string appears in an error tip.

num2str(z)   Returns a string formed by converting the real or complex number z into a decimal-valued string.

search(*S, S1, m*)   Returns the starting position of the substring *S1* in string *S* beginning from position *m*, or -1 if no substring is found. *m* must be a nonnegative integer.

str2num(S)	Returns a constant formed by converting the characters in string S to a number. S must contain only characters which constitute an integer, a floating-point or complex number, or an e-format number such as 4.51e-3 (for $4.51 \cdot 10^{-3}$). Spaces are ignored.
str2vec(S)	Returns a vector of ASCII codes corresponding to the characters in string S.
strlen(S)	Returns the number of characters in string S.
substr(S, m, n)	Returns a substring of S beginning with the character in the mth position and having at most n characters. m and n must be nonnegative integers.
vec2str($\mathbf{v}$)	Returns a string formed by converting a vector $\mathbf{v}$ of ASCII codes to characters. The elements of $\mathbf{v}$ must be integers between 0 and 255.

The strings used and returned by most of these functions are typed in a math placeholder by pressing the double-quote key (") and entering any combination of letters, numbers, or other ASCII characters. Mathcad automatically places double quotes around the string expression and displays quotes around a string returned as a result.

Note When evaluating the functions *search* and *substr*, Mathcad assumes that the first character in a string is at position 0.

File Access Functions

The file argument you supply to a Mathcad file access function is a *string*—or a variable to which a string is assigned—that corresponds either to:

- The name of a data or image file in the folder of the Mathcad worksheet you're currently working on.
- The name of a colormap file (see page 202) in the CMAP subfolder of your Mathcad installation folder.
- A full or relative path to a data, image, or colormap file located elsewhere on a local or network file system.

Reading and writing ASCII data files

READPRN(*file*) Reads a structured data file. Returns a matrix. Each line in the data file becomes a row in the matrix. The number of elements in each row must be the same. Usually used as follows:
A := READPRN(*file*)

WRITEPRN(*file*) Writes a matrix into a data file. Each row becomes a line in the file. Must be used in a definition of the form WRITEPRN(*file*) := **A**

APPENDPRN(*file*) Appends a matrix to an existing file. Each row in the matrix becomes a new line in the data file. Must be used in a definition of the form APPENDPRN(*file*) := **A**. Existing data must have as many columns as **A**.

Files in plain ASCII format consist only of numbers separated by commas, spaces, or carriage returns. The numbers in the data files can be integers like **3** or **−1**, floating-point numbers like **2.54**, or E-format numbers like **4.51E−4** (for $4.51 \cdot 10^{-4}$).

Tip   These ASCII data file access functions are provided mainly for compatibility with worksheets created in earlier versions of Mathcad. The Input Table and File Read/Write component provide more general methods of importing and exporting data in a variety of formats. See Chapter 11, "Vectors, Matrices, and Data Arrays."

Reading and writing image files

READBMP(*file*) Creates a matrix containing a grayscale representation of the image in BMP format *file*. Each element in the matrix corresponds to a pixel. The value of a matrix element determines the shade of gray associated with the corresponding pixel. Each element is an integer between 0 (black) and 255 (white).

READRGB(*file*) Creates a matrix in which the color information in BMP format *file* is represented by the appropriate values of red, green, and blue. This matrix consists of three submatrices, each with the same number of columns and rows. Three matrix elements, rather than one, correspond to each pixel. Each element is an integer between 0 and 255. The three corresponding elements, when taken together, establish the color of the pixel.

WRITEBMP(*file*) Creates a grayscale BMP file from the matrix. Must be used in a definition of the form WRITEBMP(*file*) := **A**.

WRITERGB(*file*) Creates a color BMP file from a matrix in which the image is stored in RGB format. Must be used in a definition of the form WRITERGB(*file*) := **A**.

READ_IMAGE(*file*) Creates a matrix containing a grayscale representation of the image in BMP, GIF, JPG, PCX, or TGA format *file*.

READ_HLS(*file*)	Creates a matrix in which the color information in BMP, GIF,
READ_HSV(*file*)	JPG, PCX, or TGA format *file* is represented by the
	appropriate values of hue, lightness, and saturation (HLS) or
	hue, saturation, and value (HSV).

READ_RED(*file*)	Extracts only the red, green, or blue component from a color
READ_GREEN(*file*)	image in BMP, GIF, JPG, PCX, or TGA format *file*. The result
READ_BLUE(*file*)	has one-third the number of columns that the matrix returned
	by *READRGB* would have had.

READ_HLS_HUE(*file*)	Extracts only the hue, lightness, or saturation component
READ_HLS_LIGHT(*file*)	from a color image in BMP, GIF, JPG, PCX, or TGA format
READ_HLS_SAT(*file*)	*file*. The result has one-third the number of columns that the
	matrix returned by *READ_HLS* would have had.

READ_HSV_HUE(*file*)	Extracts only the hue, saturation, or value component from
READ_HSV_SAT(*file*)	a color image in BMP, GIF, JPG, PCX, or TGA format *file*.
READ_HSV_VALUE(*file*)	The result has one-third the number of columns that the
	matrix returned by *READ_HSV* would have had.

WRITE_HLS(*file*)	Creates a color BMP file out of a matrix in which the image
	is stored in HLS format. Must be used in a definition of the
	form WRITE_HLS(*file*) := **A**.

WRITE_HSV(*file*)	Creates a color BMP file out of a matrix in which the image
	is stored in HSV format. Must be used in a definition of the
	form WRITE_HSV(*file*) := **A**.

Reading and writing WAV files

Use these functions to read, write, and get format information from pulse code modulated (PCM) Microsoft WAV files.

| READWAV(*file*) | Creates an *n*-column matrix containing data values |
| | corresponding to *n* channels of a WAV file, *file*. |

WRITEWAV(*file*, *r*, *b*)	Creates a WAV file, *file*, from a matrix, with a specified
	sample rate, *r*, and number of bits per sample, or bit
	resolution, *b*. Both *r* and *b* must be integers. Must be used in
	a definition of the form WRITEWAV(*file*, *r*, *b*) := **A**.

GETWAVINFO(*file*)	Returns a vector containing, in order, the number of
	channels, the sample rate, the bit resolution, and the average
	bytes per second of a WAV file, *file*.

Functions Related to 3D Graphs

Loading and saving colormaps

LoadColormap(*file*)   Returns an array containing the values in the colormap *file*.

SaveColormap(*file*, **M**)   Creates a colormap *file* containing the values in the three-column array **M**. Returns the number of rows written to *file*.

A colormap is a .CMP file containing three columns of values that represent levels of red, green, and blue. You can apply a colormap to a 3D plot as described in "Fill Color" on page 248. Each value in a colormap should be an integer between 0 and 255, inclusive. By default Mathcad saves and loads colormaps from the CMAPS subfolder of the location where you installed Mathcad.

Graphing 3D polyhedra

PolyLookup(*n*)   Returns a vector containing the name, the dual name, and the Wythoff symbol for the uniform polyhedron whose number code is *n*. *n* is a positive integer less than 81, a name typed as a string, or a Wythoff symbol typed as a string.

Polyhedron(S)   Generates the uniform polyhedron whose name, number code, or Wythoff symbol is string S.

The uniform polyhedra are regular polyhedra whose vertices are congruent. Each has a name, a number, a dual (the name of another polyhedron), and a Wythoff symbol associated with it. To look up the name, Wythoff symbol, and dual name of a polyhedron, use *PolyLookup*.

To graph a uniform polyhedron:

1. Click in a blank spot of your worksheet. Choose **Graph⇒Surface Plot** from the **Insert** menu.

2. In the placeholder, enter the *Polyhedron* function with an appropriate string argument.

3. Click outside the plot or press [**Enter**].

Polyhedron("tetrahedron" **)**

Chapter 11
Vectors, Matrices, and Data Arrays

♦ Creating Arrays

♦ Accessing Array Elements

♦ Displaying Arrays

♦ Working with Arrays

♦ Nested Arrays

Creating Arrays

As introduced in "Inserting Math" on page 35, one technique of creating an array is to use the **Matrix** command on the **Insert** menu to create an array of empty placeholders and then to enter expressions directly into the placeholders. This technique can only be used for small arrays, but it can be used to create arrays of any kind of Mathcad expression, not just numbers. This section describes this technique and other approaches for creating arrays of arbitrary size:

• Using range variables to fill in the elements. This technique is useful when you have some explicit formula for the array elements in terms of their indices.

• Using the File Read/Write component to import data from external files in a variety of formats.

• Entering numbers manually in a spreadsheet-like input table.

Unlike the Insert Matrix command, however, these procedures can be used *only* for creating arrays of numbers, as opposed to arbitrary math expressions.

Note The effective array size limit depends on the memory available on your system—usually at least 1 million elements. In no system is it higher than 8 million elements.

Insert Matrix Command

To insert a vector or matrix in Mathcad, follow these steps:

1. Click in either a blank space or on a math placeholder.

2. Choose **Matrix** from the **Insert** menu, or click on the Matrix toolbar. A dialog box appears, as shown at right.

3. Enter the appropriate number of elements in the text boxes for "Rows" and "Columns." For example, to create a three-element vector, enter **3** and **1**.

4. An array with blank placeholders appears in your worksheet.

Next, fill in the array elements. You can enter any Mathcad expression into the placeholders of an array created in this way. Simply click in a placeholder and type a number or Mathcad expression. Use the [**Tab**] key to move from placeholder to placeholder.

Note Arrays created using the **Matrix** command on the **Insert** menu are limited to 100 elements.

Changing the size of a vector or matrix

You can change the size of a matrix by inserting and deleting rows and columns:

1. Click on one of the matrix elements to place it between the editing lines. Mathcad begins inserting or deleting with this element.

$$\begin{pmatrix} 2| & 5 & 17 \\ 3.5 & 3.9 & -12.9 \end{pmatrix}$$

2. Choose **Matrix** from the **Insert** menu. Type the number of rows and/or columns you want to insert or delete. Then press either "Insert" or "Delete." For example, to delete the column that holds the selected element, type **1** in the box next to "Columns," **0** in the box next to "Rows," and press "Delete."

$$\begin{pmatrix} 5 & 17 \\ 3.9 & -12.9 \end{pmatrix}$$

Note If you insert rows or columns, Mathcad inserts rows *below* the selected element and inserts columns to the *right* of the selected element. If you delete rows or columns, Mathcad begins with the row or column occupied by the selected element and deletes rows from that element downward and columns from that element rightward. To insert a row above the top row or a column to the left of the first column, first place the entire matrix between the editing lines.

Creating Arrays with Range Variables

As introduced in "Range Variables" on page 106, you can use one or more range variables to fill up the elements of an array. If you use two range variables in an equation, for example, Mathcad runs through each value of each range variable. This is useful for defining matrices. For example, to define a 5×5 matrix whose i,jth element is $i + j$, enter the equations shown in Figure 11-1.

Recall that you enter the range variable operator by pressing the semicolon key (**;**) or clicking on the Calculator toolbar. You enter the subscript operator by clicking $\boxed{x_n}$ on the Matrix toolbar.

The $x_{i,j}$ equation is evaluated for each value of each range variable, for a total of 25 evaluations. The result is the matrix shown at the bottom of Figure 11-1, with 5 rows and 5 columns. The element in the ith row and jth column of this matrix is $i + j$.

$$i := 0 .. 4 \qquad j := 0 .. 4$$

$$x_{i,j} := i + j$$

$$x = \begin{pmatrix} 0 & 1 & 2 & 3 & 4 \\ 1 & 2 & 3 & 4 & 5 \\ 2 & 3 & 4 & 5 & 6 \\ 3 & 4 & 5 & 6 & 7 \\ 4 & 5 & 6 & 7 & 8 \end{pmatrix}$$

Figure 11-1: Defining a matrix using range variables.

Note To be used to define an array element, a range variable can take on only whole-number values.

Tip You can also define individual array elements using the subscript operator, as described in "Accessing Array Elements" on page 208.

Reading a Data File

Mathcad provides the *File Read/Write component* to read a data file and store the data in a Mathcad array variable.

Note A component is a specialized OLE object that you insert into a Mathcad worksheet to create a link between the worksheet and either a data source or another application containing data. For more information on components, including specialized components for linking other computational applications dynamically to arrays in a Mathcad worksheet, see Chapter 16, "Advanced Computational Features."

You can read data from files in a variety of formats, including:

- Excel (*.XLS)
- MATLAB (*.MAT)
- Lotus 1-2-3 (*.WK*)
- ASCII editors (*.DAT, *.CSV, *.PRN, *.TXT)

Tip Mathcad also provides a number of built-in functions for importing ASCII data files and image files. See "File Access Functions" on page 199.

To read in data using the File Read/Write component:

1. Click in a blank spot of your worksheet.

2. Choose **Component** from the **Insert** menu.

3. Choose File Read or Write from the list and click "Next." This launches the File Read or Write Wizard.

4. Choose "Read from a file" and press "Next" to continue through the Wizard.

5. Specify the type of data file you want to read. Enter the path to the data file or use the "Browse" button to locate it.

6. Press "Finish." You'll see the File Read/Write component icon and the path to the data file. For example, if you specify a data file called data.txt in the C:\WINDOWS folder, you'll see the component at right.

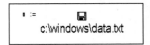

In the placeholder that appears, enter the name of the Mathcad variable to which the data from the file will be assigned. When you click outside the component, the data file is read in and the data is assigned to the Mathcad array variable you entered into the placeholder.

Each time you calculate the worksheet, Mathcad re-reads the data from the file you have specified. Figure 11-2 shows an example of reading in data using the File Read/Write component. If you want to import data from a file just once into Mathcad, refer to"Importing Once from a Data File" on page 208.

Figure 11-2: Reading in data from a data file. Whenever you calculate the worksheet, the data file is read in.

To read in a different data file or a different type of data file:

1. Click with the right mouse button on the component and select **Choose File** from the component pop-up menu.

2. In the "Files of type" text box, choose the type of file you'd like to import. Use the dialog box to browse to the data file, select the data file, and click "Open."

Tip   By default, Mathcad reads in the entire data file and creates an array with the variable name you provide. To read in only certain rows or columns of a data file, click once on the component to select it, then click with the right mouse button on the component and choose **Properties** from the pop-up menu. Use the Properties dialog box to specify the row and columns at which to start and stop reading.

Entering Data into a Table

To get the convenience of a spreadsheet-like interface for entering data, you can create an array using the Input Table component:

1. Click in a blank spot in your worksheet and choose **Component** from the **Insert** menu.

2. Select **Input Table** from the list and click "Next." The Input Table component is inserted into your worksheet.

3. Enter the name of the Mathcad variable to which the data will be assigned in the placeholder that appears.

4. Click in the component and enter data into the cells. Each row must have the same number of data values. If you do not enter a number into a cell, Mathcad inserts 0 into the cell.

Figure 11-3 shows two input tables. Notice that when you create an input table, you're actually assigning elements to an array that has the name of the variable you entered into the placeholder.

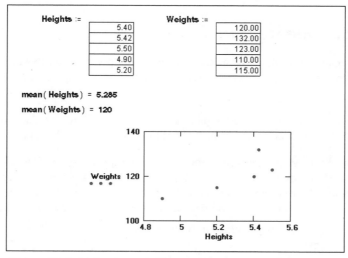

Figure 11-3: Using input tables to create arrays of data.

When you click the table, you can edit the values in it. The scroll bars let you scroll through the table. To resize the table, move the cursor to one of these handles along the sides of the region so that it changes to a double-headed arrow. Then press and hold down the mouse button and drag the cursor to change the table's dimensions.

Tip You can copy data from an input table as follows: first select some data, then click with the right mouse button on the component and choose **Copy** from the pop-up menu. You can paste a single number from the Clipboard into the table by selecting a cell and choosing **Paste** from the pop-up menu. Choosing **Paste Table** from the pop-up menu overwrites the entire table with values in the Clipboard.

Importing Once from a Data File

You can use an input table to import data a single time from a data file. To do so:

1. Insert an input table by following the instructions given above.
2. In the placeholder that appears to the left, enter the name of the Mathcad variable to which this data will be assigned.
3. Click on the table to select it. Then click on it with the right mouse button on the input table so that you see the pop-up menu.
4. Choose **Import**.
5. The Read from File dialog box appears. In the "Files of type" text box, choose the type of file you'd like to import. Use the dialog box to browse to the data file and click "Open."

The data from the data file appears in your worksheet in the input table.

Note Unlike the File Read/Write component, the Import feature of an input table reads the data only when you choose **Import**, not each time you calculate the worksheet. If you want the data to be imported each time you calculate, use the File Read/Write component as described in "Reading a Data File" on page 205.

Accessing Array Elements

You can access all the elements of an array simply by using its variable name, or you can access the elements individually or in groups.

Subscripts

You access individual elements of a vector or matrix by using the subscript operator described in "Vector and Matrix Operators" on page 133. Insert the subscript operator by clicking $\boxed{\times_n}$ on the Matrix toolbar or by typing **[**. To access an element of a vector, enter one number in the subscript. To access a matrix element, enter two numbers separated by a comma. To refer to the ith element of a vector, type **v[i**. In general, to refer to the element in the ith row, jth column of matrix **M**, type **M[i,j**.

Figure 11-4 shows examples of how to define individual matrix elements and how to view them.

Chapter 11 Vectors, Matrices, and Data Arrays

$$M_{0,0} := 1 \qquad M_{0,1} := 3 \qquad M_{0,2} := 5$$

$$M_{1,0} := 2 \qquad M_{1,2} := 6$$

Now show the values of the elements of M . . .

$$M = \begin{pmatrix} 1 & 3 & 5 \\ 2 & 0 & 6 \end{pmatrix}$$

$$M_{1,2} = 6 \qquad M_{1,1} = 0$$

$$M_{2,2} =$$

Value of subscript or superscript is too big (or too small) for this array.

<- Since the array ORIGIN is zero, there is a zeroth row and a first row...but no second row.

Figure 11-4: Defining and viewing matrix elements.

Note   When you define vector or matrix elements, you may leave gaps in the vector or matrix. For example, if **v** is undefined and you define v_3 as 10, then v_0, v_1, and v_2 are all undefined.

Mathcad fills these gaps with zeros until you enter specific values for them, as shown in Figure 11-4. Be careful of inadvertently creating very large vectors and matrices by doing this. Also note that vector and matrix elements by default are numbered starting with row zero and column zero unless the built-in variable ORIGIN has a value other than zero (see page 209).

You can use this kind of subscript notation in Mathcad to perform parallel calculations on the elements of an array. See "Doing Calculations in Parallel" on page 213.

Tip   If you want to define or access a group of array elements at once, you can use a range variable in a subscript.

Accessing Rows and Columns

Although you can use a range variable to access all the elements in a row or column of an array, Mathcad provides a column operator for quickly accessing all the elements in a column. Click $M^{\langle \rangle}$ on the Matrix toolbar for the column operator. Figure 11-5 shows how to extract the third column of the matrix **M**.

To extract a single row from a matrix, transpose the matrix using the transpose operator (click M^T on the Matrix toolbar) and then extract a column using the column operator. This is shown on the right-hand side of Figure 11-5.

Changing the Array Origin

When you use subscripts to refer to array elements, Mathcad assumes the array begins at the current value of the built-in variable ORIGIN. By default, ORIGIN is 0, but you can change its value. See "Built-in Variables" on page 102 for details.

Figure 11-6 shows a worksheet with the ORIGIN set to 1. If you try to refer to the zeroth element of an array in this case, Mathcad displays an error message.

$$M = \begin{pmatrix} 1 & 3 & 5 \\ 2 & 0 & 6 \end{pmatrix} \qquad M^{\langle 2 \rangle} = \begin{pmatrix} 5 \\ 6 \end{pmatrix} \qquad$$ **Note: the origin is 0. Thus, the superscript of 2 refers to the third column of the matrix M.**

$$M^{T} = \begin{pmatrix} 1 & 2 \\ 3 & 0 \\ 5 & 6 \end{pmatrix} \qquad w := (M^{T})^{\langle 1 \rangle} \qquad w = \begin{pmatrix} 2 \\ 0 \\ 6 \end{pmatrix}$$

Figure 11-5: Extracting a column from a matrix.

ORIGIN $\equiv 1$
Matrices:

$$M := \begin{pmatrix} 1 & 2 & 7 \\ 2 & 4 & 6 \\ 3 & 6 & 9 \end{pmatrix}$$

$M_{1,1} = 1 \qquad M_{3,3} = 9 \qquad M_{1,3} = 7 \qquad M_{0,0} =$

Value of subscript or superscript is too big (or too small) for this array.

Vectors:

$v_1 := 1 \qquad v_2 := 3 \qquad v_3 := 5$

Since the array ORIGIN is now one, there is no longer a zeroth row or column.

$$v = \begin{pmatrix} 1 \\ 3 \\ 5 \end{pmatrix} \qquad v_0 =$$

Value of subscript or superscript is too big (or too small) for this array.

Figure 11-6: Arrays beginning at element one instead of at element zero.

Displaying Arrays

As described in "Formatting Results" on page 115, Mathcad automatically displays matrices and vectors having more than nine rows or columns as output tables rather than as matrices or vectors. Smaller arrays are displayed by default in traditional matrix notation. Figure 11-7 shows an example.

Note An output table displays a portion of an array. To the left of each row and at the top of each column, there is a number indicating the index of the row or column. Click with the right mouse button on the output table and select **Properties** from the pop-up menu to control whether row and column numbers appear and the font used for values in the table. If your results extend beyond the table, a scroll bar appears along the appropriate edge of the table. You can scroll through the table using these scroll bars just as you would scroll through any window.

$i := 0 .. 2$ $j := 0 .. 2$ $A_{i,j} := \sin(i) + \dfrac{\pi}{2} - j$

$A = \begin{pmatrix} 1.571 & 0.571 & -0.429 \\ 2.412 & 1.412 & 0.412 \\ 2.48 & 1.48 & 0.48 \end{pmatrix}$ <-- Array displayed as a matrix.

$A =$

	0	1	2
0	1.571	0.571	-0.429
1	2.412	1.412	0.412
2	2.48	1.48	0.48

<-- Array displayed as an output table.

Figure 11-7: Display results as a matrix or in an output table.

To resize an output table:

1. Click the output table. You'll see handles along the sides of the table.

2. Move the cursor to one of these handles so that it changes to a double-headed arrow.

3. Press and hold down the mouse button and drag the cursor in the direction you want the table's dimensions to change.

Tip   You can change the alignment of the table with respect to the expression on the left-hand side of the equal sign. Click with the right mouse button on the table, then choose one of the **Alignment** options from the pop-up menu.

Changing the Display of Arrays — Table versus Matrix

Although matrices and vectors having more than nine rows or columns are automatically displayed as scrolling output tables, you can have Mathcad display them as matrices. You can also change matrices to output tables. To do so:

1. Click on the scrolling output table.

2. Choose **Result** from the **Format** menu.

3. Click on the Display Options tab.

4. Choose Matrix or Table in the "Matrix display style" drop-down box.

5. Click "OK."

To display all the results in your worksheet as matrices or as tables regardless of their size, click "Set as Default" in the Result Format dialog box rather than "OK."

Note   Mathcad cannot display extremely large arrays in matrix form. You should display a large array as a scrolling output table.

Changing the Format of Displayed Elements

You format the numbers in the array the same way you format other numerical results, as described in "Formatting Results" on page 115. Just click on the displayed array and choose **Result** from the **Format** menu, and modify the settings there. When you click "OK," Mathcad applies the selected format to all the numbers in the table, vector, or matrix. It is not possible to format the numbers individually.

Copying and Pasting Arrays

You can copy an array of numbers directly from a spreadsheet or database into Mathcad where you can take advantage of its free-form interface and its advanced mathematical tools. Once you've performed the necessary computations, you can paste the resulting array of numbers back to its source or even into another application.

To copy just one number from a result array, simply click the number and choose **Copy**

from the **Edit** menu, or click 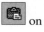 on the Standard toolbar. Copying multiple numbers from a vector or matrix result differs depending on whether the array is displayed as a matrix or as an output table. See "Formatting Results" on page 115 for more information on how vector and matrix results are displayed.

To copy a result array displayed as a matrix:

1. Drag-select the array to the right of the equal sign to place the entire array between the editing lines.

2. Choose **Copy** from the **Edit** menu. This places the entire array on the Clipboard.

3. Click wherever you want to paste the result. If you're pasting into another application, choose **Paste** from that application's **Edit** menu. If you're pasting into

   a Mathcad worksheet, choose **Paste** from Mathcad's **Edit** menu, or click ![icon] on the Standard toolbar.

Note You may only paste an array into a math placeholder or into a blank space in a Mathcad worksheet.

When you display array results as a table, you can copy some or all of the numbers from the table and use them elsewhere:

1. Click on the first number you want to copy.

2. Drag the mouse in the direction of the other values you want to copy while holding the mouse button down.

3. Click on the selected values with the right mouse button and choose **Copy Selection** from the pop-up menu.

To copy all the values in a row or column, click on the column or row number shown to the left of the row or at the top of the column. All the values in the row or column are selected. Then choose **Copy** from the **Edit** menu.

After you have copied one or more numbers from an output table, you can paste them into another part of your worksheet or into another application. Figure 11-8 shows an example of a new matrix created by copying and pasting numbers from an output table.

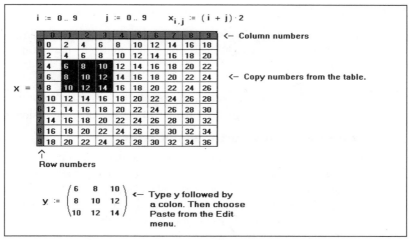

$i := 0 .. 9 \qquad j := 0 .. 9 \qquad x_{i,j} := (i + j) \cdot 2$

<--- Column numbers

<--- Copy numbers from the table.

$x =$

↑
Row numbers

$y := \begin{pmatrix} 6 & 8 & 10 \\ 8 & 10 & 12 \\ 10 & 12 & 14 \end{pmatrix}$ <--- Type y followed by
a colon. Then choose
Paste from the Edit
menu.

Figure 11-8: Copying and pasting results from an output table.

Working with Arrays

Once you create an array, you can use it in calculations. There are many operators and functions designed for use with vectors and matrices. See "Vector and Matrix Operators" on page 133 and "Vector and Matrix Functions" on page 159 for an overview. This section highlights the vectorize operator, which permits efficient parallel calculations on the elements of arrays. You can also display the values of an array graphically or export them to a data file or another application.

Doing Calculations in Parallel

Any calculation Mathcad can perform with single values, it can also perform with vectors or matrices of values. There are two ways to do this:

- Iterate over each element using range variables. See for example "Creating Arrays with Range Variables" on page 204.

- Use the *vectorize operator*, which allows Mathcad to perform the same operation efficiently on each *element* of a vector or matrix.

Mathematical notation often shows repeated operations with subscripts. For example, to define a matrix **P** by multiplying corresponding elements of the matrices **M** and **N**, you would write:

$$\mathbf{P}_{i,j} = \mathbf{M}_{i,j} \cdot \mathbf{N}_{i,j}$$

Note that this is not matrix multiplication, but multiplication element by element. It *is* possible to perform this operation in Mathcad using subscripts, but it is much faster to perform exactly the same operation with a vectorized equation.

Here's how to apply the vectorize operator to an expression like $\mathbf{M} \cdot \mathbf{N}$:

1. Select the whole expression by clicking inside it and pressing [**Space**] until the right-hand side is surrounded by the editing lines.

2. Click on the Matrix toolbar to apply the vectorize operator. Mathcad puts an arrow over the top of the selected expression.

Properties of the vectorize operator

*   The vectorize operator changes the meaning of the other *operators* and *functions* to which it applies. The vectorize operator tells Mathcad to apply the operators and functions with their scalar meanings, element by element. It does not change the meaning of the actual names and numbers. If you apply the vectorize operator to a single name, it simply draws an arrow over the name. You can use this arrow for cosmetic purposes only if you like.

*   Since operations between two arrays are performed element by element, all arrays under a vectorize operator must be the same size. Operations between an array and a scalar are performed by applying the scalar to each element of the array.

*   You can use any of the following matrix operations under a vectorize operator: dot product, matrix multiplication, matrix powers, matrix inverse, determinant, or magnitude of a vector. The vectorize operator transforms these operations into element-by-element scalar multiplication, exponentiation, or absolute value, as appropriate.

Tip   A number of Mathcad's built-in functions and operators ordinarily take scalar arguments but *implicitly* vectorize arguments that are vectors (one-column arrays): they automatically compute a result element by element, whether you apply the vectorize operator or not. Functions that implicitly vectorize vector arguments include the trigonometric, logarithmic, Bessel, and probability distribution functions. Operators that implicitly vectorize vector arguments include the factorial, square and *n*th root, and relational operators. You must continue to use the vectorize operator on arrays of other sizes with these functions and operators.

For example, suppose you want to apply the quadratic formula to three vectors containing coefficients *a*, *b*, and *c*. Figure 11-9 shows how to do this with the vectorize operator.

The vectorize operator, appearing as an arrow above the quadratic formula in Figure 11-9, is essential in this calculation. Without it, Mathcad would interpret $\mathbf{a} \cdot \mathbf{c}$ as a vector dot product and also flag the square root of a vector as illegal. But with the vectorize operator, both $\mathbf{a} \cdot \mathbf{c}$ and the square root are performed element by element.

Coefficients as follows . . . $a := \begin{pmatrix} 1 \\ 1 \\ 2 \\ 2 \end{pmatrix}$ $b := \begin{pmatrix} 3 \\ 2 \\ 1 \\ 0 \end{pmatrix}$ $c := \begin{pmatrix} 2 \\ 1 \\ 1 \\ 1 \end{pmatrix}$

Compute a root . . .

$$x := \overrightarrow{\left(\frac{-b + \sqrt{b^2 - 4 \cdot a \cdot c}}{2 \cdot a} \right)} \qquad x = \begin{pmatrix} -1 \\ -1 \\ -0.25 + 0.661i \\ 0.707i \end{pmatrix}$$

$$\overrightarrow{(a \cdot x^2 + b \cdot x + c)} = \begin{pmatrix} 0 \\ 0 \\ 0 \\ 0 \end{pmatrix} \quad \text{. . . should be zero}$$

Figure 11-9: Quadratic formula with vectors and the vectorize operator.

Graphical Display of Arrays

In addition to looking at the actual numbers making up an array, you can also see a graphical representation of those same numbers. There are several ways to do this:

- For an arbitrary array, you can use the various three-dimensional plot types discussed in Chapter 13, "3D Plots."

- For an array of integers between 0 and 255, you can look at a grayscale image by choosing **Picture** from the **Insert** menu and entering the array's name in the placeholder.

- For three arrays of integers between 0 and 255 representing the red, green, and blue components of an image, choose **Picture** from the **Insert** menu and enter the arrays' names, separated by commas, in the placeholder.

See Chapter 6, "Working with Graphics and Other Objects," for more on viewing a matrix (or three matrices, in the case of a color image) in the picture operator.

Writing to a Data File

The File Read/Write component allows you to write the values stored in a Mathcad variable to a data file in a variety of formats, including the following:

- Excel (*.XLS)
- MATLAB (*.MAT)
- Lotus 1-2-3 (*.WK*)
- ASCII editors (*.DAT, *.CSV, *.PRN, *.TXT)

Tip Mathcad also provides a number of built-in functions to export arrays as ASCII data files or image files. See "File Access Functions" on page 199.

To export data using the File Read/Write component:

1. Click in a blank spot in your worksheet.

2. Choose **Component** from the **Insert** menu.

3. Select File Read or Write from the list and click "Next." This launches the File Read or Write Wizard.

4. Choose "Write to a file" and press "Next" to continue through the Wizard.

5. Specify the type of data file you want to create. Also enter the path to the data file you want to write or click the "Browse" button to locate it.

6. Press "Finish." You'll see the File Read/Write component icon and the path to the data file. For example, if you specify a data file called data.txt, you'll see the component at right.

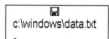

In the placeholder, enter the name of the Mathcad variable containing the data to be written to the data file. When you click outside the component, all the values in the array are written to the file you specified. Each time you calculate the worksheet, the data file is rewritten. See Figure 11-10 for an example.

Figure 11-10: Exporting data with the File Read/Write component

To change the name of the data file or the file type being created:

1. Click once on the component to select it.

2. Click with the right mouse button on the component and select **Choose File** from the pop-up menu to open the Write to File dialog box.

3. Choose the type of file you'd like to create in the "Files of type" text box. Use the dialog box to browse to the folder in which the data file will be created and click "Open."

Tip   When you display an array as an output table, as described in "Displaying Arrays" on page 210, you can export data directly from the table. Click with the right mouse button on the output table, choose **Export** from the pop-up menu, and enter the name of the file that will receive the data. Unlike the File Read/Write component, the output table writes the data only when you choose **Export**, not each time you calculate the worksheet.

Nested Arrays

An array element need not be a scalar. It's possible to make an array element itself be another array. This allows you to create arrays within arrays.

These arrays behave very much like arrays whose elements are all scalars. However, there are some distinctions, as described below.

Note   Most of Mathcad's operators and functions do not work with nested arrays, since there is no universally accepted definition of what constitutes correct behavior in this context. Certain operators and functions are nevertheless useful and appropriate for nested arrays. Functions that enumerate rows or columns, or that partition, augment, and stack matrices, can be applied to nested arrays. The transpose, subscript, and column array operators and the Boolean equal sign likewise support nested arrays.

Defining a Nested Array

You define a nested array in much the same way you would define any array. The only difference is that you cannot use the **Matrix** command from the **Insert** menu when you've selected a placeholder within an existing array. You can, however, click on a placeholder in an array and type the *name* of another array. Figure 11-11 shows several ways to define a nested array. Additional methods include using a file access function such as READPRN in the array of placeholders created using the Insert Matrix command, and using the programming operators in Mathcad Professional to build up an array whose elements are themselves arrays.

Note   The display of a nested array is controlled by Display Styles settings in the Result Format dialog box (see page 115). You can expand a nested array when the array is displayed in matrix form; otherwise, whenever an array element is itself an array, you see bracket notation showing the number of rows and columns rather than the array itself. If the nested array is displayed as an output table, you can see the underlying array temporarily. Click on the array element, then click with the right mouse button and choose **Down One Level** from the pop-up menu. Choose **Up One Level** from the pop-up menu to restore the array element to non-expanded form.

Three ways to define nested arrays...

Using range variables	Using the Matrices command	Defining element by element
$m := 0 .. 3$	$u := \begin{pmatrix} 1 \\ 2 \end{pmatrix}$	$B_0 := 1$
$n := 0 .. 3$		$B_1 := identity(2)$
	$v := (2 \quad 4)$	$B_2 := \begin{pmatrix} B_0 & 2 & v \end{pmatrix}$
$M_{m,n} := identity(m+1)$	$V := \begin{pmatrix} u \\ v \end{pmatrix}$	

── **Displaying the elements** ──────────

$$M_{0,0} = (1)$$

$$M_{1,1} = \begin{pmatrix} 1 & 0 \\ 0 & 1 \end{pmatrix}$$

$$M_{2,2} = \begin{pmatrix} 1 & 0 & 0 \\ 0 & 1 & 0 \\ 0 & 0 & 1 \end{pmatrix}$$

$$V_0 = \begin{pmatrix} 1 \\ 2 \end{pmatrix}$$

$$V_1 = (2 \quad 4)$$

$$V = \begin{pmatrix} \{2,1\} \\ \{1,2\} \end{pmatrix}$$

$$B_0 = 1$$

$$B_1 = \begin{pmatrix} 1 & 0 \\ 0 & 1 \end{pmatrix}$$

$$B = \begin{pmatrix} 1 \\ \{2,2\} \\ \{1,3\} \end{pmatrix}$$

Figure 11-11: Defining nested arrays.

Chapter 12
2D Plots

♦ Overview of 2D Plotting

♦ Graphing Functions and Expressions

♦ Plotting Vectors of Data

♦ Formatting a 2D Plot

♦ Modifying Your 2D Plot's Perspective

Overview of 2D Plotting

To visually represent a function or expression of a single variable or X-Y data in Mathcad, you can create a 2D plot. You can create either a Cartesian X-Y plot or a polar plot. A typical X-Y plot shows horizontal x-values versus vertical y-values, while a typical polar plot shows angular values, θ, versus radial values, r. Figure 12-1 shows several examples of 2D plots.

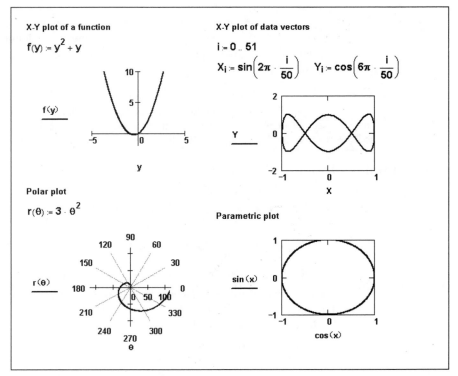

Figure 12-1: Examples of 2D plots.

Creating an X-Y Plot

In general, to create an X-Y plot:

1. Click in your worksheet where you want the graph to appear.

2. Choose **Graph⇒X-Y Plot** from the **Insert** menu or click on the Graph toolbar. Alternatively, type [**Shift**] 2 or **@**. Mathcad inserts a blank X-Y plot.

3. Fill in both the *x*-axis placeholder (bottom center) and the *y*-axis placeholder (left center) with a function, expression, or variable.

4. Click outside the plot or press [**Enter**].

Mathcad automatically chooses axis limits for you. If you want to specify the axis limits yourself, click in the plot and type over the numbers in the placeholders at the ends of the axes.

Mathcad creates the plot over a default range using default limits. See "Formatting a 2D Plot" on page 229 for information on modifying these defaults.

Note If a point is complex, Mathcad does not graph it. To graph the real or imaginary part of a point or expression, use the *Re* and *Im* functions to extract the real and imaginary parts, respectively.

To resize a plot, click in the plot to select it. Then move the cursor to a handle along the right or bottom edge of the plot until the cursor changes to a double-headed arrow. Hold the mouse button down and drag the mouse in the direction that you want the plot's dimension to change.

Note If some points in a function or expression are valid and others are not, Mathcad plots only the valid ones. If the points are not contiguous, Mathcad does not connect them with a line. You may therefore see a blank plot if none of the points are contiguous. To see the points, format the trace to have symbols. See "Formatting a 2D Plot" on page 229 for information on formatting traces.

Creating a polar plot

In general, to create a polar plot:

1. Click in your worksheet where you want the graph to appear.

2. Choose **Graph⇒Polar Plot** from the **Insert** menu or click 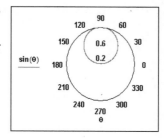 on the Graph toolbar.

3. Fill in both the angular-axis placeholder (bottom center) and the radial-axis placeholder (left center) with a function, expression, or variable.

4. Click outside the plot or press [**Enter**].

Mathcad creates the plot over a default range using default limits. See "Formatting a 2D Plot" on page 229 for information on modifying these defaults.

The remaining sections in this chapter focus on plotting functions, expressions, and data. Although the instructions and figures typically show X-Y plots, the instructions apply to polar plots as well.

Graphing Functions and Expressions

2D QuickPlots

A 2D *QuickPlot* is a plot created from an expression or function which represents the *y*-coordinates of the plot. With a *QuickPlot*, there is no need to define the independent or *x*-axis variable.

To create an X-Y plot of a single expression or function:

1. Click in your worksheet where you want the graph to appear.

2. Enter the expression or function of a single variable you want to plot. Make sure the editing lines remain in the expression.

3. Choose **Graph⇒X-Y Plot** from the **Insert** menu or click 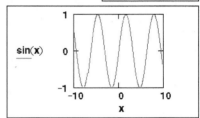 on the Graph toolbar.

4. Click outside the graph or press [**Enter**].

Mathcad automatically produces a plot over a default domain for the independent variable, from −10 to 10.

To change the default domain for the independent variable in a 2D QuickPlot, change the axis limits on the plot:

1. Click on the plot, and then click on one of the four axis limit placeholders located at the ends of the axes.

2. Type the value of the axis limit you want. There is no restriction on the values you can enter in these placeholders.

3. Click outside the graph or press [**Enter**] to see the updated graph.

Defining an independent variable

If you don't want Mathcad to use a default range for the independent variable, you can define the independent variable as a range variable before creating the plot. For example:

1. Define a range variable, such as *x*, that takes on the values you want to graph. The range variable need not be called *x*; you can use any valid name. See "Range Variables" on page 106. $x := 0, 0.1 .. 2\pi$

2. Enter an expression or function you want to plot using that variable. Make sure the editing lines remain in the expression. $\sin(x)$

3. Choose **Graph⇒X-Y Plot** from the **Insert** menu or click 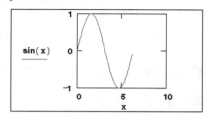 on the Graph toolbar.

4. Type the name of the variable into the x-axis placeholder.

5. Click outside the graph or press [**Enter**].

Mathcad graphs one point for every value of the range variable, and, unless you specify otherwise, connects each pair of points with a straight line.

Tip To override Mathcad's choices for the axis limits on a plot, click in the plot and type over the limits in the placeholders at the ends of the axes (see "Setting Axis Limits" on page 229).

Plotting Multiple 2D Curves

You can graph several traces on the same X-Y or polar plot. A graph can show several y-axis (or radial) expressions against the same x-axis (or angular) expression. See Figure 12-3. Or it can match up several y-axis (or radial) expressions with the corresponding number of x-axis (or angular) expressions. See Figure 12-2.

To create a *QuickPlot* containing more than one trace:

1. Enter the expressions or functions of a single variable you want to plot, separated by commas. Make sure the editing lines remain in the expression.

2. Choose **Graph⇒X-Y Plot** from the **Insert** menu or click 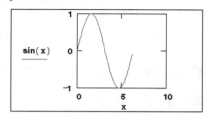 on the Graph toolbar.

3. Click outside the graph or press [**Enter**].

Mathcad produces a single graph containing plots of all the expressions or functions, over a default range for the independent variable(s), from –10 to 10. You can change the axis range by editing the upper and lower limits on the x-axis as described in "Setting Axis Limits" on page 229.

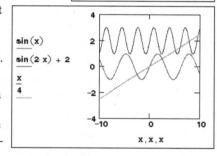

Note In a *QuickPlot* with multiple traces, you need not use the same independent variable in every y-axis (or radial-axis) expression. Mathcad will provide the appropriate corresponding variable in the x-axis (or angular-axis) placeholder.

In general, to create a graph containing several independent curves:

1. Choose **Graph⇒X-Y Plot** from the **Insert** menu or click 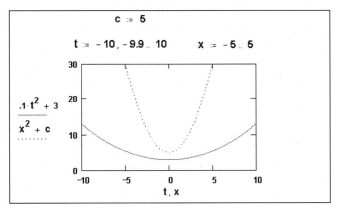 on the Graph toolbar.
2. Enter two or more expressions separated by commas in the *y*-axis placeholder.
3. Enter the same number of expressions separated by commas in the *x*-axis placeholder.

Mathcad matches up the expressions in pairs—the first *x*-axis expression with first *y*-axis expression, the second with the second, and so on. It then draws a trace for each pair. Figure 12-2 shows an example.

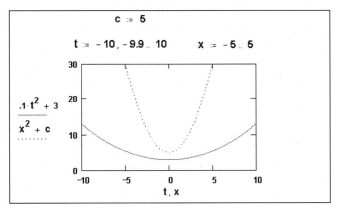

Figure 12-2: Graph with multiple expressions on both axes.

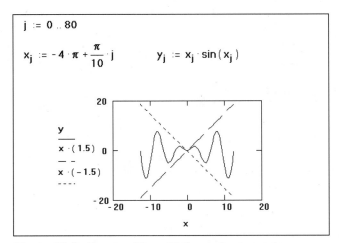

Figure 12-3: Graph with multiple y-axis expressions.

Note All traces on a graph share the same axis limits. For each axis, all expressions and limits on that axis must have compatible units.

Creating a parametric plot

A parametric plot is one in which a function or expression is plotted against another function or expression that uses the same independent variable. You can create either an X-Y or polar parametric plot.

To create an X-Y parametric plot:

1. Click in your worksheet where you want the graph to appear.

2. Choose **Graph⇒X-Y Plot** from the **Insert** menu or click on the Graph toolbar. Mathcad inserts a blank X-Y plot with empty placeholders.

3. In both the *x*-axis and *y*-axis placeholders, enter a function or expression.

4. Click outside the plot or press [**Enter**].

Mathcad produces a *QuickPlot* over a default range for the independent variable. Figure 12-1 shows an example of a parametric plot.

If you don't want Mathcad to use a default range for the plot, define the independent variable as a range variable before creating the plot. Mathcad graphs one point for each value of the independent variable and connects each pair of points with a straight line. Figure 12-4 shows two functions of θ plotted against each other. The range variable θ was previously defined. For more information, see "Range Variables" on page 106.

Figure 12-4: Graphing one function against another.

Plotting Vectors of Data

To graph a vector of data, you can create either an X-Y plot or a polar plot. When creating either type of plot, you need to use the vector subscript (see "Vector and Matrix Operators" on page 133) to specify which elements to plot. Additionally, you can use Axum LE (see "Using Axum to Plot Data" on page 227) to create a 2D plot of your vectors or data. Some graphs of data vectors are shown in Figure 12-5.

Plotting a single vector of data

To create an X-Y plot of a single vector of data:

1. Define a range variable, such as i, that references the subscript of each element of the vector you want to plot. For example, for a vector with 10 elements, your subscript range variable would be $i := 0 .. 9$.

2. Click in your worksheet where you want the graph to appear.

3. Choose **Graph⇒X-Y Plot** from the **Insert** menu or click ![xy plot icon] on the Graph toolbar. Mathcad inserts a blank X-Y plot.

4. Enter i in the bottom placeholder and the vector name with the subscript (y_i for example) in the placeholder on the left. Type **[** as a shortcut to create the subscript.

5. Click outside the graph or press [**Enter**].

Note   Subscripts must be integers greater than or equal to ORIGIN. This means that the x-axis or angular variable used in the graphs in Figure 12-5 can run through whole-number values only. If you want to graph fractional or negative values on the x-axis, graph a function or graph one vector against another, as described in the next section.

Tip   If you have a handful of data points, you can use an input table to create a vector as shown in the second graph in Figure 12-5 or in Figure 12-7. For more information, see "Entering Data into a Table" on page 207.

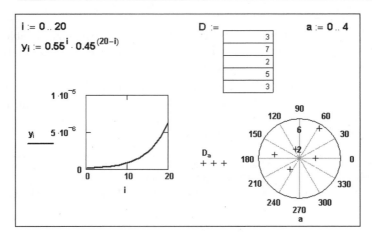

Figure 12-5: Graphing a vector.

Plotting one data vector against another

To graph all the elements of one data vector against all the elements in another, enter the names of the vectors in the axis placeholders of an X-Y plot or polar plot.

For example, to create an X-Y plot of two data vectors *x* and *y*:

1. Define the vectors *x* and *y*.

2. Click in your worksheet where you want the graph to appear.

3. Choose **Graph**⟹**X-Y Plot** from the **Insert** menu, or click ![toolbar icon] on the Graph toolbar.

4. Enter *y* in the *y*-axis placeholder and *x* in the *x*-axis placeholder.

5. Click outside the graph or press [**Enter**].

Mathcad plots the elements in the vector *x* against the elements in the vector *y*.

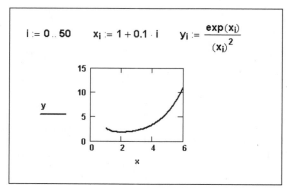

Figure 12-6: Graphing two vectors.

Note If the vectors being plotted are not the same length, Mathcad plots the number of elements in the shorter vector.

If you want to plot only certain vector elements, define a range variable and use it as a subscript on the vector names. In the example above, to plot the fifth through tenth elements of *x* and *y* against each other:

1. Define a range variable, such as *k*, going from 4 to 9 in increments of 1. (Note that the first elements of the vectors *x* and *y* are x_0 and y_0 by default.)

2. Enter y_k and x_k in the axis placeholders.

Note If you have a set of data values to graph, create a vector by reading in data from a data file, by pasting in the data from the Clipboard, or by typing data directly into an input table. See Chapter 11, "Vectors, Matrices, and Data Arrays." See Figure 12-7 for an example showing the use of an input table.

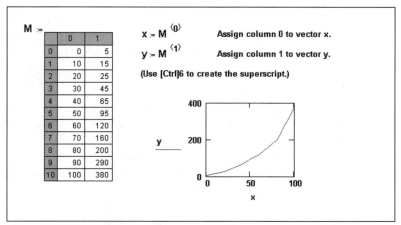

Figure 12-7: Plotting vectors from input table data.

Using Axum to Plot Data

Included on your Mathcad CD is the application Axum LE. Axum LE is a version of Axum that features numerous 2D plot types, complete control over graph formatting, and a full set of annotation tools. Axum LE gives you fine control over every aspect of your 2D plots, and you can integrate these plots into your Mathcad worksheets.

There are two basic methods for integrating plots from Axum into your Mathcad worksheet. You can create a graph in Axum and insert it into your Mathcad worksheet as an object. Or, you can define data in your Mathcad worksheet, send it to Axum, and create a dynamic Axum graph directly in your Mathcad worksheet. Here are brief instructions for each method.

Inserting an Axum graph object

To insert an Axum graph object:

1. Create and save a graph in Axum. For more information about using Axum, see Axum's on line Help.

2. In Mathcad, choose **Object** from the **Insert** menu. In the Insert Object dialog box, click Create from File, and browse for your saved Axum graph sheet. Once you have selected your graph sheet, click OK.

3. The Axum graph appears into your Mathcad worksheet. If you check Link in the Insert Object dialog, you may activate the plot from within your Mathcad worksheet, by double-clicking, and make changes to the original Axum graph.

For more information about inserting objects, refer to "Chapter 6: Working with Graphics and Other Objects."

Inserting a Dynamic Axum graph

To insert an Axum graph linked to data in your Mathcad worksheet:

1. In Mathcad, define the vector(s) of data you wish to plot.

2. Click in a blank spot in your worksheet. Be sure to click below or to the right of your vector(s) of data.

3. Choose **Component** from the **Insert** menu. Select Axum Graph from the list and click Next. Choose a plot type and specify as many input variables as you have data vectors. Click Finish.

4. A blank Axum graph appears in your Mathcad worksheet. Enter the name(s) of your data vector(s) in the placeholders in the bottom left corner of the graph. Click outside the graph or press [**Enter**].

If you change the vectors of data upon which your Axum graph component is dependent, your graph updates automatically. For more information about using components, refer to "Chapter 16: Advanced Computational Features." Figure 12-8 shows an Axum graph that has been customized with axes labels, a title, and text and graphic annotations.

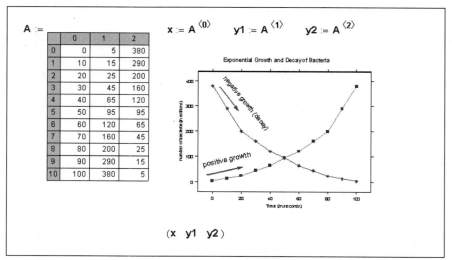

Figure 12-8: An Axum graph in a Mathcad worksheet.

Note If you want to create an Axum graph component with multiple independent traces, define x- and y-vectors for each plot. Then, choose the plot type "Scatter Plots of XY Pairs" from the Axum Graph dialog, and specify as many input variables as you have vectors of data. Enter the vector names in the placeholders in xy-pairs, i.e., (x1 y1 x2 y2 etc.)

Formatting a 2D Plot

When you create an X-Y plot or a polar plot, Mathcad uses the default settings to format the axes and traces. You can, however, reformat the axes and traces. You can also add titles and labels and control the default settings of the graph.

To format a 2D graph:

1. Double-click the graph. Alternatively, click once on the graph and choose **Graph⇒X-Y Plot** or **Graph⇒Polar Plot** from the **Format** menu. You'll see the dialog box for formatting a selected graph.

2. Click the tab for the page you want to work with. Use the Axes tab to determine the appearance of the axes and grid lines. Use the Traces tab to set the color, type, and width of the traces. Use the Labels tab to insert labels on the axes. Use the Defaults tab to specify the default appearance of your graphs.

3. Make the appropriate changes in the dialog box.

4. Click Apply to see the effect of your changes *without* closing the dialog box.

5. Close the dialog by clicking OK.

Note   In the Axes page, make sure you turn options on and off in the appropriate axis column. In the Traces page, click on a trace's name in the Legend Label column and change characteristics by clicking on the arrow beside each of the drop-down options.

Tip   If you double-click an axis on a graph, you'll see a formatting dialog box for that axis alone.

On-line Help   Click Help in the dialog box for details on particular formatting options.

Setting Axis Limits

When you create a 2D graph, the Autoscale option is turned on. Use the Axes page of the plot formatting dialog box to turn Autoscale on or off:

• With Autoscale on, Mathcad automatically sets each axis limit to the first major tick mark beyond the end of the data. This is a reasonably round number large enough to display every point being graphed.

• With Autoscale off, Mathcad automatically sets the axis limits exactly at the data limits.

Specifying Other Limits

You can override Mathcad's automatic limits by entering limits directly on the graph. To do so:

1. Click the graph to select it. Mathcad displays four additional numbers, one by each axis limit. These numbers are enclosed within corner symbols, as illustrated in the selected plot in Figure 12-9.

2. Click on one of these numbers and type a number to replace it. Do the same for the other numbers if you want to change more than one limit.

3. Click outside the graph. Mathcad redraws it using the new axis limits you specified. The corner symbols below the limits you changed disappear. Figure 12-9 shows the effect of manually setting limits on a graph.

Figure 12-9: Data limits set automatically and manually.

Setting Default Formats

Mathcad uses default settings to format the axes and traces of new graphs you create.

Copying Defaults from an Existing Graph

One way to create a new set of defaults is to use the format settings of an existing graph. The advantage of this method is that you can actually see how the format settings look as you define them.

To use the format of a particular graph as the default graph format:

1. Double-click the graph, or click in the graph and choose **Graph⇒X-Y Plot** (or **Graph⇒Polar Plot**) from the **Format** menu. Mathcad displays the dialog box for formatting a selected graph.

2. Click the Defaults tab to see the Defaults page.

3. Check Use for Defaults. When you click OK, to close the dialog box, Mathcad saves these settings as your default settings.

Setting Defaults Without Using a Graph

You can use the Setting Default Formats dialog box to change default plot settings. To set defaults this way:

1. Make sure that you don't have any graphs selected.

2. Choose **Graph⇒X-Y Plot** (or **Graph⇒Polar Plot**) from the **Format** menu. You'll see the Setting Default Formats dialog box.

3. Change the appropriate settings on the Axes and Traces pages.

4. Click OK to accept your changes and close the dialog box.

Adding Custom Titles, Labels, and Other Annotations

One way to add titles and labels to your 2D graph is to use the options on the Labels tab of the 2D Plot Format dialog box. A second way to add titles and labels, as well as annotations, is to create text or some other object in your worksheet and then move it on top of the graph.

To create an annotation for your 2D graph:

1. Create a text region, or insert a graphic object in your worksheet by pasting it in or by choosing **Object** from the **Insert** menu.

2. Drag the text or object onto your 2D graph and position it appropriately.

Figure 12-10 shows a graph containing both a text region ("inflection pt") and a graphic object (an arrow).

Note   If you choose **Separate Regions** from the **Format** menu, all overlapping regions in your worksheet will separate. In the case of annotated graph, such as the one shown above, all annotations move below the graph when you separate regions.

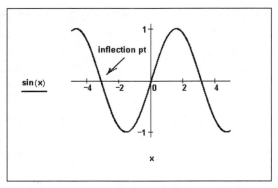

Figure 12-10: Mathcad graph with annotations.

Modifying Your 2D Plot's Perspective

Mathcad provides the following options for manipulating your 2D graph:

- You can zoom in on a portion of the graph.

- You can get the *x*- and *y*-coordinates for any point that was plotted to construct an individual plot.

- You can get the *x*- and *y*-coordinates for any location within the graph.

Zooming in on a Plot

Mathcad allows you to select a region of a graph and magnify it. To zoom in on a portion of a graph, follow these steps:

1. Click in the graph and choose **Graph⇒Zoom** from the **Format** menu, or click [magnifier icon] on the Graph toolbar. The Zoom dialog box appears. The X-Y Zoom dialog box is shown to the right.

2. If necessary, reposition the Zoom dialog box so that you can see the entire region of the graph you want to zoom.

3. Click the mouse at one corner of the region in the graph you want to magnify.

4. Press and hold down the mouse button and drag the mouse. A dashed selection outline emerges from the anchor point. The coordinates of the selected region are listed in the Min and Max text boxes (or the Radius text box of the Polar Zoom dialog box).

5. When the selection outline just encloses the region you want to magnify, let go of the mouse button. If necessary, click on the selection outline, hold the mouse button down, and move the outline to another part of the graph.

6. Click Zoom to redraw the graph. The axis limits are temporarily set to the coordinates specified in the Zoom dialog box. To make these axis limits permanent, click OK.

Tip   If you're working with a graph that has already been zoomed, you can restore the default appearance of the graph. To do so, click Full View in the Zoom dialog box.

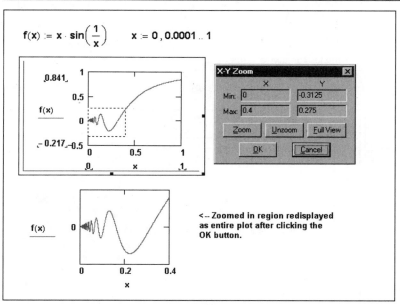

Figure 12-11: A zoomed-in region of an X-Y plot.

Getting a Readout of Plot Coordinates

To see a readout of coordinates of the specific points that make up a trace, follow these steps:

1. Click in the graph and choose **Graph⇒Trace** from the **Format** menu, or click on the Graph toolbar. The X-Y Trace dialog box appears as in the example at right. Check Track Data Points if it isn't already checked. If necessary, reposition the Trace dialog box so that you can see the entire graph.

2. Click and drag the mouse along the trace whose coordinates you want to see. A dotted crosshair jumps from one point to the next as you move the pointer along the trace.

3. If you release the mouse button, you can use the left and right arrows to move to the previous and next data points. Use the up and down arrows to select other traces.

4. As the pointer reaches each point on the trace, Mathcad displays the values of that point in the X-Value and Y-Value boxes (or the Radius and Angle boxes in the Polar Trace dialog box).

5. The values of the last point selected are shown in the boxes. The crosshair remains until you click outside the plot. .

Tip When Track Data Points is unchecked in the Trace dialog box, you can see a readout of coordinates for any location in a graph, not just the data points that created an individual plot.

Figure 12-12 shows an example of a plot whose coordinates are being read.

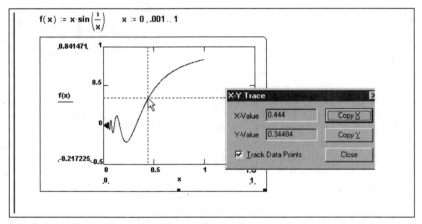

Figure 12-12: Reading coordinates from a graph.

To copy and paste a coordinate using the Clipboard:

1. Click Copy X or Copy Y (or Copy Radius or Copy Angle in the case of a polar plot).

2. You can then paste that value into a math or text region in your Mathcad worksheet, into a spreadsheet, or into any other application that allows pasting from the Clipboard.

Chapter 13
3D Plots

- ◆ Overview of 3D Plotting
- ◆ Creating 3D Plots of Functions
- ◆ Creating 3D Plots of Data
- ◆ Formatting a 3D Plot
- ◆ Rotating and Zooming on 3D Plots

Overview of 3D Plotting

To visually represent in three dimensions a function of one or two variables or to plot data in the form of x-, y-, and z-coordinates, you can create a surface plot, a contour plot, a 3D bar plot, a 3D scatter plot, or a vector field plot. Create these different plot types using commands from the **Insert** menu or the 3D Plot Wizard. You can also place more than one 3D plot on the same graph. Mathcad renders 3D plots with sophisticated, high performance OpenGL graphics.

Inserting a 3D Plot

In general, to create a three-dimensional plot:

1. Define a function of two variables or a matrix of data.

2. Click in the worksheet where you want the plot to appear. Then choose **Graph** from the **Insert** menu and select a 3D plot. Alternatively, click one of the 3D graph buttons on the Graph toolbar. Mathcad inserts a blank 3D plot with axes and an empty placeholder.

3. Enter the name of the function or matrix in the placeholder.

4. Click outside the plot or press [**Enter**]. Mathcad creates the plot according to the function or matrix of data.

For example, the surface plot shown below was created in Mathcad from the function:

$$F(x, y) := \sin(x) + \cos(y)$$

When you create a 3D plot from a function, it's called a *QuickPlot*. A *QuickPlot* uses default ranges and grids for the independent variables. To change these settings, double-click on the graph and use the QuickPlot Data page of the 3D Plot Format dialog. For more information on modifying these and other plot characteristics, see "Formatting a 3D Plot" on page 246.

To learn how to create a plot from a matrix of values, see the shown in Figure 13-2 on page 241.

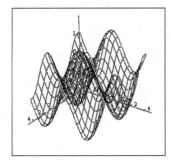

F

3D Plot Wizard

The *3D Plot Wizard* gives you more control over the format settings of the plot as you insert it. To use the Wizard:

1. Click in your worksheet wherever you want the graph to appear.

2. Choose **Graph⇒3D Plot Wizard** from the **Insert** menu. The first page of the 3D Plot Wizard appears.

3. Select the type of three-dimensional graph you want to see and click "Next."

4. Make your selections for the appearance and coloring of the plot on subsequent pages of the Wizard. Click "Finish" and a graph region with a blank placeholder appears.

5. Enter appropriate arguments (a function name, data vectors, etc.) for the 3D plot into the placeholder.

6. Click outside the plot or press [**Enter**].

The plot is created using the settings you specified in the Wizard. For information on modifying the appearance of your plot, see "Formatting a 3D Plot" on page 246.

Creating 3D Plots of Functions

This section describes how to create various 3D plots from functions in Mathcad, also known as *QuickPlots*. Although the instructions focus on using commands on the **Insert** menu and changing settings through the 3D Plot Format dialog box, you can also use the 3D Plot Wizard, as described on page 236.

Tip   To see a variety of two- and three-dimensional functions and data sets visualized in plots, open the "Practical Curves and Surfaces" section of QuickSheets in the Mathcad Resource Center (choose **Resource Center** from the **Help** menu and click on "QuickSheets").

Creating a Surface, Bar, Contour, or Scatter Plot

You can visualize any function of two variables as a surface, bar, contour, or scatter plot in three dimensions.

Step 1: Define a function or set of functions

First, define the function in your worksheet in any one of the following forms:

$$F(x, y) := \sin(x) + \cos(y) \qquad G(u, v) := \begin{pmatrix} 2 \cdot u \\ 2 \cdot u \cdot \cos(v) \\ 2 \cdot \cos(v) \end{pmatrix} \qquad \begin{matrix} X(u, v) := v \\ Y(u, v) := v \cdot \cos(u) \\ Z(u, v) := \sin(u) \end{matrix}$$

F(x,y) is a function of two variables. In this type of function, the *x*- and *y*-coordinates of the plot vary, by default, from –5 to 5 with a step size of 0.5. Each *z*-coordinate is determined by the function using these *x*- and *y*-values.

G(u,v) is a vector-valued function of two variables. In this type of function, the independent variables *u* and *v* vary, by default, from –5 to 5 with a step size of 0.5. The *x*-, *y*-, and *z*-coordinates are plotted parametrically according to the definitions in the three elements of the vector using these *u*- and *v*-values.

X(u,v), *Y(u,v)*, and *Z(u,v)* are functions of two variables. In this type of function triple, the independent variables *u* and *v* vary, by default, from –5 to 5 with a step size of 0.5. The *x*-, *y*-, and *z*-coordinates are plotted parametrically according to the three function definitions using these *u*- and *v*-values.

Note The function descriptions above assume that you are working in Cartesian coordinates. If your function represents spherical or cylindrical, rather than Cartesian, coordinates, you can automatically convert the function to Cartesian coordinates. Double-click on the plot, go to the QuickPlot Data page of the 3D Plot Format dialog box, and click "Spherical" or "Cylindrical" under Coordinate System.

Step 2: Insert a 3D plot

After you define a function or set of functions to plot, choose **Graph** from the **Insert** menu and select a 3D plot type.

For example, to create a surface plot from the functions X, Y, and Z, defined above:

1. Choose **Graph⇒Surface Plot** from the **Insert** menu or click [image] on the Graph toolbar. Mathcad inserts a blank 3D plot.

2. Enter the name of the functions in the placeholder. When you have more than one function definition for a single surface, separate the function names by commas and enclose the function names in parentheses. For this example, type:

(X, Y, Z)

3. Press [**Enter**] or click outside the plot.

(X, Y, Z)

To change your plot to a different plot type:

1. Double-click on the graph to bring up the 3D Plot Format dialog box.
2. In the Display As section on the General tab, select Bar Plot, Contour Plot, or Data Points from the array of plot types.
3. Click "OK."

Figure 13-1 shows a 3D scatter plot created from the function G, and a contour plot created from the function F, both defined above:

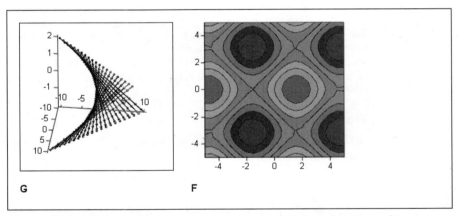

Figure 13-1: A scatter plot and a contour plot created from functions of two variables.

Note   All 3D *QuickPlots* are parametric curves or surfaces. In other words, all *QuickPlots* are created from three vectors or matrices of data representing the x-, y-, and z-coordinates of the plot. In the case of a single function of two variables, Mathcad internally creates two matrices of x- and y-data over the default range -5 to 5 with a step size of 0.5, and then generates z-data using these x- and y-coordinates.

To change the default ranges and grids for the independent variables, double-click on the graph and use the QuickPlot Data page of the 3D Plot Format dialog. For more information on modifying these and other plot characteristics, see "Formatting a 3D Plot" on page 246.

Creating a Space Curve

You can visualize any parametrically-defined function of one variable as a scatter plot in three dimensions.

Step 1: Define a function or set of functions

First, define the function in your worksheet in one of the following forms:

$$H(u) := \begin{pmatrix} \sin(u) \\ \cos(u) \\ \sin(u) \cdot \cos(u) \end{pmatrix} \qquad \begin{array}{l} R(u) := 2 \cdot u \\ S(u) := u^2 \\ T(u) := \cos(u) \end{array}$$

$H(u)$ is a vector-valued function of one variable. In this type of function, the independent variable u varies, by default, from –5 to 5 with a step size of 0.5. The x-, y-, and z-coordinates of the plot are determined by the functions in each element of the vector using these u-values.

$R(u)$, $S(u)$, and $T(u)$ are functions of one variable. In this type of function triple, the independent variable u varies, by default, from –5 to 5 with a step size of 0.5. The x-, y-, and z-coordinates are plotted according to the function definitions using these u-values.

Note A space curve often represents the path of a particle in motion through space where u is a time parameter.

Step 2: Insert a 3D scatter plot

To create a space curve from a single function or set of functions:

1. Choose **Graph⇒3D Scatter Plot** from the **Insert** menu or click on the Graph toolbar. Mathcad inserts a blank 3D plot.

2. Enter the name of function or functions in the placeholder. When you have more than one function definition, separate the function names by commas and enclose the function names in parentheses. To create a space curve from the functions R, S, and T, defined above, type:

$$(R, S, T)$$

---

3. Press [**Enter**] or click outside the plot.

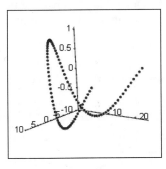

(R, S, T)

For general information on formatting 3D plots, refer to "Formatting a 3D Plot" on page 246. For specific information on formatting a scatter plot, refer to the topic "Scatter Plots" in the on-line Help.

Creating 3D Plots of Data

This section describes how to create various 3D plots from data in Mathcad. Although the instructions focus on using commands on the **Insert** menu and changing settings through the 3D Plot Format dialog, you can also use the 3D Plot Wizard, as described on page 236.

Creating a Surface, Bar, or Scatter Plot

Surface, bar, and scatter plots are useful for visualizing two-dimensional data contained in an array as either a connected surface, bars above and below the zero plane, or points in space.

For example, to create a surface plot from data:

1. Create or import a matrix of values to plot. The row and column numbers represent the x- and y-coordinate values. The matrix elements themselves are the z-coordinate values plotted as heights above and below the xy-plane (at $z = 0$).

2. Choose **Graph⇒Surface Plot** from the **Insert** menu or click ▨ on the Graph toolbar. Mathcad inserts a blank 3D plot.

3. Enter the name of the matrix in the placeholder.

4. Press [**Enter**] or click outside the plot. Figure 13-2 shows a 3D bar plot created from a matrix, M:

In the default perspective, the first row of the matrix extends from the back left corner of the grid to the right, while the first column extends from the back left corner out toward the viewer. See "Formatting a 3D Plot" on page 246 to learn how to change this default view.

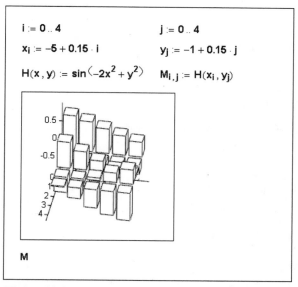

$$i := 0 .. 4 \qquad j := 0 .. 4$$

$$x_i := -5 + 0.15 \cdot i \qquad y_j := -1 + 0.15 \cdot j$$

$$H(x, y) := \sin\left(-2x^2 + y^2\right) \qquad M_{i,j} := H(x_i, y_j)$$

M

Figure 13-2: Defining a matrix of data and plotting it as a 3D bar plot.

Creating a Parametric Surface Plot

A parametric surface plot is created by passing three matrices representing the x-, y-, and z- coordinates of your points in space to the surface plot.

To create a parametric surface plot:

1. Create or import three matrices having the same number of rows and columns.

2. Choose **Graph**⇒**Surface Plot** from the **Insert** menu or click ![icon] on the Graph toolbar. Mathcad inserts a blank 3D plot.

3. Type the names of the three matrices separated by commas and enclosed in parentheses in the placeholder. For example:

    (X, Y, Z)

4. Press [**Enter**] or click outside the plot.

Figure 13-3 shows a parametric surface plot created from the matrices, X, Y, and Z, defined above the plot.

Note   The underlying parameter space is a rectangular sheet covered by a uniform mesh. In effect, the three matrices map this sheet into three-dimensional space. For example, the matrices **X, Y**, and **Z** defined in Figure 13-3 carry out a mapping that rolls the sheet into a tube and then joins the ends of the tube to form a torus.

For general information on formatting 3D plots, refer to "Formatting a 3D Plot" on page 246. For specific information on formatting a parametric surface plot, refer to the topic "Surface Plots" in the on-line Help.

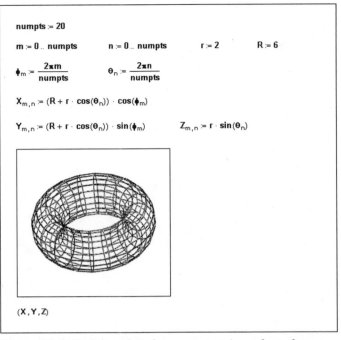

$$numpts := 20$$

$$m := 0 .. numpts \qquad n := 0 .. numpts \qquad r := 2 \qquad R := 6$$

$$\phi_m := \frac{2\pi m}{numpts} \qquad \theta_n := \frac{2\pi n}{numpts}$$

$$X_{m,n} := (R + r \cdot \cos(\theta_n)) \cdot \cos(\phi_m)$$

$$Y_{m,n} := (R + r \cdot \cos(\theta_n)) \cdot \sin(\phi_m) \qquad Z_{m,n} := r \cdot \sin(\theta_n)$$

$$(X, Y, Z)$$

Figure 13-3: Defining data for a parametric surface plot.

Creating a Three-dimensional Parametric Curve

A three-dimensional parametric curve is created by passing three vectors representing the x-, y-, and z-coordinates of your points in space to the surface plot.

To create a three-dimensional parametric curve:

1. Create or import three vectors having the same number of rows.

2. Choose **Graph$\Rightarrow$Scatter Plot** from the **Insert** menu or click ▦ on the Graph toolbar. Mathcad inserts a blank 3D plot.

3. Type the names of the three vectors separated by commas and enclosed in parentheses in the placeholder. For example:

    (X, Y, Z)

4. Press [**Enter**] or click outside the plot.

Figure 13-4 shows a three-dimensional parametric curve created from the vectors, P, Q, and R, defined above the plot:

For general information on formatting 3D plots, refer to "Formatting a 3D Plot" on page 246. For specific information on formatting a scatter plot, refer to the topic "Scatter Plots" in the on-line Help.

$i := -5, -4.9 .. 5 \qquad x(i) := i \cdot 10 + 50$

$P_{x(i)} := \cos(i) \qquad Q_{x(i)} := \sin(2 \cdot i) \qquad R_{x(i)} := \cos(i) + \sin(2 \cdot i)$

(P, Q, R)

Figure 13-4: Defining data for a space curve.

Creating a Contour Plot

To view three-dimensional data as a two-dimensional contour map, you can create a contour plot:

1. Define or import a matrix of values to plot.

2. Choose **Graph⇒Contour Plot** from the **Insert** menu or click 🖼 on the Graph toolbar. Mathcad shows a blank plot with a single placeholder.

3. Type the name of the matrix in the placeholder.

4. Press [**Enter**] or click outside the plot.

Figure 13-5 shows a contour plot created from the matrix, C, defined above the plot:

The contour plot is a visual representation of the matrix's level curves. Mathcad assumes that the rows and columns represent equally spaced intervals on the axes, and then linearly interpolates the values of this matrix to form level curves or contours. Each level curve is formed such that no two cross. By default, the *z*-contours are shown on the *x*-*y* plane. Mathcad plots the matrix such that the element in row 0 and column 0 is in the lower left corner. Thus the rows of the matrix correspond to values on the *x*-axis, increasing to the right, and the columns correspond to values along the *y*-axis, increasing toward the top.

For general information on formatting 3D plots, refer to "Formatting a 3D Plot" on page 246. For specific information on formatting a contour plot, refer to the topic "Contour Plots" in the on-line Help.

Note If you create a contour plot of a function as described above, the positive *x*-axis of the plot extends to the right and the positive *y*-axis extends toward the top of the plot.

Figure 13-5: Defining data for a contour plot.

Creating a Vector Field Plot

In a vector field plot, each point in the *x-y* plane is assigned a two-dimensional vector. There are two ways to set up the data needed for a vector field plot:

1. Create a matrix of complex numbers in which the following conditions exist:

    *   The row and column numbers represent the *x-* and *y*-coordinates

    *   The real part of each matrix element is the *x*-component of the vector associated with that row and column

    *   The imaginary part of each element is the *y*-component of the vector associated with that row and column.

2. Create two matrices having the same number of rows and columns. The first matrix should have the *x*-components of the vectors, the second the *y*-components.

Once you have defined your data, as described above, to create a vector field plot:

1. Choose **Graph⇒Vector Field Plot** from the **Insert** menu or click ▦ on the Graph toolbar.

2. Type the name(s) of the matrix or matrices in the placeholder. If you have more than one matrix for a vector field plot, separate the matrix names by commas and enclose the matrix name set in parentheses. For example:

    (X, Y)

3. Press [**Enter**] or click outside the plot.

Figure 13-6 shows a vector field plot created from the matrix, Q, defined above the plot:

$m := 0 .. 11$ $n := 0 .. 11$

$Q_{m,n} := 0.2i \cdot (m - 5) - 0.1 - 0.1i$ $g(z) := \dfrac{z^2}{0.1 + |z|}$

$M := \overrightarrow{g(Q)}$

M

Figure 13-6: Defining data for a vector field plot.

For general information on formatting 3D plots, refer to "Formatting a 3D Plot." For specific information on formatting a vector field plot, refer to the topic "Vector field plots" in the on-line Help.

Graphing Multiple 3D Plots

Just as you can plot more than one trace on a two-dimensional graph, you can place more than one surface, curve, contour, bar, or scatter plot on a three-dimensional graph.

For example, to create a 3D graph with a contour plot and a surface plot:

1. Define two functions of two variables or any combination of two acceptable argument sets for a 3D plot (two matrices, two sets of three vectors, etc.).

2. Choose **Graph⇒Contour Plot** from the **Insert** menu or click 🖼 on the Graph toolbar. Mathcad inserts a blank 3D plot.

3. Enter the name of the function or matrix for the contour plot into the placeholder. Then type **,** (a comma).

4. Enter the name of the function or matrix for the surface plot.

5. Press [**Enter**] or click outside the plot. You see two contour plots.

6. Double-click the graph to bring up the 3D Plot Format dialog box. In the Display As section of the General tab, click the tab labeled Plot 2 and select Surface from the array of plot types. Click "OK."

Both the contour plot and the surface plot, with default format settings, appear in a single graph.

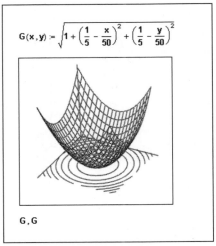

$$G(x,y) := \sqrt{1 + \left(\frac{1}{5} - \frac{x}{50}\right)^2 + \left(\frac{1}{5} - \frac{y}{50}\right)^2}$$

G,G

Figure 13-7: Two plots, one contour and one surface, shown on the same graph.

Tip   As a general rule, you will not want to create a 3D graph with more than two or three plots together since they may obscure each other and make the graph difficult to interpret.

Formatting a 3D Plot

A three-dimensional plot's default appearance depends on how you insert it. When you choose **Graph⇒3D Plot Wizard** from the **Insert** menu, you make selections in the pages of the Wizard that determine a plot's appearance. When you insert a plot by choosing a plot type from the **Insert** menu, however, the plot automatically acquires default characteristics.

You can change the appearance of any 3D plot after it is inserted. To do so, you use the many options available in the 3D Plot Format dialog box. For example, you can use the options to change a plot's color, format the axes, add backplanes, and format the lines or points.

To bring up the 3D Plot Format dialog box:

1. Click once on the plot to select it and choose **Graph⇒3D Plot** from the **Format** menu. Alternatively, double-click the plot itself. Mathcad brings up the 3D Plot Format dialog box. The General page is shown at right. The remaining tabs take you to additional pages.

2. Click the tab for the page you want to work with.

3. Make the appropriate changes in the dialog box.

4. Click Apply to see the effect of your changes *without* closing the dialog box.

5. Close the dialog by clicking OK.

The 3D Plot Format Dialog Box

The tabs in the 3D Plot Format dialog box bring you to pages containing options for formatting various aspects of a three-dimensional plot. Some options available on certain pages in the dialog box depend on the kind of plot you are formatting. Options on other pages are available for any three-dimensional graph.

- The **General** page gives you access to basic options that control the overall appearance of the graph. Use these options to control the position of a plot, set the axis style, draw a border or a box, or convert a plot to another type.

- The options on the **Axes** page allow you to control exactly how each axis looks. You can specify the weight of each axis and whether it has numbers or tick marks. You can also specify the axis limits. Use the tabs at the top of the page to format the *x*-, *y*-, or *z*-axis.

- The **Backplanes** page has options for specifying whether a backplane is filled with a color, has a border, or has grid lines or tick marks. Use the tabs at the top of the page to format the *xy*-, *yz*-, or *xz*-backplane.

Note Both the Backplanes page and the Axes page have options for setting and formatting grid lines. When you set the grid lines for an axis on the Axes tab, you set them for the two backplanes shared by the axis. When you set the grid lines on the Backplanes tab, you set them for one backplane only.

- Use the options on the **Appearance** page to format the surfaces, lines, and points that make up a plot. For example, you can apply color directly to a plot's surface, its contours, or its lines and points. The following sections discuss how to control the surfaces, lines, and points of a plot.

- The **Lighting** page options control both the overall lighting of the plot as well as individual lights directed onto it. See "Lighting" on page 253 for more information on lighting.

- The **Title** page provides a text box for entering a title for the graph and options for specifying the location of the title on the graph.

- The **Special** page allows you to control options related to specific kinds of plots. For example, the Bar Plot Layout options let you specify the way the bars are arranged in a 3D bar plot.

- The **Advanced** page has options used only when you need very fine control over the appearance of a plot, such as the vertical scale.

- The **QuickPlot Data** page contains the range and grid settings for the independent variables that control a 3D QuickPlot. Additionally, you can specify whether your function(s) are in Cartesian, spherical, or cylindrical coordinates.

On-line Help   For details on the options available on a particular page in the 3D Plot Format dialog box, click the Help button at the bottom of the dialog box.

Some options in the 3D Plot Format dialog box work together to control the appearance of a plot. For example, the choices on the Appearance page, the Lighting page, and the Special and Advanced pages together control the color of a plot.

Note   When you format a graph containing more than one plot (using Mathcad Professional), as described in "Graphing Multiple 3D Plots" on page 245, some options in the 3D Plot Format dialog box apply to an entire graph while others apply to individual plots. For example, all the options on the Axes, Backplanes, and Lighting pages are for the graph as a whole: each plot on the graph uses common axes, backplanes, and lighting. However, options on the Appearance tab are specific to each plot on the graph. That is, each plot can be filled with its own color, have its own lines drawn, etc. The tabs labeled Plot 1, Plot 2, etc. control the settings for individual plots.

Fill Color

The color of a plot is primarily determined by its fill color. This section describes the ways to apply color to a plot by filling its surfaces or contours. A plot's color and shading are also affected by *lighting*, as described in more detail in page 253.

Mathcad allows you to apply either a solid color or a colormap to the surface or contours of a plot. A solid color is useful when you don't want to overcomplicate a plot with many colors or when you want to use lighting to shade a plot. A colormap applies an array of color to a plot according to its coordinates.

Note Mathcad comes with a variety of colormaps for applying rainbow colors and shades of gray, red, green, and blue. You can also create and load custom colormaps in Mathcad Professional by using the *SaveColormap* and *LoadColormap* functions, described on page 202. By default, a colormap is applied in the direction of the *z*-values, or according to the height of the plot. You can apply the colormap in the direction of the *x*-values or *y*-values by clicking the Advanced tab and choosing a direction in the Colormap section. For more information, see on-line Help.

Filling the Surface

The options on the Appearance page of the 3D Plot Format dialog box allow you to fill the plot's surface with a solid color or a colormap. For example, to color the bars in a 3D bar plot according to a colormap:

1. Double-click the graph to bring up the 3D Plot Format dialog box.

2. Click the Appearance tab.

3. Click both Fill Surface in Fill Options and Colormap in Color Options.

4. Click Apply to preview the plot. Click OK to close the dialog box.

Figure 13-8 shows an example.

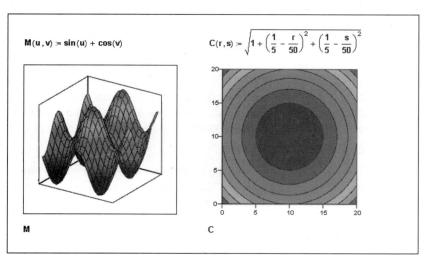

Figure 13-8: Filling the surface or contours of a plot.

The plot is shaded using the default colormap "Rainbow." To choose a different colormap, click the Advanced tab of the 3D Plot Format dialog box and select a colormap from the Choose Colormap drop-down menu.

If you wanted to fill the bars of the plot with a solid color, choose Solid Color instead of Colormap and click the color box next to Solid Color to select a color.

Filling Contours

When you format a surface plot, you can choose Fill Contours instead of Fill Surface in the Fill Options section of the Appearance page. If you fill the contours of a surface plot, the plot is filled according to its contours rather than directly by its data. You can fill according to the x-, y-, or z-contours or two at the same time. For a contour plot, you must choose Fill Contours instead of Fill Surface to fill the contours of the plot.

For example, to fill a contour plot with color:

1. Double-click the graph to bring up the tabbed dialog box.

2. Click the Appearance tab.

3. In the Fill Options section, click Fill Contours.

4. Click Apply to preview the plot. Click OK to close the dialog box.

The plot is shaded using the default colormap Rainbow. To choose a different colormap, click the Advanced tab of the 3D Plot Format dialog box and select a colormap from the Choose Colormap drop-down menu.

Note   If you have a contour plot projected on a plane other than the x-y plane, you can fill the contour using options on the Special page of the 3D Plot Format dialog box. To do so, click the Special tab, then choose a contour direction from the drop-down menu. Click Fill for each contour you want to color. For example, if you have Fill checked for the z-contours and x-contours, you will see contour color on both the x-y backplane and the y-z backplane.

Lines

Mathcad provides many ways to control the appearance of the lines on a three-dimensional plot. You can draw the lines so they form a wireframe, or you can draw only the contour lines. You can also control the weight and color of the lines on a plot.

Drawing a Wireframe

To control whether lines form a wireframe on a plot, use the options on the Appearance page of the 3D Plot Format dialog box. For example, to remove the wireframe on a surface plot as shown in Figure 13-9:

1. Double-click the graph to bring up the tabbed dialog box.

2. Click the Appearance tab.

3. In the Line Options section, click No Lines.

4. Click Apply to preview the plot. Click OK to close the dialog box.

To turn lines on again later, choose Wireframe on the Appearance page.

Drawing Contour Lines

When you format a surface plot, you can choose Contour instead of Wireframe in the Line Options section of the Appearance page. Contour lines are those drawn according to the contours of a surface. You can draw either the *x*-, *y*-, or *z*- contour lines, two of these contours lines, or all three.

Note	For contour plots, Mathcad always chooses Contour instead of Wireframe to draw contour lines.

For example, to draw lines showing the *x*-contours of a surface plot:

1. Double-click the graph to bring up the tabbed dialog box.
2. Click the Appearance tab.
3. Click Contour in the Line Options section.
4. Click the Special tab.
5. Verify that Z-Contours is selected in the drop-down menu at the bottom of the Contour Options section. Click Draw Lines to remove the check mark. This turns lines off for the *z*-contours.
6. Choose Z-Contours from the drop-down menu on the Special page.
7. Check Draw Lines.
8. Click Apply to preview the plot. Click OK to close the dialog box.

The surface plot is drawn with contour lines perpendicular to the *z*-axis, as shown in Figure 13-9.

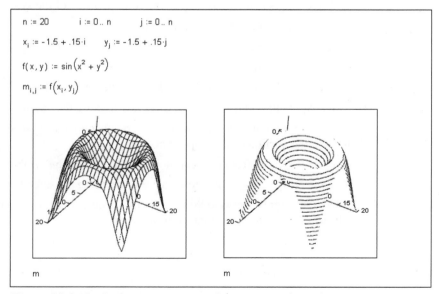

$$n := 20 \qquad i := 0..n \qquad j := 0..n$$

$$x_i := -1.5 + .15 \cdot i \qquad y_j := -1.5 + .15 \cdot j$$

$$f(x, y) := \sin\left(x^2 + y^2\right)$$

$$m_{i,j} := f\left(x_i, y_j\right)$$

Figure 13-9: A wireframe vs. contour lines on a surface plot.

Note When you format a contour plot on a multi-plot graph (see page 236), the options in the drop-down menu on the Special tab determine on which backplane the contour lines are drawn. For example, if you have Draw Lines checked for the z-contours and x-contours, you will see contour lines on both the x-y backplane and the y-z backplane.

Line Color

You can control the color of the lines in a plot using the color options in the Line Options section of the Appearance page. Just as you can fill a plot's surface with a colormap or a solid color, described on page 249, you can also apply a colormap or solid color to the lines in a plot.

For example, to make the lines of a contour plot orange:

1. Double-click the graph to bring up the tabbed dialog box.
2. Click the Appearance tab.
3. In the Line Options section, click Contour to draw contour lines and Solid Color.
4. Click the color box next to Solid Color, click the orange box, and click OK.
5. Click Apply to preview the plot. Click OK to close the dialog box.

Points

You can draw and format points on most three-dimensional plots, since all 3D plots are constructed from discrete data points. (The exceptions are vector field plots, contour plots, bar plots, and patch plots.) Points are most useful, however, on a 3D scatter plot in which points are the main focus of the plot. Mathcad allows you to control the symbol used for the points in a plot as well as the color and size of the symbol.

To draw or remove points on a surface plot:

1. Double-click the graph to bring up the 3D Plot Format dialog box.
2. Click the Appearance tab.
3. In the Points Options section, check (or uncheck) Draw Points.
4. Click Apply to preview the plot. Click OK to close the dialog box.

To format the symbol, color, and size of the points on your 3D scatter plot using the Points Options section of the Appearance tab:

- Choose a Symbol from the drop-down list to change the symbol displayed.
- Use the arrows next to Size to increase or decrease the size of the symbol.
- Click the color box next to Solid Color and choose a hue from the color palette, or click Colormap to change the coloring of the symbols.

Lighting

The color of a three-dimensional plot is a result of color you use to fill its surface, lines, and points as well as the color of any ambient light or directed lights shining on it. This behavior is identical to the effect of light on object color in the real world. Objects reflect and absorb light depending on their color. For example, a yellow ball reflects mostly yellow light and absorbs others, and it can look grayish under dim lighting, green under blue lighting, and bright yellow in bright lighting.

You can fill a plot's surfaces, contours, lines, and points with either a solid color or a colormap using the options on the Appearance and Advanced pages of the 3D Plot Format dialog box.

Light is controlled using the options on the Lighting page of the 3D Plot Format dialog box. If you are content to fill a plot with a colormap, you may not need to use lighting at all. However, if you want to shade the plot differently, or if you fill the plot with a solid color and want to shade it, you can enable lighting.

Note If your 3D graph contains multiple plots, lighting affects all the plots in a graph, but you can fill individual plots with color independently.

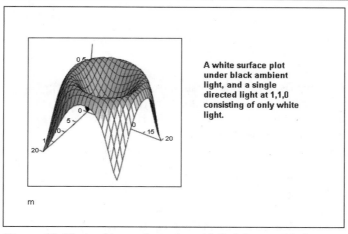

A white surface plot under black ambient light, and a single directed light at 1,1,0 consisting of only white light.

Figure 13-10: A white surface plot with lighting enabled.

Note If you want lighting to be the sole determinant of the color of a plot, use the Appearance page options in the 3D Plot Format dialog box to fill the plot with solid white.

To enable lighting:

1. Double-click the plot to open the tabbed dialog box.
2. Click the Lighting tab.
3. Check Enable Lighting in the Lighting section.

4. Click the options on tabs labeled Light 1, Light 2, etc. to enable a directed light and set its color and location. Mathcad lets you set up to eight directed lights.

5. Click the Ambient Light Color box to set the ambient light color. Note that black corresponds to no ambient light.

6. Click Apply to preview the plot. Click OK to close the dialog box.

On-line Help   For details on the options available on the Lighting page, click the Help button at the bottom of the dialog box. For additional information on lighting, see "Advanced Topics" under Overview and Tutorial in the Mathcad Resource Center.

Changing One 3D Plot to Another

You can change almost any three-dimensional plot into another kind of three-dimensional plot by using the Display As options on the General tab in the 3D Plot Format dialog box. Simply select another available 3D plot type and click Apply or OK to change the plot instantaneously to another type. Figure 13-11 shows the same matrix displayed as three different plot types.

Note   Some three-dimensional plots cannot be converted to other forms. For example, you cannot convert a vector field plot into any other kind of plot. If a plot cannot be converted to another kind of plot, that plot type is grayed in the 3D Plot Format dialog box.

Annotations

In addition to adding a title to your three-dimensional plot by using options on the Title page of the 3D Plot Format dialog box, you can annotate a three-dimensional plot by placing text or bitmaps anywhere on it. This allows you to label or highlight any part of the plot that you wish.

To add a text annotation to a three-dimensional plot:

1. Create a text region in your worksheet using the methods described in Chapter 5, "Working with Text."

2. Drag the text region from its location in your worksheet and drop it directly onto the plot. See "Moving and Copying Regions" on page 10 for more on dragging and dropping regions.

You can select the text annotation on your plot to reposition it. To edit a text annotation on a plot, select the text and drag it off the plot to your worksheet. You can now edit the text region. Then drag the text region back onto the plot.

Tip   You can drag a bitmap image from your Mathcad worksheet onto a three-dimensional plot just as you drag and drop text annotations. To place a bitmap you created in another application onto a three-dimensional plot, copy the bitmap from the other application to the Clipboard, click on the plot with the right mouse button, and choose **Paste Special** from the pop-up menu.

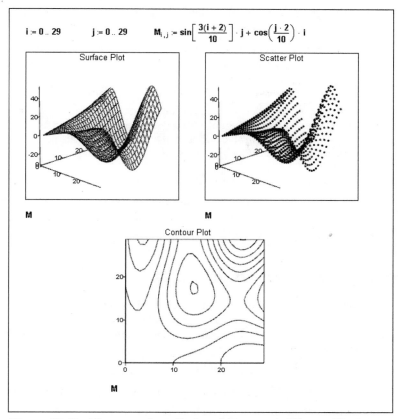

$$i := 0 \ldots 29 \qquad j := 0 \ldots 29 \qquad M_{i,j} := \sin\left[\frac{3(i+2)}{10}\right] \cdot j + \cos\left(\frac{j \cdot 2}{10}\right) \cdot i$$

Figure 13-11: The same data displayed in several different 3D plots.

Modifying 3D QuickPlot Data

When you create a 3D QuickPlot, as described on page 236, you can change the range and step size of each independent variable by using the settings on the QuickPlot Data page of the 3D Plot Format dialog box.

To change the range of either independent variable:

1. Set the start and end values of either range using the text boxes for each range.

2. Click Apply to keep the dialog box open. Click OK to close the dialog box.

To change the step size, the number of grids generated along each variable's axis between the start and end values:

1. Use the arrows next to # of Grids for each range to increase or decrease the grid value. Alternatively, you can type in a value in the text box.

2. Click Apply to keep the dialog box open. Click OK to close the dialog box.

Note The ranges you set for the independent variables in the QuickPlot Data page do not necessarily control the axis limits of the plot, unless you are plotting a single function of two variables in Cartesian coordinates. In all other cases, the axis limits are determined by the x-, y-, and z-data generated for the QuickPlot by your function(s).

To perform automatic coordinate system conversions on your QuickPlot data:

1. Click the radio button under Coordinate System corresponding the coordinate system of the function you are plotting.

2. Click Apply to keep the dialog box open. Click OK to close the dialog box.

Rotating and Zooming on 3D Plots

You can resize a three-dimensional plot using the same methods you use to resize any graph region in Mathcad. Click on it and use the handles that appear along the edges to drag out the edges. Mathcad provides several additional options for manipulating the presentation of your 3D plot:

- You can rotate the plot to see it from a different perspective.

- You can set the plot in motion about an axis of rotation so that it spins continuously.

- You can zoom in or out on a portion of the plot.

Note When you rotate, spin, or zoom a three-dimensional plot, any visible axes move or resize themselves with the plot. Text or graphic annotations you add to the plot (see page 254) remain anchored at their original sizes and positions.

Rotating a Plot

You can rotate a plot interactively with the mouse or by specifying parameters in the 3D Plot Format dialog box.

To rotate a three-dimensional plot interactively by using the mouse:

1. Click in the plot, and hold the mouse button down.

2. Drag the mouse in the direction you want the plot to turn.

3. Release the mouse button when the plot is in the desired position.

To rotate a three-dimensional plot by using the 3D Plot Format dialog box:

1. Click once on the plot to select it and choose **Graph⇒3D Plot** from the **Format** menu. Alternatively, double-click the plot.

2. Click the General tab.

3. Edit the settings for Rotation, Tilt, and Twist in the View options.

4. Click Apply to preview the plot. Click OK to close the dialog box.

Spinning a Plot

You can set a plot in motion so that it spins continuously about an axis of rotation:

1. Click in the plot, and hold the [**Shift**] key and the mouse button down.

2. Drag the mouse in the direction you want the plot to spin.

3. Release the mouse button to set the plot in motion.

The plot spins continuously until you click again inside the plot.

Note   If you make changes to equations that affect a plot, the plot recomputes even when it is spinning!

Tip   To create an AVI file of a spinning plot, see the techniques in "Animation" on page 124.

Zooming a Plot

You can zoom in or out of a plot interactively or by specifying a zoom factor in the 3D Plot Format dialog box.

To zoom in on a three-dimensional plot by using the mouse:

1. Click in the plot, and hold the [**Ctrl**] key and the mouse button down.

2. Drag the mouse toward the top of the plot to zoom out, or drag the mouse toward the bottom to zoom in.

3. Release the mouse button when the plot is at the desired zoom factor.

Tip   If you use an IntelliMouse-compatible mouse with a center wheel, you can rotate the wheel to zoom in or out of a three-dimensional plot.

To zoom in or out of a three-dimensional plot by using the 3D Plot Format dialog box:

1. Click once on the plot to select it and choose **Graph⇒3D Plot** from the **Format** menu. Alternatively, double-click the plot.

2. Click the General tab.

3. Edit the Zoom setting in the View options.

4. Click Apply to preview the plot. Click OK to close the dialog box.

Chapter 14
Symbolic Calculation

♦ Overview of Symbolic Math

♦ Live Symbolic Evaluation

♦ Using the Symbolics Menu

♦ Examples of Symbolic Calculation

♦ Symbolic Optimization

Overview of Symbolic Math

Elsewhere in this *User's Guide*, you've seen Mathcad engaging in *numeric* calculations. This means that whenever you evaluate an expression, Mathcad returns one or more *numbers*, as shown at the top of Figure 14-1. When Mathcad engages in *symbolic* mathematics, however, the result of evaluating an expression is generally another expression, as shown in the bottom of Figure 14-1.

A numerical calculation gives nothing but numbers:

$$F(x) := \sum_{k=0}^{3} \frac{3!}{k! \cdot (3-k)!} \cdot x^k \cdot 2^{3-k}$$

$$F(2) = 64$$

$$F(-5) = -27$$

But a symbolic transformation can yield insight into the underlying expression:

$$F(x) \rightarrow 8 + 12 \cdot x + 6 \cdot x^2 + x^3$$

Figure 14-1: A numeric and symbolic evaluation of the same expression.

There are three ways to perform a symbolic transformation on an expression.

- You can use the symbolic equal sign as described in "Live Symbolic Evaluation" on page 260. This method feels very much as if you're engaging in numeric math. If you need more control over the symbolic transformation, you can use *keywords* with the symbolic equal sign.

- You can use commands from the **Symbolics** menu. See "Using the Symbolics Menu" on page 269.

- You can make the numeric and symbolic processors work together, the latter simplifying an expression behind the scenes so that the former can work with it more efficiently. This is discussed in "Symbolic Optimization" on page 280.

Note For a computer, symbolic operations are, in general, much more difficult than the corresponding numeric operations. In fact, many complicated functions and deceptively simple-looking functions have no closed-forms as integrals or roots.

Live Symbolic Evaluation

The symbolic equal sign provides a way to extend Mathcad's live document interface beyond the numeric evaluation of expressions. You can think of it as being analogous to the equal sign "=." Unlike the equal sign, which always gives a numeric result on the right-hand side, the symbolic equal sign is capable of returning *expressions*. You can use it to symbolically evaluate expressions, variables, functions, or programs.

To use the symbolic equal sign:

1. Make sure that **Automatic Calculation** on the **Math** menu has a check beside it. If it doesn't, choose it from the menu.

2. Enter the expression you want to evaluate.

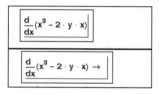

3. Click [→] on the Symbolic toolbar or press [**Ctrl**]. (the Control key followed by a period). Mathcad displays a symbolic equal sign, "→."

4. Click outside the expression. Mathcad displays a simplified version of the original expression. If an expression cannot be simplified further, Mathcad simply repeats it to the right of the symbolic equal sign.

The symbolic equal sign is a live operator just like any Mathcad operator. When you make a change anywhere above or to the left of it, Mathcad updates the result. The symbolic equal sign "knows" about previously defined functions and variables and uses them wherever appropriate. You can force the symbolic equal sign to ignore prior definitions of functions and variables by defining them recursively just before you evaluate them, as shown in Figure 14-6 on page 269.

Figure 14-2 shows some examples of how to use the symbolic equal sign, "→."

Figure 14-2: Using the symbolic equal sign.

Note The symbolic equal sign, "→," applies to an entire expression. You cannot use the symbolic equal sign to transform only part of an expression.

Tip Figure 14-2 also illustrates the fact that the symbolic processor treats numbers containing a decimal point differently from numbers without a decimal point. When you send numbers with decimal points to the symbolic processor, any numeric results you get back are decimal approximations to the exact answer. Otherwise, any numeric results you get back are expressed without decimal points whenever possible.

Customizing the Symbolic Equal Sign Using Keywords

The "→" takes the left-hand side and places a simplified version of it on the right-hand side. Of course, exactly what "simplify" means is a matter of opinion. You can, to a limited extent, control how the "→" transforms the expression by using one of the *symbolic keywords*.

To do so:

1. Enter the expression you want to evaluate.

2. Click on the Symbolic toolbar or press **[Ctrl]**
   [Shift]. (Press the Control and Shift keys and type a
   period.) Mathcad displays a placeholder to the left of the symbolic equal sign, "→."

3. Click on the placeholder to the left of the symbolic equal sign
   and type any of the keywords from the following table. If the
   keyword requires any additional arguments, separate the
   arguments from the keyword with commas.

   $$(x + y)^3 \text{ expand } \rightarrow$$

4. Press **[Enter]** to see the result.

   $$(x + y)^3 \text{ expand } \rightarrow x^3 + 3 \cdot x^2 \cdot y + 3 \cdot x \cdot y^2 + y^3$$

Tip Another way to use a keyword is to enter the expression you want to evaluate and click on a keyword button from the Symbolic toolbar. This inserts the keyword, placeholders for any additional arguments, and the symbolic equal sign, "→." Just press **[Enter]** to see the result.

Keyword	Function
complex	Carries out symbolic evaluation in the complex domain. Result is usually in the form $a + i \cdot b$.
float,m	Displays a floating point value with m places of precision whenever possible. If the argument m, an integer, is omitted, the precision is 20. $1 \leq m \leq 250$
simplify	Simplifies an expression by performing arithmetic, canceling common factors, and using basic trigonometric and inverse function identities.
expand,expr	Expands all powers and products of sums in an expression except for the subexpression *expr*. The argument *expr* is optional. The entire expression is expanded if the argument *expr* is omitted.
	If the expression is a fraction, expands the numerator and writes the expression as a sum of fractions. Expands sines, cosines, and tangents of sums of variables or integer multiples of variables as far as possible into expressions involving only sines and cosines of single variables.

Keyword	Function
factor, *expr*	Factors an expression into a product, if the entire expression can be written as a product. Factors with respect to *expr*, a single radical or a list of radicals separated by commas. The argument *expr* is optional.
	Usually factors a single variable into powers of primes. Otherwise, attempts to convert the expression into a product of simpler functions. Combines a sum of fractions into a single fraction and often simplifies a complex fraction with more than one fraction bar.
solve, *var*	Solves an equation for the variable *var* or solves a system of equations for the variables in a vector *var*.
collect, *var1,...,varn*	Collects like terms with respect to the variables or subexpressions *var1* through *varn*.
coeffs, *var*	Finds coefficients of an expression when it is rewritten as a polynomial in the variable or subexpression *var*.
substitute, *var1=var2*	Replaces all occurrences of a variable *var1* with an expression or variable *var2*. Press **[Ctrl]**= for the bold equal sign.
series, *var=z,m*	Expands an expression in one or more variables, *var*, around the point z. The order of expansion is m. Arguments z and m are optional. By default, the expansion is taken around zero and is a polynomial of order six. By default, finds Taylor series (series in nonnegative powers of the variable) for functions that are analytic at 0 and Laurent series for functions that have a pole of finite order at 0.
convert, **parfrac,** *var*	Converts an expression to a partial fraction expansion in *var,* the variable in the denominator of the expression on which to convert. Usually factors the denominator of the expression into linear or quadratic factors having integer coefficients and expands the expression into a sum of fractions with these factors as denominators.
fourier, *var*	Evaluates the Fourier transform of an expression with respect to the variable *var*. Result is a function of ω given by:
	$$\int_{-\infty}^{+\infty} f(t)e^{-i\omega t}dt$$
	where $f(t)$ is the expression to be transformed.
invfourier, *var*	Evaluates the inverse Fourier transform of an expression with respect to the variable *var*. Result is a function of t given by:
	$$\frac{1}{2\pi}\int_{-\infty}^{+\infty} F(\omega)e^{i\omega t}d\omega$$
	where $F(\omega)$ is the expression to be transformed.

laplace, var	Evaluates the Laplace transform of an expression with respect to the variable *var*. Result is a function of *s* given by:

$$\int_0^{+\infty} f(t)e^{-st}dt$$

where $f(t)$ is the expression to be transformed. |
| **invlaplace, var** | Evaluates the inverse Laplace transform of an expression with respect to the variable *var*. Result is a function of *t* given by:

$$\frac{1}{2\pi i}\int_{\sigma-i\infty}^{\sigma+i\infty} F(s)e^{st}dt$$

where $F(s)$ is the expression to be transformed and all singularities of $F(s)$ are to the left of the line $\mathrm{Re}(s) = \sigma$. |
| **ztrans, var** | Evaluates the *z*-transform of an expression with respect to the variable *var*. Result is a function of *z* given by:

$$\sum_{n=0}^{+\infty} f(n)z^{-n}$$

where $f(n)$ is the expression to be transformed. |
| **invztrans, var** | Evaluates the inverse *z*-transform of an expression with respect to the variable *var*. Result is a function of *n* given by a contour integral around the origin:

$$\frac{1}{2\pi i}\int_C F(z)z^{n-1}dz$$

where $F(z)$ is the expression to be transformed and C is a contour enclosing all singularities of the integrand. |
| **assume constraint** | Imposes constraints on one or more variables according to the expression *constraint*. |

Many of the keywords take at least one additional argument, typically the name of a variable with respect to which you are performing the symbolic operation. Some of the arguments are optional. See Figure 14-3 and Figure 14-4 for examples.

Note Keywords are case sensitive and must therefore be typed exactly as shown. Unlike variables, however, they are not font sensitive.

By itself, the symbolic equal sign simply evaluates the expression to the left of it and places it on the right:

$$\frac{d}{dx}(x + y)^3 \rightarrow 3 \cdot (x + y)^2$$

But when preceded by an appropriate keyword, the symbolic equal can change its meaning:

$$(x + y)^3 \text{ expand } \rightarrow x^3 + 3 \cdot x^2 \cdot y + 3 \cdot x \cdot y^2 + y^3$$

The keyword "float" makes the result display as a floating point number whenever possible:

$$x \cdot \text{acos}(0) \rightarrow \frac{1}{2} \cdot x \cdot \pi \qquad\qquad x \cdot \text{acos}(0) \text{ float}, 4 \rightarrow 1.571 \cdot x$$

The keyword "laplace" returns the Laplace transform of a function:

$$\exp(-a \cdot t) \text{ laplace}, t \rightarrow \frac{1}{(s + a)}$$

Figure 14-3: Using keywords with a symbolic evaluation sign.

Symbolic evaluation   Complex evaluation

$$\int_0^\infty e^{-x^2} dx \rightarrow \frac{1}{2} \cdot \pi^{\frac{1}{2}} \qquad e^{i \cdot n \cdot \theta} \text{ complex } \rightarrow \cos(n \cdot \theta) + i \cdot \sin(n \cdot \theta)$$

Floating point evaluation

$$\int_0^\infty e^{-x^2} dx \text{ float}, 10 \rightarrow .8862269255$$

Constrained evaluation

$$x \cdot \int_0^\infty e^{-\alpha \cdot t} dt \text{ assume}, \alpha > 1 \rightarrow \frac{x}{\alpha} \qquad (\text{``}\alpha\text{'' is constrained to be greater than 1})$$

Figure 14-4: Evaluating expressions symbolically.

Keyword modifiers

Some keywords take additional modifiers that specify the kind of symbolic evaluation even further.

To use a modifier, separate it from its keyword with a comma. For example, to use the "assume=real" modifier with the **simplify** keyword on an expression:

1. Enter the expression to simplify.

2. Click [■→] on the Symbolic toolbar or press **[Ctrl] [Shift].** (hold down the Control and Shift keys and type a period). Mathcad displays a placeholder to the left of the symbolic equal sign, "→."

3. Enter **simplify,assume=real** into the placeholder (press **[Ctrl]=** for the equal sign).

4. Press **[Enter]** to see the result.

Modifiers for "assume"

var=real
Evaluates the expression on the assumption that the variable *var* is real.

var= RealRange(a,b)
Evaluates on the assumption that all the indeterminates are real and are between *a* and *b*, where *a* and *b* are real numbers or infinity (**[Ctrl][Shift]z**).

Modifiers for "simplify"

assume=real
Simplifies on the assumption that all the indeterminates in the expression are real.

assume= RealRange(a,b)
Simplifies on the assumption that all the indeterminates are real and are between *a* and *b*, where *a* and *b* are real numbers or infinity (**[Ctrl][Shift]z**).

trig
Simplifies a trigonometric expression by applying only the following identities:

$$\sin(x)^2 + \cos(x)^2 = 1$$

$$\cosh(x)^2 - \sinh(x)^2 = 1$$

It does not simplify the expression by simplifying logs, powers, or radicals.

Figure 14-5 shows some examples using the **simplify** keyword with and without additional modifiers.

Tip Keyword modifiers can be typed or inserted from the buttons on the Modifier toolbar.

$$\frac{x^2 - 3 \cdot x - 4}{x - 4} + 2 \cdot x - 5 \; \text{simplify} \; \rightarrow 3 \cdot x - 4$$

$$e^{2 \ln(a)} \; \text{simplify} \; \rightarrow a^2$$

$$\sin(\ln(a \cdot b))^2 \; \text{simplify} \; \rightarrow 1 - \cos(\ln(a \cdot b))^2$$

$$\left(2^b\right)^c \; \text{simplify} \; \rightarrow \left(2^b\right)^c$$

$$\left(2^b\right)^c \; \text{simplify, assume} = \text{real} \; \rightarrow 2^{(b \cdot c)} \quad \text{<-- Press [Ctrl] = for the equal sign.}$$

$$\sqrt{x^2} \; \text{simplify} \; \rightarrow \text{csgn}(x) \cdot x$$

$$\sqrt{x^2} \; \text{simplify, assume} = \text{RealRange}(-10, -5) \; \rightarrow -x \quad \text{<-- Press [Ctrl] = for the equal sign.}$$

Figure 14-5: Modifiers such as "assume=real" allow you to control simplification.

Using More Than One Keyword

In some cases, you may want to perform two or more types of symbolic evaluation consecutively on an expression. Mathcad allows you to apply several symbolic keywords to a single expression. There are two ways of applying multiple keywords. The method you choose depends on whether you want to see the results from each keyword or only the final result.

To apply several keywords and see the results from each:

1. Enter the expression you want to evaluate.

2. Press $\boxed{\blacksquare \rightarrow}$ on the Symbolic toolbar or type [**Ctrl**] [**Shift**] **.** (Hold down the Control and Shift keys and type a period.) Mathcad displays a placeholder to the left of the symbolic equal sign, "→."

3. Enter the first keyword into the placeholder to the left of the symbolic equal sign, including any comma-delimited arguments the keyword takes.

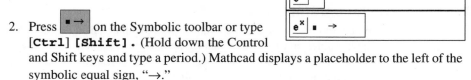

4. Press [**Enter**] to see the result from the first keyword.

5. Click on the result and press **[Ctrl]**
[Shift]. again. The first result disappears
temporarily. Enter a second keyword and any
modifiers into the placeholder.

$$e^x \;\; \text{series}, x, 3 \;\; \rightarrow \text{float}, 1| \rightarrow$$

6. Press **[Enter]** to see
the result from the
second keyword.

$$e^x \;\; \text{series}, x, 3 \;\; \rightarrow \;\; 1 + x + \frac{1}{2} \cdot x^2 \;\; \text{float}, 1 \;\; \rightarrow \;\; 1. + x + .5 \cdot x^2$$

Continue applying keywords to the intermediate results in this manner.

To apply several keywords and see only the final result:

1. Enter the expression you want to evaluate.

$$e^x|$$

2. Click [■→] on the Symbolic toolbar or press
[Ctrl] [Shift]. so that Mathcad displays a
placeholder to the left of the symbolic equal sign, "→."

$$e^x \; ■ \; \rightarrow$$

3. Enter the first keyword into the placeholder,
including any comma-delimited arguments it
takes.

$$e^x \; \text{series}, x, 3| \; \rightarrow$$

4. Press **[Ctrl] [Shift]**. again and enter a
second keyword into the placeholder. The
second keyword is placed immediately below
the first keyword.

$$e^x \; \begin{vmatrix} \text{series}, x, 3 \\ \text{float}, 1| \end{vmatrix} \rightarrow$$

5. Continue adding keywords by pressing **[Ctrl]**
[Shift]. after each one. Press **[Enter]** to
see the final result.

$$e^x \; \begin{vmatrix} \text{series}, x, 3 \\ \text{float}, 1 \end{vmatrix} \rightarrow 1. + x + .5 \cdot x^2$$

Ignoring Previous Definitions

When you use the symbolic equal sign to evaluate an expression, Mathcad checks all
the variables and functions making up that expression to see if they've been defined
earlier in the worksheet. If Mathcad does find a definition, it uses it. Any other variables
and functions are evaluated symbolically.

There are two exceptions to this. In evaluating an expression made up of previously
defined variables and functions, Mathcad *ignores* prior definitions:

- When the variable has been defined recursively.

- When the variable has been defined as a range variable.

These exceptions are illustrated in Figure 14-6.

Note Although Mathcad does not evaluate range variables symbolically, it does symbolically evaluate
any vectors or matrices that you define using range variables.

```
x := 3

(x + 1)·(z - 1) expand  → 4·z - 4    ◄─── Mathcad substitutes the value of 3 for
                                          "x" before evaluating this expression.


x := x    ◄─── recursive definition.

(x + 1)·(x - 1) expand  → x² - 1      ◄─── Although "x" is defined to be 3, Mathcad
                                          ignores that definition for symbolic
                                          evaluation because of the recursive
                                          definition.


m := 1..10

m → m    ◄─── Since "m" is defined as a range variable, Mathcad ignores this
             definition.
```

Figure 14-6: Defining a variable in terms of itself makes the symbolic processor ignore previous definitions of that variable.

Using the Symbolics Menu

One advantage to using the symbolic equal sign, sometimes together with keywords and modifiers as discussed in the last section, is that it is "live," just like the numeric processing in Mathcad. That is, Mathcad checks all the variables and functions making up the expression being evaluated to see if they've been defined earlier in the worksheet. If Mathcad does find a definition, it uses it. Any other variables and functions are evaluated symbolically. Later on, whenever you make a change to the worksheet, the results automatically update. This is useful when the symbolic and numeric equations in the worksheet are tied together.

There may be times, however, when a symbolic calculation is quite separate from the rest of your worksheet and does not need to be tied to any previous definitions. In these cases, you can use commands from the **Symbolics** menu. These commands are not live: you apply them on a case by case basis to selected expressions, they do not "know" about previous definitions, and they do not automatically update.

The commands on the **Symbolics** menu perform the same manipulations as many of the keywords listed on page 261. For example, the **Symbolics** menu command **Polynomial Coefficients** evaluates an expression just as the keyword `coeffs` does. The only differences are that the menu command does not recognize previous definitions and does not automatically update.

The basic steps for using the **Symbolics** menu are the same for all the menu commands:

1. Place whatever math expression you want to evaluate *between the two editing lines*. You can drag-select a part of the expression to place it between the editing lines.

2. Choose the appropriate command from the **Symbolics** menu. Mathcad then places the evaluated expression into your document.

For example, to evaluate an expression symbolically using the **Symbolics** menu, follow these steps:

1. Enter the expression you want to evaluate.

2. Surround the expression with the editing lines.

3. Choose **Evaluate⇒Symbolically** from the **Symbolics** menu. Mathcad places the evaluated expression into your worksheet. The location of the result in relation to the original expression depends on the Evaluation Style you've selected (see "Displaying Symbolic Results" on page 270).

$$\frac{d}{dx}\left(x^3 - 2 \cdot y \cdot x\right)$$

$$\frac{d}{dx}\left(x^3 - 2 \cdot y \cdot x\right)$$

$$3 \cdot x^2 - 2 \cdot y$$

Some commands on the **Symbolics** menu require that you click on or select the variable of interest rather than select the entire expression. If a menu command is unavailable, try selecting a single variable rather than an entire expression.

Tip   Since the commands on the **Symbolics** menu operate only on the part of the expression currently selected by the editing lines, they are useful when you want to address parts of an expression. For example, if evaluating or simplifying the entire expression doesn't give the answer you want, try selecting a subexpression and choose a command from the **Symbolics** menu.

Long Results

Symbolic calculations can easily produce results so long that they don't fit conveniently in your window. If you obtain a symbolic result consisting of several terms by using commands on the **Symbolics** menu, you can reformat such a result by using Mathcad's "Addition with line break" operator (see "Operators" on page 447).

Sometimes, a symbolic result is so long that you can't conveniently display it in your worksheet. When this happens, Mathcad asks if you want the result placed in the Clipboard. If you click "OK," Mathcad places a string representing the result on the Clipboard. When you examine the contents of the clipboard, you'll see a result written in a Fortran-like syntax. See the topic "Special functions and syntax used in Symbolic results" in the on-line Help for more information on this syntax.

Displaying Symbolic Results

If you're using the symbolic equal sign, "→," the result of a symbolic transformation always goes to the right of the "→." However, when you use the **Symbolics** menu, you can tell Mathcad to place the symbolic results in one of the following ways:

• The symbolic result can go below the original expression.

• The symbolic result can go to the right of the original expression.

• The symbolic result can simply replace the original expression.

In addition, you can choose whether you want Mathcad to generate text describing what had to be done to get from the original expression to the symbolic result. This text goes between the original expression and the symbolic result, creating a narrative for the symbolic evaluation. These text regions are referred to as "evaluation comments."

To control both the placement of the symbolic result and the presence of narrative text, choose **Evaluation Style** from the **Symbolics** menu to bring up the "Evaluation Style" dialog box.

Examples of Symbolic Calculation

Just as you can carry out a variety of numeric calculations in Mathcad, you can carry out all kinds of symbolic calculations. As a general rule, any expression involving variables, functions, and operators can be evaluated symbolically using either the symbolic equal sign or the menu commands, as described earlier in this chapter.

Tip When deciding whether to use the symbolic equal sign or menu commands from the **Symbolics** menu, remember that unlike the keyword-modified expressions, expressions modified by commands from the **Symbolics** menu do not update automatically, as described in the section "Using the Symbolics Menu" on page 269.

This section describes how to symbolically evaluate definite and indefinite integrals, derivatives, and limits. It also covers how to symbolically transpose, invert, and find the determinant of a matrix. Finally, this section describes how to perform symbolic transforms and solve equations symbolically. Keep in mind that these are just a few of the calculations you can perform symbolically.

Note Functions and variables you define yourself are recognized by the symbolic processor when you use the symbolic equal sign. They are not, however, recognized when you use the **Symbolics** menu commands. Figure 14-7 shows the difference.

Derivatives

To evaluate a derivative symbolically, you can use Mathcad's derivative operator and the live symbolic equal sign as shown in Figure 14-8:

1. Click $\frac{d}{dx}$ on the Calculus toolbar or type **?** to insert the derivative operator.

    Alternatively, click $\frac{d^n}{dx^n}$ on the Calculus toolbar or type **[Ctrl]?** to insert the nth order derivative operator.

2. Enter the expression you want to differentiate and the variable with respect to which you are differentiating in the placeholders.

3. Click $\rightarrow$ on the Symbolic toolbar or press **[Ctrl].** (the Control key followed by a period). Mathcad displays a symbolic equal sign, "$\rightarrow$."

4. Press **[Enter]** to see the result.

Mathcad's symbolic processor recognizes many of its built-in math functions and constants....

$$e^{\ln(x)} \rightarrow x \qquad\qquad \sin\left(\frac{\pi}{4}\right) \rightarrow \frac{1}{2} \cdot \sqrt{2}$$

....but not the ones that don't have a commonly accepted meaning.

$$\text{rnd}(x) \rightarrow \text{rnd}(x)$$

Functions and variables you define yourself are recognized when you use the symbolic equal sign...

$$F(x) := \frac{\ln(x)}{2} \qquad\qquad a := 3$$

$$e^{F(x)} \rightarrow x^{\left(\frac{1}{2}\right)} \qquad\qquad a^2 \cdot \sin(a) \rightarrow 9 \cdot \sin(3)$$

....but not when you use commands from the Symbolics menu.

$$e^{F(x)} \qquad\qquad a^2 \cdot \sin(a)$$

simplifies to   simplifies to

$$\exp(F(x)) \qquad\qquad a^2 \cdot \sin(a)$$

Figure 14-7: The symbolic processor recognizes certain built-in functions. Functions and variables you define yourself are only recognized when you use the symbolic equal sign.

Some integrals evaluated symbolically using the symbolic equal sign ([Ctrl] + Period)

$$\int_1^c x^3 \, dx \rightarrow \frac{1}{4} \cdot c^4 - \frac{1}{4} \qquad \leftarrow \text{Press \& for definite integral}$$

$$\int_0^\infty e^{-x^2} \, dx \rightarrow \frac{1}{2} \cdot \pi^{\left(\frac{1}{2}\right)} \qquad \leftarrow \text{Press [Ctrl][Shift]Z for "}\infty\text{" in upper limit}$$

$$\int a \cdot x^2 \, dx \rightarrow \frac{1}{3} \cdot a \cdot x^3 \qquad \leftarrow \text{Press [Ctrl]i for indefinite integral}$$

A second derivative:

$$\frac{d^2}{dz^2} z \cdot \text{atan}(z) \rightarrow \frac{2}{\left(1 + z^2\right)} - 2 \cdot \frac{z^2}{\left(1 + z^2\right)^2} \qquad \begin{array}{l} \leftarrow \text{Press [Ctrl] ? to} \\ \text{get the nth derivative} \\ \text{operator.} \end{array}$$

Figure 14-8: Evaluating integrals and derivatives symbolically.

Figure 14-9 shows you how to differentiate an expression without using the derivative operator. The **Symbolics** menu command **Variable⇒Differentiate** differentiates an expression with respect to a selected variable. For example, to differentiate $2 \cdot x^2 + y$ with respect to x:

Click on "x" and choose Variable ⇒ Differentiate from the Symbolics menu.

$2 \cdot x^2 + y$ by differentiation, yields $4 \cdot x$

⇒

$\dfrac{x}{\cosh(x)}$ by differentiation, yields $\dfrac{1}{\cosh(x)} - \dfrac{x}{\cosh(x)^2} \cdot \sinh(x)$

Click on "x" and choose Variable ⇒ Integrate from the Symbolics menu.

$x^2 \cdot e^x$ by integration, yields $x^2 \cdot \exp(x) - 2 \cdot x \cdot \exp(x) + 2 \cdot \exp(x)$

$\dfrac{x + a}{x^2 + b}$ by integration, yields $\dfrac{1}{2} \cdot \ln(x^2 + b) + \dfrac{a}{b^{\left(\frac{1}{2}\right)}} \cdot \operatorname{atan}\left[\dfrac{x}{b^{\left(\frac{1}{2}\right)}}\right]$

Figure 14-9: Differentiating and integrating with menu commands.

1. Enter the expression.

2. Click on or select the x.

3. Choose **Variable⇒Differentiate** from the **Symbolics** menu. Mathcad displays the derivative, $4 \cdot x$. Note that y is treated as a constant.

If the expression in which you've selected a variable is one element of an array, Mathcad differentiates only that array element. To differentiate an entire array, differentiate each element individually: select a variable in that element and choose **Variable⇒Differentiate** from the **Symbolics** menu.

Tip   Be sure to select a variable in an expression before choosing from the **Symbolics** menu. Otherwise, the **Variable⇒Differentiate** menu command is not available.

Integrals

To symbolically evaluate a definite or indefinite integral:

1. Click $\int_a^b$ or $\int$ on the Calculus toolbar to insert the definite or indefinite integral operator.

2. Fill in the placeholder for the integrand and, if applicable, the placeholders for the limits of integration.

3. Place the integration variable in the placeholder next to the "d." This can be any variable name.

4. Click [→] on the Symbolic toolbar or press **[Ctrl].** (the Control key followed by a period). Mathcad displays a symbolic equal sign, "→."

5. Press **[Enter]** to see the result.

See Figure 14-8 for examples of integrals evaluated symbolically.

When evaluating a definite integral, the symbolic processor attempts to find an indefinite integral of your integrand before substituting the limits you specified. If the symbolic integration succeeds and the limits of integration are integers, fractions, or exact constants like π, you get an exact value for your integral. If the symbolic processor can't find a closed form for the integral, you'll see an appropriate error message.

Another way to integrate an expression indefinitely is to enter the expression and click on the variable of integration. Then choose **Variable⇒Integrate** from the **Symbolics** menu. See Figure 14-9 for an example. Be sure to select a variable in an expression before choosing from the **Symbolics** menu. Otherwise, the **Variable⇒Integrate** menu command is unavailable.

Tip   When you apply the **Variable⇒Integrate** command on the **Symbolics** menu, the expression you select should not usually include the integral operator. You should select only an expression to integrate. If you include the integral operator in the selected expression, you are taking a double integral.

Limits

Mathcad provides three limit operators. These can only be evaluated symbolically. To use the limit operators:

1. Click [lim →a] on the Calculus toolbar or press **[Ctrl]L** to insert the limit operator.

   To insert the operator for a limit from the left or right, click [lim →a⁻] or [lim →a⁺] on the Calculus toolbar or press **[Ctrl][Shift]B** or **[Ctrl][Shift]A**.

2. Enter the expression in the placeholder to the right of the "lim."

3. Enter the limiting variable in the left-hand placeholder below the "lim."

4. Enter the limiting value in the right-hand placeholder below the "lim."

5. Click [→] on the Symbolic toolbar or press **[Ctrl].** (the Control key followed by a period). Mathcad displays a symbolic equal sign, "→."

6. Press **[Enter]** to see the result.

Mathcad returns a result for the limit. If the limit does not exist, Mathcad returns an error message. Figure 14-10 shows some examples of evaluating limits.

Figure 14-10: Evaluating limits.

Solving an Equation for a Variable

To solve an equation symbolically for a variable, use the keyword **solve**:

1. Type the equation. Make sure you click $\boxed{=}$ on the Boolean toolbar or type [**Ctrl**]= to create the bold equal sign.

Note   When solving for the root of an expression, there is no need to set the expression equal to zero. See Figure 14-11 for an example.

2. Click $\boxed{\scriptsize ■ \to}$ on the Symbolic toolbar or type [**Ctrl**] [**Shift**] . (hold down the Control and Shift keys and type a period). Mathcad displays a placeholder to the left of the symbolic equal sign, "→."

3. Type **solve** in the placeholder, followed by a comma and the variable for which to solve.

4. Press [**Enter**] to see the result.

Mathcad solves for the variable and inserts the result to the right of the "→." Note that if the variable was squared in the original equation, you may get *two* results back when you solve. Mathcad displays these in a vector. Figure 14-11 shows an example.

Tip   Another way to solve for a variable is to enter the equation, click on the variable you want to solve for in the equation, and choose **Variable⇒Solve** from the **Symbolics** menu.

$$A1 = \frac{L}{r^2} + 2 \cdot C \text{ solve}, r \rightarrow \begin{bmatrix} \frac{1}{(A1 - 2 \cdot C)} \cdot [(A1 - 2 \cdot C) \cdot L]^{\left(\frac{1}{2}\right)} \\ \frac{-1}{(A1 - 2 \cdot C)} \cdot [(A1 - 2 \cdot C) \cdot L]^{\left(\frac{1}{2}\right)} \end{bmatrix}$$

$a := 34$

Use [Crtr] = for the equal sign.

$$\frac{1}{2} \cdot x + x = -2 + a \text{ solve}, x \rightarrow \frac{64}{3}$$

$$x^3 - 5 \cdot x^2 - 4 \cdot x + 20 > 0 \text{ solve}, x \rightarrow \begin{bmatrix} (-2 < x) \cdot (x < 2) \\ 5 < x \end{bmatrix}$$

$$e^t + 1 \text{ solve}, t \rightarrow i \cdot \pi$$

You don't need =0 when finding roots.

Figure 14-11: Solving equations, solving inequalities, and finding roots.

Solving a System of Equations Symbolically: "Solve" Keyword

One way to symbolically solve a system of equations is to use the same **solve** keyword used to solve one equation in one unknown. To solve a system of *n* equations for *n* unknowns:

1. Press [▦] on the Matrix toolbar or type **[Ctrl]M** to insert a vector having *n* rows and 1 column.

2. Fill in each placeholder of the vector with one of the *n* equations making up the system. Make sure you click **=** on the Boolean toolbar or type **[Ctrl]=** to enter the bold equal sign.

3. Press **▪→** on the Symbolic toolbar or type **[Ctrl] [Shift] .** (hold down the Control and Shift keys and type a period). Mathcad displays a placeholder to the left of the symbolic equal sign, "→."

4. Type **solve** followed by a comma in the placeholder.

5. Type **[Ctrl]M** or press [▦] on the Matrix toolbar to create a vector having *n* rows and 1 column. Then enter the variables you are solving for.

6. Press **[Enter]** to see the result.

Mathcad displays the *n* solutions to the system of equations to the right of the symbolic equal sign. Figure 14-12 shows an example.

Using the "solve" keyword (press [Ctrl]+[Shift]+Period):

$$\begin{pmatrix} x + 2 \cdot \pi \cdot y = a \\ 4 \cdot x + y = b \end{pmatrix} \text{ solve, } \begin{pmatrix} x \\ y \end{pmatrix} \rightarrow \left[\begin{array}{cc} \dfrac{-(-2 \cdot \pi \cdot b + a)}{(-1 + 8 \cdot \pi)} & \dfrac{(4 \cdot a - b)}{(-1 + 8 \cdot \pi)} \end{array} \right]$$

Using a solve block:

Given

$$x + 2 \cdot \pi \cdot y = a \qquad \text{<- Use [Ctrl]= to type the equal sign.}$$

$$4 \cdot x + y = b$$

$$\text{Find}(x, y) \rightarrow \left[\begin{array}{c} \dfrac{-(-2 \cdot \pi \cdot b + a)}{(-1 + 8 \cdot \pi)} \\[2mm] \dfrac{(4 \cdot a - b)}{(-1 + 8 \cdot \pi)} \end{array} \right]$$

Figure 14-12: Two methods for solving a system of equations symbolically.

Solving a System of Equations Symbolically: Solve Block

Another way to solve a system of equations symbolically is to use a solve block, similar to the numeric solve blocks described in "Solving and Optimization Functions" on page 166:

1. Type the word *Given*. This tells Mathcad that what follows is a system of equations. You can type *Given* in any combination of upper- and lowercase letters and in any font. Just be sure you don't type it while in a text region.

2. Now enter the equations in any order below the word *Given*. Make sure that for every equation you click ☐ on the Boolean toolbar or type [**Ctrl**]= to insert the bold equal sign for each equation.

3. Enter the *Find* function with arguments appropriate for your system of equations. This function is described in "Linear/Nonlinear System Solving and Optimization" on page 167.

4. Click ☐ on the Symbolic toolbar or press [**Ctrl**]. (the Control key followed by a period). Mathcad displays the symbolic equal sign.

5. Click outside the *Find* function or press [**Enter**].

Mathcad displays the solutions to the system of equations to the right of the symbolic equal sign. Figure 14-12 shows an example.

Most of the guidelines for solve blocks described in "Linear/Nonlinear System Solving and Optimization" on page 167 apply to the symbolic solution of systems of equations. The main difference is that when you solve equations symbolically, you do not enter guess values for the solutions.

Symbolic Matrix Manipulation

You can use Mathcad to find the symbolic transpose, inverse, or determinant of a matrix using a built-in operator and the symbolic equal sign. To find the transpose of a matrix, for example:

1. Place the entire matrix between the two editing lines by clicking [**Space**] one or more times.

2. Click ▉ on the Matrix toolbar or press [**Ctrl**] | to insert the matrix transpose operator.

3. Click ▉ on the Symbolic toolbar or press [**Ctrl**]. (the Control key followed by a period). Mathcad displays the symbolic equal sign, "→."

4. Press [**Enter**] to see the result.

Mathcad returns the result to the right of the "→." Figure 14-13 shows some examples.

Transposing a matrix

$$\begin{pmatrix} x & 1 & a \\ -b & x^2 & -a \\ 1 & b & x^3 \end{pmatrix}^T \rightarrow \begin{pmatrix} x & -b & 1 \\ 1 & x^2 & b \\ a & -a & x^3 \end{pmatrix}$$

Press [Ctrl] M to create a matrix.
Press [Ctrl] . for the arrow.

Finding the inverse

$$\begin{pmatrix} \lambda & 2 & 1-\lambda \\ 0 & 1 & -2 \\ 0 & 0 & -\lambda \end{pmatrix}^{-1} \rightarrow \begin{bmatrix} \dfrac{1}{\lambda} & \dfrac{-2}{\lambda} & \dfrac{-(\lambda-5)}{\lambda^2} \\ 0 & 1 & \dfrac{-2}{\lambda} \\ 0 & 0 & \dfrac{-1}{\lambda} \end{bmatrix}$$

Finding the determinant

$$\begin{vmatrix} x & 1 & a \\ -b & x^2 & -a \\ 1 & b & x^3 \end{vmatrix} \rightarrow x^6 + x \cdot a \cdot b + b \cdot x^3 - a \cdot b^2 - a - a \cdot x^2$$

Figure 14-13: Symbolic matrix operations.

Another way to find the transpose, inverse, or determinant of a matrix is to use the **Matrix** commands on the **Symbolics** menu. For example, to find the transpose of a matrix:

1. Place the entire matrix between the two editing lines by pressing [**Space**] one or more times.

2. Choose **Matrix⇒Transpose** from the **Symbolics** menu.

Unlike matrices evaluated with the symbolic equal sign, matrices modified by commands from the **Symbolics** menu do not update automatically, as described in the section "Using the Symbolics Menu" on page 269.

Chapter 14 Symbolic Calculation

Transformations

You can use symbolic keywords to evaluate the Fourier, Laplace, or z- transform of a expression and to evaluate the inverse transform. For example, to evaluate the Fourier transform of an expression:

1. Enter the expression you want to transform.

2. Click ▪→ on the Symbolic toolbar or type **[Ctrl] [Shift] .** (hold down the Control and Shift keys and type a period). Mathcad displays a placeholder to the left of the symbolic equal sign, "→."

3. Type **fourier** in the placeholder, followed by a comma and the name of the transform variable.

4. Press **[Enter]** to see the result.

Note Mathcad returns a function in a variable commonly used for the transform you perform. If the expression you are transforming already contains this variable, Mathcad avoids ambiguity by returning a function of a double variable. For example, Mathcad returns a function in the variable ω when you perform a Fourier transform. If the expression you are transforming already contains an ω, Mathcad returns a function of the variable $\omega\omega$ instead.

The Fourier transform result is a function of ω given by:

$$\int_{-\infty}^{+\infty} f(t)e^{-i\omega t}dt$$

Use the keyword **invfourier** to return the inverse Fourier transform as a function given by:

$$\frac{1}{2\pi}\int_{-\infty}^{+\infty} F(\omega)e^{i\omega t}d\omega$$

where $f(t)$ and $F(\omega)$ are the expressions to be transformed.

Use the keywords **laplace**, **invlaplace**, **ztrans**, and **invztrans** to perform a Laplace or z-transform or their inverses.

The Laplace transform result is a function of s given by:

$$\int_{0}^{+\infty} f(t)e^{-st}dt$$

Its inverse is given by:

$$\frac{1}{2\pi}\int_{\sigma-i\infty}^{\sigma+i\infty} F(s)e^{st}dt$$

where $f(t)$ and $F(s)$ are the expressions to be transformed. All singularities of $F(s)$ are to the left of the line $\text{Re}(s) = \sigma$.

The z-transform result is a function of z given by:

$$\sum_{n=0}^{+\infty} f(n)z^{-n}$$

Its inverse is given by:

$$\frac{1}{2\pi i}\int_C F(z)z^{n-1}dz$$

where $f(n)$ and $F(z)$ are the expressions to be transformed and C is a contour enclosing all singularities of the integrand.

Tip   You can substitute a different variable for the one Mathcad returns from a transform or its inverse by using the **substitute** keyword.

Another way to evaluate the Fourier, Laplace, or z- transform or their inverses on an expression is to use commands on the **Symbolics** menu. For example, to find the Laplace transform of an expression:

- Enter the expression.

- Click on the transform variable.

- Choose **Transform⇒Laplace** from the **Symbolics** menu.

Keep in mind that, unlike keyword-modified expressions, expressions modified by commands from the **Symbolics** menu do not update automatically, as described in the section "Using the Symbolics Menu" on page 269.

Note   Results from symbolic transformations may contain functions that are recognized by Mathcad's symbolic processor but not by its numeric processor. An example is the function *Dirac* shown in the middle of Figure 14-14. You'll find numeric definitions for this and other such functions in "Special Functions" on page 486 in the Appendices as well as in the Resource Center QuickSheet titled "Special Functions."

Symbolic Optimization

In general, Mathcad's symbolic and numeric processors don't communicate with one another. You can, however, make the numeric processor ask the symbolic processor for advice before starting what could be a needlessly complicated calculation.

For example, if you were to evaluate an expression such as:

$$\int_0^u\int_0^v\int_0^w x^2 + y^2 + z^2 dx\, dy\, dz$$

Mathcad would undertake the task of evaluating a numeric approximation of the triple integral even though one could arrive at an exact solution by first performing a few elementary calculus operations.

This happens because by itself, Mathcad's numeric processor does not simplify before plunging ahead into the calculation. Although Mathcad's symbolic processor knows

Figure 14-14: Performing symbolic transforms.

all about simplifying complicated expressions, these two processors do not consult with each other, although for certain definitions, it would be helpful. To make these two processors talk to each other for a particular definition click on a definition with the right mouse button and choose **Optimize** from the pop-up menu.

Once you've done this, Mathcad's live symbolic processor simplifies the expression to the right of a ":=" *before* the numeric processor begins its calculations. This helps Mathcad's numeric processor evaluate the expression more quickly. It can also avoid any computational issues inherent in the numeric calculation.

If Mathcad finds a simpler form for the expression, it responds by doing the following:

• It marks the region with a red asterisk.

• It *internally* replaces what you've typed with a simplified form.

• The equivalent expression is evaluated instead of the expression you specified. To see this equivalent expression, double-click the red asterisk beside the region.

If Mathcad is unable to find a simpler form for the expression, it places a *blue* asterisk next to it.

In the previous example, the symbolic processor would examine the triple integral and return the equivalent, but much simpler expression:

$$\frac{1}{3}(w^3 vu + wv^3 u + wvu^3)$$

Then it uses any definitions that exist in your worksheet and simplifies the expression further. To see this expression in a pop-up window, click the red asterisk with the right mouse button and choose **Show Popup** from the pop-up menu (see Figure 14-15).

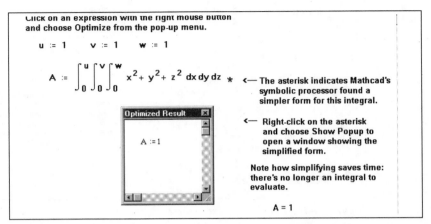

Figure 14-15: A pop-up window showing the equivalent expression that Mathcad actually evaluates.

To enable optimization for an entire worksheet, choose **Optimization** from the **Math** menu. To disable optimization for an expression, right-click it and uncheck **Optimize** on the pop-up menu. Mathcad evaluates the expression exactly as you typed it.

To disable optimization for all expressions, remove the check from **Optimization** on the **Math** menu.

Chapter 15
Programming

♦ Defining a Program
♦ Conditional Statements
♦ Looping
♦ Controlling Program Execution
♦ Error Handling
♦ Programs Within Programs

Defining a Program

A Mathcad program is a special kind of expression you can
create in Mathcad Professional. It's an expression made up of a
sequence of statements created using *programming operators*,

available on the Programming toolbar. Click on the Math
toolbar, or choose **Toolbars⇒Programming** from the **View**
menu, to open the Programming toolbar.

You can think of a program as a compound expression that
involves potentially many programming operators. Like any expression, a program
returns a value—a scalar, vector, array, nested array, or string—when followed by the
equal sign or the symbolic equal sign. Just as you can define a variable or function in
terms of an expression, you can also define them in terms of a program.

The following example shows how to make a simple program to define the function:

$$f(x, w) = \log\left(\frac{x}{w}\right)$$

Although the example chosen is simple enough not to require programming, it
illustrates how to separate the statements that make up a program and how to use the
local assignment operator, "←."

1. Type the left side of the function definition, followed by a ":=". Make sure the placeholder is selected.

2. Click **Add Line** on the Programming toolbar. Alternatively, press **]**. You'll see a vertical bar with two placeholders, which will hold the statements that comprise your program.

3. Click in the top placeholder. Type **z**, then click **←** on the Programming toolbar. Alternatively, press **{** to insert a "←," which is also known as the local definition symbol.

4. Type **x/w** in the placeholder to the right of the local definition symbol. Then press [**Tab**] to move to the bottom placeholder, or click on the bottom placeholder.

$$f(x,w) := \left| \begin{array}{l} z \leftarrow \dfrac{x}{w} \\ \blacksquare \end{array} \right.$$

5. Enter the value to be returned by the program in the remaining placeholder. Type **log(z)**.

$$f(x,w) := \left| \begin{array}{l} z \leftarrow \dfrac{x}{w} \\ \log(z) \end{array} \right.$$

You can now use this function just as you would any other function in your worksheet.

Note   You cannot use Mathcad's usual assignment operator, ":=," inside a program. You must use the local assignment operator, represented by "←," instead. Variables defined inside a program with the local assignment operator, such as z in the example above, are local to the program and are undefined elsewhere in the worksheet. However, within a program, you can refer to Mathcad variables and functions defined previously in the worksheet.

Figure 15-1 shows a more complex example involving the quadratic formula. Although you can define the quadratic formula with a single statement as shown in the top half of the figure, you may find it easier to define it with a series of simple statements as shown in the bottom half.

$$q(a,b,c) := \frac{-b + \sqrt{b^2 - 4 \cdot a \cdot c}}{2 \cdot a}$$

Although you can define complicated functions all on one line...

$$r(a,b,c) := \left| \begin{array}{l} discr \leftarrow b^2 - 4 \cdot a \cdot c \\ num \leftarrow -b + \sqrt{discr} \\ denom \leftarrow 2 \cdot a \\ \dfrac{num}{denom} \end{array} \right.$$

...it's sometimes easier to break them up into simpler steps anyway.

Figure 15-1: A more complex function defined in terms of both an expression and a program.

Tip
A program can have any number of statements. To add a statement, click Add Line on the Programming toolbar or press **[**. Mathcad inserts a placeholder below whatever statement you've selected. To delete the placeholder, click on it and press [**Bksp**].

As with any expression, a Mathcad program must have a value. This value is simply the value of the last statement executed by the program. It can be a string expression, a single number, or an array of numbers. It can even be an array of arrays (see "Nested Arrays" on page 217).

You can also write a Mathcad program to return a *symbolic* expression. When you evaluate a program using the symbolic equal sign, "→," described in Chapter 14, "Symbolic Calculation," Mathcad passes the expression to its symbolic processor and, when possible, returns a simplified symbolic expression. You can use Mathcad's ability to evaluate programs symbolically to generate complicated symbolic expressions, polynomials, and matrices. Figure 15-2 shows a function that, when evaluated symbolically, generates symbolic polynomials.

A function to generate a polynomial.

$$f(n) := \begin{vmatrix} a \leftarrow 0 \\ i \leftarrow 0 \\ \text{while} \quad i \le n \\ \quad \begin{vmatrix} a \leftarrow \left[a + (1 + x)^i \right] \\ i \leftarrow i + 1 \end{vmatrix} \\ a \end{vmatrix}$$

<-- Mathcad can evaluate the program symbolically even though x is undefined.

Evaluate symbolically . . .

$$f(3) \text{ expand } \rightarrow 4 + 6 \cdot x + 4 \cdot x^2 + x^3$$

<-- Expand symbolic keyword expands the result. Press [Ctrl][Shift][period] for the symbolic keyword operator.

Figure 15-2: Using a Mathcad program to generate a symbolic expression.

Note
Programs that include the **return** and **on error** statements, described on page 290 and page 292, cannot be evaluated symbolically since the symbolic processor does not recognize these operators.

On-line Help
For programming examples, see the "Programming" section in the Resource Center QuickSheets. The Resource Center also includes a special section, "The Treasury Guide to Programming," which provides detailed examples and applications of Mathcad programs.

Defining a Program

285

Conditional Statements

In general, Mathcad evaluates each statement in your program from the top down. There may be times, however, when you want Mathcad to evaluate a statement only when a particular condition is met. You can do this by including an **if** statement.

For example, suppose you want to define a function that forms a semicircle around the origin but is otherwise constant. To do this:

1. Type the left side of the function definition, followed by a "**:=**". Make sure the placeholder is selected.

    $$f(x) := \blacksquare$$

2. Click **Add Line** on the Programming toolbar. Alternatively, press **]**. You'll see a vertical bar with two placeholders. These placeholders will hold the statements making up your program.

    $$f(x) := \begin{vmatrix} \blacksquare \\ \blacksquare \end{vmatrix}$$

3. Click **if** on the Programming toolbar in the top placeholder. Alternatively, press **}**. Do not type "if."

    $$f(x) := \begin{vmatrix} \blacksquare \ \text{if} \ \blacksquare \\ \blacksquare \end{vmatrix}$$

4. Enter a Boolean expression in the right placeholder using one of the relational operators on the Boolean toolbar. In the left placeholder, type the value you want the program to return whenever the expression in the right placeholder is true. If necessary, add more placeholders by clicking **Add Line**.

    $$f(x) := \begin{vmatrix} 0 \ \text{if} \ |x| > 2 \\ \blacksquare \end{vmatrix}$$

5. Select the remaining placeholder and click **otherwise** on the Programming toolbar or press **[Ctrl] 3**.

    $$f(x) := \begin{vmatrix} 0 \ \text{if} \ |x| > 2 \\ \blacksquare \ \text{otherwise} \end{vmatrix}$$

6. Type the value you want the program to return if the condition in the first statement is false.

    $$f(x) := \begin{vmatrix} 0 \ \text{if} \ |x| > 2 \\ \sqrt{4 - x^2} \ \text{otherwise} \end{vmatrix}$$

Figure 15-3 shows a plot of this function.

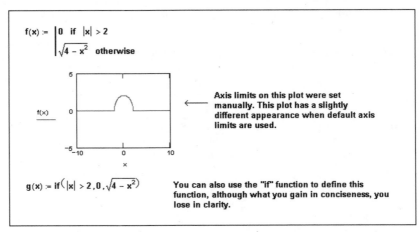

$$f(x) := \begin{vmatrix} 0 \ \text{if} \ |x| > 2 \\ \sqrt{4 - x^2} \ \text{otherwise} \end{vmatrix}$$

Axis limits on this plot were set manually. This plot has a slightly different appearance when default axis limits are used.

$$g(x) := \text{if}\left(|x| > 2, 0, \sqrt{4 - x^2}\right)$$

You can also use the "if" function to define this function, although what you gain in conciseness, you lose in clarity.

Figure 15-3: Using the **if** *statement to define a piecewise continuous function.*

The **if** statement in a Mathcad program is not the same as the *if* function (see "Piecewise Continuous Functions" on page 155). Although it is not hard to define a simple program using the *if* function, as shown in Figure 15-3, the *if* function can become unwieldy as the number of branches exceeds two.

Looping

One of the greatest strengths of programmability is the ability to execute a sequence of statements repeatedly in a loop. Mathcad provides two loop structures. The choice of which loop to use depends on how you plan to tell the loop to stop executing.

- If you know exactly how many times you want a loop to execute, use a **for** loop.

- If you want the loop to stop when a condition has been met, but you don't know how many loops will be required, use a **while** loop.

Tip   See "Controlling Program Execution" on page 289 for methods to interrupt calculation within the body of a loop.

"For" Loops

A **for** loop terminates after a predetermined number of iterations. Iteration is controlled by an *iteration variable* defined at the top of the loop. The definition of the iteration variable is local to the program.

To create a **for** loop:

1. Click [for] on the Programming toolbar or press **[Ctrl] "**. Do not type the word "for."

2. Type the name of the iteration variable in the placeholder to the left of the "∈ ."

3. Enter the range of values the iteration variable should take in the placeholder to the right of the "∈ ." You usually specify this range the same way you would for a range variable (see page 106).

4. Type the expression you want to evaluate in the remaining placeholder. This expression generally involves the iteration variable. If necessary, add placeholders by clicking [Add Line] on the Programming toolbar.

The upper half of Figure 15-4 shows this **for** loop being used to add a sequence of integers.

Note Although the expression to the right of the "∈" is usually a range, it can also be a vector or a list of scalars, ranges, and vectors separated by commas. The lower half of Figure 15-4 shows an example in which the iteration variable is defined as the elements of two vectors.

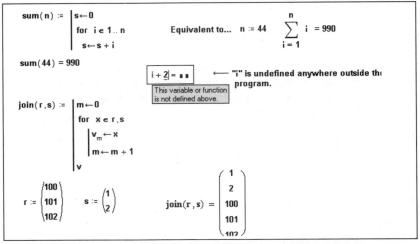

Figure 15-4: Using a for *loop with two different kinds of iteration variables.*

"While" Loops

A **while** loop is driven by the truth of some condition. Because of this, you don't need to know in advance how many times the loop will execute. It is important, however, to have a statement somewhere, either within the loop or elsewhere in the program, that eventually makes the condition false. Otherwise, the loop executes indefinitely.

To create a **while** loop:

1. Click ▢ while ▢ on the Programming toolbar or press [**Ctrl**] **]**. Do not type the word "while."

2. Click in the top placeholder and type a condition. This is typically a Boolean expression like the one shown.

3. Type the expression you want evaluated in the remaining placeholder. If necessary, add placeholders by clicking ▢ Add Line ▢ on the Programming toolbar.

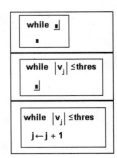

Figure 15-5 shows a larger program incorporating the above loop.

Upon encountering a **while** loop, Mathcad checks the condition. If the condition is true, Mathcad executes the body of the loop and checks the condition again. If the condition is false, Mathcad exits the loop.

Figure 15-5: Using a while *loop to find the first occurrence of a particular number in a matrix.*

Controlling Program Execution

The Programming toolbar in Mathcad Professional includes three statements for controlling program execution:

- Use the **break** statement within a **for** or **while** loop to interrupt the loop when a condition occurs and move execution to the next statement outside the loop.

- Use the **continue** statement within a **for** or **while** loop to interrupt the current iteration and force program execution to continue with the next iteration of the loop.

- Use the **return** statement to stop a program and return a particular value from within the program rather than from the last statement evaluated.

The "Break" Statement

It is often useful to break out of a loop upon the occurrence of some condition. For example, in Figure 15-6 a **break** statement is used to stop a loop when a negative number is encountered in an input vector.

To insert a **break** statement, click on a placeholder inside a loop and click ▊break▊ on the Programming toolbar or press [**Ctrl**] **{**. Do not type the word "break." You typically insert **break** into the left-hand placeholder of an **if** statement. The **break** is evaluated only when the right-hand side of the **if** is true.

Tip   To create the program on the left in Figure 15-6, for example, you would click ▊break▊ first, then click ▊if▊.

The "Continue" Statement

To ignore an iteration of a loop, use **continue**. To insert the **continue** statement, click on a placeholder inside a loop and click ▒continue▒ on the Programming toolbar or press [**Ctrl**] [. Do not type the word "continue." As with **break**, you typically insert **continue** into the left-hand placeholder of an **if** statement. The **continue** statement is evaluated only when the right-hand side of the **if** is true.

For example, in Figure 15-6 a **continue** statement is used to ignore nonpositive numbers in an input vector.

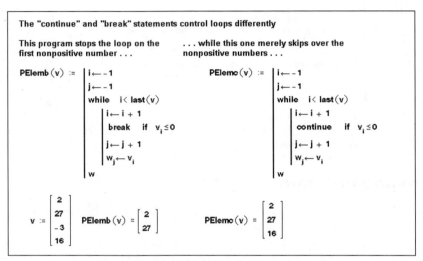

Figure 15-6: The break *statement halts the loop. Program execution resumes on the next iteration when* continue *is used.*

The "Return" Statement

A Mathcad program returns the value of the last expression evaluated in the program. In simple programs, the last expression evaluated is in the last line of the program. As you create more complicated programs, you may need more flexibility. The **return** statement allows you to interrupt the program and return particular values other than the default value.

A **return** statement can be used anywhere in a program, even within a deeply nested loop, to force program termination and the return of a scalar, vector, array, or string. As with **break** and **continue**, you typically use **return** on the left-hand side of an **if** statement, and the **return** statement is evaluated only when the right-hand side of the **if** statement is true.

The following program fragment shows how a **return** statement is used to return a string upon the occurrence of a particular condition:

1. Click [if] on the Programming toolbar.

   > ■ if ■

2. Now click [return] on the Programming toolbar or press [**Ctrl**]|. Do not type "return."

   > return ▪ if ■

3. Create a string by typing the double-quote key (**"**) on the placeholder to the right of **return**. Then type the string to be returned by the program. Mathcad displays the string between a pair of quotes.

   > return "int"   if ■

4. Type a condition in the placeholder to the right of **if**. This is typically a Boolean expression like the one shown. (Type [**Ctrl**]= for the bold equal sign.)

   > return "int"   if   floor$(x) = x$

In this example, the program returns the string "int" when the expression $floor(x) = x$ is true.

Tip   You can add more lines to the expression to the right of **return** by clicking [Add Line] on the Programming toolbar.

Error Handling

Errors may occur during program execution that cause Mathcad to stop calculating the program. For example, because of a particular input, a program may attempt to divide by 0 in an expression and therefore encounter a singularity error. In these cases Mathcad treats the program as it does any math expression: it marks the offending expression with an error message and highlights the offending name or operator in a different color, as described in Chapter 8, "Calculating in Mathcad."

Mathcad Professional gives you two features to improve error handling in programs:

- The **on error** statement on the Programming toolbar allows you to trap a numerical error that would otherwise force Mathcad to stop calculating the program.

- The *error* string function gives you access to Mathcad's error tip mechanism and lets you customize error messages issued by your program.

"On Error" Statement

In some cases you may be able to anticipate program inputs that lead to a numerical error (such as a singularity, an overflow, or a failure to converge) that would force Mathcad to stop calculating the program. In more complicated cases, especially when your programs rely heavily on Mathcad's numerical operators or built-in function set, you may not be able to anticipate or enumerate all of the possible numerical errors that can occur in a program. The **on error** statement is designed as a general-purpose error trap to compute an alternative expression when a numerical error occurs that would otherwise force Mathcad to stop calculating the program.

To use the **on error** statement, click on error on the Programming toolbar or type [**Ctrl**] **'**. Do not type "on error." In the placeholder to the right of **on error**, create the program statement(s) you ordinarily expect to evaluate but in which you wish to trap any numerical errors. In the placeholder to the left of **on error**, create the program statement(s) you want to evaluate should the default expression on the right-hand side fail. Figure 15-7 shows **on error** operating in a program to find a root of an expression.

Figure 15-7: The on error *statement traps numerical errors in a program.*

Issuing Error Messages

Just as Mathcad automatically stops further evaluation and produces an appropriate "error tip" on an expression that generates an error (see the bottom of Figure 15-7 for an example), you can cause evaluation to stop and make custom error tips appear when your programs or other expressions are used improperly or cannot return answers.

Mathcad Professional's *error* string function gives you this capability. This function (see "String Functions" on page 198) suspends further numerical evaluation of an expression and produces an error tip whose text is the string it takes as an argument.

Typically you use the *error* string function in the placeholder on the left-hand side of an **if** or **on error** programming statement so that an error and appropriate error tip are generated when a particular condition is encountered. Figure 15-8 shows how custom errors can be used even in a small program.

Figure 15-8: Generating custom errors via the error *string function.*

Note   Some error strings are automatically translated to a Mathcad error message that is similar to the error string. For example "must be real" is translated to "This value must be real. Its imaginary part must be zero."

Programs Within Programs

The examples in previous sections have been chosen more for illustrative purposes rather than their power. This section shows examples of more sophisticated programs.

Much of the flexibility inherent in programming arises from the ability to embed programming structures inside one another. In Mathcad, you can do this in the following ways:

- You can make one of the statements in a program be another program, or you can define a program elsewhere and call it from within another program as if it were a subroutine.

- You can define a function recursively.

Subroutines

Figure 15-9 shows two examples of programs containing a statement which is itself a program. In principle, there is no limit to how deeply you can nest a program.

Figure 15-9: Programs in which statements are themselves programs.

One way many programmers avoid overly complicated programs is to bury the complexity in *subroutines*. Figure 15-10 shows an example of this technique.

INTEGRATION IN WHICH WIDTHS OF INTERVALS ARE CHOSEN ADAPTIVELY

$$\text{intsimp}(f,a,b,N) := \begin{vmatrix} s \leftarrow 0 \\ w \leftarrow \dfrac{b-a}{N} \\ \text{for } i \in 1..N \\ \quad s \leftarrow s + w \cdot \dfrac{\left[f(a + (i-1) \cdot w) + 4 \cdot f\left(a - \dfrac{w}{2} + i \cdot w\right) \right] + f(a + i \cdot w)}{6} \\ s \end{vmatrix}$$

$$\text{adapt}(f,a,b) := \begin{vmatrix} x \leftarrow \text{intsimp}(f,a,b,10) \\ x \quad \text{if } |x - \text{intsimp}(f,a,b,5)| \leq \text{TOL} \\ \text{adapt}\left(f,a,\dfrac{a+b}{2}\right) + \text{adapt}\left(f,\dfrac{a+b}{2},b\right) \quad \text{otherwise} \end{vmatrix}$$

$$\text{adapt}(\log,10^{-15},1) = -0.434958018397141$$

Figure 15-10: Using a subroutine to manage complexity.

Tip Breaking up long programs with subroutines is good programming practice. Long programs and those containing deeply nested statements can become difficult for other users to understand at a glance. They are also more cumbersome to edit and debug.

In Figure 15-10, the function *adapt* carries out an adaptive quadrature or integration routine by using *intsimp* to approximate the area in each subinterval. By defining *intsimp* elsewhere and using it within *adapt*, the program used to define *adapt* becomes considerably simpler.

Recursion

Recursion is a powerful programming technique that involves defining a function in terms of itself, as shown in Figure 15-11. See also the definition of *adapt* in Figure 15-10. Recursive function definitions should always have at least two parts:

- A definition of the function in terms of a previous value of the function.
- An initial condition to prevent the recursion from continuing forever.

The idea is similar to mathematical induction: if you can determine $f(n + 1)$ from $f(n)$, and you know $f(0)$, then you know all there is to know about f.

Tip Recursive function definitions, despite their elegance and conciseness, are not always computationally efficient. You may find that an equivalent definition using one of the iterative loops described earlier will evaluate more quickly.

Factorial function

$$\text{factorial}(n) := \begin{vmatrix} 1 & \text{if } n = 1 \\ n \cdot \text{factorial}(n - 1) & \text{otherwise} \end{vmatrix}$$

$$\text{factorial}(5) = 120$$

Compound interest

$$P(n, i, Po) := \begin{vmatrix} Po & \text{if } n = 0 \\ P(n - 1, i, Po) \cdot (1 + i \cdot \%) & \text{otherwise} \end{vmatrix}$$

$$P(3, 12, 100) = 140.493$$ **Type Ctrl= to generate the boolean equals signs used inside the programs.**

Figure 15-11: Defining functions recursively.

Chapter 16
Advanced Computational Features

- ◆ Overview
- ◆ Exchanging Data with Other Applications
- ◆ Scripting Custom OLE Automation Objects
- ◆ Accessing Mathcad from Within Another Application

Overview

In this chapter, you will learn how to extend Mathcad's functionality by bringing the feature sets of other applications into your Mathcad worksheet. Likewise, you can expand the usefulness of other programs by interfacing with Mathcad. In both cases, you take advantage of Mathcad's OLE (Object Linking and Embedding) capabilities.

Exchanging Data with Other Applications

Components are specialized OLE objects in your Mathcad worksheet. They allow you to exchange data with other applications or sources. *Application components* allow you to access functions and data from other computational applications such as Excel, SmartSketch, and MATLAB. Unlike other kinds of OLE objects you insert into a worksheet, as described in the section "Inserting Objects" in Chapter 6, a component can receive data from Mathcad, return data to Mathcad, or do both, dynamically linking the object to your Mathcad computations.

Tip   As described in Chapter 11, "Vectors, Matrices, and Data Arrays," Mathcad also provides the File Read/Write component for you to import and export *static* data files in a variety of formats compatible with other computational programs. For linking dynamically to an object for which Mathcad does not have a dedicated component, see "Scripting Custom OLE Automation Objects" on page 308.

Components that connect Mathcad to other applications include:

- Axum, for creating highly customizable Axum graphs
- Excel, for accessing cells and formulas in a Microsoft Excel spreadsheet
- MATLAB, for accessing the programming environment of MATLAB
- ODBC Read, for retrieving data from an ODBC-compliant database that supports SQL

- SmartSketch, for creating 2D drawings and designs
- S-PLUS Graph, for creating S-PLUS graphs
- S-PLUS Script, for accessing the programming environment of S-PLUS

Note To use an application component, you must have the application for that component installed, but not necessarily running, on your system.

Other built-in components that may be customized using scripting:

- Data Acquisition, for sending data to or getting data from a measurement device
- MathSoft Controls, for creating custom forms controls like buttons and text boxes

These components are described in detail in the next section, "Scripting Custom OLE Automation Objects" on page 308.

Tip See the SAMPLES folder of your Mathcad installation for a variety of example files that use components.

How to Use Application Components

In general, components receive *input* from one or more Mathcad variables, perform operations on the data you specify, and return *output* to other Mathcad variables. An "input variable" is a scalar, vector, matrix, or, in some cases, a string, that you have already defined in your Mathcad worksheet. It contains the data that is passed into a component. Output from a component (again, either a scalar, vector, matrix, or string) is then assigned to a Mathcad variable. This variable is referred to as an "output variable."

The basic steps for using a component are as follows:

- Insert the component.
- Specify the input variable(s) and output variable(s).
- Configure the component to handle inputs from and return outputs to Mathcad.

Since some components only take input or only send output, these steps differ slightly for each component. The ideas presented in the steps that follow provide an overview of the process.

Step 1: Inserting a component

To insert a component into a Mathcad worksheet:

1. Click in a blank area of your Mathcad worksheet where you want the component to appear. Click below or to the right of definitions for any variables that will become inputs to the component.

2. Choose **Component** from the **Insert** menu. This launches the Component Wizard.

3. Choose a component from the list and click "Next" or "Finish," depending on the component you choose. You may see additional dialog boxes that let you specify properties of the component before it is inserted. When you click "Finish," the component is inserted into your worksheet.

If you don't see a Wizard when you choose one of the components from the Insert Component dialog box, you'll immediately see the component inserted into your worksheet with some default properties.

Each component has its own particular appearance, but all components have one or more placeholders to the left of the :=, if it returns data to Mathcad, and/or at the bottom of the component, if it receives data from Mathcad. For example, the Excel component (with one input and two outputs) looks like this when inserted into your worksheet:

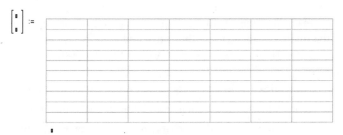

The placeholder(s) at the bottom of the component are for the names of previously defined input variables. The placeholder(s) you see to the left of the := are for the output variables.

After you fill in the placeholders for the input and output variables, you can hide the variables by clicking with the right mouse button on the component and choosing **Hide Arguments** from the pop-up menu.

Note To add an input or output variable, click with the right mouse button on the component and choose **Add Input Variable** or **Add Output Variable** from the pop-up menu. To eliminate an input or output, choose **Remove Input Variable** or **Remove Output Variable** from the menu.

Step 2: Configuring a component

Once you've inserted a component into a worksheet, you can configure its properties so that the component knows how to handle any inputs it receives from Mathcad and what to send as output. To configure the properties for a component:

1. Click on the component once to select it.

2. Click on the component with the right mouse button to see a pop-up menu.

3. Choose **Properties** from the pop-up menu.

The settings in the Properties dialog box differ for each component. For example, the Properties dialog box for the Excel component lets you specify the starting cells in which the input values are stored and the cell range from which the output is sent.

Tip When you insert an application component, you see a small window on that application's environment embedded in your Mathcad worksheet. When you *double-click* the component, the component is *in-place activated* and Mathcad's menus and toolbars change to those of the other application. This gives you access to the features of that application without leaving the Mathcad environment.

Step 3: Exchanging data

Once you've configured the component, click outside it elsewhere in the worksheet. At that point, the region recalculates and data exchange takes place: data passes from the input variable(s) into the component, the component processes the data, and the output variable(s) receive output from the component. This exchange happens whenever:

- You click on the component and press **[F9]** to recalculate the region.
- The input variables change and Automatic Calculation is turned on.
- You choose **Calculate Worksheet** from the **Math** menu.

Tip Some components allow you to save the file with which the component exchanges data as a separate file. Click on a component with the right mouse button and choose **Save As...** from the pop-up menu.

Excel Component

The Excel component allows you to exchange data with and access the functions of Microsoft Excel (version 7 or higher), if it is installed on your system.

Tip If you only need to import or export a static data file in Excel format, use the File Read/Write component as described in Chapter 11, "Vectors, Matrices, and Data Arrays."

Inserting an Excel component

To insert an Excel component into a Mathcad worksheet:

1. Click in a blank spot in your worksheet. If you want to send values to the component from a Mathcad variable defined in your worksheet, click below or to the right of the variable definition.
2. Choose **Component** from the **Insert** menu.

3. Select Excel from the list and click "Next." To create an object based on a file you've already created, choose "Create from file," and type the path name in the text box or use the Browse button to locate the file; then click "Open." Otherwise, choose "Create an empty Excel Worksheet."

4. Click Display as Icon if you want to see an icon in your Mathcad worksheet rather than a portion of the Excel spreadsheet object.

Successive pages of the Wizard allow you to specify:

- **The number of input and output variables.** Supply multiple input and output variables. The number of input and output variables you can pass between Mathcad and Excel is only limited by the memory and speed of your computer. There is no set limit.

- **Input ranges.** The cells in which the values of each input variable from Mathcad will be stored. Enter the starting cell, which is the cell that will hold the element in the upper left corner of an input array. For example, for an input variable containing a 3×3 matrix of values, you can specify A1 as the starting cell, and the values will be placed in cells A1 through C3.

- **Output ranges.** The cells whose values will define the output variables in Mathcad. For example, enter C2:L11 to extract the values in cells C2 through L11 and create a 10×10 matrix.

Tip You can specify a particular Excel worksheet and cell range using standard Excel notation such as Sheet2!B2:C2. You can also specify named cells and cell ranges.

When you finish using the Wizard, the Excel component appears in your worksheet with placeholders for the input and output variables. Enter the names of input variables in the bottom placeholders. Enter the names of the output variables into the placeholders to the left of the :=. When you click outside the component, input variables are sent to Excel from Mathcad and a range of cells are returned to Mathcad.

Figure 16-1 shows an example of an Excel component in a Mathcad worksheet.

Note By default, the Excel component displays only some of the rows and columns of the underlying spreadsheet object. To see more or fewer rows and columns, click the component so that you see handles along its sides. Resize the component by dragging a handle. To see different rows or columns than the ones shown in the view, double-click the component and use the scroll bars to find the rows or columns of interest.

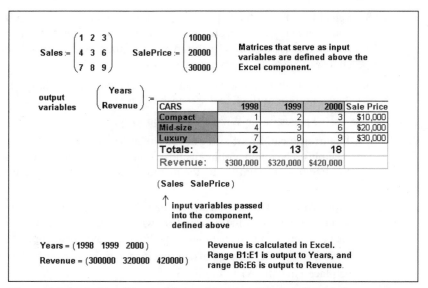

Figure 16-1: An Excel spreadsheet object in a Mathcad worksheet.

Changing the inputs and outputs

If you add input or output variables, you need to specify which cells in the component will store the new input and which will provide the new output. To do so:

1. Click on the component with the right mouse button and choose **Properties** from the pop-up menu.

2. Click on the Inputs tab and specify a starting cell for each input; click on the Outputs tab and specify a range of cells for each output.

You should also follow these steps if you want to change the cell ranges for inputs and outputs you initially specified in the Setup Wizard.

Note Strings can be passed as input to and outputs from an Excel component.

Accessing Excel

After inserting an Excel component into a Mathcad worksheet, you can use the component to perform calculations in Excel. To do so:

1. Double-click the Excel component in the Mathcad worksheet. The Excel component opens and the menus and toolbars change to Excel's menus and toolbars. This is called *in-place activation* of the component application, i.e. Excel.

2. Edit the Excel component.

3. Click back in the Mathcad worksheet to have the component recalculate and to resume working in Mathcad.

MATLAB Component

The MATLAB component allows you to exchange data with and access the programming environment of The MathWorks' MATLAB Professional 4.2c or higher, if it is installed on your system.

Tip If you only need to import or export a static data file in MATLAB format, use the File Read/Write component as described in Chapter 11, "Vectors, Matrices, and Data Arrays."

Inserting a MATLAB component

To insert a MATLAB component into a Mathcad worksheet:

1. Click in a blank spot in your worksheet. If you want to send values to the MATLAB component from a Mathcad variable, click below or to the right of the variable definition.

2. Choose **Component** from the **Insert** menu. Select MATLAB from the list and click "Finish." The MATLAB component is inserted into your worksheet.

3. In the placeholder that appears at the bottom, enter the name of the Mathcad input variable to pass into the MATLAB component. In the placeholder that appears to the left of the component, enter the name of the Mathcad output variable to be defined.

Note By default, the data in the Mathcad input variables are sent into MATLAB variables named **in0**, **in1**, **in2**, and so on. The MATLAB variables **out0**, **out1**, **out2**, and so on define the data to be passed to the Mathcad output variables. To change these names, choose **Properties** from the component's pop-up menu and type in new names in the Inputs and Outputs tabs.

To use the MATLAB component to perform calculations in MATLAB:

1. Right-click the MATLAB component in your Mathcad worksheet and select **Edit Script...** from the pop-up menu. This action opens a text window for entering MATLAB commands.

2. Edit the MATLAB script to your liking. Be sure to use appropriate MATLAB variable names to take input from Mathcad and provide output.

When you click outside the component, input variables from Mathcad are sent to MATLAB, and arrays from MATLAB are assigned to output variables in Mathcad.

Note Some versions of MATLAB support multidimensional arrays and other complex data structures. While you may use these structures within the MATLAB component, you may pass only scalars, vectors, and two-dimensional arrays from Mathcad to the MATLAB component and vice versa.

ODBC Component

The ODBC (Open Database Connectivity) component allows you to retrieve information from a database that supports SQL in its ODBC driver, like Microsoft Access or FoxPro. There are some programs that have SQL support within their application, but do not support SQL in their ODBC driver, like Microsoft Excel.

A link to your database must be established before you insert an ODBC component into your worksheet. In order to establish a link to a database on your system or network, in the Control Panel, go to Administrative Tools\Data Sources (ODBC), in Windows 2000, or ODBC Data Sources, in Windows 95, 98, and NT. For more information about ODBC and SQL support, check the documentation that comes with your database application.

Inserting an ODBC component

To insert an ODBC component into a Mathcad worksheet:

1. Click in a blank spot in your worksheet and choose **Component** from the **Insert** menu.
2. Select ODBC Read from the list and click "Next."
3. Choose a database from which to collect data. Depending on the data source, you also may need to enter a username and password. Click "Next."
4. Select a table and specify the fields in the database that you would like to read. Click "Finish."
5. In the placeholder that appears to the left of the component, enter the name of the Mathcad output variable to be defined.

Once a link to a particular database has been established, you may want to change the data source, the table, or the columns of data to be imported to your Mathcad worksheet.

To change the data source in an ODBC component:

1. Right-click the component and select **Properties** from the pop-up menu.
2. In the Properties dialog box under the Data Source tab, select a database, table, and columns of data.
3. Click "OK" to close the dialog box and update your worksheet.

Note   You can change the order in which the fields of your database are stored in the columns of the output matrix in Mathcad. To do so, right-click the ODBC component in your Mathcad worksheet and choose **Properties** from the pop-up menu. Navigate to the Advanced tab of the dialog box, and rearrange the order of the fields in the columns of the matrix using the "move up" and "move down" buttons.

To filter your data before bringing it into a Mathcad output variable, you can query your database directly through the ODBC component using a SQL "where" statement.

To filter your data through the ODBC component:

1. Right-click the component and select **Properties** from the pop-up menu.

2. Under the Advanced tab, check the "Use SQL" option and type a "where" statement in the text box.

3. Click "OK" to close the dialog box and update your worksheet.

Figure 16-2 shows the use of a SQL "where" statement.

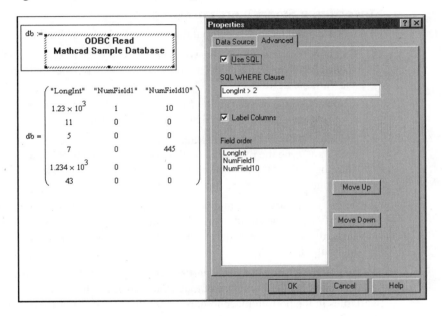

Figure 16-2: Using a SQL "where" statement to filter data through the ODBC component.

Tip Checking the "Show all fields" option in the ODBC component Wizard or on the Data Source page of the **Properties** dialog box displays all data fields, even those not supported by Mathcad variables. For example, Mathcad does not support any time data types, but you can select and display time indices from your database in a Mathcad output variable.

SmartSketch Component

SmartSketch is a 2D drawing and design tool developed by Intergraph. The Smart-Sketch component allows you to create in a Mathcad worksheet SmartSketch drawings whose dimensions are computationally linked to your Mathcad calculations. For example, your Mathcad equations can drive the size of drawing objects.

The SmartSketch component makes Mathcad the ideal platform for creating technical illustrations and specification-driven designs. You can use the SmartSketch component if you have installed SmartSketch LE for Mathcad (included on your Mathcad CD), SmartSketch 3 or higher, Imagination Engineer, or Imagineer Technical 2.

Inserting a SmartSketch drawing

To insert a drawing that is computationally linked to your Mathcad worksheet:

1. Click in a blank spot in your worksheet. If you want to send values to the drawing from a Mathcad variable defined in your worksheet, click below or to the right of the variable definition.

2. Choose **Component** from the **Insert** menu. Select SmartSketch and click "Next." The first page of the SmartSketch component Wizard appears.

3. To insert a SmartSketch drawing you've already created, choose "From Existing File," and type the path name in the text box or use the Browse button to locate the file; then click "Open." Otherwise, choose "New SmartSketch Document." The next page of the Wizard appears.

4. Specify the number of inputs and outputs. If you are using an existing file, also specify the names of the variables, dimensions, or symbols in the drawing to send input to and retrieve output from. Use the drop-down list boxes next to each input and output.

When you click "Finish," the SmartSketch component appears in your worksheet with placeholders for the input and output variables. Enter the names of Mathcad input variables in the bottom placeholders. Enter the output variables in the placeholders to the left of the :=.

Figure 16-3 shows a SmartSketch drawing inserted into a Mathcad worksheet. The values from the variables *RadiusA*, *RadiusB*, and *Distance* are sent to SmartSketch as input and used to create the drawing. The variables *WrapB*, *BLength*, and *Beta1* are output variables.

Figure 16-3: Integrating a SmartSketch drawing into a Mathcad worksheet.

Note Input values that do not have units attached are passed in SI units. For example, if you send 2.0 as input for a length, it is assumed to be 2.0 meters. SmartSketch, by default, converts this to the display units (inches by default) and creates the drawing.

Creating a new drawing

If you choose "New SmartSketch Document" when inserting the SmartSketch component, you need to create a new SmartSketch drawing after the component appears. To do so:

1. Double-click on the component and use SmartSketch's menus and toolbars to create a drawing. Use the Dimensions toolbar to add dimensions to your drawing.

2. Choose **Variables** from the **Tools** menu to define variables or edit dimensions. Close the Variable Table before clicking back in the Mathcad worksheet.

Next you need to bind variables, dimensions, or symbols to the inputs or outputs. To do so, right-click on the component in Mathcad and choose **Properties** from the pop-up menu. Use the Properties dialog to specify:

- **Input names.** The dimension, symbol, or variable names used in the SmartSketch drawing that are controlled by the inputs to the SmartSketch component. Choose a dimension or variable name from the drop-down list.

- **Output names.** The dimension, symbol, or variable names used in the SmartSketch drawing that define the output variables in Mathcad. Choose a dimension or variable name from the drop-down list.

When you click outside the component, input values are sent to the SmartSketch drawing from Mathcad and values are returned to Mathcad as output.

Tip   If the drawing is so large that it extends beyond the component window, click on the component with the right mouse button, choose **Properties** from the pop-up menu, and click the box next to Automatic Resizing.

Note   In order for the dimensions in a drawing to resize relative to any changes to the dimensions, check the box next to **Maintain Relationships** under the **Tools** menu in SmartSketch. To verify this setting, double-click on the component and choose **Tools** from the menu bar.

For more information on SmartSketch, refer to the tutorials and documentation available from the Help menu in SmartSketch. Sample Mathcad files containing Smart-Sketch components are located in the SAMPLES\CAD folder of your Mathcad installation.

Note   To learn about other built-in application components in Mathcad, see Mathcad's online Help.

Scripting Custom OLE Automation Objects

As described in the previous section, Mathcad has several specialized components for accessing the functionality of other technical computing environments within your Mathcad worksheet. However, you can dynamically exchange data between a Mathcad worksheet and any other application that supports OLE Automation, even if Mathcad does not have a specific component for that application. To do so, you must use the *Scriptable Object component* (SOC).

In addition to programming the SOC to interface with other OLE applications, you can build customized *Controls* that respond to user input in the worksheet, such as buttons and text boxes. Also, you can use the SOC to retrieve data from measurement devices attached to your system. Scripted objects to perform these tasks come pre-installed with Mathcad. Brief descriptions of their use appear later in this section, under "Customizing and Redistributing Components" on page 310 and "Data Acquisition Component (DAC)" on page 313. These components appear in the Insert Component list, but they still need to be customized through modifications to their scripts.

How to Use Scriptable Object Components

In general, you can create a custom scriptable object from any object you can insert into a Mathcad worksheet as well as any ActiveX controls installed on your computer.

To create a Scriptable Object component, you must:

1. Be proficient in a supported scripting language, such as Microsoft VBScript or JScript, that is installed on your system.

2. Know something about the Object Model of the other application. In other words, you must know how the application has implemented Automation.

3. Have the other application or control installed on your system, if you're interfacing with another application.

Scripting Languages

To use a Scriptable Object component, you must have a supported scripting language installed on your system. Two scripting languages are supported by Mathcad: Microsoft VBScript (Visual Basic Scripting Edition) and Microsoft JScript (an implementation of JavaScript). Both of these scripting languages are included with Microsoft Internet Explorer, which can be installed from the Mathcad CD. These scripting languages can also be downloaded at no charge from Microsoft, Inc. at:

http://msdn.microsoft.com/scripting

For more information on scripting languages and syntax associated with their usage, see the **Developer's Reference** under the **Help** menu in Mathcad.

Inserting a Scriptable Object

To insert a Scriptable Object component into a Mathcad worksheet:

1. Click in a blank spot in your worksheet. If you want to send values to the object from a Mathcad variable, click below or to the right of the variable definition.

2. Choose **Component** from the **Insert** menu.

3. Select Scriptable Object from the list in the Wizard and click "Next."

This launches the Scripting Wizard. The Object to Script scrolling list shows the available server applications on your system. Choose an application that supports the OLE 2 automation interface (consult documentation for the application for details).

You must specify:

- Whether the component is a new file or whether you will insert an existing file.
- Whether you will see the actual file or an icon in your Mathcad worksheet.

In the remaining pages of the Wizard you specify: the type of object you want to script, the scripting language you are using, the name of the object, and the number of inputs and outputs the object will accept and provide.

A Scriptable Object component appears in your worksheet with placeholders for the input and output variables. Enter the input variables in the bottom placeholders. Enter the output variables into the placeholders to the left of the :=.

Note There are two Properties dialog boxes for any customized Scripted Object component, one for the *object* and one for the *embedded control*. Access the one for the object by right-clicking on the object and choosing **Properties** from the pop-up menu. This dialog box allows you to specify the number of inputs and outputs and the name of the object. Access the one for the control by right-clicking on the object and choosing **Properties (Control Name) Object**. This dialog box allows you to modify the setting for the embedded control. For example, in the Data Acquisition Control (see page 313), you use it to change the data collection mode from single point to waveform.

Customizing and Redistributing Components

Once you have scripted an object to your liking, you can save it as a customized Scripted Object component for future use. The scripted object will be saved as an MCM file and, once registered, it will be available every time you start Mathcad 2001. You can share any MCM file you have created with other Mathcad 2001 users.

Saving Scripted Objects as customized components

To save a Scripted Object as a customized component:

1. Create a Scripted Object component in your Mathcad worksheet.
2. Right-click on the component and choose **Export as Component** from the pop-up menu.
3. Specify the name of the component, as you would like it to appear on the Insert Component list, and provide a file name. Click "Next."
4. Enter a password to prevent others from editing the script of the component and verify the password. Click "Finish" to save the component. This step is optional.

Once you have exported your component, which saves the component information in an MCM file, it automatically becomes available on your system. The component will appear in the Insert Component list.

To start using a component defined in an MCM file you have received:

1. Copy the MCM file to the MCM folder of your Mathcad installation.
2. Double-click the MCM file to register it with Mathcad.
3. Start Mathcad and the customized component defined in the MCM file will appear on your Insert Component list.

MathSoft Control Components

The MathSoft Control components allow you to insert buttons, text boxes, list boxes, combo boxes, and sliders into your Mathcad worksheet. These components operate in a fashion similar to Microsoft Forms Controls.

Note For more information about the properties and methods associated with MathSoft Controls and other Scriptable Object components, see the **Developer's Reference** under the **Help** menu in Mathcad.

Inserting a MathSoft Control component

To insert a MathSoft Control component into a Mathcad worksheet:

1. Click in a blank spot in your worksheet. If you want to send values to the component from a Mathcad variable, click below or to the right of the variable definition.

2. Choose **Component** from the **Insert** menu. Select MathSoft TextBox Control or one of the other MathSoft Controls from the list and click "Finish."

3. In the placeholder that appears to the left of the component, enter the name of the Mathcad output variable to be defined.

To add input or output variables to your component, right-click the embedded control (i.e. the button, list box, text box, etc.) and select **Add Input Variable** or **Add Output Variable** from the pop-up menu. If you add or remove input or output variables from the component, you must make changes to the script. To edit the script, right-click the embedded control and select **Edit Script...** from the pop-up menu.

You are allowed a maximum of four inputs and four outputs for any MathSoft Control component. For information on inputs, outputs, and scripting your control component see the **Developer's Reference** under **Help** in Mathcad.

Tip For most MathSoft Control components, you will specify outputs only. For example, if you have a TextBox control you will get 0 inputs and 1 output, the output being based on the text entered in the text box.

To change the appearance of a MathSoft Control component:

1. Right-click on the component and select **Mathsoft (Control) Object** ⇒ **Properties** from the pop-up menu.

2. In the **Properties** dialog box you will see various options that let you change the appearance of the control. For example, for a MathSoft Button Control, you can change the default check box to a push button within this dialog box. Make your selections.

3. Click "Apply" to keep the Properties dialog box open and preview the changes in your worksheet. Click "OK" to close the Properties dialog box and return to the worksheet.

Tip   To customize a button quickly with a specific graphic image, create an image and copy it into your clipboard. Right-click on your MathSoft Control component and select MathSoft (Control) Object ⇒ Paste Bitmap from the pop-up menu. Alternatively, you can browse for a bitmap or icon file through the Pictures tab in the Properties dialog box.

To edit the script of a MathSoft Control component:

1. Right-click on the component and select **MathSoft (Control) Object** ⇒ **Edit Script...** from the pop-up menu.

2. Make your changes and close the Script Editor.

3. To update the component in your Mathcad worksheet, select **Calculate Worksheet** from the **Math** menu or click on the component and press **[F9]**.

Note   You cannot send a string as input to any MathSoft Control component. The only types of input variables allowed are scalars, vectors, and matrices. However, you can define an output variable as a string in a MathSoft Control component. See CONTROLS.MCD in the SAMPLES directory of your Mathcad installation for examples of MathSoft Control components.

Data Acquisition Component (DAC)

The Data Acquisition component (DAC) allows you to read data directly from or send data directly to a measurement device installed in your system. The DAC eliminates the step of saving data to an external file before importing the data into Mathcad for display and analysis. To some degree, the DAC also allows for "real time" data logging and analysis. At this time, the DAC only supports National Instruments E-Series data acquisition boards and PC cards. See the **Developer's Reference** for a complete list of supported data acquisition boards.

Note The degree to which "real time" data logging and analysis is possible depends on the size of the data being transferred, the complexity of the calculations being performed, and the speed of your computer. If at some point Mathcad is unable to keep up with the data transfer or calculations, real-time analysis is no longer possible.

Inserting a Data Acquisition component

To insert a Data Acquisition component into a Mathcad worksheet:

1. Click in a blank spot in your worksheet. If you want to send values to the component from a Mathcad variable, click below or to the right of the variable definition.

2. Choose **Component** from the **Insert** menu.

3. Select Data Acquisition Component (DAC) from the list and click "Finish."

The DAC is inserted into the worksheet with default properties, namely, one output and single point analog data collection. These properties are easily modified, however, using either the object's Properties dialog box, the Edit Script… window, or the user interface for the control, shown in Figure 16-4.

Figure 16-4: User Interface of the Data Acquisition copmonent (DAC).

To modify DAC settings using the object's Properties dialog box:

1. Right-click the DAC and select **Properties MathcadDAQ.AnalogIO Object** from the pop-up menu.

2. Use this properties dialog box to specify properties for the embedded data acquisition control.

The number of inputs and outputs for the component can be specified by right-clicking on the component and selecting **Add** or **Remove Inputs** or **Outputs** from the pop-up menu or by selecting **Properties...** from the pop-up menu and using the Scripted Object Component Properties dialog box.

Note   For more information about the properties and methods associated with the DAC and other Scriptable Object components, see the **Developer's Reference** under the **Help** menu in Mathcad.

Tip   If you are using the DAC component to bring analog waveform data into Mathcad for "real time" analysis, be sure that Automatic Calculation, under the Math menu, is turned on.

Example worksheets are provided in the SAMPLES folder of your Mathcad installation showing usage of the component for single point and waveform analog input and output. Context sensitive help is available for all methods, properties, and events associated with the Mathcad Data Acquisition control. You can access context sensitive help by looking at the AnalogIO object in the Visual Basic object browser and clicking on the help button.

Accessing Mathcad from Within Another Application

The previous section describes how to script a custom OLE object in Mathcad. Mathcad's OLE automation interface provides a mechanism for the complementary process of using Mathcad as an automation server from *within* another Windows application. Using Mathcad's OLE automation interface, you can send data dynamically to Mathcad from another application, use Mathcad to perform calculations or other data manipulations, and send results back to the original application.

Mathcad Add-ins

There are several applications for which specialized Mathcad Add-ins have been created. An Add-in allows you to insert a Mathcad object into another application. Visit the Download area of the Mathcad web site at **http://www.mathcad.com/** for a complete list of available Mathcad Add-ins and information about how to download them for use.

Note   The OLE automation interface is supported in Mathcad 7.02 and higher and supersedes the DDE interface supported in Mathcad 5 and 6. For information on the interface, see the **Developer's Reference** under the **Help** menu in Mathcad. For specific examples, see TRAJECTORY.XLS in the \SAMPLES\EXCEL and DOUGHNUT.EXE in the \SAMPLES\VBASIC in your Mathcad installation.

Mathcad

Reference Manual

Mathcad 2001 Professional

Chapter 17
Functions

This chapter lists and describes Mathcad's built-in mathematical and statistical functions. The functions are listed alphabetically.

Certain features described here accompany the *Solving and Optimization Extension Pack*, which requires Mathcad and is available for sale separately.

Function names are case-sensitive, but not font-sensitive. Type them in any font, but use the same capitalization as shown in the syntax section.

Many functions described here as accepting scalar arguments will, in fact, accept vector arguments. For example, while the input z for the acos function is specified as a "real or complex number," acos will in fact evaluate correctly at each of a vector input of real or complex numbers.

Other functions may possess optional arguments, for example, cumint or fv. For such functions f and g, the notation $f(x,[y])$ means that y can be omitted, while the notation $g(x,[[y],[z]])$ means that both x and y can be omitted (but not just x or just y).

Some functions don't accept input arguments with units. For such a function f, an error message "must be dimensionless" will arise when evaluating $f(x)$, if x has units.

Function Categories

Each function falls within one of the following categories:

- Bessel
- Complex numbers
- Differential equation solving
- Expression type
- File access
- Finance
- Fourier transform
- Hyperbolic
- Interpolation and prediction
- Log and exponential
- Number theory/combinatorics
- Piecewise continuous

- Probability density
- Probability distribution
- Random number
- Regression and smoothing
- Solving
- Sorting
- Special
- Statistics
- String
- Trigonometric
- Truncation and round-off
- Vector and matrix
- Wavelet transform

The category name is indicated in the upper right corner of each entry. To see all the functions that belong to a given category, check the index of this book.

Finding More Information

You can also find information about functions using either of these methods:

- To quickly see a short description of each function from within Mathcad, choose **Function** from the **Insert** menu. Select a function in the Function field, then read the description in the Description field. Click on the **Help** button to see the Help topic on a selected function.
- Refer to the Resource Center QuickSheets for more detailed information about functions, categories, and related topics. Select **Resource Center** from the **Help** menu. Then click on the QuickSheets icon and select a specific topic.

About the References

References are provided in the Appendices for you to learn more about the numerical algorithm underlying a given Mathcad function or operator. References are not intended to give a description of the actual underlying source code. Some references (such as *Numerical Recipes*) do contain actual C code for the algorithms discussed therein, but the use of the reference does not necessarily imply that the code is what is implemented in Mathcad. The references are cited for background information only.

Functions

acos

Syntax   acos(*z*)

Description   Returns the inverse cosine of *z* (in radians). The result is between 0 and π if *z* is real. For complex *z*, the result is the principal value.

Arguments
z   real or complex number

acosh

Syntax   acosh(*z*)

Description   Returns the inverse hyperbolic cosine of *z*. The result is the principal value for complex *z*.

Arguments
z   real or complex number

acot

Syntax   acot(*z*)

Description   Returns the inverse cotangent of *z* (in radians). The result is between 0 and π if *z* is real. For complex *z*, the result is the principal value.

Arguments
z   real or complex number

acoth

Syntax   acoth(*z*)

Description   Returns the inverse hyperbolic cotangent of *z*. The result is the principal value for complex *z*.

Arguments
z   real or complex number

acsc

Syntax   acsc(*z*)

Description   Returns the inverse cosecant of *z* (in radians). The result is the principal value for complex *z*.

Arguments
z   real or complex number

acsch

Syntax   acsch(*z*)

Description   Returns the inverse hyperbolic cosecant of *z*. The result is the principal value for complex *z*.

Arguments
z   real or complex number

Ai

Syntax	Ai(x)
Description	Returns the value of the Airy function of the first kind.
Arguments	
x	real number
Example	

Comments	This function is a solution of the differential equation: $\frac{d^2}{dx^2}y - x \cdot y = 0$.
Algorithm	Asymptotic expansion (Abramowitz and Stegun, 1972)
See also	Bi

angle

Syntax	angle(x, y)
Description	Returns the angle (in radians) from positive x-axis to point (x, y) in x-y plane. The result is between 0 and 2π.
Arguments	
x, y	real numbers
See also	arg, atan, atan2

APPENDPRN

Syntax	APPENDPRN(*file*) := **A**
Description	Appends a matrix **A** to an existing structured ASCII data file. Each row in the matrix becomes a new line in the data file. Existing data must have as many columns as **A**. The function must appear alone on the left side of a definition.
Arguments	
file	string variable corresponding to structured ASCII data filename or path
See also	WRITEPRN for more details

arg
Complex Numbers

Syntax	arg(z)
Description	Returns the angle (in radians) from the positive real axis to point z in the complex plane. The result is between $-\pi$ and π. Returns the same value as that of θ when z is written as $r \cdot e^{i \cdot \theta}$.
Arguments	
z	real or complex number
See also	angle, atan, atan2

asec
Trigonometric

Syntax	asec(z)
Description	Returns the inverse secant of z (in radians). The result is the principal value for complex z.
Arguments	
z	real or complex number

asech
Hyperbolic

Syntax	asech(z)
Description	Returns the inverse hyperbolic secant of z. The result is the principal value for complex z.
Arguments	
z	real or complex number

asin
Trigonometric

Syntax	asin(z)
Description	Returns the inverse sine of z (in radians). The result is between $-\pi/2$ and $\pi/2$ if z is real. For complex z, the result is the principal value.
Arguments	
z	real or complex number

asinh
Hyperbolic

Syntax	asinh(z)
Description	Returns the inverse hyperbolic sine of z. The result is the principal value for complex z.
Arguments	
z	real or complex number

atan
Trigonometric

Syntax	atan(z)
Description	Returns the inverse tangent of z (in radians). The result is between $-\pi/2$ and $\pi/2$ if z is real. For complex z, the result is the principal value.
Arguments	
z	real or complex number
See also	angle, arg, atan2

atan2

Syntax   atan2(x, y)

Description   Returns the angle (in radians) from positive x-axis to point (x, y) in x-y plane. The result is between $-\pi$ and π.

Arguments
x, y real numbers

See also   angle, arg, atan

atanh

Syntax   atanh(z)

Description   Returns the inverse hyperbolic tangent of z. The result is the principal value for complex z.

Arguments
z real or complex number

augment

Syntax   augment(**A**, **B**, **C**, ...)

Description   Returns a matrix formed by placing the matrices **A**, **B**, **C**, ... left to right.

Arguments
A, B, C, ... at least two matrices or vectors; **A**, **B**, **C**, ... must have the same number of rows

Example

$$A := \begin{bmatrix} \sqrt{2} \\ e \\ \pi \end{bmatrix} \qquad B := \mathbf{identity}(3) \qquad B = \begin{bmatrix} 1 & 0 & 0 \\ 0 & 1 & 0 \\ 0 & 0 & 1 \end{bmatrix} \qquad \mathbf{augment}(3,5,7) = (3 \quad 5 \quad 7)$$

$$\mathbf{augment}(A,B) = \begin{bmatrix} 1.41421 & 1 & 0 & 0 \\ 2.71828 & 0 & 1 & 0 \\ 3.14159 & 0 & 0 & 1 \end{bmatrix} \qquad \mathbf{stack}(A^T, B) = \begin{bmatrix} 1.41421 & 2.71828 & 3.14159 \\ 1 & 0 & 0 \\ 0 & 1 & 0 \\ 0 & 0 & 1 \end{bmatrix}$$

See also   stack

bei

Syntax   bei(n, x)

Description   Returns the value of the imaginary Bessel Kelvin function of order n.

Arguments
n integer, $n \geq 0$
x real number

Comments   The function $\mathrm{ber}(n, x) + i \cdot \mathrm{bei}(n, x)$ is a solution of the differential equation:

$$x^2 \frac{d^2}{dx^2}y + x \cdot \frac{d}{dx}y - (i \cdot x^2 + n^2) \cdot y = 0 \cdot$$

Algorithm   Series expansion (Abramowitz and Stegun, 1972)

See also   ber

---

ber

Syntax   ber(n, x)

Description   Returns the value of the real Bessel Kelvin function of order n.

Arguments
n integer, $n \geq 0$
x real number

Comments   The function $\text{ber}(n, x) + i \cdot \text{bei}(n, x)$ is a solution of the differential equation:

$$x^2 \frac{d^2}{dx^2} y + x \cdot \frac{d}{dx} y - (i \cdot x^2 + n^2) \cdot y = 0.$$

Algorithm   Series expansion (Abramowitz and Stegun, 1972)

See also   bei

Bi

Syntax   Bi(x)

Description   Returns the value of the Airy function of the second kind.

Arguments
x real number

Comments   This function is a solution of the differential equation:

$$\frac{d^2}{dx^2} y - x \cdot y = 0.$$

Algorithm   Asymptotic expansion (Abramowitz and Stegun, 1972)

See also   Ai for example

bspline

Syntax   bspline(**vx**, **vy**, **u**, n)

Description   Returns the vector of coefficients of a B-spline of degree n, given the knot locations indicated by the values in **u**. The output vector becomes the first argument of the interp function.

Arguments
vx, vy   real vectors of the same size; elements of **vx** must be in ascending order

u   real vector with $n - 1$ fewer elements than **vx**; elements of **u** must be in ascending order; first element of **vx** is $\geq$ first element of **u**; last element of **vx** is $\leq$ last element of **u**

n integer equal to 1, 2, or 3; represents the degree of the individual piecewise linear, quadratic, or cubic polynomial fits

Comments   The knots, those values where the pieces fit together, are contained in the input vector **u**. This is unlike traditional splines (lspline, cspline, and pspline) where the knots are forced to be the values contained in the vector **vx**. The fact that knots are chosen or modified by the user gives bspline more flexibility than the other splines.

See also   lspline for more details

---

bulstoer

Syntax   bulstoer(**y**, *x1*, *x2*, *acc*, **D**, *kmax*, *save*)

Description Solves a differential equation using the smooth Bulirsch-Stoer method. Provides DE solution estimate at *x2*.

Arguments   Several arguments for this function are the same as described for rkfixed.

y   real vector of initial values

x1, *x2*   real endpoints of the solution interval

acc   real *acc* > 0 controls the accuracy of the solution; a small value of *acc* forces the algorithm to take smaller steps along the trajectory, thereby increasing the accuracy of the solution. Values of *acc* around 0.001 will generally yield accurate solutions.

D(*x*, **y**) real vector-valued function containing the derivatives of the unknown functions

kmax   integer *kmax* > 0 specifies maximum number of intermediate points at which the solution is approximated; places an upper bound on the number of rows of the matrix returned by these functions

save   real *save* > 0 specifies the smallest allowable spacing between values at which the solutions are approximated; places a lower bound on the difference between any two numbers in the first column of the matrix returned by the function

Comments   The specialized DE solvers Bulstoer, Rkadapt, Stiffb, and Stiffr provide the solution *y(x)* over a number of uniformly spaced *x*-values in the integration interval bounded by *x1* and *x2*. When you want the value of the solution at only the endpoint, *y(x2)*, use bulstoer, rkadapt, stiffb, and stiffr instead.

Algorithm   Adaptive step Bulirsch-Stoer method (Press *et al.*, 1992)

See also   rkfixed, a more general differential equation solver, for information on output and arguments.

Bulstoer

Syntax   Bulstoer(**y**, *x1*, *x2*, *npts*, **D**)

Description Solves a differential equation using the smooth Bulirsch-Stoer method. Provides DE solution at equally spaced *x*-values by repeated calls to bulstoer.

Arguments   All arguments for this function are the same as described for rkfixed.

y   real vector of initial values

x1, *x2*   real endpoints of the solution interval

npts   integer *npts* > 0 specifies the number of points beyond initial point at which the solution is to be approximated; controls the number of rows in the matrix output

D(*x*,**y**) real vector-valued function containing the derivatives of the unknown functions

Comments   When you know the solution is smooth, use the Bulstoer function instead of rkfixed. The Bulstoer function uses the Bulirsch-Stoer method which is slightly more accurate under these circumstances than the Runge-Kutta method used by rkfixed.

Algorithm   Fixed step Bulirsch-Stoer method with adaptive intermediate steps (Press *et al.*, 1992)

See also   rkfixed, a more general differential equation solver, for information on output and arguments.

Syntax	bvalfit(**v1**, **v2**, *x1*, *x2*, *xf*, **D**, **load1**, **load2**, **score**)
Description	Converts a boundary value differential equation to initial/terminal value problems. Useful when derivatives have a single discontinuity at an intermediate point *xf*.
Arguments	
v1	real vector containing guesses for initial values left unspecified at *x1*
v2	real vector containing guesses for initial values left unspecified at *x2*
x1, *x2*	real endpoints of the interval on which the solution to the DEs are evaluated
xf	point between *x1* and *x2* at which the trajectories of the solutions beginning at *x1* and those beginning at *x2* are constrained to be equal
D(*x*, **y**)	real *n*-element vector-valued function containing the derivatives of the unknown functions
load1(*x1*, **v1**)	real vector-valued function whose *n* elements correspond to the values of the *n* unknown functions at *x1*. Some of these values are constants specified by your initial conditions. If a value is unknown, you should use the corresponding guess value from **v1**
load2(*x2*, **v2**)	analogous to **load1** but for values taken by the *n* unknown functions at *x2*
score(*xf*, **y**)	real *n*-element vector-valued function used to specify how you want the solutions to match at *xf* One usually defines score(*xf*, **y**) := **y** to make the solutions to all unknown functions match up at *xf*
Example	

Solve $\quad y'' = \begin{pmatrix} y \\ -y \end{pmatrix} \quad \begin{array}{l} \text{for } x < 0 \\ \text{for } x \geq 0 \end{array} \quad$ where y(-1)=1 and y(1)=2

$$D(x, y) := \begin{bmatrix} y_1 \\ (x < 0) \cdot y_0 + (x \geq 0) \cdot -y_0 \end{bmatrix}$$

$v1_0 := 1 \qquad \leftarrow$ guess value for y'(-1)

$v2_0 := 1 \qquad \leftarrow$ guess value for y'(1) $\qquad$ xf := 0 $\quad \leftarrow$ point of discontinuity

$\text{load1}(x1, v1) := \begin{pmatrix} 1 \\ v1_0 \end{pmatrix} \quad \begin{array}{l} \leftarrow y(-1) \\ \leftarrow \text{guess value for y'(-1)} \end{array}$

$\text{load2}(x2, v2) := \begin{pmatrix} 2 \\ v2_0 \end{pmatrix} \quad \begin{array}{l} \leftarrow y(1) \\ \leftarrow \text{guess value for y'(1)} \end{array}$

$\text{score}(xf, y) := y \quad \leftarrow$ tells Mathcad to match the two halves of the solution at x=xf

$S := \text{bvalfit}(v1, v2, -1, 1, 0, D, \text{load1}, \text{load2}, \text{score})$

$S = (\ 0.092 \quad -0.678\ ) \qquad \leftarrow$ contains (y'(-1) $\quad$ y'(1))

Comments	If you have information at the initial and terminal points, use sbval. If you know something about the solution and its first *n* − 1 derivatives at some intermediate value *xf*, use bvalfit.
	bvalfit solves a two-point boundary value problem of this type by shooting from the endpoints and matching the trajectories of the solution and its derivatives at the intermediate point. bvalfit is especially useful when a derivative has a discontinuity somewhere in the integration interval, as the above example illustrates. bvalfit does not return a solution to a differential equation. It merely computes the initial values the solution must have in order for the solution to match the final values you specify. You must then take the initial values returned by bvalfit and solve the resulting initial value problem using rkfixed or any of the other more specialized DE solvers.

Algorithm	Shooting method with 4th order Runge-Kutta method (Press *et al.*, 1992)
See also	rkfixed, for more information on output and arguments.

ceil

Syntax	ceil(x)
Description	Returns the least integer $\geq x$.
Arguments	
x	real number
See also	floor for more details, round, trunc

cfft

Syntax	cfft($\mathbf{A}$)
Description	Returns the fast discrete Fourier transform of complex data (representing measurements at regular intervals in the time domain). Returns an array of the same size as its argument.
Arguments	
$\mathbf{A}$	real or complex matrix or vector
Example	

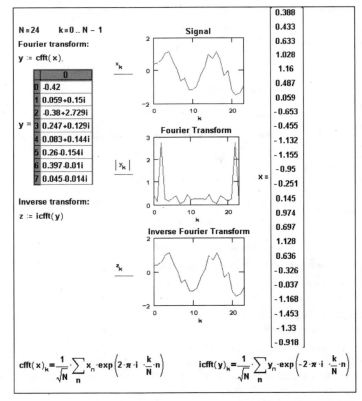

$$cfft(x)_k = \frac{1}{\sqrt{N}} \cdot \sum_n x_n \cdot \exp\left(2 \cdot \pi \cdot i \cdot \frac{k}{N} \cdot n\right) \qquad icfft(y)_k = \frac{1}{\sqrt{N}} \cdot \sum_n y_n \cdot \exp\left(-2 \cdot \pi \cdot i \cdot \frac{k}{N} \cdot n\right)$$

Comments	There are two reasons why you may not be able to use the fft/ifft Fourier transform pair:

- The data may be complex-valued, hence Mathcad can no longer exploit the symmetry present in the real-valued case.

- The data vector might not have exactly 2^n data points in it, hence Mathcad cannot take advantage of the efficient FFT algorithm used by the fft/ifft pair.

Although the cfft/icfft pair works on arrays of any size, the functions work significantly faster when the number of rows and columns contains many smaller factors. Vectors with length 2^n fall into this category, as do vectors having lengths like 100 or 120. Conversely, a vector whose length is a large prime number slows down the Fourier transform algorithm.

Algorithm	Singleton method (Singleton, 1986)
See also	fft for more details

CFFT
Fourier Transform

Syntax	CFFT(**A**)
Description	Returns the fast discrete Fourier transform of complex data (representing measurements at regular intervals in the time domain). Returns an array of the same size as its argument.
	Identical to cfft(**A**), except uses a different normalizing factor and sign convention (see example).
Arguments	
A	real or complex matrix or vector
Example	

$$\mathrm{CFFT}(x)_k = \frac{1}{N} \cdot \sum_n x_n \cdot \exp\left(-2 \cdot \pi \cdot i \cdot \frac{k}{N} \cdot n\right) \qquad \mathrm{ICFFT}(Y)_k = \sum_n Y_n \cdot \exp\left(2 \cdot \pi \cdot i \cdot \frac{k}{N} \cdot n\right)$$

Algorithm	Singleton method (Singleton, 1986)
See also	fft for more details

cholesky

Syntax	cholesky(**M**)
Description	Returns a lower triangular matrix **L** satisfying the equation $\mathbf{L} \cdot \mathbf{L^T} = \mathbf{M}$.
Arguments	
M	real, symmetric, positive definite, square matrix
Comments	cholesky takes **M** to be symmetric, in the sense that it uses only the upper triangular part of **M** and assumes it to match the lower triangular part.

cnorm

Syntax	cnorm(x)
Description	Returns the cumulative standard normal distribution. Same as pnorm(x, 0, 1).
Arguments	
x	real number
Comments	cnorm is provided mainly for compatibility with documents created in earlier versions of Mathcad.

cnper

Syntax	cnper($rate$, pv, fv)
Description	Returns the number of compounding periods required for an investment to yield a specified future value, fv, given a present value, pv, and an interest rate period, $rate$.
Arguments	
$rate$	real rate, $rate > -1$
pv	real present value, $pv > 0$
fv	real future value, $fv > 0$
Comments	If you know the annual interest rate for the investment, ann_rate, you must calculate the interest rate per period as $rate = ann\_rate/nper$.
See also	crate, nper

cols

Syntax	cols(**A**)
Description	Returns the number of columns in array **A**.
Arguments	
A	matrix or vector
Example	

Matrix M . . .

$$M := \begin{pmatrix} 0 & 1 \\ 5 & 3 \\ 6 & -2 \end{pmatrix} \quad \begin{matrix} \text{cols}(M) = 2 \\ \text{rows}(M) = 3 \end{matrix} \quad \begin{matrix} \leftarrow \text{Return no. of rows and} \\ \text{columns in M} \end{matrix}$$

See also	rows

combin

Syntax | combin(n, k)

Description | Returns the number of subsets each of size k that can be formed from n objects.

Arguments
n, k | integers, $0 \leq k \leq n$

Comments | Each such subset is known as a combination. The number of combinations is $C^n_k = \dfrac{n!}{k! \cdot (n-k)!}$.

See also | permut

concat

Syntax | concat($S1, S2, S3, ...$)

Description | Appends string $S2$ to the end of string $S1$, string $S3$ to the end of string $S2$, and so on.

Arguments
$S1, S2, S3, ...$ | string expressions

cond1

Syntax | cond1($\mathbf{M}$)

Description | Returns the condition number of the matrix $\mathbf{M}$ based on the L_1 norm.

Arguments
$\mathbf{M}$ | real or complex square matrix

cond2

Syntax | cond2($\mathbf{M}$)

Description | Returns the condition number of the matrix $\mathbf{M}$ based on the L_2 norm.

Arguments
$\mathbf{M}$ | real or complex square matrix

Algorithm | Singular value computation (Wilkinson and Reinsch, 1971)

conde

Syntax | conde($\mathbf{M}$)

Description | Returns the condition number of the matrix $\mathbf{M}$ based on the Euclidean norm.

Arguments
$\mathbf{M}$ | real or complex square matrix

condi

Syntax | condi($\mathbf{M}$)

Description | Returns the condition number of the matrix $\mathbf{M}$ based on the infinity norm.

Arguments
$\mathbf{M}$ | real or complex square matrix

corr

Syntax   corr($\mathbf{A}$, $\mathbf{B}$)

Description   Returns the Pearson correlation coefficient for the elements in two $m \times n$ arrays $\mathbf{A}$ and $\mathbf{B}$:

$$\text{corr}(\mathbf{A}, \mathbf{B}) = \frac{\text{cvar}(\mathbf{A}, \mathbf{B})}{\text{stdev}(\mathbf{A}) \cdot \text{stdev}(\mathbf{B})}$$

Arguments

$\mathbf{A}$, $\mathbf{B}$ real or complex $m \times n$ matrices or vectors of the same size

See also   cvar

cos

Syntax   cos(z), for z in radians;
cos($z \cdot$deg), for z in degrees

Description   Returns the cosine of z.

Arguments

z real or complex number

cosh

Syntax   cosh(z)

Description   Returns the hyperbolic cosine of z.

Arguments

z real or complex number

cot

Syntax   cot(z), for z in radians;
cot($z \cdot$deg), for z in degrees

Description   Returns the cotangent of z.

Arguments

z real or complex number; z is not a multiple of π

coth

Syntax   coth(z)

Description   Returns the hyperbolic cotangent of z.

Arguments

z real or complex number

crate

Syntax   crate($nper$, pv, fv)

Description   Returns the fixed interest rate required for an investment at present value, pv, to yield a specified future value, fv, over a given number of compounding periods, $nper$.

Arguments

$nper$ integer number of compounding periods, $nper \geq 1$

pv real present value, $pv > 0$

fv real future value, $fv > 0$

See also   cnper, rate

CreateMesh

Vector and Matrix

Syntax | CreateMesh(**F**, *s0*, *s1*, *t0*, *t1*, *sgrid*, *tgrid*, **fmap**)

Description | Returns a nested array containing points on the parametric surface in 3D space defined by **F**.

Arguments

F | real three-dimensional vector-valued function of two variables *s* and *t*; defines a parametric surface in (u,v,w)-space

s0, s1 | (optional) real endpoints for the domain for *s*, $s0 < s1$

t0, t1 | (optional) real endpoints for the domain for *t*, $t0 < t1$

sgrid | (optional) integer number of gridpoints in *s*, $sgrid > 0$

tgrid | (optional) integer number of gridpoints in *t*, $tgrid > 0$

fmap | (optional) real three-dimensional vector-valued function of three variables *u*, *v* and *w*; defines Cartesian coordinates (x,y,z) in terms of (u,v,w)

Comments | CreateMesh is used internally by Mathcad when making 3D QuickPlots of surfaces. The default value for *s0* and *t0* is -5, for *s1* and *t1* it is 5, for *sgrid* and *tgrid* it is 20, and for **fmap** it is the identity mapping. If *s0* and *s1* are explicitly specified, then *t0* and *t1* must also be specified. The number of cells in the grid determined by *sgrid* and *tgrid* is $(sgrid-1)(tgrid-1)$.

There is flexibility in specifying the function **F**. Calls to CreateMesh might look like CreateMesh(**G**), where **G** is a real scalar-valued function of *u* and *v* (and $w=\mathbf{G}(u,v)$); or CreateMesh(*h1,h2,h3*), where *h1*, *h2*, and *h3* are real scalar-valued functions of *s* and *t* (and $u=h1(s,t)$, $v=h2(s,t)$, $w=h3(s,t)$).

Also, the mapping **fmap** may be defined to be sph2xyz, a Mathcad built-in function which converts spherical coordinates (r,θ,ϕ) to Cartesian coordinates (x,y,z):

$$x = u \sin(w) \cos(v) = r \sin(\phi) \cos(\theta)$$

$$y = u \sin(w) \sin(v) = r \sin(\phi) \sin(\theta)$$

$$z = u \cos(w) = r \cos(\phi)$$

or cyl2xyz, which converts cylindrical coordinates (r,θ,z) to (x,y,z) :

$$x = u \cos(v) = r \cos(\theta)$$

$$y = u \sin(v) = r \sin(\theta)$$

$$z = w = z.$$

CreateSpace

Vector and Matrix

Syntax | CreateSpace(**F**, *t0*, *t1*, *tgrid*, **fmap**)

Description | Returns a nested array containing points on the parametric curve in 3D space defined by **F**.

Arguments

F | real three-dimensional vector-valued function of one variable *t*; defines a parametric curve in (u,v,w)-space

t0, t1 | (optional) real endpoints for the domain for *t*, $t0 < t1$

tgrid | (optional) integer number of gridpoints in *t*, $tgrid > 0$

fmap | (optional) real three-dimensional vector-valued function of three variables *u*, *v* and *w*; defines Cartesian coordinates (x,y,z) in terms of (u,v,w)

Comments	CreateSpace is used internally by Mathcad when making 3D QuickPlots of curves. The default value for *t0* is -5, for *t1* it is 5, for *tgrid* it is 20, and for **fmap** it is the identity mapping. The number of cells in the grid determined by *tgrid* is *tgrid*–1.
	There is flexibility in specifying the function **F**. Calls to CreateSpace might look like CreateSpace(*g1,g2,g3*), where *g1*, *g2*, and *g3* are real scalar-valued functions of *t* and *u*=*g1*(*t*), *v*=*g2*(*t*), *w*=*g3*(*t*).
See also	CreateMesh for information about the mapping **fmap**.

csc

Trigonometric

Syntax	csc(*z*), for *z* in radians;
	csc(*z*·deg), for *z* in degrees
Description	Returns the cosecant of *z*.
Arguments	
z	real or complex number; *z* is not a multiple of π

csch

Hyperbolic

Syntax	csch(*z*)
Description	Returns the hyperbolic cosecant of *z*.
Arguments	
z	real or complex number

csgn

Complex Numbers

Syntax	csgn(*z*)
Description	Returns 0 if *z*=0, 1 if Re(*z*)>0 or (Re(*z*)=0 and Im(*z*)>0), −1 otherwise.
Arguments	
z	real or complex number
See also	sign, signum

csort

Sorting

Syntax	csort(**A**, *j*)
Description	Sorts the rows of the matrix **A** by placing the elements in column *j* in ascending order. The result is the same size as **A**.
Arguments	
A	$m \times n$ matrix or vector
j	integer, $0 \le j \le n-1$
Algorithm	Heap sort (Press *et al.*, 1992)
See also	sort for more details, rsort

cspline

Interpolation and Prediction

One-dimensional Case

Syntax	cspline(**vx**, **vy**)
Description	Returns the vector of coefficients of a cubic spline with cubic ends. This vector becomes the first argument of the interp function.
Arguments	
vx, vy	real vectors of the same size; elements of **vx** must be in ascending order

Two-dimensional Case

Syntax	cspline(**Mxy**, **Mz**)
Description	Returns the vector of coefficients of a two-dimensional cubic spline, constrained to be cubic at region boundaries spanned by **Mxy**. This vector becomes the first argument of interp.
Arguments	
Mxy	$n \times 2$ matrix whose elements, $Mxy_{i, 0}$ and $Mxy_{i, 1}$, specify the x- and y-coordinates along the *diagonal* of a rectangular grid. This matrix plays exactly the same role as **vx** in the one-dimensional case described above. Since these points describe a diagonal, the elements in each column of **Mxy** must be in ascending order ($Mxy_{i, k} < Mxy_{j, k}$ whenever $i < j$).
Mz	$n \times n$ matrix whose ijth element is the z-coordinate corresponding to the point $x = Mxy_{i, 0}$ and $y = Mxy_{j, 1}$. **Mz** plays exactly the same role as **vy** does in the one-dimensional case above.
Algorithm	Tridiagonal system solving (Press *et al.*, 1992; Lorczak)
See also	lspline for more details

cumint

Syntax	cumint(*rate*, *nper*, *pv*, *start*, *end*, [*type*])
Description	Returns the cumulative interest paid on a loan between a starting period, *start*, and an ending period, *end*, given a fixed interest rate, *rate*, the total number of compounding periods, *nper*, and the present value of the loan, *pv*.
Arguments	
rate	real rate, $rate \geq 0$
nper	integer number of compounding periods, $nper \geq 1$
pv	real present value
start	integer starting period of the accumulation, $start \geq 1$
end	integer ending period of the accumulation, $end \geq 1$, $start \leq end$, $end \leq nper$
type	(optional) indicator payment timing, 0 for payment made at the end of the period, 1 for payment made at the beginning, default is $type = 0$
Comments	If you know the annual interest rate for the loan, *ann_rate*, you must calculate the interest rate per period as $rate = ann\_rate/nper$.
See also	cumprn, ipmt, pmt

cumprn

Syntax	cumprn(*rate*, *nper*, *pv*, *start*, *end*, [*type*])
Description	Returns the cumulative principal paid on a loan between a starting period, *start*, and an ending period, *end*, given a fixed interest rate, *rate*, the total number of compounding periods, *nper*, and the present value of the loan, *pv*.
Arguments	
rate	real rate, $rate \geq 0$
nper	integer number of compounding periods, $nper \geq 1$
pv	real present value
start	integer starting period of the accumulation, $start \geq 1$
end	integer ending period of the accumulation, $end \geq 1$, $start \leq end$, $end \leq nper$
type	(optional) indicator payment timing, 0 for payment made at the end of the period, 1 for payment made at the beginning, default is $type = 0$

Comments	If you know the annual interest rate for the loan, *ann_rate*, you must calculate the interest rate per period as *rate = ann_rate/nper*.
See also	cumint, pmt, ppmt

cvar

Syntax	cvar(**A**, **B**)
Description	Returns the covariance of the elements in two $m \times n$ arrays **A** and **B**:

$$\text{cvar}(\mathbf{A}, \mathbf{B}) = \frac{1}{mn} \sum_{i=0}^{m-1} \sum_{j=0}^{n-1} [A_{i,j} - \text{mean}(\mathbf{A})]\overline{[B_{i,j} - \text{mean}(\mathbf{B})]}, \text{ where the bar indicates}$$

complex conjugation.

Arguments	
A, **B**	real or complex $m \times n$ matrices or vectors
See also	corr

cyl2xyz

Syntax	cyl2xyz(r, θ, z)
Description	Converts the cylindrical coordinates of a point in 3D space to rectangular coordinates.
Arguments	
r, θ, z	real numbers
Comments	$x = r \cos(\theta)$, $y = r \sin(\theta)$, $z = z$
See also	xyz2cyl

dbeta

Syntax	dbeta(x, $s1$, $s2$)
Description	Returns the probability density for a beta distribution: $\frac{\Gamma(s_1 + s_2)}{\Gamma(s_1) \cdot \Gamma(s_2)} \cdot x^{s_1 - 1} \cdot (1 - x)^{s_2 - 1}$.
Arguments	
x	real number, $0 < x < 1$
s_1, s_2	real shape parameters, $s_1 > 0$, $s_2 > 0$

dbinom

Syntax	dbinom(k, n, p)
Description	Returns $\Pr(X = k)$ when the random variable X has the binomial distribution: $\frac{n!}{k!(n-k)!}p^k(1-p)^{n-k}$.
Arguments	
k, n	integers, $0 \le k \le n$
p	real number, $0 \le p \le 1$

dcauchy

Syntax	dcauchy(x, l, s)
Description	Returns the probability density for the Cauchy distribution: $(\pi s(1 + ((x - l)/s)^2))^{-1}$.

Chapter 17 Functions

Arguments

x	real number
l	real location parameter
s	real scale parameter, $s > 0$

dchisq Probability Density

Syntax   dchisq(x, d)

Description   Returns the probability density for the chi-squared distribution: $\dfrac{e^{-x/2}}{2\Gamma(d/2)}\left(\dfrac{x}{2}\right)^{(d/2-1)}$.

Arguments

x	real number, $x \geq 0$
d	integer degrees of freedom, $d > 0$

dexp Probability Density

Syntax   dexp(x, r)

Description   Returns the probability density for the exponential distribution: re^{-rx}.

Arguments

x	real number, $x \geq 0$
r	real rate, $r > 0$

dF Probability Density

Syntax   dF(x, $d1$, $d2$)

Description   Returns the probability density for the F distribution:

$$\frac{d_1^{d_1/2} d_2^{d_2/2} \Gamma((d_1 + d_2)/2)}{\Gamma(d_1/2)\Gamma(d_2/2)} \cdot \frac{x^{(d_1-2)/2}}{(d_2 + d_1 x)^{(d_1+d_2)/2}}.$$

Arguments

x	real number, $x \geq 0$
d_1, d_2	integer degrees of freedom, $d_1 > 0$, $d_2 > 0$

dgamma Probability Density

Syntax   dgamma(x, s)

Description   Returns the probability density for the gamma distribution: $\dfrac{x^{s-1}e^{-x}}{\Gamma(s)}$.

Arguments

x	real number, $x \geq 0$
s	real shape parameter, $s > 0$

dgeom Probability Density

Syntax   dgeom(k, p)

Description   Returns $\Pr(X = k)$ when the random variable X has the geometric distribution: $p(1 - p)^k$.

Arguments

k	integer, $k \geq 0$
p	real number, $0 < p \leq 1$

dhypergeom

Syntax   dhypergeom(m, a, b, n)

Description   Returns $\Pr(X = m)$ when the random variable X has the hypergeometric distribution:

$$\binom{a}{m} \cdot \binom{b}{n-m} \Big/ \binom{a+b}{n} \text{ where } max\{0, n-b\} \le m \le min\{n, a\} \text{ ; } 0 \text{ for } m \text{ elsewhere.}$$

Arguments
m, a, b, n integers, $0 \le m \le a$, $0 \le n - m \le b$, $0 \le n \le a + b$

diag

Syntax   diag($\mathbf{v}$)

Description   Returns a diagonal matrix containing, on its diagonal, the elements of $\mathbf{v}$.

Arguments
$\mathbf{v}$ real or complex vector

dlnorm

Syntax   dlnorm(x, μ, σ)

Description   Returns the probability density for the lognormal distribution: $\dfrac{1}{\sqrt{2\pi}\sigma x} \exp\left(-\dfrac{1}{2\sigma^2}(\ln(x) - \mu)^2\right)$.

Arguments
x real number, $x \ge 0$
μ real logmean
σ real logdeviation, $\sigma > 0$

dlogis

Syntax   dlogis(x, l, s)

Description   Returns the probability density for the logistic distribution: $\dfrac{\exp(-(x - l)/s)}{s(1 + \exp(-(x - l)/s))^2}$.

Arguments
x real number
l real location parameter
s real scale parameter, $s > 0$

dnbinom

Syntax   dnbinom(k, n, p)

Description   Returns $\Pr(X = k)$ when the random variable X has the negative binomial distribution:

$$\binom{n+k-1}{k} p^n (1-p)^k$$

Arguments
k, n integers, $n > 0$ and $k \ge 0$
p real number, $0 < p \le 1$

dnorm

Syntax   dnorm(x, μ, σ)

Description   Returns the probability density for the normal distribution: $\dfrac{1}{\sqrt{2\pi}\sigma}\exp\left(-\dfrac{1}{2\sigma^2}(x-\mu)^2\right)$.

Arguments

x real number

μ   real mean

σ   real standard deviation, σ > 0

Example

```
x := -10, -9.8 .. 10
```

The "dnorm" function generates the familiar bell curve, here shown with mean = 2.
The "pnorm" function is the running area under the "dnorm" curve.

dpois

Syntax   dpois(k, λ)

Description   Returns Pr($X = k$) when the random variable X has the Poisson distribution: $\dfrac{\lambda^k}{k!}e^{-\lambda}$.

Arguments

k integer, $k \geq 0$

λ   real mean, λ > 0.

dt function

Syntax   dt(x, d)

Description   Returns the probability density for Student's t distribution: $\dfrac{\Gamma((d+1)/2)}{\Gamma(d/2)\sqrt{\pi d}}\left(1+\dfrac{x^2}{d}\right)^{-(d+1)/2}$.

Arguments

x real number

d integer degrees of freedom, $d > 0$.

dunif

Syntax   dunif(x, a, b)

Description   Returns the probability density for the uniform distribution: $\dfrac{1}{b-a}$.

Arguments

x real number, $a \leq x \leq b$

a, b real numbers, $a < b$

dweibull

Syntax   dweibull(x, s)

Description   Returns the probability density for the Weibull distribution: $sx^{s-1}\exp(-x^s)$.

Arguments
x real number, $x \geq 0$
s real shape parameter, $s > 0$

eff

Syntax   eff(*rate*, *nper*)

Description   Returns the effective annual interest rate given the nominal interest rate, *rate*, and the number of compounding periods per year, *nper*.

Arguments
rate   real rate
nper   real number of compounding periods, *nper* ≥ 1

Comments   Effective annual interest rate is also known as annual percentage rate (APR).

See also   nom

eigenvals

Syntax   eigenvals(**M**)

Description   Returns a vector of eigenvalues for the matrix **M**.

Arguments
M   real or complex square matrix

Example

$$A := \begin{pmatrix} 1 & -7 & 6 \\ 3 & 0 & 10 \\ 2 & 5 & -1 \end{pmatrix} \quad c := \text{eigenvals}(A) \quad c = \begin{pmatrix} 3.805 + 1.194i \\ 3.805 - 1.194i \\ -7.609 \end{pmatrix}$$

Algorithm   Reduction to Hessenberg form coupled with QR decomposition (Press *et al.*, 1992)

See also   eigenvec, eigenvecs

eigenvec

Syntax   eigenvec(**M**, z)

Description   Returns a vector containing the normalized eigenvector corresponding to the eigenvalue z of the square matrix **M**.

Arguments
M   real or complex square matrix
z real or complex number

Algorithm   Inverse iteration (Press *et al.*, 1992; Lorczak)

See also   eigenvals, eigenvecs

eigenvecs

Syntax   eigenvecs(**M**)

Description Returns a matrix containing the normalized eigenvectors corresponding to the eigenvalues of the matrix **M**. The nth column of the matrix is the eigenvector corresponding to the nth eigenvalue returned by eigenvals.

Arguments
M   real or complex square matrix

Algorithm   Reduction to Hessenberg form coupled with QR decomposition (Press *et al.*, 1992)

See also   eigenvals, eigenvec

Example

Finding eigenvalues and eigenvectors of a real matrix . .

$$A := \begin{pmatrix} 1 & -2 & 6 \\ 3 & 0 & 10 \\ 2 & 5 & -1 \end{pmatrix} \qquad c := \text{eigenvals}(A) \qquad c = \begin{pmatrix} 0.105 \\ 7.497 \\ -7.602 \end{pmatrix}$$

To find all the corresponding eigenvectors at once (Mathcad Professional)

$$v := \text{eigenvecs}(A) \qquad v = \begin{pmatrix} 0.873 & 0.244 & -0.554 \\ -0.408 & 0.81 & -0.574 \\ -0.266 & 0.534 & 0.603 \end{pmatrix}$$

The first column of v is the eigenvector corresponding to 0.105, the first element of c. Similarly, the second column of v is the eigenvector corresponding to 7.497, the second element of c.

---

erf

Syntax   erf(x)

Description Returns the error function $\text{erf}(x) = \int_0^x \frac{2}{\sqrt{\pi}} e^{-t^2} dt$.

Arguments
x real number

Algorithm   Continued fraction expansion (Abramowitz and Stegun, 1972; Lorczak)

See also   erfc

erfc

Syntax   erfc(x)

Description Returns the complementary error function $\text{erfc}(x) := 1 - \text{erf}(x)$.

Arguments
x real number

Algorithm   Continued fraction expansion (Abramowitz and Stegun, 1972; Lorczak)

See also   erf

error

Syntax   error(S)

Description   Returns the string S as an error message.

Arguments
  S string

Example

$$f(x) := if\left(x<5, x\cdot\frac{2}{\pi}, error\,(\text{"x should be less than 5"})\right)$$

$f(7) = $ ▯ ▯

x should be less than 5

Comments   Mathcad's built-in error messages appear as "error tips" when a built-in function is used incorrectly or could not return a result.

Use the string function error to define specialized error messages that will appear when your user-defined functions are used improperly or cannot return answers.This function is especially useful for trapping erroneous inputs to Mathcad programs you write.

When Mathcad encounters the error function in an expression, it highlights the expression in red. When you click on the expression, the error message appears in a tool tip that hovers over the expression. The text of the message is the string argument you supply to the error function.

exp

Syntax   exp(z)

Description   Returns the value of the exponential function e^z .

Arguments
  z real or complex number

expfit

Syntax   expfit(**vx**, **vy**, **vg**)

Description   Returns a vector containing the parameters (a, b, c) that make the function $a \cdot e^{b \cdot x} + c$ best approximate the data in **vx** and **vy**.

Arguments
  vx, vy   real vectors of the same size
  vg   real vector of guess values for (a, b, c)

Comments   This is a special case of the genfit function. A vector of guess values is needed for initialization. By decreasing the value of the built-in TOL variable, higher accuracy in expfit might be achieved.

See Also   line, linfit, genfit, logfit, lnfit, pwrfit, lgsfit, sinfit, medfit

Syntax   fft(**v**)

Description   Returns the fast discrete Fourier transform of real data. Returns a vector of size $2^{n-1}+1$.

Arguments
   v   real vector with 2^n elements (representing measurements at regular intervals in the time domain), where n is an integer, $n > 0$.

Example

Comments   When you define a vector **v** for use with Fourier or wavelet transforms, be sure to start with v_0 (or change the value of ORIGIN). If you do not define v_0 , Mathcad automatically sets it to zero. This can distort the results of the transform functions.

Mathcad comes with two types of Fourier transform pairs: fft/ifft and cfft/icfft. These functions can be applied only to discrete data (i.e., the inputs and outputs are vectors and matrices only). You cannot apply them to continuous data.

Use the fft and ifft functions if:

- the data values in the time domain are real, and
- the data vector has 2^n elements.

Use the cfft and icfft functions in all other cases.

The first condition is required because the fft/ifft pair takes advantage of the fact that, for real data, the second half of the transform is just the conjugate of the first. Mathcad discards the second half of the result vector to save time and memory. The cfft/icfft pair does not assume symmetry in the transform; therefore you *must* use this pair for complex valued data. Because the real numbers are just a subset of the complex numbers, you can use the cfft/icfft pair for real numbers as well.

The second condition is required because the fft/ifft transform pair uses a highly efficient fast Fourier transform algorithm. In order to do so, the vector you use with fft must have 2^n elements. The cfft/icfft Fourier transform pair uses an algorithm that permits vectors as well as matrices of arbitrary size. When you use this transform pair with a matrix, you get back a two-dimensional Fourier transform.

If you used fft to get to the frequency domain, you *must* use ifft to get back to the time domain. Similarly, if you used cfft to get to the frequency domain, you *must* use icfft to get back to the time domain.

Different sources use different conventions concerning the initial factor of the Fourier transform and whether to conjugate the results of either the transform or the inverse transform. The functions fft, ifft, cfft, and icfft use as a normalizing factor and a positive exponent in going from the time to the frequency domain. The functions FFT, IFFT, CFFT, and ICFFT use $1/n$ as a normalizing factor and a negative exponent in going from the time to the frequency domain. Be sure to use these functions in pairs. For example, if you used CFFT to go from the time domain to the frequency domain, you *must* use ICFFT to transform back to the time domain.

The elements of the vector returned by fft satisfy the following equation:

$$c_j = \frac{1}{\sqrt{n}} \sum_{k=0}^{n-1} v_k e^{2\pi i (j/n)k}$$

In this formula, n is the number of elements in **v** and i is the imaginary unit.

The elements in the vector returned by the fft function correspond to different frequencies. To recover the actual frequency, you must know the sampling frequency of the original signal. If **v** is an n-element vector passed to the fft function, and the sampling frequency is f_s, the frequency corresponding to c_k is

$$f_k = \frac{k}{n} \cdot f_s$$

Therefore, it is impossible to detect frequencies above the sampling frequency. This is a limitation not of Mathcad, but of the underlying mathematics itself. In order to correctly recover a signal from the Fourier transform of its samples, you must sample the signal with a frequency of at least twice its bandwidth. A thorough discussion of this phenomenon is outside the scope of this manual but within that of any textbook on digital signal processing.

Algorithm   Cooley-Tukey (Press *et al.*, 1992)

FFT

Syntax   FFT(**v**)

Description   Identical to fft(**v**), except uses a different normalizing factor and sign convention. Returns a vector of size $2^{n-1}+1$.

Arguments

v   real vector with 2^n elements (representing measurements at regular intervals in the time domain), where n is an integer, $n > 0$.

Comments   The definitions for the Fourier transform discussed in the fft entry are not the only ones used. For example, the following definitions for the discrete Fourier transform and its inverse appear in Ronald Bracewell's *The Fourier Transform and Its Applications* (McGraw-Hill, 1986):

$$F(\upsilon) = \frac{1}{n}\sum_{\tau=1}^{n} f(\tau)e^{-2\pi i(\upsilon/n)\tau} \quad f(\tau) = \sum_{\upsilon=1}^{n} F(\upsilon)e^{2\pi i(\tau/n)\upsilon}$$

These definitions are very common in engineering literature. To use these definitions rather than those presented in the last section, use the functions FFT, IFFT, CFFT, and ICFFT. These differ from those discussed in the last section as follows:

- Instead of a factor of $1/\sqrt{n}$ in front of both forms, there is a factor of $1/n$ in front of the transform and no factor in front of the inverse.
- The minus sign appears in the exponent of the transform instead of in its inverse.

The functions FFT, IFFT, CFFT, and ICFFT are used in exactly the same way as the functions fft, ifft, cfft, and icfft.

Algorithm   Cooley-Tukey (Press *et al.*, 1992)

See also   fft for more details

fhyper

Syntax   fhyper(a, b, c, x)

Description   Returns the value of the Gauss hypergeometric function $_2F_1(a, b;c;x)$.

Arguments

a, b, c, x real numbers, $-1 < x < 1$

Comments   The hypergeometric function is a solution of the differential equation

$$x \cdot (1-x) \cdot \frac{d^2}{dx^2}y + (c - (a+b+1) \cdot x) \cdot \frac{d}{dx}y - a \cdot b \cdot y = 0 .$$

Many functions are special cases of the hypergeometric function, e.g., elementary ones like

$$\ln(1+x) = x \cdot \text{fhyper}(1, 1, 2, -x), \text{asin}(x) = x \cdot \text{fhyper}\left(\frac{1}{2}, \frac{1}{2}, \frac{3}{2}, x^2\right)$$

and more complicated ones like Legendre functions.

Algorithm   Series expansion (Abramowitz and Stegun, 1972)

Find

Syntax Find(*var1*, *var2*, ...)

Description Returns values of *var1*, *var2*, ... which solve a prescribed system of equations, subject to prescribed inequalities. The number of arguments matches the number of unknowns. Output is a scalar if only one argument; otherwise it is a vector of answers.

Arguments

var1, *var2*, ... real or complex variables; *var1*, *var2*,.. must be assigned guess values before using Find.

Examples

Solve the equation: $x^2 + 10 = e^x$

Guess value: $x := 2$

Given

$$x^2 + 10 = e^x$$

$$a := Find(x)$$

Result is: $a = 2.919$

Verify result: $a^2 + 10 = 18.52$

$$e^a = 18.52$$

Figure 17-1: Example 1: A solve block with one equation in one unknown.

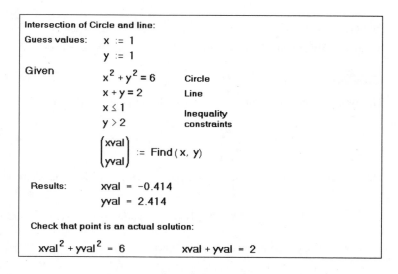

Intersection of Circle and line:

Guess values: $x := 1$
$y := 1$

Given

$x^2 + y^2 = 6$ Circle

$x + y = 2$ Line

$x \le 1$

$y > 2$ Inequality constraints

$$\begin{pmatrix} xval \\ yval \end{pmatrix} := Find(x, y)$$

Results: $xval = -0.414$
$yval = 2.414$

Check that point is an actual solution:

$xval^2 + yval^2 = 6$ $xval + yval = 2$

Figure 17-2: Example 2: A solve block with both equations and inequalities.

$f := 0.02$

Given

$$\frac{1}{\sqrt{f}} = -2.0 \cdot \log\left(\frac{\varepsilon \cdot D^{-1}}{3.7} + \frac{2.51}{R \cdot \sqrt{f}}\right)$$

$\text{FricFac}(\varepsilon, D, R) := \text{Find}(f)$

Same problem,
solved for a vector
of answers . . .

$D := 2.5 \cdot in$

$\varepsilon := .00085 \cdot in$

$i := 0 .. 19$

$R_i := 10000 + 10000 \cdot i$

$ff_i := \text{FricFac}(\varepsilon, D, R_i)$

ff_i

| 0.031 |
| 0.027 |
| 0.024 |
| 0.023 |
| 0.022 |
| 0.021 |

Figure 17-3: Example 3: Solving an equation repeatedly (by defining the Reynolds number R to be a range variable).

$$M := \begin{bmatrix} 13 & 4 & 4 \\ 4 & 9 & -3 \\ 4 & -3 & 57 \end{bmatrix}$$

Two methods for computing a matrix square root

$\text{Vec} := \text{eigenvecs}(M)$ $\text{Vals} := \text{diag}(\text{eigenvals}(M))$ $S := \text{Vec} \cdot \overrightarrow{\sqrt{\text{Vals}} \cdot \text{Vec}^T}$

$$S = \begin{bmatrix} 3.528 & 0.639 & 0.38 \\ 0.639 & 2.915 & -0.31 \\ 0.38 & -0.31 & 7.534 \end{bmatrix}$$ $$S^2 = \begin{bmatrix} 13 & 4 & 4 \\ 4 & 9 & -3 \\ 4 & -3 & 57 \end{bmatrix}$$ *using eigenanalysis*

$X := M$ *(initial guess)*

Given

$X^2 = M$

$$\text{Find}(X) = \begin{bmatrix} 2.095 & 2.867 & 0.623 \\ 2.867 & -0.55 & -0.69 \\ 0.623 & -0.69 & 7.492 \end{bmatrix}$$ *using solve block*

Figure 17-4: Example 4: A solve block for computing the square root of a matrix.

$$A := \begin{bmatrix} 0 & 0 \\ 0 & 1 \end{bmatrix} \qquad B := \begin{bmatrix} 0 & 1 \\ 0 & -1 \end{bmatrix} \qquad C := \begin{bmatrix} 1 & 0 \\ 0 & 0 \end{bmatrix} \qquad P := \text{identity}(2)$$

(initial guess)

Given

$$-P \cdot A \cdot P + P \cdot B + B^T \cdot P + C = 0$$

$$\text{Find}(P) = \begin{bmatrix} 1.732051 & 1 \\ 1 & 0.732051 \end{bmatrix}$$

Solution of algebraic Riccati equation from system and control theory

Figure 17-5: Example 5: A solve block for computing the solution of a matrix equation.

Comments
Mathcad lets you numerically solve a system of up to 200 simultaneous equations in 200 unknowns. If you aren't sure that a given system possesses a solution but need an approximate answer which minimizes error, use Minerr instead. To solve an equation symbolically, that is, to find an exact answer in terms of elementary functions, choose **Solve for Variable** from the **Symbolic** menu or use the solve keyword.

There are four steps to solving a system of simultaneous equations:

1. Provide initial guesses for all the unknowns you intend to solve for. These give Mathcad a place to start searching for solutions. Use complex guess values if you anticipate complex solutions; use real guess values if you anticipate real solutions.

2. Type the word Given. This tells Mathcad that what follows is a system of equality or inequality constraints. You can type Given or given in any style. Just don't type it while in a text region.

3. Type the equations and inequalities in any order below the word Given. Use [**Ctrl**]= to type "=."

4. Finally, type the Find function with your list of unknowns. You can't put numerical values in the list of unknowns: for example, Find(2) in Example 1 isn't permitted. Like given, you can type Find or find in any style.

The word Given, the equations and inequalities that follow, and the Find function form a *solve block*.

Example 1 shows a worksheet that contains a solve block for one equation in one unknown. For one equation in one unknown, you can also use the root or polyroots functions.

Mathcad is very specific about the types of expressions that can appear between Given and Find. See Example 2. The types of allowable constraints are $z=w$, $x>y$, $x<y$, $x\geq y$ and $x\leq y$. Mathcad does not allow the following inside a solve block:

- Constraints with "$\neq$"

- Range variables or expressions involving range variables of any kind

- Any kind of assignment statement (statements like **x:=1**)

If you want to include the outcome of a solve block in an iterative calculation, see Example 3.

Solve blocks cannot be nested inside each other. Each solve block can have only one Given and one Find. You can however, define a function like $f(x) := \text{Find}(x)$ at the end of one solve block and use this same function in another solve block.

If the solver cannot make any further improvements to the solution but the constraints are *not* all satisfied, then the solver stops and marks Find with an error message. This happens whenever the difference between successive approximations to the solution is greater than TOL *and*:

- The solver reaches a point where it cannot reduce the error any further.

- The solver reaches a point from which there is no preferred direction. Because of this, the solver has no basis on which to make further iterations.

- The solver reaches the limit of its accuracy. Round-off errors make it unlikely that further computation would increase accuracy of the solution. This often happens if you set TOL to a value below 10^{-15}.

The following problems may cause this sort of failure:
- There may actually be no solution.

- You may have given real guesses for an equation with no real solution. If the solution for a variable is complex, the solver will not find it unless the starting value for that variable is also complex.

- The solver may have become trapped in a local minimum for the error values. To find the actual solution, try using different starting values or add an inequality to keep Mathcad from being trapped in the local minimum.

- The solver may have become trapped on a point that is not a local minimum, but from which it cannot determine where to go next. Again, try changing the initial guesses or adding an inequality to avoid the undesirable stopping point.

- It may not be possible to solve the constraints to within the desired tolerance. Try defining TOL with a larger value somewhere above the solve block. Increasing the tolerance changes what Mathcad considers close enough to call a solution.

The pop-up menu (right mouse click) associated with Find contains the following options:

- AutoSelect – chooses an appropriate algorithm

- Linear option – indicates that the problem is linear (and thus applies linear programming methods to the problem); guess values for *var1*, *var2*,... are immaterial (can all be zero)

- Nonlinear option – indicates that the problem is nonlinear (and thus applies these general methods to the problem: the conjugate gradient solver; if that fails to converge, the Levenberg-Marquardt solver; if that too fails, the quasi-Newton solver); guess values for *var1*, *var2*,... greatly affect the solution

- Quadratic option (appears only if the Solving and Optimization Extension Pack or Expert Solver product is installed) – indicates that the problem is quadratic (and thus applies quadratic programming methods to the problem); guess values for *var1*, *var2*,... are immaterial (can all be zero)

- Advanced options – applies only to the nonlinear conjugate gradient and the quasi-Newton solvers

These options provide you more control in trying different algorithms for testing and comparison. You may also adjust the values of the built-in variables CTOL and TOL. The *constraint tolerance* CTOL controls how closely a constraint must be met for a solution to be acceptable; if CTOL were 0.001, then a constraint such as x < 2 would be considered satisfied if the value of x satisfied x < 2.001. This can be defined or changed in the same way as the *convergence tolerance* TOL. The default value for CTOL is 10^{-3}.

Other Solving and Optimization Extension Pack features include mixed integer programming and constraint sensitivity report generation. See on-line Help for details.

Algorithm	For the non-linear case: Levenberg-Marquardt, Quasi-Newton, Conjugate Gradient. For the linear case: simplex method with branch/bound techniques (Press *et al.*, 1992; Polak, 1997; Winston, 1994)
See also	Minerr, Maximize, Minimize

floor
Truncation and Round-off

Syntax	floor(*x*)
Description	Returns the greatest integer $\leq x$.
Arguments	
x	real number
Example	

```
    ceil( 3.25 )  =  4            floor( 3.25 )  =  3

mantissa( x )  :=  x - floor( x )

        mantissa( 3.45 )  =  0.45
```

Comments	Can be used to define the positive fractional part of a number: mantissa(*x*) := *x* - floor(*x*).
See also	ceil, round, trunc

fv
Finance

Syntax	fv(*rate*, *nper*, *pmt*, [[*pv*], [*type*]])
Description	Returns the future value of an investment or loan over a specified number of compounding periods, *nper*, given a periodic, constant payment, *pmt*, and a fixed interest rate, *rate*.
Arguments	
rate	real rate
nper	integer number of compounding periods, $nper \geq 1$
pmt	real payment
pv	(optional) real present value, default is $pv = 0$
type	(optional) indicator payment timing, 0 for payment made at the end of the period, 1 for payment made at the beginning, default is $type = 0$

Comments	If you know the annual interest rate, *ann_rate*, you must calculate the interest rate per period as *rate = ann_rate/nper*.
	Payments you make, such as deposits into a savings account or payments toward a loan, must be entered as negative numbers. Cash you receive, such as dividend checks, must be entered as positive numbers.
See also	fvadj, fvc, nper, pmt, pv, rate

fvadj
Finance

Syntax	fvadj(*prin*, **v**)
Description	Returns the future value of an initial principal, *prin*, after applying a series of compound interest rates stored in a vector, **v**.
Arguments	
prin	real principal
v	real vector of interest rates
Comments	Use fvadj to calculate the future value of an investment with a variable or adjustable interest rate.
See also	fv, fvc

fvc
Finance

Syntax	fvc(*rate*, **v**)
Description	Returns the future value of a list of cash flows occurring at regular intervals, **v**, earning a specified interest rate, *rate*.
Arguments	
rate	real rate
v	real vector of cash flows
Comments	In **v**, payments must be entered as negative numbers and income must be entered as positive numbers.
	fvc assumes that the payment is made at the end of the period.
See also	fv, fvadj

gcd
Number Theory/Combinatorics

Syntax	gcd(**A**)
Description	Returns the largest positive integer that is a divisor of all the values in the array **A**. This integer is known as the greatest common divisor of the elements in **A**.
Arguments	
A	integer matrix or vector; all elements of **A** are greater than zero
Comments	gcd(**A, B, C, ...**) is also permissible and returns the greatest common divisor of the elements of **A, B, C, ...**.
Algorithm	Euclid's algorithm (Niven and Zuckerman, 1972)
See also	lcm

genfit

Syntax	genfit(**vx**, **vy**, **vg**, **F**)

Description Returns a vector containing the parameters that make a function f of x and n parameters $u_0, u_1, \ldots, u_{n-1}$ best approximate the data in **vx** and **vy**.

Arguments

vx, vy real vectors of the same size

vg real vector of guess values for the n parameters

F a function that returns an $n+1$ element vector containing f and its partial derivatives with respect to its n parameters

Example

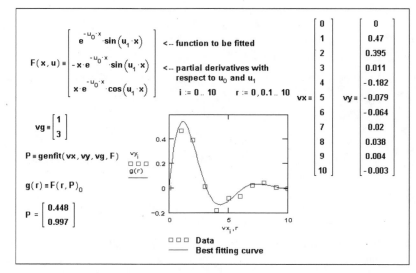

Comments The functions linfit and genfit are closely related. Anything you can do with linfit you can also do, albeit less conveniently, with genfit. The difference between these two functions is analogous to the difference between solving a system of linear equations and solving a system of nonlinear equations. The former is easily done using the methods of linear algebra. The latter is far more difficult and generally must be solved by iteration. This explains why genfit needs a vector of guess values as an argument and linfit does not.

The example above uses genfit to find the exponent that best fits a set of data. By decreasing the value of the built-in TOL variable, higher accuracy in genfit might be achieved.

Algorithm Levenberg-Marquardt (Press *et al.*, 1992)

See also line, linfit, expfit, logfit, lnfit, pwrfit, lgsfit, sinfit, medfit

geninv

Syntax	geninv(**A**)

Description Returns the left inverse of a matrix **A**.

Arguments

A real $m \times n$ matrix, where $m \geq n$.

Comments If **L** denotes the left inverse, then $\mathbf{L} \cdot \mathbf{A} = \mathbf{I}$ where **I** is the identity matrix with cols(**I**)=cols(**A**).

Algorithm SVD-based construction (Nash, 1979)

genvals

Syntax	genvals(**M**, **N**)
Description	Returns a vector **v** of eigenvalues each of which satisfies the generalized eigenvalue equation $\mathbf{M} \cdot \mathbf{x} = v_j \cdot \mathbf{N} \cdot \mathbf{x}$ for nonzero eigenvectors **x**.
Arguments	
M, N	real square matrices of the same size
Example	

$$\mathbf{M} := \begin{bmatrix} -3 & 6 & 0 \\ 3 & 0 & -4 \\ 6 & 6 & -5 \end{bmatrix} \qquad \mathbf{N} := \begin{bmatrix} -5 & 9 & -1 \\ 0 & 4 & -7 \\ -3 & 10 & 4 \end{bmatrix}$$

Vector of generalized eigenvalues:

$$\mathbf{v} := \text{genvals}(\,\mathbf{M}, \mathbf{N}\,) \qquad \mathbf{v} = \begin{bmatrix} 2.177 \\ 0.803 \\ 0.285 \end{bmatrix}$$

Matrix of generalized eigenvectors which correspond to the generalized eigenvalues in vector v:

$$\mathbf{x} := \text{genvecs}(\,\mathbf{M}, \mathbf{N}\,) \qquad \mathbf{x} = \begin{bmatrix} 0.839 & 0.562 & -0.597 \\ 0.515 & 0.725 & -0.21 \\ 0.175 & 0.397 & -0.774 \end{bmatrix}$$

$$\mathbf{x0} := \text{submatrix}(\,\mathbf{x}, 0, 2, 0, 0\,)$$
$$\mathbf{x1} := \text{submatrix}(\,\mathbf{x}, 0, 2, 1, 1\,)$$
$$\mathbf{x2} := \text{submatrix}(\,\mathbf{x}, 0, 2, 2, 2\,)$$

Compare:

$$\mathbf{M} \cdot \mathbf{x0} = \begin{bmatrix} 0.571 \\ 1.818 \\ 7.25 \end{bmatrix} \qquad \mathbf{M} \cdot \mathbf{x1} = \begin{bmatrix} 2.666 \\ 0.1 \\ 5.744 \end{bmatrix} \qquad \mathbf{M} \cdot \mathbf{x2} = \begin{bmatrix} 0.534 \\ 1.306 \\ -0.969 \end{bmatrix}$$

$$v_0 \cdot (\,\mathbf{N} \cdot \mathbf{x0}\,) = \begin{bmatrix} 0.571 \\ 1.818 \\ 7.25 \end{bmatrix} \qquad v_1 \cdot (\,\mathbf{N} \cdot \mathbf{x1}\,) = \begin{bmatrix} 2.666 \\ 0.1 \\ 5.744 \end{bmatrix} \qquad v_2 \cdot (\,\mathbf{N} \cdot \mathbf{x2}\,) = \begin{bmatrix} 0.534 \\ 1.306 \\ -0.969 \end{bmatrix}$$

Comments	To compute the eigenvectors, use genvecs.
Algorithm	Stable QZ method (Golub and Van Loan, 1989)

genvecs

Syntax	genvecs(**M**, **N**)
Description	Returns a matrix of normalized eigenvectors corresponding to the eigenvalues in **v**, the vector returned by genvals. The *j*th column of this matrix is the eigenvector **x** satisfying the generalized eigenvalue problem $\mathbf{M} \cdot \mathbf{x} = v_j \cdot \mathbf{N} \cdot \mathbf{x}$.
Arguments	
M, N	real square matrices of the same size
Algorithm	Stable QZ method (Golub and Van Loan, 1989)
See also	genvals for example

GETWAVINFO

Syntax	GETWAVINFO(*file*)
Description	Creates a vector with four elements containing information about *file*. The elements corresponds to the number of channels, the sample rate, the number of bits per sample (resolution), and average number of bytes per second, respectively.
Arguments	
file	string variable corresponding to pulse code modulated (PCM) Microsoft WAV filename or path
Comments	Data from a WAV file is not scaled.
See also	READWAV and WRITEWAV

gmean

Syntax	gmean(**A**)
Description	Returns the geometric mean of the elements of **A**: $\text{gmean}(\mathbf{A}) = \left(\prod_{i=0}^{m-1} \prod_{j=0}^{n-1} \mathbf{A}_{i,j} \right)^{1/(mn)}$.
Arguments	
A	real $m \times n$ matrix or vector with all elements greater than zero
Comments	gmean(**A**, **B**, **C**, **...**) is also permissible and returns the geometric mean of the elements of **A**, **B**, **C**, ...
See also	hmean, mean, median, mode

Her

Syntax	Her(*n*, *x*)
Description	Returns the value of the Hermite polynomial of degree *n* at *x*.
Arguments	
n	integer, $n \geq 0$
x	real number
Comments	The *n*th degree Hermite polynomial is a solution of the differential equation:

$$x \cdot \frac{d^2}{dx^2} y - 2 \cdot x \cdot \frac{d}{dx} y + 2 \cdot n \cdot y = 0 .$$

Algorithm	Recurrence relation (Abramowitz and Stegun, 1972)

hist

Uniform Bin Case

Syntax	hist(*n*, **A**)
Description	Returns a vector containing the frequencies with which values in **A** fall in *n* subintervals of the range $\min(\mathbf{A}) \leq \text{value} \leq \max(\mathbf{A})$ of equal length. The resulting histogram vector has *n* elements.
Arguments	
n	integer, $n > 0$
A	real matrix

Comments	This is identical to hist(**intervals**, **A**) with $intervals_i = min(\mathbf{A}) + \dfrac{max(\mathbf{A}) - min(\mathbf{A})}{n} \cdot i$ and $0 \le i \le n$ (see below).

Non-uniform Bin Case

Syntax	hist(**intervals**, **A**)
Description	Returns a vector containing the frequencies with which values in **A** fall in the intervals represented by the **intervals** vector. The resulting histogram vector is one element shorter than **intervals**.
Arguments	
intervals	real vector with elements in ascending order
A	real matrix
Example	

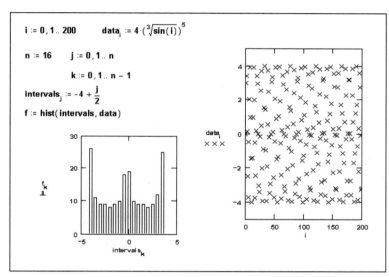

Comments	The **intervals** vector contains the endpoints of subintervals constituting a partition of the data. The result of the hist function is a vector **f**, in which f_i is the number of values in **A** satisfying the condition $intervals_i \le value < intervals_{i+1}$.
	Mathcad ignores data points less than the first value in **intervals** or greater than the last value in **intervals**.

See also	histogram

histogram

Uniform Bin Case

Syntax	histogram(n, **A**)
Description	Returns a matrix with two columns. The first column contains midpoints of the n subintervals of the range $min(\mathbf{A}) \le value \le max(\mathbf{A})$ of equal length. The second column is identical to hist(n, **A**), and hence the resulting matrix has n rows.
Arguments	
n	integer, $n > 0$
A	real matrix

Comments	Using histogram rather than hist saves you the additional step of defining horizontal axis data when plotting.

Non-uniform Bin Case

Syntax	histogram(**intervals**, **A**)
Description	Returns a matrix with two columns. The first column contains midpoints of the intervals represented by the **intervals** vector. The second column is identical to hist(**intervals**, **A**), and hence the resulting matrix has one less row than **intervals**.
Arguments	
intervals	real vector with elements in ascending order
A	real matrix

See also	hist

hlookup
Vector and Matrix

Syntax	hlookup(z, **A**, r)
Description	Looks in the first row of a matrix, **A**, for a given value, z, and returns the value(s) in the same column(s) in the row specified, r. When multiple values are returned, they appear in a vector.
Arguments	
z	real or complex number, or string
A	real, complex or string $m \times n$ matrix
r	integer, $ORIGIN \leq r \leq ORIGIN + m - 1$
Comments	The degree of precision to which the comparison adheres is determined by the *TOL* setting of the worksheet.
See Also	lookup, vlookup, match

hmean
Statistics

Syntax	hmean(**A**)
Description	Returns the harmonic mean of the elements of **A**: $hmean(\mathbf{A}) = \left(\dfrac{1}{mn} \displaystyle\sum_{i=0}^{m-1} \sum_{j=0}^{n-1} \dfrac{1}{\mathbf{A}_{i,j}} \right)^{-1}$.
Arguments	
A	real $m \times n$ matrix or vector with all elements greater than zero
Comments	hmean(**A**, **B**, **C**, ...) is also permissible and returns the harmonic mean of the elements of **A**, **B**, **C**, ...
See also	gmean, mean, median, mode

I0
Bessel

Syntax	I0(x)
Description	Returns the value of the modified Bessel function $I_0(x)$ of the first kind. Same as In(0, x).
Arguments	
x	real number
Algorithm	Small order approximation (Abramowitz and Stegun, 1972)

I1

Syntax — I1(*x*)

Description — Returns the value of the modified Bessel function $I_1(x)$ of the first kind. Same as In(1, *x*).

Arguments

x — real number

Algorithm — Small order approximation (Abramowitz and Stegun, 1972)

ibeta

Syntax — ibeta(*a*, *x*, *y*)

Description — Returns the value of the incomplete beta function with parameter *a*, at (*x*, *y*).

Arguments

a — real number, $0 \le a \le 1$

x, *y* — real numbers, $x > 0$, $y > 0$

Comments — The incomplete beta function often arises in probabilistic applications. It is defined by the following formula:

$$\text{ibeta}(a, x, y) = \frac{\Gamma(x + y)}{\Gamma(x) \cdot \Gamma(y)} \cdot \int_0^a t^{x-1} \cdot (1 - t)^{y-1} dt .$$

Algorithm — Continued fraction expansion (Abramowitz and Stegun, 1972)

icfft

Syntax — icfft(**A**)

Description — Returns the inverse Fourier transform corresponding to cfft. Returns an array of the same size as its argument.

Arguments

A — real or complex matrix or vector

Comments — The cfft and icfft functions are exact inverses; $\text{icfft}(\text{cfft}(\mathbf{A})) = \mathbf{A}$.

Algorithm — Singleton method (Singleton, 1986)

See also — fft for more details and cfft for example

ICFFT

Syntax — ICFFT(**A**)

Description — Returns the inverse Fourier transform corresponding to CFFT. Returns an array of the same size as its argument.

Arguments

A — real or complex matrix or vector

Comments — The CFFT and ICFFT functions are exact inverses; $\text{ICFFT}(\text{CFFT}(\mathbf{A})) = \mathbf{A}$.

Algorithm — Singleton method (Singleton, 1986)

See also — fft for more details and CFFT for example

identity

Syntax   identity(n)

Description Returns the $n \times n$ identity matrix.

Arguments
n integer, $n > 0$

if

Syntax   if($cond, x, y$)

Description Returns x or y depending on the value of *cond*.
             If *cond* is true (non-zero), returns x. If *cond* is false (zero), returns y.

Arguments
cond   arbitrary expression (usually a Boolean expression)
x, y arbitrary real or complex numbers, arrays, or strings

Example

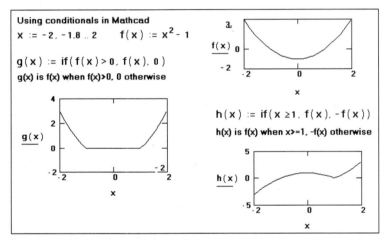

Comments   Use if to define a function that behaves one way below a certain number and a different way
            above that number. That point of discontinuity is specified by its first argument, *cond*. The
            remaining two arguments let you specify the behavior of the function on either side of that
            discontinuity. The argument *cond* is usually a Boolean expression (made up using the Boolean
            operators $=$, $>$, $<$, $\geq$, $\leq$, $\neq$, $\wedge$, $\vee$, $\oplus$, or $\neg$).

            To save time, Mathcad evaluates only the necessary arguments. For example, if *cond* is false,
            there is no need to evaluate x because it will not be returned anyway. Therefore, errors in the
            unevaluated argument can escape detection. For example, Mathcad will never detect the fact that
            $\ln(0)$ is undefined in the expression if($|z| < 0$, $\ln(0)$, $\ln(z)$).

            You can combine Boolean operators to create more complicated conditions. For example, the
            condition $(x < 1) \wedge (x > 0)$ acts like an "and" gate, returning 1 if and only if x is between
            0 and 1. Similarly, the expression $(x < 1) \vee (x > 0)$ acts like an "or" gate, returning a 1 if and
            only if $x > 1$ or $x < 0$.

Chapter 17 Functions

ifft   Fourier Transform

Syntax	ifft(**v**)
Description	Returns the inverse Fourier transform corresponding to fft. Returns a real vector of size 2^n.
Arguments	
v	real or complex vector of size $1 + 2^{n-1}$, where n is an integer.
Comments	The argument **v** is a vector similar to those generated by the fft function. To compute the result, Mathcad first creates a new vector **w** by taking the conjugates of the elements of **v** and appending them to the vector **v**. Then Mathcad computes a vector **d** whose elements satisfy this formula:

$$d_j = \frac{1}{\sqrt{n}} \sum_{k=0}^{n-1} w_k e^{-2\pi i (j/n)k}.$$

	This is the same formula as the fft formula, except for the minus sign in the exponent. The fft and ifft functions are exact inverses. For all real **v**, $\mathrm{ifft}(\mathrm{fft}(\mathbf{v})) = \mathbf{v}$.
Algorithm	Cooley-Tukey (Press *et al.*, 1992)
See also	fft for more details

IFFT   Fourier Transform

Syntax	IFFT(**v**)
Description	Returns the inverse transform corresponding to FFT. Returns a real vector of size 2^n.
Arguments	
v	real or complex vector of size $1 + 2^{n-1}$, where n is an integer.
Algorithm	Cooley-Tukey (Press *et al.*, 1992)
See also	fft for more details

Im   Complex Numbers

Syntax	Im(z)
Description	Returns the imaginary part of z.
Arguments	
z	real or complex number
See also	Re

In   Bessel

Syntax	In(m, x)
Description	Returns the value of the modified Bessel function $\mathrm{I}_m(x)$ of the first kind.
Arguments	
m	integer, $0 \le m \le 100$
x	real number
Comments	Solution of the differential equation $x^2 \cdot \dfrac{d^2}{dx^2}y + x \cdot \dfrac{d}{dx}y - (x^2 + m^2) \cdot y = 0$.
Algorithm	Small order approximation, upward recurrence relation (Abramowitz and Stegun, 1972; Press *et al.*, 1992)
See also	Kn

---

intercept

Syntax	intercept(**vx**, **vy**)
Description	Returns the y-intercept of the least-squares regression line.
Arguments	
vx, **vy**	real vectors of the same size
See also	slope for more details, line, stderr, medfit

interp

One-dimensional Case

Syntax	interp(**vs**, **vx**, **vy**, x)
Description	Interpolates the value from spline coefficients or regression coefficients. Takes three vector arguments **vx**, **vy** (of the same size) and **vs**. Returns the interpolated y value corresponding to the point x.
Arguments	
vs	real vector output from interpolation routine bspline, cspline, lspline, or pspline or regression routine regress or loess
vx, **vy**	real vectors of the same size
x	real number
Comments	Let us first discuss interp on the output of cubic spline routines. To find the interpolated value for a particular x, Mathcad finds the two points which x falls between. It then returns the y value on the cubic section enclosed by these two points. For x values less than the smallest point in **vx**, Mathcad extrapolates the cubic section connecting the smallest two points of **vx**. Similarly, for x values greater than the largest point in **vx**, Mathcad extrapolates the cubic section connecting the largest two points of **vx**.
	For best results, do not use the interp function on values of x far from the fitted points. Splines are intended for interpolation, not extrapolation. Consequently, computed values for such x values are unlikely to be useful. See predict for an alternative.
	In the regress case, interp simply computes the value of the regression polynomial; for loess, interp uses the local least-squares polynomial on the interval.

Two-dimensional Case

Syntax	interp(**vs**, **Mxy**, **Mz**, **v**)
Description	Interpolates the value from spline coefficients or regression coefficients. Takes two matrix arguments **Mxy** and **Mz** (with the same number of rows) and one vector argument **vs**. Returns the interpolated z value corresponding to the point $x = v_0$ and $y = v_1$.
Arguments	
vs	real vector output from interpolation routine bspline, cspline, lspline, or pspline or regression routine regress or loess
Mxy, Mz	real matrices (with the same number of rows)
v	real two-dimensional vector
Comments	For best results, do not use the interp function on values of x and y far from the grid points. Splines are intended for interpolation, not extrapolation. Consequently, computed values for such x and y values are unlikely to be useful. See predict for an alternative.
See also	lspline for example, bspline, cspline, pspline, regress, loess

---

Chapter 17 Functions

ipmt

Syntax	ipmt(*rate*, *per*, *nper*, *pv*, [[*fv*], [*type*]])
Description	Returns the interest payment of an investment or loan for a given period, *per*, based on periodic constant payments over a given number of compounding periods, *nper*, using a fixed interest rate, *rate*, and a specified present value, *pv*.
Arguments	
rate	real rate
per	integer period number, $per \geq 1$
nper	integer number of compounding periods, $1 \leq per \leq nper$
pv	real present value
fv	(optional) real future value, default is $fv = 0$
type	(optional) indicator payment timing, 0 for payment made at the end of the period, 1 for payment made at the beginning, default is $type = 0$
Comments	If you know the annual interest rate, *ann_rate*, you must calculate the interest rate per period as $rate = ann\_rate/nper$.
	Payments you make, such as deposits into a savings account or payments toward a loan, must be entered as negative numbers. Cash you receive, such as dividend checks, must be entered as positive numbers.
See also	cumint, pmt, ppmt

irr

Syntax	irr(**v**, [*guess*])
Description	Returns the internal rate of return for a series of cash flows, **v**, occurring at regular intervals.
Arguments	
v	real vector of cash flows
guess	(optional) real guess value, default is $guess = 0.1$ (10%)
Comments	In **v**, payments must be entered as negative numbers and income must be entered as positive numbers. There must be at least one negative value and one positive value in **v**.
	If irr cannot find a result that is accurate to within $1 \cdot 10^{-5}$ percent after 20 iterations, it returns an error. In such a case, a different guess value should be tried, although it will not guarantee a solution.
See also	mirr, npv

IsArray

Syntax	IsArray(*x*)
Description	Returns 1 if *x* is a matrix or vector; 0 otherwise.
Arguments	
x	arbitrary real or complex number, array, or string

IsScalar
Expression Type

Syntax   IsScalar(*x*)

Description   Returns 1 if *x* is a real or complex number; 0 otherwise.

Arguments

    x   arbitrary real or complex number, array, or string

IsString
Expression Type

Syntax   IsString(*x*)

Description   Returns 1 if *x* is a string; 0 otherwise.

Arguments

    x   arbitrary real or complex number, array, or string

iwave
Wavelet Transform

Syntax   iwave(**v**)

Description   Returns the inverse wavelet transform corresponding to wave.

Arguments

    v   real vector of 2^n elements, where *n* is an integer, $n > 0$.

Algorithm   Pyramidal Daubechies 4-coefficient wavelet filter (Press *et al.*, 1992)

See also   wave for example

J0
Bessel

Syntax   J0(*x*)

Description   Returns the value of the Bessel function $J_0(x)$ of the first kind. Same as Jn(0, *x*).

Arguments

    x   real number

Algorithm   Steed's method (Press *et al.*, 1992)

J1
Bessel

Syntax   J1(*x*)

Description   Returns the value of the Bessel function $J_1(x)$ of the first kind. Same as Jn(1, *x*).

Arguments

    x   real number

Algorithm   Steed's method (Press *et al.*, 1992)

Jac
Special

Syntax   Jac(*n*, *a*, *b*, *x*)

Description   Returns the value of the Jacobi polynomial of degree *n* with parameters *a* and *b*, at *x*.

Arguments

    n   integer, $n \geq 0$

    a, *b*   real numbers, $a > -1, b > -1$

    x   real number

Comments	The Jacobi polynomials are solutions of the differential equation:

$$(1 - x^2) \cdot \frac{d^2}{dx^2}y + (b - a - (a + b + 2) \cdot x) \cdot \frac{d}{dx}y + n \cdot (n + a + b + 1) \cdot y = 0$$

and include the Chebyshev and Legendre polynomials as special cases.

Algorithm	Recurrence relation (Abramowitz and Stegun, 1972)

Jn
Bessel

Syntax	Jn(m, x)
Description	Returns the value of the Bessel function $J_m(x)$ of the first kind.
Arguments	
m	integer, $0 \le m \le 100$.
x	real number
Comments	Solution of the differential equation $x^2 \cdot \frac{d^2}{dx^2}y + x \cdot \frac{d}{dx}y + (x^2 - m^2) \cdot y = 0$.
Algorithm	Steed's method (Press *et al.*, 1992)
See also	Yn

js
Bessel

Syntax	js(n, x)
Description	Returns the value of the spherical Bessel function of the first kind, of order n, at x.
Arguments	
n	integer, $-200 \le n$
x	real number, $x > 0$; $x = 0$ is permitted for js if $n \ge 0$
Comments	Solution of the differential equation: $x^2 \cdot \frac{d^2}{dx^2}y + 2x \cdot \frac{d}{dx}y + (x^2 - n \cdot (n + 1))y = 0$.
Algorithm	Small order approximation, upward recurrence relation (Abramowitz and Stegun, 1972; Press *et al.*, 1992)
See also	ys

K0
Bessel

Syntax	K0(x)
Description	Returns the value of the modified Bessel function $K_0(x)$ of the second kind. Same as Kn(0, x).
Arguments	
x	real number, $x > 0$
Algorithm	Small order approximation (Abramowitz and Stegun, 1972)

K1
Bessel

Syntax	K1(x)
Description	Returns the value of the modified Bessel function $K_1(x)$ of the second kind. Same as Kn(1, x).
Arguments	
x	real number, $x > 0$
Algorithm	Small order approximation (Abramowitz and Stegun, 1972)

Kn

Syntax   Kn(m, x)

Description   Returns the value of the modified Bessel function $K_m(x)$ of the second kind.

Arguments

m integer, $0 \le m \le 100$.

x real number, $x > 0$

Comments   Solution of the differential equation $x^2 \cdot \dfrac{d^2}{dx^2}y + x \cdot \dfrac{d}{dx}y - (x^2 + m^2) \cdot y = 0$.

See also   In

Algorithm   Small order approximation, upward recurrence relation (Abramowitz and Stegun, 1972; Press *et al.*, 1992)

ksmooth

Syntax   ksmooth(**vx**, **vy**, b)

Description   Creates a new vector, of the same size as **vy**, by using a Gaussian kernel to return weighted averages of **vy**.

Arguments

vx, vy   real vectors of the same size; elements of **vx** must be in ascending order

b real bandwidth $b > 0$; controls the smoothing window and should be set to a few times the spacing between your data points on the x-axis, depending on how big of a window you want to use when smoothing

Comments   The ksmooth function uses a Gaussian kernel to compute local weighted averages of the input vector **vy**. This smoother is most useful when your data lies along a band of relatively constant width. If your data lies scattered along a band whose width fluctuates considerably, you should use an adaptive smoother like supsmooth.

For each vy_i in the n-element vector **vy**, the ksmooth function returns a new vy'_i given by:

$$vy'_i = \frac{\displaystyle\sum_{j=1}^{n} K\left(\frac{vx_i - vx_j}{b}\right) vy_j}{\displaystyle\sum_{j=1}^{n} K\left(\frac{vx_i - vx_j}{b}\right)} \quad \text{where: } K(t) = \frac{1}{\sqrt{2\pi} \cdot (0.37)} \cdot \exp\left(-\frac{t^2}{2 \cdot (0.37)^2}\right)$$

and b is a bandwidth which you supply to the ksmooth function. The bandwidth is usually set to a few times the spacing between data points on the x axis, depending on how big a window you want to use when smoothing.

Algorithm   Moving window Gaussian kernel smoothing (Lorczak)

See also   "medsmooth" on page 377 for more details, "supsmooth" on page 437

---

kurt

Syntax   kurt(**A**)

Description   Returns the kurtosis of the elements of **A**:

$$\text{kurt}(\mathbf{A}) = \left(\frac{mn(mn+1)}{(mn-1)(mn-2)(mn-3)} \sum_{i=0}^{m-1} \sum_{j=0}^{n-1} \left(\frac{\mathbf{A}_{i,j} - \text{mean}(\mathbf{A})}{\text{Stdev}(\mathbf{A})} \right)^4 \right) - \frac{3(mn-1)^2}{(mn-2)(mn-3)}$$

Arguments

A   real or complex $m \times n$ matrix or vector; $m \cdot n \geq 4$

Comments   kurt(**A**, **B**, **C**, ...) is also permissible and returns the kurtosis of the elements of **A**, **B**, **C**, ...

Lag

Syntax   Lag(n, x)

Description   Returns the value of the Laguerre polynomial of degree n at x.

Arguments

n integer, $n \geq 0$

x real number

Comments   The Laguerre polynomials are solutions of the differential equation

$$x \cdot \frac{d^2}{dx^2} y + (1-x) \cdot \frac{d}{dx} y + n \cdot y = 0 .$$

Algorithm   Recurrence relation (Abramowitz and Stegun, 1972)

last

Syntax   last(**v**)

Description   Returns the index of the last element in vector **v**.

Arguments

v   vector

Comments   last(**v**) = length(**v**) − 1 + ORIGIN

See also   rows

lcm

Syntax   lcm(**A**)

Description   Returns the smallest positive integer that is a multiple of all the values in the array **A**. This integer is known as the least common multiple of the elements in **A**.

Arguments

A   integer matrix or vector; all elements of **A** are greater than zero

Comments   lcm(**A**, **B**, **C**, ...) is also permissible and returns the least common multiple of the elements of **A**, **B**, **C**, ...

Algorithm   Euclid's algorithm (Niven and Zuckerman, 1972)

See also   gcd

Leg

Syntax   Leg(n, x)

Description   Returns the value of the Legendre polynomial of degree n at x.

Arguments
    n integer, $n \geq 0$
    x real number

Comments   The Legendre polynomials are solution of the differential equation

$$(1 - x^2) \cdot \frac{d^2}{dx^2}y - 2 \cdot x \cdot \frac{d}{dx}y + n \cdot (n+1) \cdot y = 0 \, .$$

Algorithm   Recurrence relation (Abramowitz and Stegun, 1972)

length

Syntax   length($\mathbf{v}$)

Description   Returns the number of elements in vector $\mathbf{v}$.

Arguments
    $\mathbf{v}$ vector

Comments   Same as rows($\mathbf{v}$)

lgsfit

Syntax   lgsfit($\mathbf{vx}$, $\mathbf{vy}$, $\mathbf{vg}$)

Description   Returns a vector containing the parameters (a, b, c) that make the function $a \cdot (1 + b\exp(-cx))^{-1}$ best approximate the data in $\mathbf{vx}$ and $\mathbf{vy}$.

Arguments
    $\mathbf{vx}$, $\mathbf{vy}$ real vectors of the same size
    $\mathbf{vg}$ real vector of guess values for (a, b, c)

Comments   This is a special case of the genfit function. A vector of guess values is needed for initialization. By decreasing the value of the built-in TOL variable, higher accuracy in lgsfit might be achieved.

See Also   line, linfit, genfit, expfit, logfit, lnfit, pwrfit, sinfit, medfit

line

Syntax   line($\mathbf{vx}$, $\mathbf{vy}$)

Description   Returns a vector containing the y-intercept and the slope of the least-squares regression line.

Arguments
    $\mathbf{vx}$, $\mathbf{vy}$ real vectors of the same size

See Also   slope for more details, intercept, stderr, medfit

linfit

Syntax linfit(**vx**, **vy**, **F**)

Description Returns a vector containing the coefficients used to create a linear combination of the functions in **F** which best approximates the data in **vx** and **vy**. See genfit for a more general technique.

Arguments

vx, vy real vectors of the same size; elements of **vx** should be in ascending order

F a function of a single variable that returns a vector of functions

Example

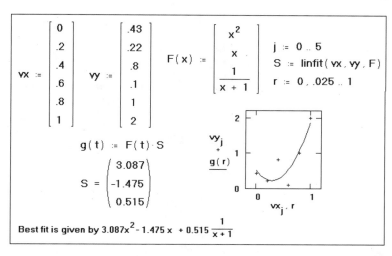

$$g(t) := F(t) \cdot S$$

$$S = \begin{pmatrix} 3.087 \\ -1.475 \\ 0.515 \end{pmatrix}$$

Best fit is given by $3.087x^2 - 1.475x + 0.515\dfrac{1}{x+1}$

Comments Not all data sets can be modeled by lines or polynomials. There are times when you need to model your data with a linear combination of arbitrary functions, none of which represent terms of a polynomial. For example, in a Fourier series you try to approximate data using a linear combination of complex exponentials. Or you may believe your data can be modeled by a weighted combination of Legendre polynomials, but you just don't know what weights to assign.

The linfit function is designed to solve these kinds of problems. If you believe your data could be modeled by a linear combination of arbitrary functions:
$y = a_0 \cdot f_0(x) + a_1 \cdot f_1(x) + \dots + a_n \cdot f_n(x)$, you should use linfit to evaluate the a_i. The example above shows a linear combination of three functions x, x^2, and $(x+1)^{-1}$ to model some data.

There are times however when the flexibility of linfit is still not enough. Your data may have to be modeled not by a linear combination of data but by some function whose parameters must be chosen. For example, if your data can be modeled by the sum:
$f(x) = a_1 \cdot \sin(2x) + a_2 \cdot \tanh(3x)$ and all you need to do is solve for the unknown weights a_1 and a_2, then the linfit function is sufficient. By contrast, if instead your data is to be modeled by the sum: $f(x) = 2 \cdot \sin(a_1 x) + 3 \cdot \tanh(a_2 x)$ and you now have to solve for the unknown parameters a_1 and a_2, you should use the genfit function.

Algorithm SVD-based least squares minimization (Press *et al.*, 1992)

See also line, genfit

linterp

Syntax   linterp(**vx**, **vy**, x)

Description   Returns a linearly interpolated value at x.

Arguments

vx, vy   real vectors of the same size; elements of **vx** should be in ascending order

x real number at which to interpolate

Example

Comments   Interpolation involves using existing data points to predict values between these data points. Mathcad allows you to either connect the data points with straight lines (linear interpolation, as with linterp) or to connect them with sections of a cubic polynomial (cubic spline interpolation, as with lspline, pspline, cspline, bspline and interp).

Unlike the regression functions discussed elsewhere, these interpolation functions return a curve which must pass through the points you specify. Therefore, the resulting function is very sensitive to spurious data points. If your data is noisy, you should consider using the regression functions instead.

Be sure that every element in the **vx** and **vy** arrays contains a data value. Because every element in an array must have a value, Mathcad assigns 0 to any elements you have not explicitly assigned.

To find the interpolated value for a particular x, linterp finds the two points between which the value falls and returns the corresponding y value on the straight line between the two points.

For x values before the first point in **vx**, linterp extrapolates the straight line between the first two data points. For x values beyond the last point in **vx**, linterp extrapolates the straight line between the last two data points.

For best results, the value of x should be between the largest and smallest values in the vector **vx**. The linterp function is intended for interpolation, not extrapolation. Consequently, computed values for x outside this range are unlikely to be useful. See predict for an alternative.

Chapter 17 Functions

ln

Syntax   ln(z)

Description   Returns the natural logarithm of nonzero z (to base e). It is the principal value (imaginary part between π and $-\pi$) for complex z.

Arguments

z real or complex nonzero number

Example

```
ln( 2 )  =  0.693    <——>    e^.693  =  2

ln( -2 )  =  0.693 + 3.142i   <— Log of a negative number is always
                                  log of the magnitude plus πi

ln( 0 )  =          <— Since anything raised to the 0 is 1,
 ┌─────────────┐        you can never have a log of zero.
 │ domain error │
 └─────────────┘
ln( 1 )  =  0    <—>    e^0  =  1
```

Comments   In general, a complex argument to the natural log function returns:

$$\ln(x + i \cdot y) = \ln|x + i \cdot y| + \text{atan}(y/x) \cdot i + 2 \cdot n \cdot \pi \cdot i$$

Mathcad's ln function returns the value corresponding to $n = 0$, namely:

$$\ln(x + i \cdot y) = \ln|x + i \cdot y| + \text{atan}(y/x) \cdot i \quad \text{(principal branch of the natural log function)}.$$

See also   log

lnfit

Syntax   lnfit(**vx, vy**)

Description   Returns a vector containing the parameters (a, b) that make the function $a \cdot \ln(x) + b$ best approximate the data in **vx** and **vy**.

Arguments

vx, vy   real vectors of the same size

Comments   This is a two-parameter alternative to the three-parameter logfit function. It uses linear regression to perform the curve fit (by taking the logarithm of y-values), hence there is no need for a guess values vector.

See Also   line, linfit, genfit, expfit, pwrfit, logfit, lgsfit, sinfit, medfit

LoadColormap

Syntax   LoadColormap(*file*)

Description   Returns an array containing the values in the colormap *file*.

Arguments

file   string variable corresponding to CMP filename

Comments   The file *file* is the name of a colormap located in the CMAPS subdirectory of your Mathcad directory. The function LoadColormap is useful when you want to edit a colormap or use it to create a new colormap. See on-line Help for more information.

See also   SaveColormap

One-dimensional Case

Syntax	loess(**vx**, **vy**, *span*)
Description	Returns the vector required by the interp function to find the set of second order polynomials that best fit particular neighborhoods of data points specified in arrays **vx** and **vy**.

Arguments

vx, vy	real vectors of the same size
span	real $span > 0$ specifies how large a neighborhood loess will consider in performing this local regression

Example

```
i := 0 .. 39    x_i := i – 10    y := stack(P, Q)

y1 := loess(x, y, 0.9)    <-- using span=0.9

y2 := loess(x, y, 0.3)    <-- using span=0.3

Smaller span causes loess to consider a smaller
neighborhood, resulting in a bumpy regression
curve that more closely tracks the data.
```

$$P = \begin{bmatrix} -3.5 \\ -1 \\ 0.9 \\ 2.11 \\ 2.78 \\ 3.41 \\ 3.65 \\ 3.65 \\ 3.79 \\ 3.53 \\ 3.55 \\ 2.95 \\ 2.54 \\ 2 \\ 1.49 \\ 1.2 \\ 1.1 \\ 1.18 \\ 1.29 \\ 1.64 \end{bmatrix} \qquad Q = \begin{bmatrix} 1.99 \\ 2.24 \\ 2.89 \\ 3.59 \\ 4.39 \\ 4.7 \\ 5.12 \\ 5.25 \\ 5.39 \\ 5.16 \\ 4.9 \\ 4.4 \\ 3.7 \\ 2.89 \\ 2.11 \\ 1.81 \\ 1.77 \\ 2 \\ 2.4 \\ 3.4 \end{bmatrix}$$

Comments

Instead of generating a single polynomial the way regress does, loess generates a different second order polynomial depending on where you are on the curve. It does this by examining the data in a small neighborhood of the point you're interested in. The argument *span* controls the size of this neighborhood. As *span* gets larger, loess becomes equivalent to regress with $n = 2$. A good default value is $span = 0.75$.

The example above shows how *span* affects the fit generated by the loess function. A smaller value of *span* makes the fitted curve track fluctuations in data more effectively. A larger value of *span* tends to smear out fluctuations in data and thereby generates a smoother fit.

Two-dimensional Case

Syntax	loess(**Mxy**, **vz**, *span*)
Description	Returns the vector required by the interp function to find the set of second order polynomials that best fit particular neighborhoods of data points specified in arrays **Mxy** and **vz**.
Arguments	
Mxy	real $m \times 2$ matrix containing x-y coordinates of the m data points
vz	real m-element vector containing the z coordinates corresponding to the points specified in **Mxy**
span	real $span > 0$ specifies how large a neighborhood loess will consider in performing this local regression
Comments	Can be extended naturally to the three- and four-dimensional cases (that is, up to four independent variables).
Algorithm	Local polynomial estimation (Cleveland and Devlin, 1988)
See also	"regress" on page 409 for more details

log
Log and Exponential

Classical Definition

Syntax	log(z)
Description	Returns the common logarithm of nonzero z to base 10. The result is the principal value (imaginary part between π and $-\pi$) for complex z.
Arguments	
z	real or complex nonzero number

Extended Definition

Syntax	log(z, b)
Description	Returns the logarithm of nonzero z to base b. The result is the principal value (imaginary part between π and $-\pi$) for complex z.
Arguments	
z	real or complex nonzero number
b	real number, $b > 0$, $b \neq 1$
See also	ln

logfit
Regression and Smoothing

Syntax	logfit(**vx**, **vy**, **vg**)
Description	Returns a vector containing the parameters (a, b, c) that make the function $a \cdot \ln(x + b) + c$ best approximate the data in **vx** and **vy**.
Arguments	
vx, **vy**	real vectors of the same size
vg	real vector of guess values for (a, b, c)
Comments	This is a special case of the genfit function. A vector of guess values is needed for initialization. By decreasing the value of the built-in TOL variable, higher accuracy in logfit might be achieved.
See Also	line, linfit, genfit, expfit, pwrfit, lnfit, lgsfit, sinfit, medfit

lookup

Syntax	lookup(z, **A**, **B**)
Description	Looks in a vector or matrix, **A**, for a given value, z, and returns the value(s) in the same position(s) (i.e., with the same row and column numbers) in another matrix, **B**. When multiple values are returned, they appear in a vector in row-wise order, starting with the top left corner of **B** and sweeping to the right.
Arguments	
z	real or complex number, or string
A, B	real, complex or string $m \times n$ matrices or vectors
Comments	The degree of precision to which the comparison adheres is determined by the *TOL* setting of the worksheet.
See Also	hlookup, vlookup, match

lsolve
Vector and Matrix

Syntax	lsolve(**M**, **v**)
Description	Returns a solution vector **x** such that $\mathbf{M} \cdot \mathbf{x} = \mathbf{v}$.
Arguments	
M	real or complex square matrix that is neither singular nor nearly singular
v	real or complex vector
Example	

```
3·x + 6·y = 9        ←— System of equations to be solved.
2·x + .54·y = 4

M := ( 3    6 )    v := ( 9 )    ←— Create your matrix and vector.
     ( 2   .54 )           ( 4 )

lsolve ( M , v ) = ( 1.844 )   ←— Value for x satisfying the system of equations.
                   ( 0.578 )   ←— Value for y satisfying the system of equations.

Note: The "lsolve" function is only available with Mathcad Professional.
```

Comments	A matrix is singular if its determinant is zero; it is nearly singular if it has a high condition number. Alternatively, you can solve a system of linear equations by using matrix inversion, via numeric or symbolic solve blocks.
Algorithm	LU decomposition and forward/backward substitution (Press *et al.*, 1992)

lspline

One-dimensional Case

Syntax   lspline(**vx**, **vy**)

Description   Returns the vector of coefficients of a cubic spline with linear ends. This vector becomes the first argument of the interp function.

Arguments

vx, vy   real vectors of the same size; elements of **vx** must be in ascending order

Example

Comments   Cubic spline interpolation lets you pass a curve through a set of points so that the first and second derivatives of the curve are continuous across each point. This curve is assembled by taking three adjacent points and constructing a cubic polynomial passing through those points. These cubic polynomials are then strung together to form the completed curve.

To fit a cubic spline curve through a set of points:

1. Create the vectors **vx** and **vy** containing the x and y coordinates through which you want the cubic spline to pass. The elements of **vx** should be in ascending order. (Although we use the names **vx**, **vy**, and **vs**, there is nothing special about these variable names; you can use whatever names you prefer.)

2. Generate the vector **vs** := lspline(**vx**, **vy**). The vector **vs** is a vector of intermediate results designed to be used with interp. It contains, among other things, the second derivatives for the spline curve used to fit the points in **vx** and **vy**.

3. To evaluate the cubic spline at an arbitrary point, say $x0$, evaluate interp(**vs**, **vx**, **vy**, $x0$) here **vs**, **vx**, and **vy** are the vectors described earlier. You could have accomplished the same task by evaluating: interp(lspline(**vx**, **vy**), **vx**, **vy**, $x0$) . As a practical matter, though, you'll probably be evaluating interp for many different points.

The call to lspline can be time-consuming and the result won't change from one point to the next, so it makes sense to do it just once and store the outcome in the **vs** array.

Be sure that every element in the input arrays contains a data value. Because every element in a array must have a value, Mathcad assigns 0 to any elements you have not explicitly assigned.

In addition to lspline, Mathcad comes with three other cubic spline functions: pspline, cspline, and bspline. The pspline function generates a spline curve that approaches a parabola at the endpoints, while the cspline function generates a spline curve that can be fully cubic at the endpoints. bspline, on the other hand, allows the interpolation knots to be chosen by the user.

For lspline, the first three components of the output vector **vs** are $vs_0=0$ (a code telling interp that **vs** is the output of a spline function as opposed to a regression function), $vs_1=3$ (the index within **vs** where the second derivative coefficients begin) and $vs_2=0$ (a code denoting lspline). The first three components for pspline and cspline are identical except $vs_2=1$ (the code denoting pspline) and $vs_2=2$ (the code denoting cspline), respectively.

Two-dimensional Case

Syntax   lspline(**Mxy**, **Mz**)

Description   Returns the vector of coefficients of a two-dimensional cubic spline, constrained to be linear at region boundaries spanned by **Mxy**. This vector becomes the first argument of the interp function.

Arguments

Mxy $n \times 2$ matrix whose elements, $Mxy_{i,0}$ and $Mxy_{i,1}$, specify the x- and y-coordinates along the *diagonal* of a rectangular grid. This matrix plays exactly the same role as **vx** in the one-dimensional case described earlier. Since these points describe a diagonal, the elements in each column of **Mxy** must be in ascending order ($Mxy_{i,k} < Mxy_{j,k}$ whenever $i < j$).

Mz $n \times n$ matrix whose ijth element is the z-coordinate corresponding to the point $x = Mxy_{i,0}$ and $y = Mxy_{j,1}$. **Mz** plays exactly the same role as **vy** does in the one-dimensional case above.

Comments   Mathcad handles two-dimensional cubic spline interpolation in much the same way as the one-dimensional case. Instead of passing a curve through a set of points so that the first and second derivatives of the curve are continuous across each point, Mathcad passes a surface through a grid of points. This surface corresponds to a cubic polynomial in x and y in which the first and second partial derivatives are continuous in the corresponding direction across each grid point.

The first step in two-dimensional spline interpolation is exactly the same as that in the one-dimensional case: specify the points through which the surface is to pass. The procedure, however, is more complicated because you now have to specify a grid of points.

To perform two-dimensional spline interpolation, follow these steps:

1. Create **Mxy**.
2. Create **Mz**.

3. Generate the vector $\mathbf{vs} := \text{lspline}(\mathbf{Mxy}, \mathbf{Mz})$. The vector $\mathbf{vs}$ is a vector of intermediate results designed to be used with interp.

To evaluate the cubic spline at an arbitrary point, say $(x0, y0)$, evaluate

$$\text{interp}\left(\mathbf{vs}, \mathbf{Mxy}, \mathbf{Mz}, \begin{bmatrix} x0 \\ y0 \end{bmatrix}\right), \text{ where } \mathbf{vs}, \mathbf{Mxy}, \text{ and } \mathbf{Mz} \text{ are as described earlier.}$$

The result is the value of the interpolating surface corresponding to the arbitrary point $(x0, y0)$. You could have accomplished exactly the same task by evaluating:

$$\text{interp}\left(\text{lspline}(\mathbf{Mxy}, \mathbf{Mz}), \mathbf{Mxy}, \mathbf{Mz}, \begin{bmatrix} x0 \\ y0 \end{bmatrix}\right).$$

As a practical matter though, you'll probably be evaluating interp for many different points. The call to lspline can be time-consuming, and the result won't change from one point to the next, so do it just once and store the outcome in the $\mathbf{vs}$ array.

In addition to lspline, Mathcad comes with two other cubic spline functions for the two-dimensional case: pspline and cspline. The pspline function generates a spline curve that approaches a second degree polynomial in x and y along the edges. The cspline function generates a spline curve that approaches a third degree polynomial in x and y along the edges.

Algorithm	Tridiagonal system solving (Press *et al.*, 1992; Lorczak)

lu

Syntax	lu(**M**)
Description	Returns an $n \times (3 \cdot n)$ matrix whose first n columns contain an $n \times n$ permutation matrix $\mathbf{P}$, whose next n columns contain an $n \times n$ lower triangular matrix $\mathbf{L}$, and whose remaining n columns contain an $n \times n$ upper triangular matrix $\mathbf{U}$. These matrices satisfy the equation $\mathbf{P} \cdot \mathbf{M} = \mathbf{L} \cdot \mathbf{U}$.
Arguments	
M	real or complex $n \times n$ matrix
Comments	This is known as the LU decomposition (or factorization) of the matrix $\mathbf{M}$, permuted by $\mathbf{P}$.
Algorithm	Crout's method with partial pivoting (Press *et al.*, 1992; Golub and Van Loan, 1989)

match

Syntax	match(z, **A**)
Description	Looks in a vector or matrix, **A**, for a given value, z, and returns the index (indices) of its positions in **A**. When multiple values are returned, they appear in a nested array in row-wise order, starting with the top left corner of **A** and sweeping to the right.
Arguments	
z	real or complex number, or string
A	real, complex or string $m \times n$ matrix or vector
Comments	The degree of precision to which the comparison adheres is determined by the *TOL* setting of the worksheet.
See Also	lookup, hlookup, vlookup

matrix

Syntax	matrix(m, n, f)
Description	Creates a matrix in which the ijth element is the value $f(i, j)$, where $i = 0, 1, ..., m - 1$ and $j = 0, 1, ..., n - 1$.
Arguments	
m, n	integers
f	scalar-valued function

max

Syntax	max(**A**)
Description	Returns the largest element in **A**. If **A** is complex, returns max(Re(**A**)) + i max(Im(**A**)).
Arguments	
A	real or complex $m \times n$ matrix or vector, or string
Comments	max(**A**, **B**, **C**, **...**) is also permissible and returns the largest element in **A**, **B**, **C**, ...
See also	min

Maximize

Syntax	Maximize(f, *var1*, *var2*,...)
Description	Returns values of *var1*, *var2*,... which solve a prescribed system of equations, subject to prescribed inequalities, and which make the function f take on its largest value. The number of arguments matches the number of unknowns, plus one. Output is a scalar if only one unknown; otherwise it is a vector of answers.
Arguments	
f	real-valued objective function
var1, *var2*, ...	real or complex variables; *var1*, *var2*, ... must be assigned guess values before using Maximize

Examples

$f(x) := 3 \cdot x_0 + 2 \cdot x_1$ *objective function*

$$M := \begin{bmatrix} 1 & 1 \\ 3 & 1 \\ -10 & 1 \end{bmatrix} \qquad v := \begin{bmatrix} 2000 \\ 3000 \\ 1000 \end{bmatrix}$$ *constraint coefficients*

$x_1 := 0$ *initialization*
             (last component of x)

Given

$M \cdot x \leq v$ *linear*
                     programming
$x \geq 0$ *solve block*

Constraint Set Boundary

$\dfrac{2000 - t}{}$
$\dfrac{3000 - 3 \cdot t}{}$
$\dfrac{1000 + 10 \cdot t}{}$

$\text{Maximize}(f, x) = \begin{bmatrix} 500 \\ 1500 \end{bmatrix}$ *solution*

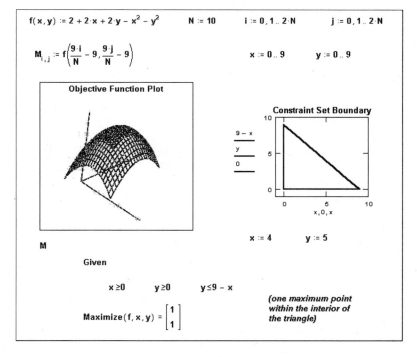

$f(x, y) := 2 + 2 \cdot x + 2 \cdot y - x^2 - y^2$ $N := 10$ $i := 0, 1 .. 2 \cdot N$ $j := 0, 1 .. 2 \cdot N$

$M_{i, j} := f\left(\dfrac{9 \cdot i}{N} - 9, \dfrac{9 \cdot j}{N} - 9\right)$ $x := 0 .. 9$ $y := 0 .. 9$

Objective Function Plot

Constraint Set Boundary

$\dfrac{9 - x}{}$
$\dfrac{y}{}$
0

M

$x := 4$ $y := 5$

Given

$x \geq 0$ $y \geq 0$ $y \leq 9 - x$

$\text{Maximize}(f, x, y) = \begin{bmatrix} 1 \\ 1 \end{bmatrix}$ *(one maximum point within the interior of the triangle)*

Comments   There are five steps to solving a maximization problem:

1. Define the objective function *f*.

2. Provide an initial guess for all the unknowns you intend to solve for. This gives Mathcad a place to start searching for solutions.

3. Type the word given. This tells Mathcad that what follows is a system of equality or inequality constraints. You can type given or Given in any style. Just be sure you don't type it while in a text region.

4. Now type the equations and inequalities in any order below the word given. Use [**Ctrl**]= to type "=."

5. Finally, type the Maximize function with *f* and your list of unknowns. You can't put numerical values in the list of unknowns; for example, Maximize(*f*, 2) isn't permitted. Like given, you can type maximize or Maximize in any style.

The Maximize function returns values as follows:

- If there is one unknown, Maximize returns a scalar value that optimizes *f*.
- If there is more than one unknown, Maximize returns a vector of answers; for example, Maximize(*f*, *var1*, *var2*) returns a vector containing values of *var1* and *var2* that satisfy the constraints and optimize *f*.

The word Given, the equations and inequalities that follow, and the Maximize function form a *solve block*.

By default, Mathcad examines your objective function and the constraints, and solves using an appropriate method. If you want to try different algorithms for testing and comparison, you can choose options from the pop-up menu associated with Maximize (available via right mouse click), which include:

- AutoSelect – chooses an appropriate algorithm for you
- Linear option – indicates that the problem is linear (and thus applies linear programming methods to the problem) – guess values for *var1*, *var2*,... are immaterial (can all be zero)
- Nonlinear option – indicates that the problem is nonlinear (and thus applies these general methods to the problem: the conjugate gradient solver; if that fails to converge, the quasi-Newton solver) – guess values for *var1*, *var2*,... greatly affect the solution
- Quadratic option (appears only if the Solving and Optimization Extension Pack or Expert Solver product is installed) – indicates that the problem is quadratic (and thus applies quadratic programming methods to the problem) – guess values for *var1*, *var2*,... are immaterial (can all be zero)
- Advanced options – applies only to the nonlinear conjugate gradient and the quasi-Newton solvers

These options provide more control for you to try different algorithms for testing and comparison. You may also adjust the values of the built-in variables CTOL and TOL. The *constraint tolerance* CTOL controls how closely a constraint must be met for a solution to be acceptable, e.g., if CTOL were 0.001, then a constraint such as x < 2 would be considered satisfied if the value of x satisfied x < 2.001. This can be defined or changed in the same way as the *convergence tolerance* TOL, which is discussed further in connection with the Find function. Since Maximize can be used without constraints, the value of CTOL will sometimes be irrelevant. Its default value is 10^{-3}.

Other Solving and Optimization Extension Pack features include mixed integer programming and constraint sensitivity report generation. See on-line Help for details.

For an unconstrained maximization problem, the word Given and constraints are unnecessary.

Algorithm	For the non-linear case: quasi-Newton, conjugate gradient
	For the linear case: simplex method with branch/bound techniques (Press *et al.*, 1992; Polak, 1997; Winston, 1994)
See also	Find for more details about solve blocks; Minerr, Minimize

mean
Statistics

Syntax	mean(**A**)
Description	Returns the arithmetic mean of the elements of **A**: $\text{mean}(\mathbf{A}) = \dfrac{1}{mn} \sum\limits_{i=0}^{m-1} \sum\limits_{j=0}^{n-1} A_{i,j}$.
Arguments	
A	real or complex $m \times n$ matrix or vector
Comments	mean(**A**, **B**, **C**, ...) is also permissible and returns the arithmetic mean of the elements of **A**, **B**, **C**, ...
See also	gmean, hmean, median, mode

medfit
Regression and Smoothing

Syntax	medfit(**vx**, **vy**)
Description	Returns a vector containing the *y*-intercept and the slope of the median-median regression line.
Arguments	
vx, vy	real vectors of the same size
Comments	medfit provides a linear fit which is more robust (less sensitive to data outliers) than line. The data is divided into three sets, the median of the first and last subsets are calculated, and the intercept and slope of the line connecting those two medians comprises the fit.
See Also	line, linfit, genfit, expfit, logfit, lnfit, pwrfit, lgsfit, sinfit

median
Statistics

Syntax	median(**A**)
Description	Returns the median of the elements of **A**. The median is the value above and below which there are an equal number of values. If **A** has an even number of elements, median is the arithmetic mean of the two central values.
Arguments	
A	real $m \times n$ matrix or vector
Comments	median(**A**, **B**, **C**, ...) is also permissible and returns the median of the elements of **A**, **B**, **C**, ...
See also	gmean, mean, median, mode

medsmooth
Regression and Smoothing

Syntax	medsmooth(**vy**, *n*)
Description	Creates a new vector, of the same size as **vy**, by smoothing **vy** with running medians.
Arguments	
vy	real vector
n	odd integer, $n > 0$, the size of smoothing window

y := stack(P, Q)	<-- raw data	$\begin{bmatrix} 0.41 \\ 0.53 \\ 0.99 \\ 0.79 \\ 0.99 \\ 1.14 \\ 1.54 \\ 1.59 \\ 2.19 \\ 2.11 \\ 2.71 \\ 2.7 \\ 2.98 \\ 4.31 \\ 3.55 \\ 3.89 \\ 4.59 \\ 4.4 \\ 4.69 \\ 4.88 \\ 4.79 \\ 4.25 \end{bmatrix}$	$\begin{bmatrix} 5.67 \\ 4.96 \\ 4.33 \\ 4.78 \\ 5.07 \\ 4.4 \\ 4.28 \\ 3.79 \\ 3.85 \\ 3.19 \\ 2.92 \\ 2.7 \\ 2.74 \\ 2.11 \\ 1.88 \\ 1.39 \\ 1.07 \\ 1.22 \\ 0.89 \\ 0.79 \\ 0.89 \\ 0.53 \end{bmatrix}$

i := 0 .. 43 ch_i := 13 + i   <-- corresponding channel number (or x value)

ys := medsmooth(**y**, 7)   <-- smoothed data

$P =$ $Q =$

○ ○ ○ Data points
——— Smoothed data

Comments

Smoothing involves taking a set of *y* (and possibly *x*) values and returning a new set of *y* values that is smoother than the original set. Unlike the interpolation functions lspline, pspline, cspline or bspline or regression functions regress or loess, smoothing results in a new set of *y* values, not a function that can be evaluated between the data points you specify. If you are interested in *y* values *between* the *y* values you specify, use an interpolation or regression function.

Whenever you use vectors in any of the functions described in this section, be sure that every element in the vector contains a data value. Because every element in a vector must have a value, Mathcad assigns 0 to any elements you have not explicitly assigned.

The medsmooth function is the most robust of Mathcad's three smoothing functions because it is least likely to be affected by spurious data points. This function uses a running median smoother, computes the residuals, smooths the residuals the same way, and adds these two smoothed vectors together.

medsmooth performs these steps:

1. Finds the running medians of the input vector **vy**. We'll call this **vy'** . The *i*th element is given by: $vy'_i = \mathrm{median}(vy_{i-(n-1/2)}, \ldots, vy_i, \ldots, vy_{i+(n-1/2)})$.

2. Evaluates the residuals: $\mathbf{vr} = \mathbf{vy} - \mathbf{vy'}$.

3. Smooths the residual vector, **vr**, using the same procedure described in step 1, to create a smoothed residual vector, **vr'** .

4. Returns the sum of these two smoothed vectors: $\mathrm{medsmooth}(\mathbf{vy}, n) = \mathbf{vy'} + \mathbf{vr'}$.

medsmooth will leave the first and last $(n-1)/2$ points unchanged. In practice, the length of the smoothing window, *n*, should be small compared to the length of the data set.

Algorithm	Moving window median method (Lorczak)
See also	ksmooth and supsmooth

mhyper

Syntax	mhyper(a, b, x)
Description	Returns the value of the confluent hypergeometric function, $_1F_1(a;b;x)$ or $M(a;b;x)$.
Arguments	
a, b, x	real numbers
Comments	The confluent hypergeometric function is a solution of the differential equation:

$$x \cdot \frac{d^2}{dx^2}y + (b - x) \cdot \frac{d}{dx}y - a \cdot y = 0 \text{ and is also known as the Kummer function.}$$

Many functions are special cases of this, e.g., elementary ones like

$$\exp(x) = \text{mhyper}(1, 1, x) \qquad \exp(x) \cdot \sinh(x) = x \cdot \text{mhyper}(1, 2, 2 \cdot x)$$

and more complicated ones like Hermite functions.

Algorithm	Series expansion, asymptotic approximations (Abramowitz and Stegun, 1972)

min

Syntax	min($\mathbf{A}$)
Description	Returns the smallest element in $\mathbf{A}$. If $\mathbf{A}$ is complex, returns min(Re($\mathbf{A}$)) + i min(Im($\mathbf{A}$)).
Arguments	
$\mathbf{A}$	real or complex $m \times n$ matrix or vector, or string
Comments	min($\mathbf{A}, \mathbf{B}, \mathbf{C}, ...$) is also permissible and returns the smallest element in $\mathbf{A}, \mathbf{B}, \mathbf{C}, ...$
See also	max

Minerr

Syntax	Minerr(*var1*, *var2*,...)
Description	Returns values of *var1*, *var2*, ... which come closest to solving a prescribed system of equations, subject to prescribed inequalities. The number of arguments matches the number of unknowns. Output is a scalar if only one argument; otherwise it is a vector of answers.
Arguments	
var1, *var2*, ...	real or complex variables; *var1*, *var2*, ... must be assigned guess values before using Minerr

The Minerr function is very similar to Find and uses exactly the same algorithm. The difference is that even if a system has no solutions, Minerr will attempt to find values which come closest to solving the system. The Find function, on the other hand, will return an error message indicating that it could not find a solution. You use Minerr exactly the way you use Find.

Like Find, type the Minerr function with your list of unknowns. You can't put numerical values in the list of unknowns; e.g., in the example above, Minerr(0.8, 1) isn't permitted. Like Find, you can type Minerr or minerr in any style.

Minerr usually returns an answer that minimizes the errors in the constraints. However, Minerr cannot verify that its answers represent an absolute minimum for the errors in the constraints.

If you use Minerr in a solve block, you should always include additional checks on the reasonableness of the results. The built-in variable ERR gives the size of the error vector for the approximate solution. There is no built-in variable for determining the size of the error for individual solutions to the unknowns.

Minerr is particularly useful for solving certain nonlinear least-squares problems. In the example, Minerr is used to obtain the unknown parameters in a Weibull distribution. The function genfit is also useful for solving nonlinear least-squares problems.

The pop-up menu (available via right mouse click) associated with Minerr contains the following options:

- AutoSelect – chooses an appropriate algorithm for you
- Linear option – not available for Minerr (since the objective function is quadratic, hence the problem can never be linear)

- Nonlinear option – indicates that the problem is nonlinear (and thus applies these general methods to the problem: the conjugate gradient solver; if that fails to converge, the Levenberg-Marquardt solver; if that too fails, the quasi-Newton solver) – guess values for *var1*, *var2*,... greatly affect the solution
- Quadratic option (appears only if the Solving and Optimization Extension Pack or Expert Solver product is installed) – indicates that the problem is quadratic (and thus applies quadratic programming methods to the problem) – guess values for *var1*, *var2*,... are immaterial (can all be zero)
- Advanced options – applies only to the nonlinear conjugate gradient and the quasi-Newton solvers

These options provide more control for you to try different algorithms for testing and comparison. You may also adjust the values of the built-in variables CTOL and TOL. The *constraint tolerance* CTOL controls how closely a constraint must be met for a solution to be acceptable, e.g., if CTOL were 0.001, then a constraint such as $x < 2$ would be considered satisfied if the value of x satisfied $x < 2.001$. This can be defined or changed in the same way as the *convergence tolerance* TOL. The default value for CTOL is 10^{-3}.

Other Solving and Optimization Extension Pack features include mixed integer programming and constraint sensitivity report generation. See on-line Help for details.

Algorithm	For the non-linear case: Levenberg-Marquardt, quasi-Newton, conjugate gradient For the linear case: simplex method with branch/bound techniques (Press *et al.*, 1992; Polak, 1997; Winston, 1994)
See also	Find for more details about solve blocks; Maximize, Minimize

Minimize

Solving

Syntax	Minimize(*f*, *var1*, *var2*,...)
Description	Returns values of *var1*, *var2*,... which solve a prescribed system of equations, subject to prescribed inequalities, and which make the function *f* take on its smallest value. The number of arguments matches the number of unknowns, plus one. Output is a scalar if only one unknown; otherwise it is a vector of answers.
Arguments	
f	real-valued function
var1, *var2*, ...	real or complex variables; *var1*, *var2*, ... must be assigned guess values before using Minimize.

Examples

$f(x) := 8 \cdot x_0 + 10 \cdot x_1 + 7 \cdot x_2 + 6 \cdot x_3 + 11 \cdot x_4 + 9 \cdot x_5$ *objective function*

$$M := \begin{bmatrix} 12 & 9 & 25 & 20 & 17 & 13 \\ 35 & 42 & 18 & 31 & 56 & 49 \\ 37 & 53 & 28 & 24 & 29 & 20 \end{bmatrix} \qquad v := \begin{bmatrix} 60 \\ 150 \\ 125 \end{bmatrix}$$ *constraint coefficients*

$x_5 := 0$ *initialization*
     (last component of x)

Given

$\quad M \cdot x \geq v$ *linear programming*
$\quad x \leq 1$ *solve block*
$\quad x \geq 0$

$$\text{Minimize}(f, x) = \begin{bmatrix} 1 \\ 0.623 \\ 0.343 \\ 1 \\ 0.048 \\ 1 \end{bmatrix}$$ *solution*

$f(x, y) := 2 + 2 \cdot x + 2 \cdot y - x^2 - y^2$ $N := 10$ $i := 0, 1 .. 2 \cdot N$ $j := 0, 1 .. 2 \cdot N$

$M_{i,j} := f\left(\dfrac{9 \cdot i}{N} - 9, \dfrac{9 \cdot j}{N} - 9\right)$ $x := 0 .. 9$ $y := 0 .. 9$

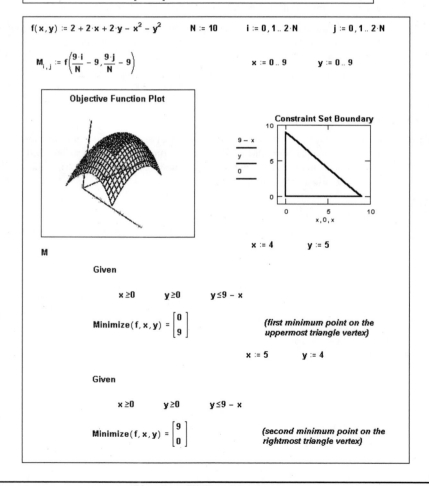

Objective Function Plot

M

Constraint Set Boundary

$\dfrac{9 - x}{y}$
$\dfrac{}{0}$

x, 0, x

$x := 4 \qquad y := 5$

Given

$\quad x \geq 0 \qquad y \geq 0 \qquad y \leq 9 - x$

$\text{Minimize}(f, x, y) = \begin{bmatrix} 0 \\ 9 \end{bmatrix}$ *(first minimum point on the uppermost triangle vertex)*

$x := 5 \qquad y := 4$

Given

$\quad x \geq 0 \qquad y \geq 0 \qquad y \leq 9 - x$

$\text{Minimize}(f, x, y) = \begin{bmatrix} 9 \\ 0 \end{bmatrix}$ *(second minimum point on the rightmost triangle vertex)*

Comments

There are five steps to solving a minimization problem:

1. Define the objective function *f.*

2. Provide an initial guess for all the unknowns you intend to solve for. This gives Mathcad a place to start searching for solutions.

3. Type the word given. This tells Mathcad that what follows is a system of equality or inequality constraints. You can type given or Given in any style. Just be sure you don't type it while in a text region.

4. Now type the equations and inequalities in any order below the word given. Use **[Ctrl]=** to type "=."

5. Finally, type the Minimize function with *f* and your list of unknowns. You can't put numerical values in the list of unknowns; for example, Minimize(*f*, 2) isn't permitted. Like given, you can type minimize or Minimize in any style.

The Minimize function returns values as follows:

- If there is one unknown, Minimize returns a scalar value that optimizes *f.*
- If there is more than one unknown, Minimize returns a vector of answers; for example, Minimize(*f*, *var1*, *var2*) returns a vector containing values of *var1* and *var2* that satisfy the constraints and optimize *f.*

The word Given, the equations and inequalities that follow, and the Minimize function form a *solve block*.

By default, Mathcad examines your objective function and the constraints, and solves using an appropriate method. If you want to try different algorithms for testing and comparison, you can choose options from the pop-up menu associated with Minimize (available via right mouse click), which include:

- AutoSelect – chooses an appropriate algorithm for you
- Linear option – indicates that the problem is linear (and thus applies linear programming methods to the problem) – guess values for *var1*, *var2*,... are immaterial (can all be zero)
- Nonlinear option – indicates that the problem is nonlinear (and thus applies these general methods to the problem: the conjugate gradient solver; if that fails to converge, the quasi-Newton solver) – guess values for *var1*, *var2*,... greatly affect the solution
- Quadratic option (appears only if the Solving and Optimization Extension Pack or Expert Solver product is installed) – indicates that the problem is quadratic (and thus applies quadratic programming methods to the problem) – guess values for *var1*, *var2*,... are immaterial (can all be zero)
- Advanced options – applies only to the nonlinear conjugate gradient and the quasi-Newton solvers

These options provide more control for you to try different algorithms for testing and comparison. You may also adjust the values of the built-in variables CTOL and TOL. The *constraint tolerance* CTOL controls how closely a constraint must be met for a solution to be acceptable, e.g., if CTOL were 0.001, then a constraint such as x < 2 would be considered satisfied if the value of x satisfied x < 2.001. This can be defined or changed in the same way as the *convergence tolerance* TOL, which is discussed further in connection with the Find function. Since Minimize can be used without constraints, the value of CTOL will sometimes be irrelevant. Its default value is 10^{-3}.

Other Solving and Optimization Extension Pack features include mixed integer programming and constraint sensitivity report generation. See on-line Help for details.

For an unconstrained minimization problem, the word Given and constraints are unnecessary.

Algorithm	For the non-linear case: quasi-Newton, conjugate gradient
	For the linear case: simplex method with branch/bound techniques
	(Press *et al.*, 1992; Polak, 1997; Winston, 1994)
See also	Find for more details about solve blocks; Maximize, Minerr

mirr
Finance

Syntax	mirr(**v**, *fin_rate*, *rein_rate*)
Description	Returns the modified internal rate of return for a series of cash flows occurring at regular intervals, **v**, given a finance rate payable on the cash flows you borrow, *fin_rate*, and a reinvestment rate earned on the cash flows as you reinvest them, *rein_rate*.
Arguments	
v	real vector of cash flows
fin_rate	real finance rate
rein_rate	real reinvestment rate
Comments	In **v**, payments must be entered as negative numbers and income must be entered as positive numbers. There must be at least one positive value and one negative value in **v**.
See also	irr

mod
Number Theory/Combinatorics

Syntax	mod(n, k)
Description	Returns the remainder of n when divided by k. The result has the same sign as n.
Arguments	
n, k	integers, $k \neq 0$

mode
Statistics

Syntax	mode(**A**)
Description	Returns the value in **A** that occurs most often.
Arguments	
A	real or complex $m \times n$ matrix or vector
Comments	mode(**A**, **B**, **C**, ...) is also permissible and returns the value in **A**, **B**, **C**, ... that occurs most often.
See also	gmean, hmean, mean, median

multigrid
Differential Equation Solving

Syntax	multigrid(**M**, *ncycle*)
Description	Solves the Poisson partial differential equation over a planar square region. The $n \times n$ matrix **M** gives source function values, where $n - 1$ is a power of 2 and zero boundary conditions on all four edges are assumed. multigrid uses a different algorithm and is faster than relax, which is more general.
Arguments	
M	$(1 + 2^k) \times (1 + 2^k)$ real square matrix containing the source term at each point in the region in which the solution is sought (for example, the right-hand side of equation below)
ncycle	positive integer specifying number of cycles at each level of the multigrid iteration; a value of 2 generally gives a good approximation of the solution

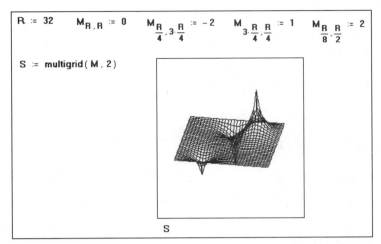

$R := 32 \quad M_{R,R} := 0 \quad M_{\frac{R}{4}, 3\cdot\frac{R}{4}} := -2 \quad M_{3\cdot\frac{R}{4}, \frac{R}{4}} := 1 \quad M_{\frac{R}{8}, \frac{R}{2}} := 2$

$S := \text{multigrid}(M, 2)$

S

Comments

Two partial differential equations that arise often in the analysis of physical systems are Poisson's equation:

$$\frac{\partial^2 u}{\partial x^2} + \frac{\partial^2 u}{\partial y^2} = \rho(x, y) \quad \text{and its homogeneous form, Laplace's equation.}$$

Mathcad has two functions for solving these equations over a square region, assuming the values taken by the unknown function $u(x, y)$ on all four sides of the boundary are known. The most general solver is the relax function. In the special case where $u(x, y)$ is known to be zero on all four sides of the boundary, you can use the multigrid function instead. This function often solves the problem faster than relax. If the boundary condition is the same on all four sides, you can simply transform the equation to an equivalent one in which the value is zero on all four sides.

The multigrid function returns a square matrix in which:

- an element's location in the matrix corresponds to its location within the square region, and
- its value approximates the value of the solution at that point.

Algorithm

Full multigrid algorithm (Press *et al.*, 1992)

See also

relax

nom

Finance

Syntax

nom(*rate*, *nper*)

Description

Returns the nominal interest rate given the effective annual interest rate, *rate*, and the number of compounding periods per year, *nper*.

Arguments

rate real rate, *rate* > −1

nper real number of compounding periods, *nper* ≥ 1

Comments

Effective annual interest rate is also known as annual percentage rate (APR).

See also

eff

norm1

Syntax | norm1(**M**)

Description | Returns the L_1 norm of the matrix **M**.

Arguments
M | real or complex square matrix

norm2

Syntax | norm2(**M**)

Description | Returns the L_2 norm of the matrix **M**.

Arguments
M | real or complex square matrix

Algorithm | Singular value computation (Wilkinson and Reinsch, 1971)

norme

Syntax | norme(**M**)

Description | Returns the Euclidean norm of the matrix **M**.

Arguments
M | real or complex square matrix

normi

Syntax | normi(**M**)

Description | Returns the infinity norm of the matrix **M**.

Arguments
M | real or complex square matrix

nper

Syntax | nper(*rate*, *pmt*, *pv*, [[*fv*], [*type*]])

Description | Returns the number of compounding periods for an investment or loan based on periodic, constant payments, *pmt*, using a fixed interest rate, *rate*, and a specified present value, *pv*.

Arguments
rate | real rate

pmt | real payment

pv | real present value

fv | (optional) real future value, default is *fv* = 0

type | (optional) indicator payment timing, 0 for payment made at the end of the period, 1 for payment made at the beginning, default is *type* = 0

Comments | If you know the annual interest rate, *ann_rate*, you must calculate the interest rate per period as *rate* = *ann_rate*/*nper*.

Payments you make, such as deposits into a savings account or payments toward a loan, must be entered as negative numbers. Cash you receive, such as dividend checks, must be entered as positive numbers. Specific to *nper*, if *pmt* > 0, *rate* and *pv* must be opposite signs.

See also | cnper, fv, pmt, pv, rate

npv

Syntax   npv(*rate*, **v**)

Description   Returns the net present value of an investment given a discount rate, *rate*, and a series of cash flows occurring at regular intervals, **v**.

Arguments

    rate   real rate

    v   real vector of cash flows

Comments   *npv* assumes that the payment is made as the end of the period.

In **v**, payments must be entered as negative numbers and income must be entered as positive numbers.

The *npv* investment begins one period before the date of the first cash flow and ends with the last cash flow in the vector. If your first cash flow occurs at the beginning of the first period, the first value must be added to the *npv* result, not included in the vector of cash flows.

See also   irr, pv

num2str

Syntax   num2str(z)

Description   Returns the string whose characters correspond to the decimal value of z.

Arguments

    z real or complex number

See also   str2num

Odesolve

Syntax   Odesolve(x, b, [*nstep*])

Description   Solves a single ordinary differential equation, subject to either initial value or boundary value constraints. The DE must be linear in the highest order derivative term. The output is a function of x, interpolated from a table of values computed via either fixed step or adaptive DE solvers.

Arguments

    x variable of integration, real

    b terminal point of integration interval, real

    nstep   (optional) integer number of steps, $nstep > 0$

Example

Given

$$100 \cdot y''(x) + 10 \cdot y'(x) + 101 \cdot y(x) = 50 \cdot \cos\left(\frac{1}{4} \cdot x\right)$$

$$y(0) = 0 \qquad y'(0) = 1$$

$$y := \text{Odesolve}(x, 150)$$

Given

$$4 \cdot \frac{d^2}{dt^2} f(t) + f(t) = t \qquad f(0) = 4 \qquad f(5) = 13.5$$

$$f := \text{Odesolve}(t, 5)$$

Comments   There are three steps to solving a DE using Odesolve:

1. Type the word Given. This tells Mathcad that what follows is a DE, along with initial value or boundary value constraints. You can type Given or given in any style. Just don't type it while in a text region.

2. Type the DE and constraints in any order below the word Given. Use [**Ctrl**]= to type "=" and [**Ctrl**]F7 to type a prime '. The DE can be written using the derivative operators d/dx, d^2/dx^2, d^3/dx^3, ... or using prime notation $y'(x)$, $y''(x)$, $y'''(x)$, ... Note that the independent variable x must be explicitly indicated throughout. A typical initial value constraint might be $y(a)=c$ or $y'(a)=d$; Mathcad does not allow more complicated constraints like $y(a)+y'(a)=e$.

3. Finally, type the Odesolve function. You can't put a numerical value in place of x: for example, Odesolve(2, 150) in the Example isn't permitted. Like given, you can type Odesolve or odesolve in any style.

The word Given, the equations that follow, and the Odesolve function form a *solve block*. This is similar to the solve block described with the Find function, except here no guess values are needed.

Mathcad is very specific about the types of expressions that can appear between Given and Odesolve. The lower derivative terms can appear nonlinearly in the DE (e.g., they can be multiplied together or raised to powers), but the highest derivative term must appear linearly. Inequality constraints are not allowed. There must be n independent equality constraints for an nth order DE. For an initial value problem, the values for $y(x)$ and its first $n-1$ derivatives at a single initial point a are required. For a boundary value problem, the n equality constraints should prescribe values for $y(x)$ and certain derivatives at exactly two points a and b. Mathcad will check for the correct type and number of conditions.

For initial value problems, the default routine employed by Odesolve is rkfixed. If you prefer Rkadapt, right-mouse click on the word Odesolve and select "Adaptive". For boundary value problems, the routine employed is sbval followed by rkfixed or Rkadapt. Internally, the output of each of these DE solvers is a table of values, which Mathcad interpolates using lspline followed by interp. Note in the Example that, although y and f are defined to be output of Odesolve (no independent variable is indicated), $y(x)$ and $f(t)$ are functions which can be plotted, etc., like any other function.

The default value for *nsteps* is ten times the length of the interval $[a, b]$ (truncated to an integer).

See also	rkfixed, Rkadapt, sbval, lspline, interp

pbeta   Probability Distribution

Syntax	pbeta(x, $s1$, $s2$)
Description	Returns the cumulative beta distribution with shape parameters $s1$ and $s2$.
Arguments	
x	real number, $0 < x < 1$
s_1, s_2	real shape parameters, $s_1 > 0$, $s_2 > 0$
Algorithm	Continued fraction expansion (Abramowitz and Stegun, 1972)

pbinom   Probability Distribution

Syntax	pbinom(k, n, p)
Description	Returns $\Pr(X \leq k)$ when the random variable X has the binomial distribution with parameters n and p.
Arguments	
k, n	integers, $0 \leq k \leq n$
p	real numbers, $0 \leq p \leq 1$
Algorithm	Continued fraction expansion (Abramowitz and Stegun, 1972)

pcauchy   Probability Distribution

Syntax	pcauchy(x, l, s)
Description	Returns the cumulative Cauchy distribution.
Arguments	
x	real number
l	real location parameter
s	real scale parameter, $s > 0$

pchisq

Syntax	pchisq(x, d)
Description	Returns the cumulative chi-squared distribution.
Arguments	
x	real number, $x \geq 0$
d	integer degrees of freedom, $d > 0$
Algorithm	Continued fraction and asymptotic expansions (Abramowitz and Stegun, 1972)

permut

Syntax	permut(n, k)
Description	Returns the number of ways of ordering n distinct objects taken k at a time.
Arguments	
n, k	integers, $0 \leq k \leq n$
Comments	Each such ordered arrangement is known as a permutation. The number of permutations is

$$P^n_k = \frac{n!}{(n-k)!}$$

See also	combin

pexp

Syntax	pexp(x, r)
Description	Returns the cumulative exponential distribution.
Arguments	
x	real number, $x \geq 0$
r	real rate, $r > 0$

pF

Syntax	pF(x, $d1$, $d2$)
Description	Returns the cumulative F distribution.
Arguments	
x	real number, $x \geq 0$
d_1, d_2	integer degrees of freedom, $d_1 > 0$, $d_2 > 0$
Algorithm	Continued fraction expansion (Abramowitz and Stegun, 1972)

pgamma

Syntax	pgamma(x, s)
Description	Returns the cumulative gamma distribution.
Arguments	
x	real number, $x \geq 0$
s	real shape parameter, $s > 0$
Algorithm	Continued fraction and asymptotic expansion (Abramowitz and Stegun, 1972)

pgeom

Syntax   pgeom(k, p)

Description   Returns $\Pr(X \leq k)$ when the random variable X has the geometric distribution with parameter p.

Arguments
  k integer, $k \geq 0$

  p real number, $0 < p \leq 1$

phypergeom

Syntax   phypergeom(m, a, b, n)

Description   Returns $\Pr(X \leq m)$ when the random variable X has the hypergeometric distribution with parameters a, b and n.

Arguments
  m, a, b, n integers, $0 \leq m \leq a$, $0 \leq n - m \leq b$, $0 \leq n \leq a + b$

plnorm

Syntax   plnorm(x, μ, σ)

Description   Returns the cumulative lognormal distribution.

Arguments

  x real number, $x \geq 0$

  μ real logmean

  σ real logdeviation, $\sigma > 0$

plogis

Syntax   plogis(x, l, s)

Description   Returns the cumulative logistic distribution.

Arguments
  x real number

  l real location parameter

  s real scale parameter, $s > 0$

pmt

Syntax   pmt(*rate*, *nper*, *pv*, [[*fv*], [*type*]])

Description   Returns the payment for an investment or loan based on periodic, constant payments over a given number of compounding periods, *nper*, using a fixed interest rate, *rate*, and a specified present value, *pv*.

Arguments
  rate   real rate

  nper   integer number of compounding periods, *nper* ≥ 1

  pv   real present value

  fv   (optional) real future value, default is *fv* = 0

  type   (optional) indicator payment timing, 0 for payment made at the end of the period, 1 for payment made at the beginning, default is *type* = 0

Comments	If you know the annual interest rate, *ann_rate*, you must calculate the interest rate per period as *rate = ann_rate/nper*.
	Payments you make, such as deposits into a savings account or payments toward a loan, must be entered as negative numbers. Cash you receive, such as dividend checks, must be entered as positive numbers.
See also	cumint, cumprn, fv, ipmt, nper, ppmt, pv, rate

pnbinom   Probability Distribution

Syntax	pnbinom(k, n, p)
Description	Returns the cumulative negative binomial distribution with parameters n and p.
Arguments	
k, n	integers, $n > 0$ and $k \geq 0$
p	real number, $0 < p \leq 1$
Algorithm	Continued fraction expansion (Abramowitz and Stegun, 1972)

pnorm   Probability Distribution

Syntax	pnorm(x, μ, σ)
Description	Returns the cumulative normal distribution.
Arguments	
x	real number
μ	real mean
σ	real standard deviation, $\sigma > 0$

Polyhedron   Vector and Matrix

Syntax	Polyhedron(S)
Description	Generates the uniform polyhedron whose name, number code, or Wytoff symbol is S.
Arguments	
S	string expression containing the name of a polyhedron, its number code, or its Wytoff symbol
Example	

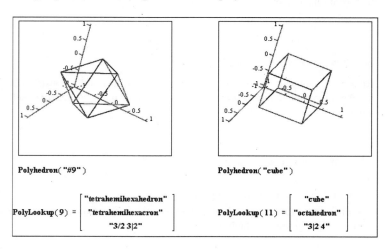

Comments	A uniform polyhedron has faces which are regular polygons and every vertex is in the same relationship to the solid. The faces, however, need not be identical. There are 75 such polyhedra, as well as two infinite families of prisms and antiprisms. The Polyhedron function can construct 80 examples of these, and is used with the 3D surface plot tool as illustrated. Its argument is either a name ("cube"), the # symbol followed by a number ("#6"), or a Wytoff symbol ("3|2 4").

PolyLookup Vector and Matrix

Syntax	PolyLookup(n)
Description	Returns a vector containing the name, the dual name, and the Wytoff symbol for the polyhedron indicated by n.
Arguments	
n	integer, is the code for a polyhedron; alternatively, a string expression containing the polyhedron's number code, name, or Wytoff symbol
See also	Polyhedron for example

polyroots Solving

Syntax	polyroots(**v**)
Description	Returns the roots of an nth degree polynomial whose coefficients are in **v**. Output is a vector of length n.
Arguments	
v	real or complex vector of length $n + 1$
Example	

$$x^3 - 10 \cdot x + 2 \qquad \leftarrow \text{ Polynomial}$$

$$\mathbf{v} := \begin{bmatrix} 2 \\ -10 \\ 0 \\ 1 \end{bmatrix} \qquad \leftarrow \begin{array}{l}\text{A vector of the coefficients, begin} \\ \text{with the constant term. Be sure to} \\ \text{include all coefficients, even if} \\ \text{they are zero.}\end{array}$$

$$\text{polyroots}(\mathbf{v}) = \begin{bmatrix} -3.258 \\ 0.201 \\ 3.057 \end{bmatrix} \qquad \leftarrow \text{ Returns all roots at once.}$$

Comments	To find the roots of an expression having the form: $v_n x^n + \ldots + v_2 x^2 + v_1 x + v_0$

you can use the polyroots function rather than the root function. Unlike root, polyroots does not require a guess value. Moreover, polyroots returns all roots at once, whether real or complex.

The polyroots function can solve only one polynomial equation in one unknown. See root for a more general equation solver. To solve several equations simultaneously, use solve blocks (Find or Minerr). To solve an equation symbolically – that is, to find an exact numerical answer in terms of elementary functions – choose **Solve for Variable** from the **Symbolics** menu or use the solve keyword.

Algorithm	Laguerre with deflation and polishing (Lorczak) is the default method; a companion matrix-based method (using Mathcad's eigenvals function) is available if you right-click on the word polyroots and change the selection on a pop-up menu.
See also	See coeff keyword for a way to create the coefficient vector **v** immediately, given a polynomial.

pol2xy   Vector and Matrix

Syntax	pol2xy(r, θ)
Description	Converts the polar coordinates of a point in 2D space to rectangular coordinates.
Arguments	
r, θ	real numbers
Comments	$x = r\cos(\theta)$, $y = r\sin(\theta)$
See also	xy2pol

ppmt   Finance

Syntax	ppmt($rate$, per, $nper$, pv, [[fv], [$type$]])
Description	Returns the payment on the principal, of an investment or loan, for a given period, per, based on periodic, constant payments over a given number of compounding periods, $nper$, using a fixed interest rate, $rate$, and a specified present value, pv.
Arguments	
$rate$	real rate
per	integer period number, $per \geq 1$
$nper$	integer number of compounding periods, $1 \leq per \leq nper$
pv	real present value
fv	(optional) real future value, default is $fv = 0$
$type$	(optional) indicator payment timing, 0 for payment made at the end of the period, 1 for payment made at the beginning, default is $type = 0$
Comments	If you know the annual interest rate, ann_rate, you must calculate the interest rate per period as $rate = ann\_rate/nper$.
	Payments you make, such as deposits into a savings account or payments toward a loan, must be entered as negative numbers. Cash you receive, such as dividend checks, must be entered as positive numbers.
See also	cumprn, ipmt, pmt

ppois   Probability Distribution

Syntax	ppois(k, λ)
Description	Returns the cumulative Poisson distribution.
Arguments	
k	integer, $k \geq 0$
λ	real mean, $\lambda > 0$
Algorithm	Continued fraction and asymptotic expansions (Abramowitz and Stegun, 1972)

predict

Syntax   predict($\mathbf{v}$, m, n)

Description   Returns n predicted values based on m consecutive values from the data vector $\mathbf{v}$. Elements in $\mathbf{v}$ should represent samples taken at equal intervals.

Arguments

$\mathbf{v}$ real vector

m, n integers, $m > 0$, $n > 0$

Example

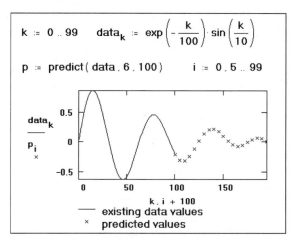

$$k := 0 \ldots 99 \qquad \text{data}_k := \exp\left(-\frac{k}{100}\right) \cdot \sin\left(\frac{k}{10}\right)$$

$$p := \text{predict}(\, \text{data}, 6, 100 \,) \qquad i := 0, 5 \ldots 99$$

existing data values
× predicted values

Comments   Interpolation functions such as cspline, lspline, or pspline, coupled with interp, allow you to find data points lying between existing data points. However, you may need to find data points that lie beyond your existing ones. Mathcad provides the function predict which uses some of your existing data to predict data points lying beyond existing ones. This function uses a linear prediction algorithm which is useful when your data is smooth and oscillatory, although not necessarily periodic. This algorithm can be seen as a kind of extrapolation method but should not be confused with linear or polynomial extrapolation.

The predict function uses the last m of the original data values to compute prediction coefficients. After it has these coefficients, it uses the last m points to predict the coordinates of the $(m+1)^{\text{st}}$ point, in effect creating a moving window that is m points wide.

Algorithm   Burg's method (Press *et al.*, 1992)

pspline

One-dimensional Case

Syntax   pspline($\mathbf{vx}$, $\mathbf{vy}$)

Description   Returns the vector of coefficients of a cubic spline with parabolic ends. This vector becomes the first argument of the interp function.

Arguments

$\mathbf{vx}$, $\mathbf{vy}$ real vectors of the same size; elements of $\mathbf{vx}$ must be in ascending order

---

Syntax	pspline(**Mxy**, **Mz**)
Description	Returns the vector of coefficients of a two-dimensional cubic spline, constrained to be parabolic at region boundaries spanned by **Mxy**. This vector becomes the first argument of the interp function.
Arguments	
Mxy	$n \times 2$ matrix whose elements, $Mxy_{i,\,0}$ and $Mxy_{i,\,1}$, specify the x- and y-coordinates along the *diagonal* of a rectangular grid. This matrix plays exactly the same role as **vx** in the one-dimensional case described earlier. Since these points describe a diagonal, the elements in each column of **Mxy** must be in ascending order ($Mxy_{i,\,k} < Mxy_{j,\,k}$ whenever $i < j$).
Mz	$n \times n$ matrix whose ijth element is the z-coordinate corresponding to the point $x = Mxy_{i,\,0}$ and $y = Mxy_{j,\,1}$. **Mz** plays exactly the same role as **vy** in the one-dimensional case above.
Algorithm	Tridiagonal system solving (Press *et al.*, 1992; Lorczak)
See also	lspline for more details

pt Probability Distribution

Syntax	pt(x, d)
Description	Returns the cumulative Student's t distribution.
Arguments	
x	real number, $x \geq 0$
d	integer degrees of freedom, $d > 0$
Algorithm	Continued fraction expansion (Abramowitz and Stegun, 1972).

punif Probability Distribution

Syntax	punif(x, a, b)
Description	Returns the cumulative uniform distribution.
Arguments	
x	real number
a, b	real numbers, $a < b$

pv Finance

Syntax	pv(*rate*, *nper*, *pmt*, [[*fv*], [*type*]])
Description	Returns the present value of an investment or loan based on periodic, constant payments over a given number of compounding periods, *nper*, using a fixed interest rate, *rate*, and a specified payment, *pmt*.

Arguments

rate	real rate
nper	integer number of compounding periods, $nper \geq 1$
pmt	real payment
fv	(optional) real future value, default is $fv = 0$
type	(optional) indicator payment timing, 0 for payment made at the end of the period, 1 for payment made at the beginning, default is $type = 0$

Comments If you know the annual interest rate, *ann_rate*, you must calculate the interest rate per period as *rate = ann_rate/nper*.

Payments you make, such as deposits into a savings account or payments toward a loan, must be entered as negative numbers. Cash you receive, such as dividend checks, must be entered as positive numbers.

See also fv, nper, pmt, rate

pweibull
Probability Distribution

Syntax pweibull(x, s)

Description Returns the cumulative Weibull distribution.

Arguments

x	real number, $x \geq 0$
s	real shape parameter, $s > 0$

pwrfit
Regression and Smoothing

Syntax pwrfit(**vx**, **vy**, **vg**)

Description Returns a vector containing the parameters (a, b, c) that make the function $a \cdot x^b + c$ best approximate the data in **vx** and **vy**.

Arguments

vx, vy	real vectors of the same size
vg	real vector of guess values for (a, b, c)

Comments This is a special case of the genfit function. A vector of guess values is needed for initialization. By decreasing the value of the built-in TOL variable, higher accuracy in pwrfit might be achieved.

See Also line, linfit, genfit, expfit, logfit, lnfit, lgsfit, sinfit, medfit

qbeta

Syntax	qbeta(p, $s1$, $s2$)
Description	Returns the inverse beta distribution with shape parameters $s1$ and $s2$.
Arguments	
p	real number, $0 \le p \le 1$
s_1, s_2	real shape parameters, $s_1 > 0$, $s_2 > 0$
Algorithm	Root finding (bisection and secant methods) (Press *et al.*, 1992)

qbinom

Syntax	qbinom(p, n, q)
Description	Returns the inverse binomial distribution function, that is, the smallest integer k so that pbinom(k, n, q) $\ge p$.
Arguments	
n	integer, $n > 0$
p, q	real numbers, $0 \le p \le 1$, $0 \le q \le 1$
Comments	k is approximately the integer for which $\Pr(X \le k) = p$, when the random variable X has the binomial distribution with parameters n and q. This is the meaning of "inverse" binomial distribution function.
Algorithm	Discrete bisection method (Press *et al.*, 1992)

qcauchy

Syntax	qcauchy(p, l, s)
Description	Returns the inverse Cauchy distribution function.
Arguments	
p	real number, $0 < p < 1$
l	real location parameter
s	real scale parameter, $s > 0$

qchisq

Syntax	qchisq(p, d)
Description	Returns the inverse chi-squared distribution.
Arguments	
p	real number, $0 \le p < 1$
d	integer degrees of freedom, $d > 0$
Algorithm	Root finding (bisection and secant methods) (Press *et al.*, 1992) Rational function approximations (Abramowitz and Stegun, 1972)

qexp

Syntax   qexp(p, r)

Description   Returns the inverse exponential distribution.

Arguments

    p real number, $0 \leq p < 1$

    r real rate, $r > 0$

qF

Syntax   qF(p, $d1$, $d2$)

Description   Returns the inverse F distribution.

Arguments

    p real number, $0 \leq p < 1$

    d_1, d_2 integer degrees of freedom, $d_1 > 0$, $d_2 > 0$

Algorithm   Root finding (bisection and secant methods) (Press *et al.*, 1992)

qgamma

Syntax   qgamma(p, s)

Description   Returns the inverse gamma distribution.

Arguments

    p real number, $0 \leq p < 1$

    s real shape parameter, $s > 0$

Algorithm   Root finding (bisection and secant methods) (Press *et al.*, 1992)
Rational function approximations (Abramowitz and Stegun, 1972)

qgeom

Syntax   qgeom(p, q)

Description   Returns the inverse geometric distribution, that is, the smallest integer k so that pgeom(k, q) $\geq p$.

Arguments

    p, q real numbers, $0 < p < 1$, $0 < q < 1$

Comments k is approximately the integer for which $\Pr(X \leq k) = p$, when the random variable X has the geometric distribution with parameter q. This is the meaning of "inverse" geometric distribution function.

qhypergeom

Syntax	qhypergeom(p, a, b, n)
Description	Returns the inverse hypergeometric distribution, that is, the smallest integer k so that phypergeom(k, a, b, n) $\geq p$.
Arguments	
p	real number, $0 \leq p \leq 1$
a, b, n	integers, $0 \leq a$, $0 \leq b$, $0 \leq n \leq a + b$
Comments	k is approximately the integer for which $\Pr(X \leq k) = p$, when the random variable X has the hypergeometric distribution with parameters a, b and n. This is the meaning of "inverse" hypergeometric distribution function.
Algorithm	Discrete bisection method (Press *et al.*, 1992)

qlnorm

Syntax	qlnorm(p, μ, σ)
Description	Returns the inverse log normal distribution.
Arguments	
p	real number; $0 \leq p < 1$
μ	logmean
σ	logdeviation; $\sigma > 0$
Algorithm	Root finding (bisection and secant methods) (Press *et al.*, 1992)

qlogis

Syntax	qlogis(p, l, s)
Description	Returns the inverse logistic distribution.
Arguments	
p	real number, $0 < p < 1$
l	real location parameter
s	real scale parameter, $s > 0$

qnbinom

Syntax	qnbinom(p, n, q)
Description	Returns the inverse negative binomial distribution function, that is, the smallest integer k so that pnbinom(k, n, q) $\geq p$.
Arguments	
n	integer, $n > 0$
p, q	real numbers, $0 < p < 1$, $0 < q < 1$
Comments	k is approximately the integer for which $\Pr(X \leq k) = p$, when the random variable X has the negative binomial distribution with parameters n and q. This is the meaning of "inverse" negative binomial distribution function.
Algorithm	Discrete bisection method (Press *et al.*, 1992)

qnorm

Syntax	qnorm(p, μ, σ)
Description	Returns the inverse normal distribution.
Arguments	
p	real number, $0 < p < 1$
m	real mean
s	standard deviation, $\sigma > 0$
Algorithm	Root finding (bisection and secant methods) (Press *et al.*, 1992)

qpois

Syntax	qpois(p, λ)
Description	Returns the inverse Poisson distribution, that is, the smallest integer k so that ppois(k, λ) $\geq p$.
Arguments	
p	real number,
λ	real mean, $\lambda > 0$
Comments	k is approximately the integer for which $\Pr(X \leq k) = p$, when the random variable X has the Poisson distribution with parameter λ. This is the meaning of "inverse" Poisson distribution function.
Algorithm	Discrete bisection method (Press *et al.*, 1992)

qr

Syntax	qr($\mathbf{A}$)
Description	Returns an $m \times (m + n)$ matrix whose first m columns contain the $m \times m$ orthonormal matrix $\mathbf{Q}$, and whose remaining n columns contain the $m \times n$ upper triangular matrix $\mathbf{R}$. These satisfy the matrix equation $\mathbf{A} = \mathbf{Q} \cdot \mathbf{R}$.
Arguments	
$\mathbf{A}$	real $m \times n$ matrix

Example

$$A := \begin{pmatrix} 1 & 2 & -1 \\ 2.3 & 4 & 4 \\ -2 & 5.1 & 1 \\ 0 & .8 & 6 \end{pmatrix} \qquad M := qr(A)$$

$$M = \begin{pmatrix} 0.312 & 0.279 & -0.411 & -0.81 & 3.208 & 0.312 & 1.933 \\ 0.717 & 0.553 & 0.117 & 0.407 & 0 & 6.823 & 3.415 \\ -0.623 & 0.776 & -0.072 & 0.064 & 0 & 0 & 6.213 \\ 0 & 0.117 & 0.901 & -0.417 & 0 & 0 & 0 \end{pmatrix}$$

$$Q := \text{submatrix}(M , 0 , 3 , 0 , 3) \qquad R := \text{submatrix}(M , 0 , 3 , 4 , 6)$$

$$Q \cdot Q^T = \begin{pmatrix} 1 & 0 & 0 & 0 \\ 0 & 1 & 0 & 0 \\ 0 & 0 & 1 & 0 \\ 0 & 0 & 0 & 1 \end{pmatrix} \qquad Q \cdot R = \begin{pmatrix} 1 & 2 & -1 \\ 2.3 & 4 & 4 \\ -2 & 5.1 & 1 \\ 0 & 0.8 & 6 \end{pmatrix}$$

qt

Syntax qt(p, d)

Description Returns the inverse Student's t distribution.

Arguments
   p real number, $0 < p < 1$
   d integer degrees of freedom, $d > 0$

Algorithm Root finding (bisection and secant methods) (Press *et al.*, 1992).

qunif

Syntax qunif(p, a, b)

Description Returns the inverse uniform distribution.

Arguments
   p real number, $0 \leq p \leq 1$
   a, b real numbers, $a < b$

qweibull

Syntax qweibull(p, s)

Description Returns the inverse Weibull distribution.

Arguments
   p real number,
   s real shape parameter, $s > 0$

rank

Syntax	rank(**A**)
Description	Returns the rank of a matrix **A**, i.e., the maximum number of linearly independent columns in **A**.
Arguments	
A	real $m \times n$ matrix
Algorithm	Singular value computation (Wilkinson and Reinsch, 1971)

rate

Syntax	rate(*nper, pmt, pv,* [[*fv*], [*type*], [*guess*]])
Description	Returns the interest rate per period of an investment or loan over a specified number of compounding periods, *nper*, given a periodic, constant payment, *pmt*, and a specified present value, *pv*.
Arguments	
nper	integer number of compounding periods, $nper \geq 1$
pmt	real payment
pv	real present value
fv	(optional) real future value, default is $fv = 0$
type	(optional) indicator payment timing, 0 for payment made at the end of the period, 1 for payment made at the beginning, default is $type = 0$
guess	(optional) real guess, default is $guess = 0.1$ (10%)
Comments	Payments you make, such as deposits into a savings account or payments toward a loan, must be entered as negative numbers. Cash you receive, such as dividend checks, must be entered as positive numbers.
	If rate cannot find a result that is accurate to within $1 \cdot 10^{-7}$ percent after 20 iterations, it returns an error. In such a case, a different guess value should be tried, but it will not guarantee a solution.
See also	crate, fv, nper, pmt, pv

rbeta

Syntax	rbeta(*m, s1, s2*)
Description	Returns a vector of *m* random numbers having the beta distribution.
Arguments	
m	integer, $m > 0$
s_1, s_2	real shape parameters, $s_1 > 0$, $s_2 > 0$
Algorithm	Best's XG algorithm, Johnk's generator (Devroye, 1986)
See also	rnd

rbinom

Syntax	rbinom(m, n, p)
Description	Returns a vector of m random numbers having the binomial distribution.
Arguments	
m, n	integers, $m > 0$, $n > 0$
p	real number, $0 \leq p \leq 1$
Algorithm	Waiting time and rejection algorithms (Devroye, 1986)
See also	rnd

rcauchy

Syntax	rcauchy(m, l, s)
Description	Returns a vector of m random numbers having the Cauchy distribution.
Arguments	
m	integer, $m > 0$
l	real location parameter
s	real scale parameter, $s > 0$
Algorithm	Inverse cumulative density method (Press *et al.*, 1992)
See also	rnd

rchisq

Syntax	rchisq(m, d)
Description	Returns a vector of m random numbers having the chi-squared distribution.
Arguments	
m	integer, $m > 0$
d	integer degrees of freedom, $d > 0$
Algorithm	Best's XG algorithm, Johnk's generator (Devroye, 1986)
See also	rnd

Re

Syntax	Re(z)
Description	Returns the real part of z.
Arguments	
z	real or complex number
See also	Im

READ_BLUE

Syntax   READ_BLUE(*file*)

Description   Extracts only the blue component from *file* of a color image in BMP, JPG, GIF, TGA, and PCX format. The result is a matrix with one-third as many columns as the matrix returned by READRGB.

Arguments
file   string variable corresponding to color image filename or path

READBMP

Syntax   READBMP(*file*)

Description   Creates a matrix containing a grayscale representation of the bitmap image in *file*. Each element in the matrix corresponds to a pixel. The value of a matrix element determines the shade of gray associated with the corresponding pixel. Each element is an integer between 0 (black) and 255 (white).

Arguments
file   string variable corresponding to grayscale image BMP filename or path

Comments   After you have read an image file into Mathcad, you can use the *picture operator* to view it.

The function READ_IMAGE which reads not only BMP files but also JPG, GIF, TGA and PCX files.

See also   For color images, see READRGB.

READ_GREEN

Syntax   READ_GREEN(*file*)

Description   Extracts only the green component from *file* of a color image in BMP, JPG, GIF, TGA, and PCX format. The result is a matrix with one-third as many columns as the matrix returned by READRGB.

Arguments
file   string variable corresponding to color image filename or path

READ_HLS

Syntax   READ_HLS(*file*)

Description   Creates a matrix in which the color information in *file* is represented by the appropriate values of hue, lightness, and saturation. *file* is in BMP, JPG, GIF, TGA, or PCX format.

Arguments
file   string variable corresponding to color image filename or path

See also   See READRGB for an overview.

READ_HLS_HUE File Access

Syntax	READ_HLS_HUE(*file*)
Description	Extracts only the hue component from *file* of a color image in BMP, JPG, GIF, TGA, or PCX format. The result is a matrix with one-third as many columns as the matrix returned by READ_HLS.
Arguments	
file	string variable corresponding to color image filename or path

READ_HLS_LIGHT File Access

Syntax	READ_HLS_LIGHT(*file*)
Description	Extracts only the lightness component from *file* of a color image in BMP, JPG, GIF, TGA, or PCX format. The result is a matrix with one-third as many columns as the matrix returned by READ_HLS.
Arguments	
file	string variable corresponding to color image filename or path

READ_HLS_SAT File Access

Syntax	READ_HLS_SAT(*file*)
Description	Extracts only the saturation component from *file* of a color image in BMP, JPG, GIF, TGA, or PCX format. The result is a matrix with one-third as many columns as the matrix returned by READ_HLS.
Arguments	
file	string variable corresponding to color image filename or path

READ_HSV File Access

Syntax	READ_HSV(*file*)
Description	Creates a matrix in which the color information in *file* is represented by the appropriate values of hue, saturation and value. *file* is in BMP, JPG, GIF, TGA, or PCX format.
Arguments	
file	string variable corresponding to color image filename or path
See also	See READRGB for an overview of reading color data files.

READ_HSV_HUE File Access

Syntax	READ_HSV_HUE(*file*)
Description	Extracts only the hue component from *file* of a color image in BMP, JPG, GIF, TGA, or PCX format. The result is a matrix with one-third as many columns as the matrix returned by READ_HSV.
Arguments	
file	string variable corresponding to color image filename or path

READ_HSV_SAT

Syntax   READ_HSV_SAT(*file*)

Description   Extracts only the saturation component from *file* of a color image in BMP, JPG, GIF, TGA, or PCX format. The result is a matrix with one-third as many columns as the matrix returned by READ_HSV.

Arguments
     file   string variable corresponding to color image filename or path

READ_HSV_VALUE

Syntax   READ_HSV_VALUE(*file*)

Description   Extracts only the value component from *file* of a color image in BMP, JPG, GIF, TGA, or PCX format. The result is a matrix with one-third as many columns as the matrix returned by READ_HSV.

Arguments
     file   string variable corresponding to color image filename or path

READ_IMAGE

Syntax   READ_IMAGE(*file*)

Description   Creates a matrix containing a grayscale representation of the image in *file*. Each element in the matrix corresponds to a pixel. The value of a matrix element determines the shade of gray associated with the corresponding pixel. Each element is an integer between 0 (black) and 255 (white). *file* is in BMP, JPG, GIF, TGA, or PCX format.

Arguments
     file   string variable corresponding to grayscale image filename or path

See also   For color images, see READRGB.

READPRN

Syntax   READPRN(*file*)

Description   Reads a structured ASCII data file and returns a matrix. Each line in the data file becomes a row in the matrix. The number of elements in each row must be the same. Used as follows:
A := READPRN(*file*).

Arguments
     file   string variable corresponding to structured ASCII data filename or path

Comments   The READPRN function reads an entire data file, determines the number of rows and columns, and creates a matrix out of the data.

When Mathcad reads data with the READPRN function:

- Each instance of the READPRN function reads an entire data file.
- All lines in the data file must have the same number of values. (Mathcad ignores lines with no values.) If the lines in the file have differing numbers of values, Mathcad marks the READPRN equation with an error message. Use a text editor to replace the missing values with zeros before you use READPRN.
- The READPRN function ignores text in the data file.
- The result of reading the data file is an m-by-n matrix **A**, where m is the number of lines containing data in the file and n is the number of values per line.

WRITEPRN and READPRN allow you to write out and read in *nested arrays* created in Mathcad.

READ_RED

Syntax	READ_RED(*file*)
Description	Extracts only the red component from *file* of a color image in BMP, JPG, GIF, TGA, or PCX format.The result is a matrix with one-third as many columns as the matrix returned by READRGB.
Arguments	
file	string variable corresponding to color image filename or path

READRGB

File Access

Syntax	READRGB(*file*)
Description	Creates a matrix in which the color information in the BMP file *file* is represented by the appropriate values of red, green, and blue. This matrix consists of three submatrices, each with the same number of columns and rows. Three matrix elements, rather than one, correspond to each pixel. Each element is an integer between 0 and 255. The three corresponding elements, when taken together, establish the color of the pixel.
Arguments	
file	string variable corresponding to color image filename or path

Example

```
color := "c:\images\monalisa.bmp"

gray := READBMP(color)
packed := READRGB(color)

r := rows( packed ) - 1        c := cols( packed )
                                     ─────────────
                                           3

red   := submatrix( packed , 0 , r , 0 , c - 1 )

green := submatrix( packed , 0 , r , c , 2·c - 1 )

blue  := submatrix( packed , 0 , r , 2·c , 3·c - 1 )
```

Comments

To partition the matrix for a color image into its red, green, and blue components, use the submatrix function formulas shown in the example above. In this example, the color bitmap file **monalisa.bmp** is read into a grayscale matrix **gray**, as well as the packed RGB matrix **packed**, and then converted into three submatrices called **red**, **green**, and **blue**.

After you have read an image file into Mathcad, you can use the *picture operator* to view it.

Mathcad includes several specialized functions for reading color images or image components, including functions for reading images in GIF, JPG, TGA and PCX formats.

Consult the following table to decide which function to use:

To separate a file into these components:	Use these functions:
red, green, and blue (RGB)	READ_RED, READ_GREEN, READ_BLUE
hue, lightness, and saturation (HLS)	READ_HLS, READ_HLS_HUE, READ_HLS_LIGHT, READ_HLS_SAT,
hue, saturation, and value (HSV)	READ_HSV, READ_HSV_HUE, READ_HSV_SAT, READ_HSV_VAL

Note   READ_HLS and READ_HSV work in exactly the same way as READRGB. All the others work in exactly the same way as READBMP.

See also   For grayscale images, see READBMP.

READWAV
File Access

Syntax   READWAV(*file*)

Description   Creates a matrix containing signal amplitudes in *file*. Each column represents a separate channel of data. Each row corresponds to a moment in time.

Arguments

file   string variable corresponding to pulse code modulated (PCM) Microsoft WAV filename or path

Comments   Data from a WAV file is not scaled.

See also   WRITEWAV and GETWAVINFO

regress
Regression and Smoothing

One-dimensional Case

Syntax   regress(**vx**, **vy**, *n*)

Description   Returns the vector required by the interp function to find the *n*th order polynomial that best fits data arrays **vx** and **vy**.

Arguments

vx, vy   real vectors of the same size

n   integer, $n > 0$

Example

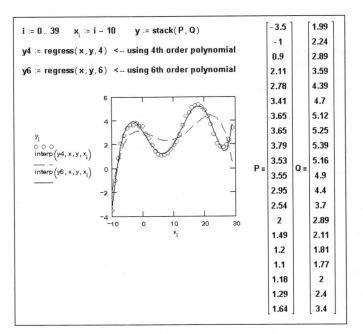

$i := 0 .. 39 \quad x_i := i - 10 \quad y := \text{stack}(P, Q)$

$y4 := \text{regress}(x, y, 4)$ <-- using 4th order polynomial

$y6 := \text{regress}(x, y, 6)$ <-- using 6th order polynomial

$$P = \begin{bmatrix} -3.5 \\ -1 \\ 0.9 \\ 2.11 \\ 2.78 \\ 3.41 \\ 3.65 \\ 3.65 \\ 3.79 \\ 3.53 \\ 3.55 \\ 2.95 \\ 2.54 \\ 2 \\ 1.49 \\ 1.2 \\ 1.1 \\ 1.18 \\ 1.29 \\ 1.64 \end{bmatrix} \quad Q = \begin{bmatrix} 1.99 \\ 2.24 \\ 2.89 \\ 3.59 \\ 4.39 \\ 4.7 \\ 5.12 \\ 5.25 \\ 5.39 \\ 5.16 \\ 4.9 \\ 4.4 \\ 3.7 \\ 2.89 \\ 2.11 \\ 1.81 \\ 1.77 \\ 2 \\ 2.4 \\ 3.4 \end{bmatrix}$$

Comments

The regression functions regress and loess are useful when you have a set of measured y values corresponding to x values and you want to fit a polynomial of degree n through those y values. (For a simple linear fit, that is, $n=1$, you may as well use the line function.)

Use regress when you want to use a single polynomial to fit all your data values. The regress function lets you fit a polynomial of any order. However as a practical matter, you would rarely need to go beyond $n = 6$.

Since regress tries to accommodate all your data points using a single polynomial, it will not work well when your data does not behave like a single polynomial. For example, suppose you expect your y_i to be linear from x_1 to x_{10} and to behave like a cubic equation from x_{11} to x_{20}. If you use regress with $n = 3$ (a cubic), you may get a good fit for the second half but a poor fit for the first half.

The loess function alleviates these kinds of problems by performing a more localized regression.

For regress, the first three components of the output vector $\mathbf{vr} := \text{regress}(\mathbf{vx}, \mathbf{vy}, n)$ are $\mathbf{vr}_0{=}3$ (a code telling interp that $\mathbf{vr}$ is the output of regress as opposed to a spline function or loess), $\mathbf{vr}_1{=}3$ (the index within $\mathbf{vr}$ where the polynomial coefficients begin), and $\mathbf{vr}_2{=}n$ (the order of the fit). The remaining $n + 1$ components are the coefficients of the fitting polynomial from the lowest degree term to the highest degree term.

Two-dimensional Case

Syntax   regress(**Mxy**, **vz**, *n*)

Description   Returns the vector required by the interp function to find the *n*th order polynomial that best fits data arrays **Mxy** and **vz**. **Mxy** is an $m \times 2$ matrix containing *x-y* coordinates. **vz** is an *m*-element vector containing the *z* coordinates corresponding to the *m* points specified in **Mxy**.

Arguments
Mxy   real $m \times 2$ matrix containing *x-y* coordinates of the *m* data points

vz   real *m*-element vector containing the *z* coordinates corresponding to the points specified in **Mxy**

n   integer, $n > 0$

Comments   Assume, for example, that you have a set of measured *z* values corresponding to *x* and *y* values and you want to fit a polynomial surface through those *z* values. The meanings of the input arguments are more general than in the one-dimensional case:

- The argument **vx**, which was an *m*-element vector of *x* values, becomes an $m \times 2$ matrix, **Mxy**. Each row of **Mxy** contains an *x* in the first column and a corresponding *y* value in the second column.

- The argument *x* for the interp function becomes a 2-element vector **v** whose elements are the *x* and *y* values at which you want to evaluate the polynomial surface representing the best fit to the data points in **Mxy** and **vz**.

This discussion can be extended naturally to higher dimensional cases. You can add independent variables by simply adding columns to the **Mxy** array. You would then add a corresponding number of rows to the vector **v** that you pass to the interp function. The regress function can have as many independent variables as you want. However, regress will calculate more slowly and require more memory when the number of independent variables and the degree are greater than four. The loess function is restricted to at most four independent variables.

Keep in mind that for regress, the number of data values, *m* must satisfy $m > \binom{n+k-1}{n} \cdot \frac{n+k}{k}$, where *k* is the number of independent variables (hence the number of columns in **Mxy**), *n* is the degree of the desired polynomial, and *m* is the number of data values (hence the number of rows in **vz**). For example, if you have five explanatory variables and a fourth degree polynomial, you will need more than 126 observations.

The loess function works better than regress when your data does not behave like a single polynomial.

Algorithm   Normal equation solution through Gauss-Jordan elimination (Press *et al.*, 1992)

relax
Differential Equation Solving

Syntax   relax(**A**, **B**, **C**, **D**, **E**, **F**, **U**, *rjac*)

Description   Returns a matrix of solution values for a Poisson partial differential equation over a planar square region. More general than multigrid, which is faster.

Arguments

A, B, C, D, E real square matrices all of the same size containing coefficients of the discretized Laplacian (for example, the left-hand side of equations below).

F real square matrix containing the source term at each point in the region in which the solution is sought (for example, the right-hand side of equations below).

U real square matrix containing boundary values along the edges of the region and initial guesses for the solution inside the region.

rjac spectral radius of the Jacobi iteration, $0 < rjac < 1$, which controls the convergence of the relaxation algorithm. Its optimal value depends on the details of your problem.

Example

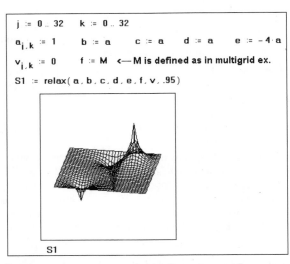

$j := 0 .. 32 \quad k := 0 .. 32$

$a_{j,k} := 1 \quad b := a \quad c := a \quad d := a \quad e := -4 \cdot a$

$v_{i,k} := 0 \quad f := M \quad \longleftarrow \text{M is defined as in multigrid ex.}$

$S1 := relax(a, b, c, d, e, f, v, .95)$

S1

Comments

Two partial differential equations that arise often in the analysis of physical systems are Poisson's equation:

$$\frac{\partial^2 u}{\partial x^2} + \frac{\partial^2 u}{\partial y^2} = \rho(x, y)$$ and its homogeneous form, Laplace's equation.

Mathcad has two functions for solving these equations over a square region, assuming the values taken by the unknown function $u(x, y)$ on all four sides of the boundary are known. The most general solver is the relax function. In the special case when $u(x, y)$ is known to be zero on all four sides of the boundary, you can use the multigrid function instead. This function will often solve the problem faster than relax. If the boundary condition is the same on all four sides, you can simply transform the equation to an equivalent one in which the value is zero on all four sides.

The relax function returns a square matrix in which:

• an element's location in the matrix corresponds to its location within the square region, and
• its value approximates the value of the solution at that point.

This function uses the relaxation method to converge to the solution. Poisson's equation on a square domain is represented by:

$$a_{j,k} u_{j+1,k} + b_{j,k} u_{j-1,k} + c_{j,k} u_{j,k+1} + d_{j,k} u_{j,k-1} + e_{j,k} u_{j,k} = f_{j,k}.$$

Algorithm

Gauss-Seidel with successive overrelaxation (Press *et al.*, 1992)

See also

multigrid

reverse

One-dimensional Case

Syntax	reverse(**v**)
Description	Reverses the order of the elements of vector **v**.
Arguments	
v	vector

Two-dimensional Case

Syntax	reverse(**A**)
Description	Reverses the order of the rows of matrix **A**.
Arguments	
A	matrix
See also	See sort for sample application.

rexp

Syntax	rexp(m, r)
Description	Returns a vector of m random numbers having the exponential distribution.
Arguments	
m	integer, $m > 0$
r	real rate, $r > 0$
See also	rnd
Algorithm	Inverse cumulative density method (Press *et al.*, 1992)

rF

Syntax	rF(m, $d1$, $d2$)
Description	Returns a vector of m random numbers having the F distribution.
Arguments	
m	integer, $m > 0$
$d1$, $d2$	integer degrees of freedom, $d1 > 0$, $d2 > 0$
Algorithm	Best's XG algorithm, Johnk's generator (Devroye, 1986)
See also	rnd

rgamma

Syntax	rgamma(m, s)
Description	Returns a vector of m random numbers having the gamma distribution.
Arguments	
m	integer, $m > 0$
s	real shape parameter, $s > 0$
Algorithm	Best's XG algorithm, Johnk's generator (Devroye, 1986)
See also	rnd

rgeom

Syntax	rgeom(*m*, *p*)
Description	Returns a vector of *m* random numbers having the geometric distribution.
Arguments	
m	integer, $m > 0$
p	real number, $0 < p < 1$
Algorithm	Inverse cumulative density method (Press *et al.*, 1992)
See also	rnd

rhypergeom

Syntax	rhypergeom(*m*, *a*, *b*, *n*)
Description	Returns a vector of *m* random numbers having the hypergeometric distribution.
Arguments	
m	integer, $m > 0$
a, *b*, *n*	integers, $0 \le a$, $0 \le b$, $0 \le n \le a + b$
Algorithm	Uniform sampling methods (Devroye, 1986)
See also	rnd

rkadapt

Syntax	rkadapt(**y**, *x1*, *x2*, *acc*, **D**, *kmax*, *save*)
Description	Solves a differential equation using a slowly varying Runge-Kutta method. Provides DE solution estimate at *x2*.
Arguments	*Several arguments for this function are the same as described for* rkfixed.
y	real vector of initial values
x1, *x2*	real endpoints of the solution interval
acc	real $acc > 0$ controls the accuracy of the solution; a small value of *acc* forces the algorithm to take smaller steps along the trajectory, thereby increasing the accuracy of the solution. Values of *acc* around 0.001 will generally yield accurate solutions.
D(*x*, **y**)	real vector-valued function containing the derivatives of the unknown functions
kmax	integer $kmax > 0$ specifies the maximum number of intermediate points at which the solution will be approximated. The value of *kmax* places an upper bound on the number of rows of the matrix returned by these functions.
save	real $save > 0$ specifies the smallest allowable spacing between the values at which the solutions are to be approximated. *save* places a lower bound on the difference between any two numbers in the first column of the matrix returned by the function.
Comments	The specialized DE solvers Bulstoer, Rkadapt, Stiffb, and Stiffr provide the solution $y(x)$ over a number of uniformly spaced *x*-values in the integration interval bounded by *x1* and *x2*. When you want the value of the solution at only the endpoint, $y(x2)$, use bulstoer, rkadapt, stiffb, and stiffr instead.
Algorithm	Adaptive step 5th order Runge-Kutta method (Press *et al.*, 1992)
See also	rkfixed, a more general differential equation solver, for information on output and arguments; Rkadapt.

Rkadapt

Syntax	Rkadapt(**y**, *x1*, *x2*, *npts*, **D**)
Description	Solves a differential equation using a slowly varying Runge-Kutta method; provides DE solution at equally spaced *x* values by repeated calls to rkadapt.
Arguments	*All arguments for this function are the same as described for* rkfixed.
y	real vector of initial values
x1, x2	real endpoints of the solution interval
npts	integer *npts* > 0 specifies the number of points beyond initial point at which the solution is to be approximated; controls the number of rows in the matrix output
D(*x*, **y**)	real vector-valued function containing the derivatives of the unknown functions

Comments

Given a fixed number of points, you can approximate a function more accurately if you evaluate it frequently wherever it's changing fast, and infrequently wherever it's changing more slowly. If you know that the solution has this property, you may be better off using **Rkadapt**. Unlike rkfixed which evaluates a solution at equally spaced intervals, **Rkadapt** examines how fast the solution is changing and adapts its step size accordingly. This "adaptive step size control" enables **Rkadapt** to focus on those parts of the integration domain where the function is rapidly changing rather than wasting time on the parts where change is minimal.

Although **Rkadapt** will use nonuniform step sizes internally when it solves the differential equation, it will nevertheless return the solution at equally spaced points.

Rkadapt takes the same arguments as rkfixed, and the matrix returned by **Rkadapt** is identical in form to that returned by rkfixed.

Algorithm	Fixed step Runge-Kutta method with adaptive intermediate steps (5th order) (Press *et al.*, 1992)
See also	rkfixed, a more general differential equation solver, for information on output and arguments; also Odesolve, for a solve block approach.

rkfixed

Syntax	rkfixed(**y**, *x1*, *x2*, *npts*, **D**)
Description	Solves a differential equation using a standard Runge-Kutta method. Provides DE solution at equally spaced *x* values.
Arguments	
y	real vector of initial values (whose length depends on the order of the DE or the size of the system of DEs). For a first order DE like that in Example 1 or Example 2 below, the vector degenerates to one point, $y(0) = y(x1)$. For a second order DE like that in Example 3, the vector has two elements: the value of the function and its first derivative at *x1*. For higher order DEs like that in Example 4, the vector has *n* elements for specifying initial conditions of $y, y', y'', ..., y^{(n-1)}$. For a first order system like that in Example 5, the vector contains initial values for each unknown function. For higher order systems like that in Example 6, the vector contains initial values for the $n - 1$ derivatives of each unknown function in addition to initial values for the functions themselves.

x1, x2	real endpoints of the interval on which the solution to the DEs will be evaluated; initial values in **y** are the values at *x1*
npts	integer *npts* > 0 specifies the number of points beyond the initial point at which the solution is to be approximated; controls the number of rows in the matrix output
D(*x*, **y**)	real vector-valued function containing derivatives of the unknown functions. For a first order DE like that in Example 1 or Example 2, the vector degenerates to a scalar function. For a second order DE like that in Example 3, the vector has two elements:

$$\mathbf{D}(t, \mathbf{y}) = \begin{bmatrix} y'(t) \\ y''(t) \end{bmatrix}$$

For higher order DEs like that in Example 4, the vector has *n* elements: $\mathbf{D}(t, \mathbf{y}) = \begin{bmatrix} y'(t) \\ y''(t) \\ \cdot \\ \cdot \\ \cdot \\ y^{(n)}(t) \end{bmatrix}$.

For a first order system like that in Example 5, the vector contains the first derivatives of each unknown function. For higher order systems like that in Example 6, the vector contains expressions for the $n - 1$ derivatives of each unknown function in addition to *n*th derivatives.

Examples

Example 1: Solving a first order differential equation.

Example 2: Solving a nonlinear differential equation.

Example 3: Solving a second order differential equation.

Solve $\quad y'''' - 2 \cdot k^2 \cdot y'' + k^4 \cdot y = 0 \qquad k := 3$

$$y := \begin{pmatrix} 0 \\ 1 \\ 2 \\ 3 \end{pmatrix} \quad \leftarrow \text{Define initial conditions}$$

$$D(t, y) := \begin{bmatrix} y_1 \\ y_2 \\ y_3 \\ 2 \cdot k^2 \cdot y_2 - k^4 \cdot y_0 \end{bmatrix} \begin{matrix} \leftarrow \text{First derivative} \\ \leftarrow \text{Second derivative} \\ \leftarrow \text{Third derivative} \\ \leftarrow \text{Fourth derivative} \end{matrix}$$

$Z := \text{rkfixed}(y, 0, 5, 100, D) \quad \leftarrow$ Evaluate solution at 100 points between t=0 and t=5.

$$Z = \begin{bmatrix}
\text{t} & \text{y(t)} & \text{y'(t)} & \text{y''(t)} & \text{y'''(t)} \\
0 & 0 & 1 & 2 & 3 \\
0.05 & 0.053 & 1.104 & 2.195 & 4.776 \\
0.1 & 0.111 & 1.221 & 2.477 & 6.543 \\
0.15 & 0.175 & 1.354 & 2.85 & 8.358 \\
0.2 & 0.246 & 1.507 & 3.315 & 10.274 \\
0.25 & 0.326 & 1.687 & 3.88 & 12.348
\end{bmatrix}$$

Example 4: Solving a higher order differential equation.

Solving a system of two non-linear first order differential equations.

$$\mu := -0.2 \qquad x := \begin{pmatrix} 0 \\ 1 \end{pmatrix} \quad \leftarrow \text{Initial conditions}$$

$$D(t, x) := \begin{bmatrix} \mu \cdot x_0 - x_1 - \left[(x_0)^2 + (x_1)^2 \right] \cdot x_0 \\ \mu \cdot x_1 + x_0 - \left[(x_0)^2 + (x_1)^2 \right] \cdot x_1 \end{bmatrix} \quad \leftarrow \text{First derivatives}$$

$Z := \text{rkfixed}(x, 0, 20, 100, D)$

$n := 0 .. 100$

$\leftarrow$ Plot $x_0(t)$ and $x_1(t)$ for t=0..20.

Example 5: Solving a system of first order linear equations.

$$\text{Solve} \quad \begin{matrix} u'' = 2v \\ v'' = 4v - 2u \end{matrix} \quad \begin{matrix} \text{subject to initial} \\ \text{conditions:} \end{matrix} \quad \begin{matrix} u(0) = 1.5 & u'(0) = 1.5 \\ v(0) = 1 & v'(0) = 1 \end{matrix}$$

$$y := \begin{pmatrix} 1.5 \\ 1.5 \\ 1 \\ 1 \end{pmatrix} \begin{matrix} \leftarrow u(0) \\ \leftarrow u'(0) \\ \leftarrow v(0) \\ \leftarrow v'(0) \end{matrix} \quad \leftarrow \text{Define vector of initial conditions.}$$

$$D(x, y) := \begin{bmatrix} y_1 \\ 2 \cdot y_2 \\ y_3 \\ 4 \cdot y_2 - 2 \cdot y_0 \end{bmatrix} \begin{matrix} u' \\ u'' \\ v' \\ v'' \end{matrix} \quad \begin{matrix} \leftarrow \text{Define vector of first and} \\ \text{second derivatives.} \end{matrix}$$

$$Z := \text{rkfixed}(y, 0, 1, 100, D)$$

x	u(x)	u'(x)	v(x)	v'(x)
0	1.5	1.5	1	1
0.01	1.515	1.52	1.01	1.01
0.02	1.53	1.54	1.02	1.02
0.03	1.546	1.561	1.03	1.03
0.04	1.562	1.582	1.041	1.041

$$Z = $$

Example 6: Solving a system of second order linear differential equations.

Comments

For a first order DE like that in Example 1 or Example 2, the output of rkfixed is a two-column matrix in which:

- The left-hand column contains the points at which the solution to the DE is evaluated.
- The right-hand column contains the corresponding values of the solution.

For a second order DE like that in Example 3, the output matrix contains three columns: the left-hand column contains the t values; the middle column contains $y(t)$; and the right-hand column contains $y'(t)$.

For higher order DEs like that in Example 4, the output matrix contains n columns: the left-hand one for the t values and the remaining columns for values of $y(t), y'(t), y''(t), \ldots, y^{(n-1)}(t)$.

For a first order system like that in Example 5, the first column of the output matrix contains the points at which the solutions are evaluated and the remaining columns contain corresponding values of the solutions. For higher order systems like that in Example 6:

- The first column contains the values at which the solutions and their derivatives are evaluated.
- The remaining columns contain corresponding values of the solutions and their derivatives. The order in which the solutions and their derivatives appear matches the order in which you put them into the vector of initial conditions.

The most difficult part of solving a DE is defining the function $\mathbf{D}(x, \mathbf{y})$. In Example 1 and Example 2, for example, it was easy to solve for $y'(x)$. In some more difficult cases, you can solve for $y'(x)$ symbolically and paste it into the definition for $\mathbf{D}(x, \mathbf{y})$. To do so, use the solve keyword or the **Solve for Variable** command from the **Symbolics** menu.

The function rkfixed uses a fourth order Runge-Kutta method, which is a good general-purpose DE solver. Although it is not always the fastest method, the Runge-Kutta method nearly always succeeds. There are certain cases in which you may want to use one of Mathcad's more specialized DE solvers. These cases fall into three broad categories:

- Your system of DEs may have certain properties which are best exploited by functions other than rkfixed. The system may be stiff (**Stiffb**, **Stiffr**); the functions could be smooth (**Bulstoer**) or slowly varying (**Rkadapt**).
- You may have a boundary value rather than an initial value problem (**sbval** and **bvalfit**).
- You may be interested in evaluating the solution only at one point (**bulstoer**, **rkadapt**, **stiffb** and **stiffr**).

You may also want to try several methods on the same DE to see which one works the best. Sometimes there are subtle differences between DEs that make one method better than another.

Algorithm	Fixed step 4th order Runge-Kutta method (Press *et al.*, 1992)
See also	Mathcad Resource Center QuickSheets and Differential Equations tutorial; also **Odesolve**, for a solve block approach.

rlnorm
Random Numbers

Syntax	rlnorm(m, μ, σ)
Description	Returns a vector of m random numbers having the lognormal distribution.
Arguments	
m	integer, $m > 0$
μ	real logmean
σ	real logdeviation, $\sigma > 0$
Algorithm	Ratio-of-uniforms method (Devroye, 1986)
See also	rnd

rlogis
Random Numbers

Syntax	rlogis(m, l, s)
Description	Returns a vector of m random numbers having the logistic distribution.
Arguments	
m	integer, $m > 0$
l	real location parameter
s	real scale parameter, $s > 0$
Algorithm	Inverse cumulative density method (Press *et al.*, 1992)
See also	rnd

rnbinom
Random Numbers

Syntax	rnbinom(m, n, p)
Description	Returns a vector of m random numbers having the negative binomial distribution.
Arguments	
m, n	integers, $m > 0$, $n > 0$
p	real number, $0 < p \leq 1$
Algorithm	Based on **rpois** and **rgamma** (Devroye, 1986)
See also	rnd

rnd

Syntax   rnd(x)

Description   Returns a random number between 0 and x. Identical to runif(1, 0, x) if $x > 0$.

Arguments

x real number

Example

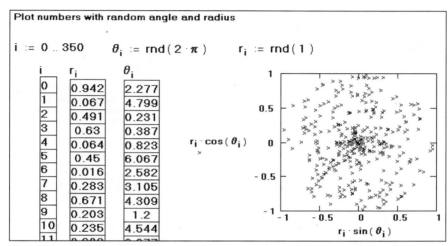

```
Plot numbers with random angle and radius

i := 0 .. 350      θ_i := rnd ( 2 · π )      r_i := rnd ( 1 )
```

i	r_i	θ_i
0	0.942	2.277
1	0.067	4.799
2	0.491	0.231
3	0.63	0.387
4	0.064	0.823
5	0.45	6.067
6	0.016	2.582
7	0.283	3.105
8	0.671	4.309
9	0.203	1.2
10	0.235	4.544
11		

Note: You won't be able to recreate this example exactly because the random number generator gives different numbers every time.

Comments   Each time you recalculate an equation containing rnd or some other random variate built-in function, Mathcad generates new random numbers. Recalculation is performed by clicking on the equation and choosing **Calculate** from the **Math** menu.

These functions have a "seed value" associated with them. Each time you reset the seed, Mathcad generates new random numbers based on that seed. A given seed value will always generate the same sequence of random numbers. Choosing **Calculate** from the **Math** menu advances Mathcad along this random number sequence. Changing the seed value, however, advances Mathcad along an altogether different random number sequence.

To change the seed value, choose **Options** from the **Math** menu and change the value of "seed" on the Built-In Variables tab. Be sure to supply an integer.

To reset Mathcad's random number generator without changing the seed value, choose **Options** from the **Math** menu, click on the Built-In Variables tab, and click "OK" to accept the current seed. Then click on the equation containing the random number generating function and choose **Calculate** from the **Math** menu. Since the randomizer has been reset, Mathcad generates the same random numbers it would generate if you restarted Mathcad.

There are many other random variate generators in Mathcad.

Algorithm   Linear congruence method (Knuth, 1997)

---

rnorm

Syntax	rnorm(*m*, μ, σ)
Description	Returns a vector of *m* random numbers having the normal distribution.
Arguments	
m	integer, $m > 0$
μ	real mean
σ	real standard deviation, $\sigma > 0$
Example	

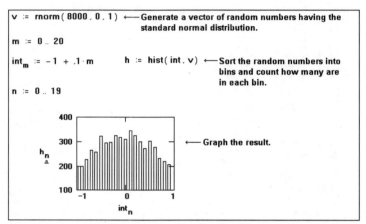

Note: You won't be able to recreate this example exactly because the random number generator gives different numbers every time.

Algorithm	Ratio-of-uniforms method (Devroye, 1986)
See also	rnd

root

Unbracketed Version

Syntax	root(*f(var)*, *var*)
Description	Returns a value of *var* at which the expression *f(var)* or function *f* is equal to 0.
Arguments	
var	real or complex scalar; *var* must be assigned a guess value before using this version of root.
f	real or complex-valued function.

Chapter 17 Functions

Example

$$x := -10, -9.9 \ldots 10$$

$$x^3 - 10 \cdot x + 2$$

Now use three initial guesses to find three zeroes . . .

$x := -2 \qquad \text{root}(x^3 - 10 \cdot x + 2, x) = -3.258$

$x := 0 \qquad \text{root}(x^3 - 10 \cdot x + 2, x) = 0.201$

$x := 3 \qquad \text{root}(x^3 - 10 \cdot x + 2, x) = 3.057$

Comments

For expressions with several roots, your guess value determines which root Mathcad returns. The example shows a situation in which the root function returns several different values, each of which depends on the initial guess value.

You can't put numerical values in the list of unknowns; for example, root($f(x)$, -2) or root(14, −2) is not permitted in the example above.

Mathcad solves for complex roots as well as real roots. To find a complex root, you must start with a complex value for the initial guess.

Solving an equation of the form $f(x) = g(x)$ is equivalent to using the root function as follows:

$\text{root}(f(x) - g(x), x)$

The root function can solve only one equation in one unknown. To solve several equations simultaneously, use Find or Minerr. To solve an equation symbolically, that is, to find an exact numerical answer in terms of elementary functions, choose **Solve for Variable** from the **Symbolics** menu or use the solve keyword.

See also polyroots for an efficient means to compute all roots of a polynomial at once.

Mathcad evaluates the unbracketed version of the root function using the *secant method*. If that method fails to find a root, then the *Mueller method* is used. The guess value you supply for x becomes the starting point for successive approximations to the root value. When the magnitude of $f(x)$ evaluated at the proposed root is less than the value of the predefined variable TOL, the root function returns a result.

If after many approximations Mathcad still cannot find an acceptable answer, it marks the root function with an error message indicating its inability to converge to a result. This error can be caused by any of the following:

- The expression has no roots.
- The roots of the expression are far from the initial guess.
- The expression has local maxima or minima between the initial guess and the roots.
- The expression has discontinuities between the initial guess and the roots.
- The expression has a complex root but the initial guess was real (or vice versa).

To find the cause of the error, try plotting the expression. This will help determine whether or not the expression crosses the x-axis and if so, approximately where. In general, the closer your initial guess is to where the expression crosses the x-axis, the more quickly the root function will converge on an acceptable result.

Here are some hints for getting the most out of the root function:

- To change the accuracy of the root function, change the value of the built-in variable TOL. If you increase TOL, the root function will converge more quickly, but the answer will be less accurate. If you decrease TOL, the root function will converge more slowly, but the answer will be more accurate. To change TOL at a specified point in the worksheet, include a definition like $TOL := 0.01$. To change TOL for the whole worksheet, choose **Options** from the **Math** menu, click on the Built-In Variables tab, and replace the number in the text box beside "TOL." After you click "OK," choose **Calculate Worksheet** from the **Math** menu to update the entire worksheet using the new value of TOL.

- If an expression has multiple roots, try different guess values to find them. Plotting the function is a good way to determine how many roots there are, where they are, and what initial guesses are likely to find them. Refer to the previous example. If two roots are close together, you may have to reduce TOL to distinguish between them.

- If $f(x)$ has a small slope near its root, then $\text{root}(f(x), x)$ may converge to a value r that is relatively far from the actual root. In such cases, even though $|f(r)| < TOL$, r may be far from the point where $f(r) = 0$. To find a more accurate root, decrease the value of TOL.

  Or, try finding $\text{root}(g(x),x)$, where $g(x) = \dfrac{f(x)}{\dfrac{d}{dx}f(x)}$.

- For an expression $f(x)$ with a known root r, solving for additional roots of $f(x)$ is equivalent to solving for roots of $h(x) = (f(x))/(x - r)$. Dividing out known roots like this is useful for resolving two roots that may be close together. It's often easier to solve for roots of $h(x)$ as defined here than it is to try to find other roots for $f(x)$ with different guesses.

Algorithm   Secant and Mueller methods (Press et al., 1992; Lorczak)

Bracketed Version

Syntax   root(*f(var)*, *var*, *a*, *b*)

Description   Returns a value of *var* lying between *a* and *b* at which the expression *f(var)* or function *f* is equal to 0.

Arguments
var   real scalar

f   real-valued function

a, b   real numbers, $a < b$

Comments   For expressions with several roots, your choice of interval endpoints *a* and *b* determines which root Mathcad returns. *f(a)* and *f(b)* must be of opposite signs. Observe that an initial guess for *var* is not required for the bracketed version of root to work.

If the optional arguments *a* and *b* are not included, then the unbracketed version of root is used. Note the restriction to real expressions and real variables in the bracketed case.

Mathcad evaluates the bracketed version of the root function using the *Ridder method*. If that method fails to find a root, then the *Brent method* is used.

The above comments concerning convergence and accuracy for the unbracketed version of root also apply to the bracketed version.

Algorithm   Ridder and Brent methods (Press *et al.*, 1992; Lorczak)

round

One-argument Version

Syntax   round(x)

Description   Rounds the real number x to the nearest integer. Same as round(x, 0).

Arguments
    x real number

Two-argument Version

Syntax   round(x, n)

Description   Rounds the real number x to n decimal places. If $n < 0$, x is rounded to the left of the decimal point.

Arguments
    x real number
    n integer

See also   ceil, floor, trunc

rows

Syntax   rows($\mathbf{A}$)

Description   Returns the number of rows in array $\mathbf{A}$.

Arguments
    $\mathbf{A}$ matrix or vector

See also   cols for example

rpois

Syntax   rpois(m, λ)

Description   Returns a vector of m random numbers having the Poisson distribution.

Arguments
    m integer, $m > 0$
    λ real mean, $\lambda > 0$

Algorithm   Devroye, 1986

See also   rnd

rref

Syntax   rref($\mathbf{A}$)

Description   Returns a matrix representing the row-reduced echelon form of $\mathbf{A}$.

Arguments
    $\mathbf{A}$ real $m \times n$ matrix

Algorithm   Elementary row reduction (Anton)

rsort

Syntax	rsort(**A**, *i*)
Description	Sorts the columns of the matrix **A** by placing the elements in row *i* in ascending order. The result is the same size as **A**.
Arguments	
A	$m \times n$ matrix or vector
i	integer, $0 \le i \le m - 1$
Algorithm	Heap sort (Press *et al.*, 1992)
See also	sort for more details, csort

rt

Syntax	rt(*m*, *d*)
Description	Returns a vector of *m* random numbers having Student's *t* distribution.
Arguments	
m	integer, $m > 0$
d	integer degrees of freedom, $d > 0$
Algorithm	Best's XG algorithm, Johnk's generator (Devroye, 1986)
See also	rnd

runif

Syntax	runif(*m*, *a*, *b*)
Description	Returns a vector of *m* random numbers having the uniform distribution
Arguments	
m	integer, $m > 0$
a, *b*	real numbers, $a < b$
Algorithm	Linear congruence method (Knuth, 1997)
See also	rnd

rweibull

Syntax	rweibull(*m*, *s*)
Description	Returns a vector of *m* random numbers having the Weibull distribution.
Arguments	
m	integer, $m > 0$
s	real shape parameter, $s > 0$
Algorithm	Inverse cumulative density method (Press *et al.*, 1992)
See also	rnd

SaveColormap

Syntax   SaveColormap(*file*, **M**)

Description   Creates a colormap *file* containing the values in the matrix **M**. Returns the number of rows written to *file*.

Arguments

file   string variable corresponding to CMP filename

M   integer matrix with three columns and whose elements $\mathbf{M}_{i,j}$ all satisfy $0 \le \mathbf{M}_{i,j} \le 255$.

Comments   The file *file* is the name of a colormap located in the CMAPS subdirectory of your Mathcad directory. After you use SaveColormap, the colormap is available on the Advanced tab in the 3D Plot Format dialog box. See on-line Help for more information.

See also   LoadColormap

sbval

Syntax   sbval(**v**, *x1*, *x2*, **D**, **load**, **score**)

Description   Converts a boundary value differential equation to an initial value problem. Useful when derivatives are continuous throughout.

Arguments

v   real vector containing guesses for missing initial values

x1, *x2*   real endpoints of the interval on which the solution to the DEs will be evaluated

D(*x*, **y**)   real *n*-element vector-valued function containing the derivatives of the unknown functions

load(*x1*, **v**)   real vector-valued function whose *n* elements correspond to the values of the *n* unknown functions at *x1*. Some of these values will be constants specified by your initial conditions. If a value is unknown, you should use the corresponding guess value from **v**.

score(*x2*, **y**)   real *n*-element vector-valued function which measures solution discrepancy at *x2*

Example

Comments	Initial value DE solvers like rkfixed assume that you know the value of the solution and its first $n-1$ derivatives at the beginning of the interval of integration. Two-point boundary value DE solvers, like sbval and bvalfit, may be used if you lack this information about the solution at the beginning of the interval of integration, but you do know something about the solution elsewhere in the interval. In particular:

- You have an nth order differential equation.
- You know some but not all of the values of the solution and its first $n-1$ derivatives at the beginning of the interval of integration, $x1$.
- You know some but not all of the values of the solution and its first $n-1$ derivatives at the end of the interval of integration, $x2$.
- Between what you know about the solution at $x1$ and what you know about it at $x2$, you have n known values.

If there is a discontinuity at a point intermediate to $x1$ and $x2$, you should use bvalfit. If continuity holds throughout, then use sbval to evaluate those initial values left unspecified at $x1$. sbval does not actually return a solution to a differential equation; it merely computes the initial values the solution must have in order for the solution to match the final values you specify. You must then take the initial values returned by sbval and solve the resulting initial value problem using rkfixed or any of the other more specialized DE solvers.

Algorithm	Shooting method with 4th order Runge-Kutta method (Press *et al.*, 1992)
See also	rkfixed for more details; also Odesolve, for a solve block approach.

search
String

Syntax	search(S, $SubS$, m)
Description	Returns the starting position of the substring $SubS$ in S beginning from position m. Returns -1 if the substring is not found.
Arguments	
S	string expression; Mathcad assumes that the first character in S is at position 0
$SubS$	substring expression
m	integer, $m \geq 0$

sec
Trigonometric

Syntax	$\sec(z)$, for z in radians;
	$\sec(z \cdot \deg)$, for z in degrees
Description	Returns the secant of z.
Arguments	
z	real or complex number; z is not an odd multiple of $\pi/2$

sech
Hyperbolic

Syntax	$\operatorname{sech}(z)$
Description	Returns the hyperbolic secant of z.
Arguments	
z	real or complex number

sign

Syntax	$\text{sign}(x)$
Description	Returns 0 if $x=0$, 1 if $x > 0$, and -1 otherwise.
Arguments	
x	real number
See also	csgn, signum

signum

Syntax	$\text{signum}(z)$
Description	Returns 1 if $z=0$ and $z/|z|$ otherwise.
Arguments	
z	real or complex number
See also	csgn, sign

sin

Syntax	$\sin(z)$, for z in radians; $\sin(z\cdot\text{deg})$, for z in degrees
Description	Returns the sine of z.
Arguments	
z	real or complex number

sinfit

Syntax	$\text{sinfit}(\mathbf{vx}, \mathbf{vy}, \mathbf{vg})$
Description	Returns a vector containing the parameters (a, b, c) that make the function $a \cdot \sin(x + b) + c$ best approximate the data in **vx** and **vy**.
Arguments	
vx, vy	real vectors of the same size
vg	real vector of guess values for (a, b, c)
Comments	This is a special case of the genfit function. A vector of guess values is needed for initialization. By decreasing the value of the built-in TOL variable, higher accuracy in sinfit might be achieved.
See Also	line, linfit, genfit, expfit, logfit, lnfit, pwrfit, lgsfit, medfit

sinh

Syntax	$\text{sinh}(z)$
Description	Returns the hyperbolic sine of z.
Arguments	
z	real or complex number

Syntax	skew(**A**)
Description	Returns the skewness of the elements of **A**:

$$\text{skew}(\mathbf{A}) = \frac{mn}{(mn-1)(mn-2)} \sum_{i=0}^{m-1} \sum_{j=0}^{n-1} \left(\frac{\mathbf{A}_{i,j} - \text{mean}(\mathbf{A})}{\text{Stdev}(\mathbf{A})} \right)^3$$

Arguments	
A	real or complex $m \times n$ matrix or vector, $m \cdot n \geq 3$
Comments	skew(**A**, **B**, **C**, **...**) is also permissible and returns the skewness of the elements of **A**, **B**, **C**, ...

slope   Regression and Smoothing

Syntax	slope(**vx**, **vy**)
Description	Returns the slope of the least-squares regression line.
Arguments	
vx, **vy**	real vector arguments of the same size
Example	

Comments	The functions intercept and slope return the intercept and slope of the line which best fits the data in a least-squares sense: $y = \text{intercept}(\mathbf{vx}, \mathbf{vy}) + \text{slope}(\mathbf{vx}, \mathbf{vy}) \cdot x$. Alternatively, you may use the line function which returns both parameter estimates via one function call.

Be sure that every element in the **vx** and **vy** arrays contains a data value. Since every element in an array must have a value, Mathcad assigns 0 to any elements not explicitly assigned.

These functions are useful not only when the data is inherently linear, but also when it is exponential. If x and y are related by $y = Ae^{kx}$, you can apply these functions to the logarithm of the data values and make use of the fact that $\ln(y) = \ln(A) + kx$, hence $A = \exp(\text{intercept}(\mathbf{vx}, \ln(\mathbf{vy})))$ and $k = \text{slope}(\mathbf{vx}, \ln(\mathbf{vy}))$.

The resulting fit weighs the errors differently from a least-squares exponential fit (which the function expfit provides) but is usually a good approximation.

See also	intercept, line, stderr, medfit

sort

Syntax | sort(**v**)

Description | Returns the elements of vector **v** sorted in ascending order.

Arguments
v | vector

Example

```
Sorting functions        i := 0 .. 3      j := 0 .. 3      x_i := sin(i)
For vectors :

        ⎡ 0    ⎤                    ⎡ 0    ⎤                            ⎡ 0.909 ⎤
        ⎢ 0.841⎥                    ⎢ 0.141⎥                            ⎢ 0.841 ⎥
x =     ⎢ 0.909⎥     sort(x) =      ⎢ 0.841⎥     reverse(sort(x)) =     ⎢ 0.141 ⎥
        ⎣ 0.141⎦                    ⎣ 0.909⎦                            ⎣ 0     ⎦

For matrices:
                                                    ⎡ 0  3  3  3 ⎤
M_(i, j) := mod(i + 3, j + 3)            M =        ⎢ 1  0  4  4 ⎥
                                                    ⎢ 2  1  0  5 ⎥
                                                    ⎣ 0  2  1  0 ⎦

Sorted on column zero . . .                 Sorted on last row . . .
                ⎡ 0  2  1  0 ⎤                           ⎡ 0  3  3  3 ⎤
                ⎢ 0  3  3  3 ⎥                           ⎢ 1  4  4  0 ⎥
csort(M, 0) =   ⎢ 1  0  4  4 ⎥            rsort(M, 3) =  ⎢ 2  5  0  1 ⎥
                ⎣ 2  1  0  5 ⎦                           ⎣ 0  0  1  2 ⎦
```

Comments | All of Mathcad's sorting functions accept matrices and vectors with complex elements. However in sorting them, Mathcad ignores the imaginary part.

To sort a vector or matrix in descending order, first sort in ascending order, then use reverse. For example, reverse(sort(**v**)) returns the elements of **v** sorted in descending order.

Unless you change the value of ORIGIN, matrices are numbered starting with row zero and column zero. If you forget this, it's easy to make the error of sorting a matrix on the wrong row or column by specifying an incorrect *n* argument for rsort and csort. To sort on the first column of a matrix, for example, you must use csort(**A**, 0).

Algorithm | Heap sort (Press *et al.*, 1992)

sph2xyz

Syntax | sph2xyz(r, θ, ϕ)

Description | Converts the spherical coordinates of a point in 3D space to rectangular coordinates.

Arguments
r, θ, ϕ | real numbers

Comments | $x = r \sin(\phi) \cos(\theta)$, $y = r \sin(\phi) \sin(\theta)$, $z = r \cos(\phi)$

See also | xyz2sph

stack

Syntax	stack(**A**, **B**, **C**, ...)
Description	Returns a matrix formed by placing the matrices **A**, **B**, **C**, ... top to bottom.
Arguments	
A, **B**, **C**, ...	at least two matrices or vectors; **A**, **B**, **C**, ... must have the same number of columns
See also	augment for example

stderr

Syntax	stderr(**vx**, **vy**)
Description	Returns the standard error associated with simple linear regression, measuring how closely data points are spread about the regression line.

$$\text{stderr}(\mathbf{vx}, \mathbf{vy}) = \sqrt{\frac{1}{n-2} \sum_{i=0}^{n-1} (\mathbf{vy}_i - (\text{intercept}(\mathbf{vx}, \mathbf{vy}) + \text{slope}(\mathbf{vx}, \mathbf{vy}) \cdot \mathbf{vx}_i))^2}.$$

Arguments	
vx, **vy**	real vector arguments of the same size
See also	slope, intercept

stdev

Syntax	stdev(**A**)
Description	Returns the standard deviation of the elements of **A**, where mn (the sample size) is used in the denominator: $\text{stdev}(\mathbf{A}) = \sqrt{\text{var}(\mathbf{A})}$.
Arguments	
A	real or complex $m \times n$ matrix or vector
Comments	stdev(**A**, **B**, **C**, ...) is also permissible and returns the standard deviation of the elements of **A**, **B**, **C**, ...
See also	Stdev, var, Var

Stdev

Syntax	Stdev(**A**)
Description	Returns the standard deviation of the elements of **A**, where $mn - 1$ (the sample size less one) is used in the denominator: $\text{Stdev}(\mathbf{A}) = \sqrt{\text{Var}(\mathbf{A})}$.
Arguments	
A	real or complex $m \times n$ matrix or vector
Comments	Stdev(**A**, **B**, **C**, ...) is also permissible and returns the standard deviation of the elements of **A**, **B**, **C**, ...
See also	stdev, var, Var

stiffb

| Syntax | stiffb(**y**, *x1, x2, acc*, **D**, **J**, *kmax, save*) |

Description
: Solves a differential equation using the stiff Bulirsch-Stoer method. Provides DE solution estimate at *x2*.

Arguments
: *Several arguments for this function are the same as described for* rkfixed.

y
: real vector of initial values.

x1, x2
: real endpoints of the solution interval.

D(x, **y**)
: real vector-valued function containing the derivatives of the unknown functions.

acc
: real *acc* > 0 controls the accuracy of the solution; a small value of *acc* forces the algorithm to take smaller steps along the trajectory, thereby increasing the accuracy of the solution. Values of *acc* around 0.001 will generally yield accurate solutions.

J(x, **y**)
: real vector-valued function which returns the $n \times (n + 1)$ matrix whose first column contains the derivatives $\partial \mathbf{D} / \partial x$ and whose remaining columns form the Jacobian matrix ($\partial \mathbf{D} / \partial y_k$) for the system of DEs.

kmax
: integer *kmax* > 0 specifies maximum number of intermediate points at which the solution will be approximated; places an upper bound on the number of rows of the matrix returned by these functions.

save
: real *save* > 0 specifies the smallest allowable spacing between values at which the solutions are to be approximated; places a lower bound on the difference between any two numbers in the first column of the matrix returned by the function.

Comments
: The specialized DE solvers Bulstoer, Rkadapt, Stiffb, and Stiffr provide the solution *y(x)* over a number of uniformly spaced *x*-values in the integration interval bounded by *x1* and *x2*. When you want the value of the solution at only the endpoint, *y(x2)*, use bulstoer, rkadapt, stiffb, and stiffr instead.

Algorithm
: Bulirsch-Stoer method with adaptive step size for stiff systems (Press *et al.*, 1992)

See also
: rkfixed, a more general differential equation solver, for information on output and arguments; Stiffb.

Stiffb

| Syntax | Stiffb(**y**, *x1, x2, npts*, **D**, **J**) |

Description
: Solves a differential equation using the stiff Bulirsch-Stoer method. Provides DE solution at equally spaced *x* values by repeated calls to stiffb.

Arguments
: *Several arguments for this function are the same as described for* rkfixed.

y
: real vector of initial values.

x1, x2
: real endpoints of the solution interval.

D(x, **y**)
: real vector-valued function containing the derivatives of the unknown functions.

npts
: integer *npts* > 0 specifies the number of points beyond initial point at which the solution is to be approximated; controls the number of rows in the matrix output.

J(x, **y**)
: real vector-valued function which returns the $n \times (n + 1)$ matrix whose first column contains the derivatives $\partial \mathbf{D} / \partial x$ and whose remaining columns form the Jacobian matrix ($\partial \mathbf{D} / \partial y_k$) for the system of DEs. For example, if:

$$\mathbf{D}(x, \mathbf{y}) = \begin{bmatrix} x \cdot y_1 \\ -2 \cdot y_1 \cdot y_0 \end{bmatrix} \quad \text{then} \quad \mathbf{J}(x, \mathbf{y}) = \begin{bmatrix} y_1 & 0 & x \\ 0 & -2 \cdot y_1 & -2 \cdot y_0 \end{bmatrix}$$

Comments	A system of DEs expressed in the form $\mathbf{y} = \mathbf{A} \cdot \mathbf{x}$ is a stiff system if the matrix $\mathbf{A}$ is nearly singular. Under these conditions, the solution returned by rkfixed may oscillate or be unstable. When solving a stiff system, you should use one of the two DE solvers specifically designed for stiff systems: Stiffb and Stiffr. These use the Bulirsch-Stoer method and the Rosenbrock method, respectively, for stiff systems.
	The form of the matrix returned by these functions is identical to that returned by rkfixed. However, Stiffb and Stiffr require an extra argument $\mathbf{J}(x, \mathbf{y})$.
Algorithm	Fixed-step Bulirsch-Stoer method with adaptive intermediate step size for stiff systems (Press *et al.*, 1992)
See also	rkfixed, a more general differential equation solver, for information on output and arguments.

stiffr

Syntax	stiffr(**y**, *x1, x2, acc,* **D, J,** *kmax, save*)
Description	Solves a differential equation using the stiff Rosenbrock method. Provides DE solution estimate at *x2*.
Arguments	*Several arguments for this function the same as described for* rkfixed.
y	real vector of initial values.
x1, x2	real endpoints of the solution interval.
D(*x, y*)	real vector-valued function containing the derivatives of the unknown functions.
acc	real *acc* > 0 controls the accuracy of the solution; a small value of *acc* forces the algorithm to take smaller steps along the trajectory, thereby increasing the accuracy of the solution. Values of *acc* around 0.001 will generally yield accurate solutions.
J(*x, y*)	real vector-valued function that returns the $n \times (n + 1)$ matrix whose first column contains the the derivatives $\partial \mathbf{D}/\partial x$ and whose remaining columns form the Jacobian matrix $(\partial \mathbf{D}/\partial y_k)$ for the system of DEs.
kmax	integer *kmax* > 0 specifies maximum number of intermediate points at which the solution will be approximated; places an upper bound on the number of rows of the matrix returned by these functions.
save	real *save* > 0 specifies the smallest allowable spacing between values at which the solutions are to be approximated; places a lower bound on the difference between any two numbers in the first column of the matrix returned by the function.
Comments	The specialized DE solvers Bulstoer, Rkadapt, Stiffb, and Stiffr provide the solution *y(x)* over a number of uniformly spaced *x*-values in the integration interval bounded by *x1* and *x2*. When you want the value of the solution at only the endpoint, *y(x2)*, use bulstoer, rkadapt, stiffb, and stiffr instead.
Algorithm	4th order Rosenbrock method with adaptive intermediate step size for stiff systems (Press *et al.*, 1992)
See also	rkfixed, a more general differential equation solver for information on output and arguments, and Stiffr

Stiffr

Syntax	Stiffb(**y**, *x1*, *x2*, *npts*, **D**, **J**)
Description	Solves a differential equation using the stiff Rosenbrock method. Provides DE solution at equally spaced *x* values by repeated calls to stiffr.
Arguments	*Several arguments for this function are the same as described for* rkfixed.
y	real vector of initial values.
x1, x2	real endpoints of the solution interval.
D(*x*, **y**)	real vector-valued function containing the derivatives of the unknown functions.
npts	integer *npts* > 0 specifies the number of points beyond initial point at which the solution is to be approximated; controls the number of rows in the matrix output.
J(*x*, **y**)	real vector-valued function which returns the $n \times (n + 1)$ matrix whose first column contains the derivatives $\partial \mathbf{D} / \partial x$ and whose remaining columns form the Jacobian matrix $(\partial \mathbf{D} / \partial y_k)$ for the system of DEs. For example, if:

$$\mathbf{D}(x, \mathbf{y}) = \begin{bmatrix} x \cdot y_1 \\ -2 \cdot y_1 \cdot y_0 \end{bmatrix} \quad \text{then} \quad \mathbf{J}(x, \mathbf{y}) = \begin{bmatrix} y_1 & 0 & x \\ 0 & -2 \cdot y_1 & -2 \cdot y_0 \end{bmatrix}$$

Comments	A system of DEs expressed in the form $\mathbf{y} = \mathbf{A} \cdot \mathbf{x}$ is a stiff system if the matrix **A** is nearly singular. Under these conditions, the solution returned by rkfixed may oscillate or be unstable. When solving a stiff system, you should use one of the two DE solvers specifically designed for stiff systems: Stiffb and Stiffr. These use the Bulirsch-Stoer method and the Rosenbrock method, respectively, for stiff systems.
	The form of the matrix returned by these functions is identical to that returned by rkfixed. However, Stiffb and Stiffr require an extra argument **J**(*x*, **y**).
Algorithm	Fixed-step 4th order Rosenbrock method with adaptive intermediate step size for stiff systems (Press *et al.*, 1992)
See also	rkfixed, a more general differential equation solver, for information on output and arguments.

str2num

Syntax	str2num(*S*)
Description	Returns the constant formed by converting the characters in *S* into a number. Characters in *S* must constitute an integer such as 17, a real floating-point number such as −16.5, a complex floating-point number such as 2.1+6i or 3.241 − 9.234j, or an e-format number such as 4.51e-3 (for $4.51 \cdot 10^{-3}$). Mathcad ignores any spaces in the string.
Arguments	
S	string expression
See also	num2str

str2vec

Syntax   str2vec(S)

Description Returns the vector of ASCII codes corresponding to the characters in string S. For a list of ASCII codes, see Appendix to the *Mathcad User's Guide*. For example, the ASCII code for letter "a" is 97, that for letter "b" is 98, and that for letter "c" is 99.

Arguments
S string expression

See also   vec2str

strlen

Syntax   strlen(S)

Description Returns the number of characters in S.

Arguments
S string expression

submatrix

Syntax   submatrix($\mathbf{A}$, ir, jr, ic, jc)

Description Returns a submatrix of $\mathbf{A}$ consisting of all elements common to rows ir through jr and columns ic through jc. Make certain that $ir \leq jr$ and $ic \leq jc$, otherwise the order of rows and/or columns will be reversed.

Arguments
$\mathbf{A}$ $m \times n$ matrix or vector

ir, jr integers, $0 \leq ir \leq jr \leq m$

ic, jc integers, $0 \leq ic \leq jc \leq n$

Example

$$M := \begin{bmatrix} 1 & 7 & 1 & 4 & 4 \\ -5 & -8 & -2 & 3 & 3 \\ -6 & -9 & -3 & 2 & 3 \\ 1 & 2 & 3 & 4 & 3 \\ 4 & 5 & 5 & 6 & 8 \end{bmatrix}$$

ORIGIN = 0

$$\text{submatrix}(M, 1, 2, 0, 2) = \begin{pmatrix} -5 & -8 & -2 \\ -6 & -9 & -3 \end{pmatrix}$$ ← Extracts all elements contained in both rows 1 and 2 and columns 0, 1 and 2.

$$\text{submatrix}(M, 1, 2, 2, 0) = \begin{pmatrix} -2 & -8 & -5 \\ -3 & -9 & -6 \end{pmatrix}$$ ← Swapping the last two arguments reverses the order of the columns.

$$\text{submatrix}(M, 2, 1, 2, 0) = \begin{pmatrix} -3 & -9 & -6 \\ -2 & -8 & -5 \end{pmatrix}$$ ← Swapping the first two arguments reverses the order of the rows.

substr String

Syntax   substr(S, m, n)

Description   Returns a substring of S beginning with the character in the mth position and having at most n characters.

Arguments

S string expression. Mathcad assumes that the first character in S is at position 0.

m, n integers, $m \geq 0$, $n \geq 0$

supsmooth Regression and Smoothing

Syntax   supsmooth($\mathbf{vx}$, $\mathbf{vy}$)

Description   Creates a new vector, of the same size as $\mathbf{vy}$, by piecewise use of a symmetric k-nearest neighbor linear least square fitting procedure in which k is adaptively chosen.

Arguments

$\mathbf{vx}$, $\mathbf{vy}$ real vectors of the same size; elements of $\mathbf{vx}$ must be in ascending order

Example

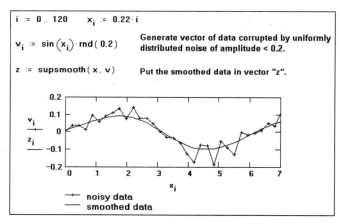

Comments   The supsmooth function uses a symmetric k nearest neighbor linear least-squares fitting procedure to make a series of line segments through the data. Unlike ksmooth which uses a fixed bandwidth for all the data, supsmooth will adaptively choose different bandwidths for different portions of the data.

Algorithm   Variable span super-smoothing method (Friedman)

See also   medsmooth and ksmooth

svd Vector and Matrix

Syntax   svd($\mathbf{A}$)

Description   Returns an $(m + n) \times n$ matrix whose first m rows contain the $m \times n$ orthonormal matrix $\mathbf{U}$, and whose remaining n rows contain the $n \times n$ orthonormal matrix $\mathbf{V}$. Matrices $\mathbf{U}$ and $\mathbf{V}$ satisfy the equation $\mathbf{A} = \mathbf{U} \cdot \mathrm{diag}(\mathbf{s}) \cdot \mathbf{V}^{\mathbf{T}}$, where $\mathbf{s}$ is the vector returned by svds($\mathbf{A}$).

Arguments

$\mathbf{A}$ $m \times n$ real matrix, where $m \geq n$

The m x n matrix A to be decomposed is defined at the bottom.

st := svd(A)   <-- (m+n) x n matrix resulting from the
                        singular value decomposition

singval := svds(A)   <-- vector contains the singular values of A

$$\text{singval} = \begin{bmatrix} 133.214 \\ 40.406 \\ 21.404 \end{bmatrix}$$

m := rows(A)   m = 6   n := cols(A)   n = 3

U := submatrix(st, 0, m − 1, 0, n − 1)   <-- extract m x n orthonormal matrix U

V := submatrix(st, m, m + n − 1, 0, n − 1)   <-- extract n x n orthonormal matrix V

Compare A with U·diag(singval)·V^T :

$$A = \begin{bmatrix} 20 & 32 & -4 \\ 4.5 & 100 & -4 \\ -5.8 & 68 & 15 \\ 1.5 & 10 & 26 \\ 7 & 30 & 18 \\ 4.2 & 28 & 25 \end{bmatrix} \quad U \cdot diag(singval) \cdot V^T = \begin{bmatrix} 20 & 32 & -4 \\ 4.5 & 100 & -4 \\ -5.8 & 68 & 15 \\ 1.5 & 10 & 26 \\ 7 & 30 & 18 \\ 4.2 & 28 & 25 \end{bmatrix}$$

$$U^T \cdot U = \begin{bmatrix} 1 & 0 & 0 \\ 0 & 1 & 0 \\ 0 & 0 & 1 \end{bmatrix}$$

$$V^T \cdot V = \begin{bmatrix} 1 & 0 & 0 \\ 0 & 1 & 0 \\ 0 & 0 & 1 \end{bmatrix}$$

Algorithm   Householder reduction with QR transformation (Wilkinson and Reinsch, 1971)

See also   svds

svds
Vector and Matrix

Syntax   svds(**A**)

Description   Returns a vector containing the singular values of **A**.

Arguments

A $m \times n$ real matrix, where $m \geq n$

Algorithm   Householder reduction with QR transformation (Wilkinson and Reinsch, 1971)

See also   svd

tan
Trigonometric

Syntax   tan(z) for z in radians;
          tan(z·deg), for z in degrees

Description   Returns the tangent of z.

Arguments
z real or complex number

tanh
Hyperbolic

Syntax   tanh(z)

Description   Returns the hyperbolic tangent of z.

Arguments
z real or complex number

Tcheb

Syntax   Tcheb(n, x)

Description   Returns the value of the Chebyshev polynomial of degree n of the first kind.

Arguments
  n integer, $n \geq 0$
  x real number

Comments   Solution of the differential equation $(1 - x^2) \cdot \dfrac{d^2}{dx^2}y - x \cdot \dfrac{d}{dx}y + n^2 \cdot y = 0$.

Algorithm   Recurrence relation (Abramowitz and Stegun, 1972)
See also   Ucheb

tr

Syntax   tr(**M**)

Description   Returns the trace of **M**, the sum of diagonal elements.

Arguments
  M   real or complex square matrix

trunc

Syntax   trunc(x)

Description   Returns the integer part of x. Same as **floor**(x) for $x > 0$ and **ceil**(x) for $x < 0$.

Arguments
  x real number

See also   ceil, floor, round

Ucheb

Syntax   Ucheb(n, x)

Description   Returns the value of the Chebyshev polynomial of degree n of the second kind.

Arguments
  n integer, $n \geq 0$
  x real number

Comments   Solution of the differential equation $(1 - x^2) \cdot \dfrac{d^2}{dx^2}y - 3 \cdot x \cdot \dfrac{d}{dx}y + n \cdot (n + 2) \cdot y = 0$.

Algorithm   Recurrence relation (Abramowitz and Stegun, 1972)
See also   Tcheb

UnitsOf

Syntax   UnitsOf(x)

Description   Returns the units of x. Returns 1 if x has no units.

Arguments
  x arbitrary real or complex number, array, or string

Comments   You can divide a value by the UnitsOf function to make it unitless. For example, some built-in functions, such as ln, require their arguments to be unitless. If an argument to ln has units, you can divide the argument by UnitsOf to remove them.

---

var

Statistics

Syntax	var(**A**)
Description	Returns the variance of the elements of **A**: $\text{var}(\mathbf{A}) = \dfrac{1}{mn}\sum_{i=0}^{m-1}\sum_{j=0}^{n-1}\left|A_{i,j}-\text{mean}(\mathbf{A})\right|^2$.

This expression is normalized by the sample size mn.

Arguments	
A	real or complex $m \times n$ matrix or array
Comments	var(**A, B, C, ...**) is also permissible and returns the variance of the elements of **A**, **B**, **C**, ...
See also	stdev, Stdev, Var

Var
Statistics

Syntax	Var(**A**)
Description	Returns the variance of the elements of **A**: $\text{var}(\mathbf{A}) = \dfrac{1}{mn-1}\sum_{i=0}^{m-1}\sum_{j=0}^{n-1}\left|A_{i,j}-\text{mean}(\mathbf{A})\right|^2$.

This expression is normalized by the sample size less one, $mn - 1$.

Arguments	
A	real or complex $m \times n$ matrix or array
Comments	Var(**A, B, C, ...**) is also permissible and returns the variance of the elements of **A**, **B**, **C**, ...
See also	stdev, Stdev, var

vec2str
String

Syntax	vec2str(**v**)
Description	Returns the string formed by converting a vector **v** of ASCII codes to characters. The elements of **v** must be integers between 0 and 255.
Arguments	
v	vector of ASCII codes
See also	str2vec

vlookup
Vector and Matrix

Syntax	vlookup(z, **A**, c)
Description	Looks in the first column of a matrix, **A**, for a given value, z, and returns the value(s) in the same row(s) in the column specified, c. When multiple values are returned, they appear in a vector.
Arguments	
z	real or complex number, or string
A	real, complex or string $m \times n$ matrix
c	integer, $ORIGIN \le c \le ORIGIN + n - 1$
Comments	The degree of precision to which the comparison adheres is determined by the *TOL* setting of the worksheet.
See Also	lookup, hlookup, match

---

wave

Syntax   wave(**v**)

Description   Returns the discrete wavelet transform of real data using Daubechies four-coefficient wavelet filter.

Arguments

   v   real vector of 2^n elements, where $n > 0$ is an integer

Example

Comments   When you define a vector **v** for use with Fourier or wavelet transforms, be sure to start with v_0 (or change the value of ORIGIN). If you do not define v_0, Mathcad automatically sets it to zero. This can distort the results of the transform functions.

Algorithm   Pyramidal Daubechies 4-coefficient wavelet filter (Press *et al.*, 1992)

See also   iwave

WRITEBMP

Syntax   WRITEBMP(*file*)

Description   Creates a grayscale BMP image file *file* out of a matrix.
Used as follows: WRITEBMP(*file*) := **M**. The function must appear alone on the left side of a definition.

Arguments

   file   string variable corresponding to BMP filename or path

   M   integer matrix, each element satisfying $0 \leq \mathbf{M}_{i,j} \leq 255$

WRITE_HLS

Syntax	WRITE_HLS(*file*)
Description	Creates a color BMP image file *file* out of a matrix formed by juxtaposing the three matrices giving the hue, lightness, and saturation components of an image.
Arguments	
file	string variable corresponding to BMP filename or path
M	integer matrix, each element satisfying $0 \le \mathbf{M}_{i,j} \le 255$
See also	See WRITERGB for an overview of creating color data files.

WRITE_HSV

Syntax	WRITE_HSV(*file*)
Description	Creates a color BMP image file *file* out of a matrix formed by juxtaposing the three matrices giving the hue, saturation, and value components of an image.
Arguments	
file	string variable corresponding to BMP filename or path
M	integer matrix, each element satisfying $0 \le \mathbf{M}_{i,j} \le 255$
See also	See WRITERGB for overview.

WRITEPRN

Syntax	WRITEPRN(*file*) := **A**
Description	Writes a matrix **A** into a structured ASCII data file *file*. Each row becomes a line in the file. The function must appear alone on the left side of a definition.
Arguments	
file	string variable corresponding to structured ASCII data filename or path
A	matrix or vector
Comments	The WRITEPRN and APPENDPRN functions write out data values neatly lined up in rows and columns. When you use these functions:

- Equations using WRITEPRN or APPENDPRN must be in a specified form. On the left should be WRITEPRN(*file*) or APPENDPRN(*file*). This is followed by a definition symbol (:=) and a matrix expression. Do not use range variables or subscripts on the matrix expression.
- Each new equation involving WRITEPRN writes a new file; if two equations write to the same file, the data written by the second equation will overwrite the data written by the first. Use APPENDPRN if you want to append values to a file rather than overwrite the file.
- The built-in variables *PRNCOLWIDTH* and *PRNPRECISION* determine the format of the data file that Mathcad creates. The value of *PRNCOLWIDTH* specifies the width of the columns (in characters). The value of *PRNPRECISION* specifies the number of significant digits used. By default, *PRNCOLWIDTH*=8 and *PRNPRECISION*=4. To change these values, choose **Options** from the **Math** menu and edit the numbers on the Built-In Variables tab, or enter definitions for these variables in your Mathcad document above the WRITEPRN function.

WRITEPRN and READPRN allow you to write out and read in *nested arrays* created in Mathcad.

If the array you are writing is either a nested array (an array whose elements are themselves arrays) or a complex array (an array whose elements are complex), then WRITEPRN will *not* create a simple ASCII file. Instead, WRITEPRN creates a file using a special format unlikely to be readable by other applications. This file can, however, be read by Mathcad's READPRN function.

By using the augment function, you can concatenate several variables and write them all using WRITEPRN to a data file.

See also APPENDPRN

WRITERGB
File Access

Syntax WRITERGB(*file*)

Description Creates a color BMP image file *file* out of a single matrix formed by juxtaposing the three matrices giving the red, green, and blue values of an image. Used as follows: WRITERGB(*file*) := **M**. The function must appear alone on the left side of a definition.

Arguments
file string variable corresponding to BMP filename or path
M integer matrix, each element satisfying $0 \le \mathbf{M}_{i,j} \le 255$

Comments The function augment is helpful for combining submatrices prior to using WRITERGB.

Mathcad has functions for creating color BMP files out of matrices in which the image is stored in HLS or HSV format. These work in exactly the same way as WRITERGB.

See also WRITE_HLS and WRITE_HSV

WRITEWAV
File Access

Syntax WRITEWAV(*file*, *s*, *b*)

Description Creates a WAV signal file *file* out of a matrix.
Used as follows: WRITEWAV(*file*, *s*, *b*) := **M**. The function must appear alone on the left side of a definition.

Arguments
file string variable corresponding to pulse code modulated (PCM) Microsoft WAV filename or path
s integer sample rate
b bit resolution
M integer matrix

Comments If the specified bit resolution is 1–8, the data is written to *file* as unsigned byte data. The limits on unsigned byte data are 0 to 256. If the bit resolution is 9–16, word data (two bytes) is written to *file*. The limits on word data are -32768 to 32767.

See also GETWAVINFO and READWAV

xyz2cyl
Vector and Matrix

Syntax xyz2cyl(*x*, *y*, *z*)

Description Converts the rectangular coordinates of a point in 3D space to cylindrical coordinates.

Arguments
x, y, z real numbers

Comments $x = r \cos(\theta)$, $y = r \sin(\theta)$, $z = z$

See also cyl2xyz

---

xy2pol

Syntax	xy2pol(x, y)
Description	Converts the rectangular coordinates of a point in 2D space to polar coordinates.
Arguments	
x, y	real numbers
Comments	$x = r \cos(\theta)$, $y = r \sin(\theta)$
See also	pol2xy

xyz2sph

Syntax	xyz2sph(x, y, z)
Description	Converts the rectangular coordinates of a point in 3D space to spherical coordinates.
Arguments	
x, y, z	real numbers
Comments	$x = r \sin(\phi) \cos(\theta)$, $y = r \sin(\phi) \sin(\theta)$, $z = r \cos(\phi)$
See also	sph2xyz

Y0

Syntax	Y0(x)
Description	Returns the value of the Bessel function $Y_0(x)$ of the second kind. Same as Yn(0, x).
Arguments	
x	real number, $x > 0$
Algorithm	Steed's method (Press *et al.*, 1992)

Y1

Syntax	Y1(x)
Description	Returns the value of the Bessel function $Y_1(x)$ of the second kind. Same as Yn(1, x).
Arguments	
x	real number, $x > 0$
Algorithm	Steed's method (Press *et al.*, 1992)

Yn

Syntax	Yn(m, x)
Description	Returns the value of the Bessel function $Y_m(x)$ of the second kind.
Arguments	
m	integer, $0 \le m \le 100$
x	real number, $x > 0$
Comments	Solution of the differential equation $x^2 \cdot \dfrac{d^2}{dx^2}y + x \cdot \dfrac{d}{dx}y + (x^2 - m^2) \cdot y = 0$.
Algorithm	Steed's method (Press *et al.*, 1992)
See also	Jn

ys

Syntax   ys(n, x)

Description   Returns the value of the spherical Bessel function of the second kind, of order n, at x.

Arguments
  x real number, $x > 0$

  n integer, $-200 \le n$

Comments   Solution of the differential equation: $x^2 \cdot \dfrac{d^2}{dx^2} y + 2 \cdot x \cdot \dfrac{d}{dx} y + (x^2 - n \cdot (n+1)) y = 0$.

Algorithm   Recurrence relation (Abramowitz and Stegun, 1972)

See also   js

δ

Syntax   δ(m, n)

Description   Returns the value of the Kronecker delta function. Output is 1 if $m=n$ and 0 otherwise. (To type δ, press **d[Ctrl]G**).

Arguments
  m, n integers

Algorithm   Continued fraction expansion (Abramowitz and Stegun, 1972; Lorczak)

ε

Syntax   ε(i, j, k)

Description   Returns the value of a completely antisymmetric tensor of rank three. Output is 0 if any two arguments are the same, 1 if the three arguments are an even permutation of (0 1 2), and –1 if the arguments are an odd permutation of (0 1 2). (To type ε, press **e[Ctrl]g**).

Arguments
  i, j, k integers between 0 and 2 inclusive (or between ORIGIN and ORIGIN+2 inclusive if ORIGIN≠0)

Γ

Classical Definition

Syntax   Γ(z)

Description   Returns the value of the classical Euler gamma function. (To type Γ, press **G[Ctrl]g**).

Arguments
  z real or complex number; undefined for $z = 0, -1, -2, \ldots$

Description   For Re(z) > 0, $\Gamma(z) = \displaystyle\int_0^{\infty} t^{z-1} e^{-t} dt$.

For Re(z) < 0, function values analytically continue the above formula. Because $\Gamma(z+1) = z!$, the gamma function extends the factorial function (traditionally defined only for positive integers).

Extended Definition

Syntax $\Gamma(x, y)$

Description   Returns the value of the extended Euler gamma function. (To type Γ, press **G[Ctrl]g**).

Arguments
x, y   real numbers, $x > 0$, $y \geq 0$

Description   Although restricted to real arguments, the function $\Gamma(x, y) = \displaystyle\int_{y}^{\infty} t^{x-1}e^{-t}dt$

extends the classical gamma function in the sense that the lower limit of integration y is free to vary. In the special case when $y=0$, the classical formulation applies and the first argument may assume complex values.

Φ Piecewise Continuous

Syntax $\Phi(x)$

Description   Returns the value of the Heaviside step function. Output is 1 if $x \geq 0$ and 0 otherwise.
(To type Φ, press **F[Ctrl]g**).

Arguments
x   real number

Example

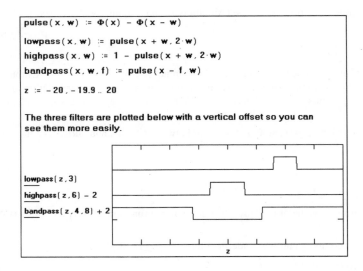

```
pulse( x , w )  :=  Φ( x )  −  Φ( x − w )

lowpass( x , w )  :=  pulse( x + w , 2·w )

highpass( x , w )  :=  1 − pulse( x + w , 2·w )

bandpass( x , w , f )  :=  pulse( x − f , w )

z  :=  −20 , −19.9 .. 20
```

The three filters are plotted below with a vertical offset so you can see them more easily.

lowpass(z , 3)

highpass(z , 6) − 2

bandpass(z , 4 , 8) + 2

Chapter 18
Operators

This chapter lists and describes Mathcad's built-in operators. The operators are listed according to the toolbar (Calculator, Matrix, Calculus, Evaluation, Boolean, or Programming) on which they appear.

Accessing Operators

You can access operators in two ways:

- Simply type in the keystroke shown for that operator, or
- Select the operator from a toolbar.

    1. First, select **View** $\Rightarrow$ **Toolbars** $\Rightarrow$ **Math**.
    The Math toolbar appears showing the various operator toolbar buttons.

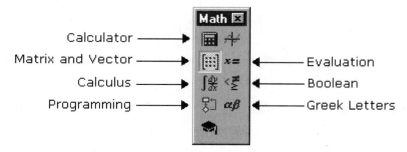

    2. Click a button for a specific toolbar. The corresponding toolbar appears.

    You can alternatively go directly to an operator toolbar from the View menu by selecting **View** $\Rightarrow$ **Toolbars**, and then selecting one of the operator toolbars listed; for example **Matrix**:

The Matrix operator toolbar appears, showing the various matrix operator buttons:

3. Click the button of the operator that you want to use.

Finding More Information

Refer to the Resource Center QuickSheets for examples involving operators. Select **Resource Center** from the **Help** menu. Then click on the QuickSheets icon and select a specific topic.

To change the appearance of certain operators (e.g., multiplication or derivatives), choose **Options** from the **Math** menu, click the Display tab and use drop-down options to make the selection. See "Changing the Display of an Operator" on page 130 for more information.

About the References

References are provided in the Appendices for you to learn more about the numerical algorithm underlying a given Mathcad function or operator. References are not intended to give a description of the actual underlying source code. Some references (such as *Numerical Recipes*) do contain actual C code for the algorithms discussed therein, but the use of the reference does not necessarily imply that the code is what is implemented in Mathcad. The references are cited for their textbook nature only.

Arithmetic Operators

To access an arithmetic operator:

- type its keystroke, or
- choose the operator from the Calculator toolbar (if it has a button):

Refer to "Accessing Operators" on page 447 for more information on how to access a toolbar.

Parentheses (X)

Keystroke	'
Description	Groups parts of an expression.

Addition $X + Y$

Keystroke	+
Description	If X and Y are real or complex numbers, adds X and Y.
	If X and Y are real or complex vectors or matrices of the same size, adds elements of X to corresponding elements of Y.
	If X is a real or complex array and Y is a real or complex number, adds Y to each element of X.

Addition with line break $X...$ $+ Y$

Keystroke	[Ctrl] [↵]
Description	Adds in the same manner as Addition, but inserts a line break for cosmetic formatting reasons.
Comments	This formatting feature cannot be used for multiplication or division. It can be used with subtraction if $X - Y$ is written instead as $X + (- Y)$.

Subtraction and Negation $X - Y$, $-X$

Keystroke   –

Subtraction

Description   If X and Y are real or complex numbers, subtracts Y from X.
If X and Y are real or complex vectors or matrices of the same size, subtracts elements of Y from corresponding elements of X.
If X is an real or complex array and Y is a real or complex number, subtracts Y from each element of X.

Negation

Description   If X is a real or complex number, reverses the sign of X.
If X is an real or complex array, reverses the sign of each element of X.

Multiplication $X \cdot Y$

Keystroke   *

Description   If X and Y are real or complex numbers, multiplies Y by X.
If Y is a real or complex array and X is a real or complex number, multiplies each element of Y by X.
If X and Y are real or complex vectors of the same size, returns the dot product (inner product).
If X and Y are real or complex conformable matrices, performs matrix multiplication.

To change the appearance of multiplication from a dot to a cross, choose **Options** from the **Math** menu, click the Display tab and use drop-down options to make the selection.

Division $\dfrac{X}{z}$

Keystroke   /

Description   If X and z are real or complex numbers and z is nonzero, divides X by z.
If X is an real or complex array and z is a nonzero real or complex number, divides each element of X by z.

Inline Division $X \div z$

Keystroke   **[Ctrl]/**

Description   If X and z are real or complex numbers and z is nonzero, divides X by z.
If X is an real or complex array and z is a nonzero real or complex number, divides each element of X by z.

Factorial $n!$

Keystroke   **!**

Description   Returns $n \cdot (n-1) \cdot (n-2) \ldots 2 \cdot 1$ if n is an integer and $n \geq 1$; 1 if $n = 0$.

Complex conjugate $\overline{X}$

Keystroke   **"**

Description   If X is a complex number, reverses the sign of the imaginary part of X.

Absolute value $|x|$

Keystroke   **|**

Description   If z is a real or complex number, |z| returns the absolute value (or modulus or magnitude) $\sqrt{\mathrm{Re}(z)^2 + \mathrm{Im}(z)^2}$ of z.

If $\mathbf{v}$ is real or complex vector, |$\mathbf{v}$| returns the magnitude (or Euclidean norm or length) $\sqrt{\mathbf{v} \cdot \overline{\mathbf{v}}}$ of $\mathbf{v}$. If all elements in $\mathbf{v}$ are real, this definition is equivalent to $\sqrt{\mathbf{v} \cdot \mathbf{v}}$.

If $\mathbf{M}$ is a real or complex square matrix, |$\mathbf{M}$| returns the determinant of $\mathbf{M}$.

Square root $\sqrt{z}$

Keystroke   ****

Description   Returns the positive square root for positive z; principal value for negative or complex z.

*n*th root $\sqrt[n]{z}$

Keystroke   **[Ctrl]**

Description   Returns the positive nth root for positive z; negative nth root for negative z and odd n; principal value otherwise. n must be an integer, $n \geq 1$.

See also   Exponentiation, Square root

Comments   This operator gives the same values as the Exponentiation operator except when $z < 0$ and n is an odd integer and $n \geq 3$ (by special convention).

Reciprocal $\dfrac{1}{z}$

Keystroke   **/ 1**

Scalar Case

Description   Returns the reciprocal (multiplicative inverse) of z, where z is a real or complex number.

Matrix Case

Description   If $\mathbf{M}$ is a real or complex square matrix, the reciprocal of $\mathbf{M}$ is the same as the inverse matrix $\mathbf{M}^{-1}$ (assuming that $\mathbf{M}$ is nonsingular).

See also   Exponentiation

Algorithm   LU decomposition used for matrix inversion (Press *et al.*, 1992)

Exponentiation z^w

Keystroke	^

Scalar Case

Description   Returns the principal value of z raised to the power w, where z and w are real or complex numbers.

See also   nth root

Comments   The principal value is given by the formula $|z|^w \cdot \exp(\pi \cdot i \cdot w)$. In the special case $z < 0$ and $w = 1/n$, where n is an odd integer and $n \geq 3$, the principal value has a nonzero imaginary part. Hence, in this special case, Exponentiation does not give the same value as the nth root operator (by convention).

Matrix Case

Description   If $\mathbf{M}$ is a real or complex square matrix and $n \geq 0$ is an integer, $\mathbf{M}^n$ returns the nth power of $\mathbf{M}$ (using iterated matrix multiplication). Under the same conditions, $\mathbf{M}^{-n}$ is the inverse of $\mathbf{M}^n$ (assuming additionally that $\mathbf{M}$ is nonsingular).

Algorithm   LU decomposition used for matrix inversion (Press *et al.*, 1992)

Equals $c =$

Keystroke	=

Description   Returns numerical value of c if c is: a variable previously defined in the worksheet; a built-in variable; a globally-defined variable; or a function of several such variables. Appears as an ordinary = on the screen. Not used for symbolic evaluation.

Definition $z := c$, $f(x,y,z,...) := expr$

Keystroke	:

Description   Gives z the numerical value c from that point onward throughout the worksheet. Gives a function $f(x,y,z,...)$ the meaning prescribed by the expression *expr* from that point onward throughout the worksheet. *expr* need not involve x, y, z, ... but it usually does; it may involve other built-in or user-defined functions.

See also   Definition (under Evaluation Operators) for example.

Mixed number $k\dfrac{m}{n}$

Keystroke	**[Ctrl][Shift]+**

Description   If k, m and n are integers, returns the value of $k + m/n$.

Comments   To display a numerical result as a mixed number, double-click on the result to bring up the Result Format dialog box. Choose Fraction for the result format on the Number Format tab. Click the box next to "Use mixed numbers" so that it is checked.

Matrix Operators

To access a matrix operator:

- type its keystroke, or

- choose the operator from the Matrix toolbar:

Refer to "Accessing Operators" on page 447 for more information on how to access a toolbar.

Insert matrix

Keystroke   [Ctrl]M

Description   Creates a vector or matrix of specified dimensions.

Vector and matrix subscript v_n, $M_{i,j}$

Keystroke   [

Description   If **v** is a vector, v_n returns the *n*th element of **v**.
If **M** is a matrix, $M_{i,j}$ returns the element in row *i* and column *j* of **M**.

Range variable

Keystroke   ;

Description   Specifies that a variable assume a range of values (for the sake of repeated or iterative calculations).

Dot product $u \cdot v$

Keystroke   *

Description   Returns the dot product (scalar or inner product) of two *n*-dimensional real or complex vectors **u** and **v**.

Cross product $u \times v$

Keystroke   [Ctrl]8

Description   Returns the cross product (vector product) of two 3-dimensional real or complex vectors **u** and **v**.

Vector sum $\Sigma \mathbf{v}$

Keystroke   **[Ctrl]4**

Description   Returns the sum (a scalar) of all elements of a real or complex vector **v**. (No range variable or vector subscripts are needed.)

Matrix Inverse

Keystroke   **^-1**

Description   Returns the multiplicative inverse of a real or complex nonsingular square matrix **M**.

Algorithm   LU decomposition used for matrix inversion (Press *et al.*, 1992)

Magnitude and Determinant $|x|$

Keystroke   **|**

Description   If z is a real or complex number, $|z|$ returns the absolute value (or modulus or magnitude) $\sqrt{\mathrm{Re}(z)^2 + \mathrm{Im}(z)^2}$ of z.

If **v** is real or complex vector, returns the magnitude (or Euclidean norm or length) $\sqrt{\mathbf{v} \cdot \overline{\mathbf{v}}}$ of **v**. If all elements in **v** are real, this definition is equivalent to $\sqrt{\mathbf{v} \cdot \mathbf{v}}$.

If **M** is a real or complex square matrix, returns the determinant of **M**.

Algorithm   LU decomposition (Press *et al.*, 1992)

Matrix superscript $\mathbf{M}^{\langle n \rangle}$

Keystroke   **[Ctrl]6**

Description   Extracts column n (a vector) from matrix **M**.

Matrix transpose $\mathbf{M}^{\mathrm{T}}$

Keystroke   **[Ctrl]1**

Description   If **M** is a vector or matrix, returns a matrix whose rows are the columns of **M** and whose columns are the rows of **M**.

Vectorize $\vec{X}$

Keystroke   **[Ctrl]-**

Description   Forces operations in expression X to take place element by element. All vectors or matrices in X must be the same size.

Comments Mathcad's vectorize operator allows parallel operations to be performed efficiently on each element of a vector or matrix. For example, to define a matrix **P** by multiplying corresponding elements of the matrices **M** and **N**, you could write $P_{i,j} = M_{i,j} \cdot N_{i,j}$ where i and j are range variables. (This is not matrix multiplication, but rather multiplication element by element.) It's faster, however, to define **P** using vectorize:

- Select the whole expression by clicking inside and pressing [**Space**] until the right-hand side is held between the editing lines.

- Press [**Ctrl**]– to apply the vectorize operator. Mathcad puts an arrow over the top of the selected expression.

Extending ordinary scalar multiplication to matrices in this fashion, element by element, is referred to as "vectorizing" an expression.

Here are some properties of the vectorize operator:

- The vectorize operator changes the meaning of functions and operators but not constants or variables.

- Operations between an array and a scalar are performed by applying the scalar to each element of the array. For example, if **v** is a vector and n is a scalar, applying the vectorize operator to $\mathbf{v}^n$ returns a vector whose elements are the nth powers of the elements of **v**.

- You cannot use any of the following matrix operations under a vectorize operator: dot product, matrix multiplication, matrix powers, matrix inverse, determinant, or magnitude of a vector. The vectorize operator will transform these operations into element-by-element scalar multiplication, exponentiation, or absolute value, as appropriate.

- The vectorize operator has no effect on operators and functions that *require* vectors or matrices: transpose, cross product, sum of vector elements, and functions like mean. These operators and functions have no scalar meaning.

Picture

Keystroke **[Ctrl]T**

Description Displays a matrix **M** as a grayscale image. Each element of **M** corresponds to a pixel. The value of an element determines the shade of gray associated with the corresponding pixel. Each element of **M** is an integer between 0 (black) and 255 (white).

Calculus Operators

To access a calculus operator:

- type its keystroke, or

- choose the operator from the Calculus toolbar:

Refer to "Accessing Operators" on page 447 for more information on how to access a toolbar.

Summation

$$\sum_{i=m}^{n} X$$

Keystroke **[Ctrl] [Shift] 4**

Description Performs iterated addition of X over $i = m, m+1, ..., n$. X can be any expression; it need not involve i but it usually does. m and n must be integers. If $m = -\infty$ or $n = \infty$, the evaluation must be performed symbolically.

Example

$$i := 0 .. 20 \qquad x_i := \sin(0.1 \cdot i \cdot \pi)$$

$$\sum_{n=0}^{20} n = 210 \qquad \prod_{n=0}^{20} (n+1) = 5.109 \cdot 10^{19}$$

$$\sum_{n=0}^{20} x_n = 0 \qquad \sum_{n=0}^{20} x_n \cdot n = -63.138$$

$$\sum_{n=0}^{20} \sum_{m=0}^{10} n^m = 2.554 \cdot 10^{13}$$

See also Range sum

Comments To evaluate multiple summations, place another summation in the final placeholder of the first summation, as illustrated in the example.

Product

$$\prod_{i=m}^{n} X$$

Keystroke [Ctrl] [Shift] 3

Description Performs iterated multiplication of X over $i = m, m + 1, ..., n$. X can be any expression; it need not involve i but it usually does. If $m = -\infty$ or $n = \infty$, the evaluation must be performed symbolically. Works similar to Summation.

See also Range product. See Summation for an example.

Range sum

$$\sum_{i} X$$

Keystroke $

Description Performs iterated addition of X over the range variable i. X can be any expression; it need not involve i but it usually does.

Example

$$i := 0 .. 20 \qquad j := 1 .. 10 \qquad x_i := \sin(0.1 \cdot i \cdot \pi)$$

$$\sum_{i} i = 210 \qquad \prod_{i} (i + 1) = 5.109 \cdot 10^{19}$$

$$\sum_{i} x_i = 0 \qquad \sum_{i} x_i \cdot i = -63.138$$

$$y_j := \sum_{i} i^j \qquad \sum_{i} \sum_{j} i^j = 2.554 \cdot 10^{13}$$

$$y_1 = 210 \qquad \sum_{j} y_j = 2.554 \cdot 10^{13}$$

$$y_{10} = 2.416 \cdot 10^{13}$$

See also Summation .

Comments When you use the Summation operator described earlier, the summation must be carried out over integers and in steps of one. Mathcad provides a more general version of this operator that can use any range variable you define as an index of summation.

The Range sum operator, unlike the Summation operator, cannot stand alone. It requires the existence of a range variable. However, a single range variable can be used with any number of these operators.

To evaluate multiple summations, place another summation in the final placeholder of the first summation and use two range variables, as illustrated in the example.

Range product $\displaystyle\prod_i X$

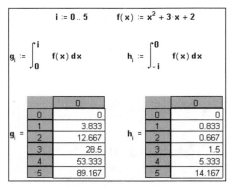

Keystroke **#**

Description Performs iterated multiplication of X over the range variable i. X can be any expression; it need not involve i but it usually does. Works similar to Range sum.

See also Product. See Range sum for an example.

Definite integral $\displaystyle\int_a^b f(t)\,dt$

Keystroke **&**

Description Returns the definite integral of $f(t)$ over the interval $[a, b]$. a and b must be real scalars. All variables in the expression $f(t)$, except the variable of integration t, must be defined. The integrand, $f(t)$, cannot return an array. $a = -\infty$, $b = \infty$, or both are permitted.

Examples

$$i := 0 .. 5 \qquad f(x) := x^2 + 3 \cdot x + 2$$

$$g_i := \int_0^i f(x)\,dx \qquad h_i := \int_{-i}^0 f(x)\,dx$$

$g_i =$

	0
0	0
1	3.833
2	12.667
3	28.5
4	53.333
5	89.167

$h_i =$

	0
0	0
1	0.833
2	0.667
3	1.5
4	5.333
5	14.167

Figure 18-1: Example 1.

Default tolerance
$$\text{TOL} := 0.001 \qquad \int_1^{e^5} \frac{1}{t}\,dt = 5.000000541364253$$

Tighter tolerance
$$\text{TOL} := 0.000001 \qquad \int_1^{e^5} \frac{1}{t}\,dt = 5.000000000007783$$

Looser tolerance
$$\text{TOL} := 0.1 \qquad \int_1^{e^5} \frac{1}{t}\,dt = 5.011533083011655$$

Figure 18-2: Example 2.

Comments   There are some important things to remember about integration in Mathcad:

- The limits of integration must be real, but the expression to be integrated can be either real or complex.
- Except for the integrating variable, all variables in the integrand must have been defined elsewhere in the worksheet.
- The integrating variable must be a single variable name.
- If the integrating variable involves units, the upper and lower limits of integration must have the same units.

Like all numerical methods, Mathcad's integration algorithm can have difficulty with ill-behaved integrands. If the expression to be integrated has singularities, discontinuities, or large and rapid fluctuations, Mathcad's solution may be inaccurate.

In some cases, you may be able to find an exact expression for your definite integral or even the indefinite integral (antiderivative) by using Mathcad's symbolics.

Although the result of an integration is a single number, you can always use an integral with a range variable to obtain results for many numbers at once (as illustrated in Example 1). Such repeated evaluations may take considerable time depending on the complexity of the integrals, the length of the interval, and the value of TOL.

Mathcad's numerical integration algorithm makes successive estimates of the value of the integral and returns a value when the two most recent estimates differ by less than the value of the built-in variable TOL. Figure 18-2 above shows how changing TOL affects the accuracy of integral calculations (not to be confused with the mere formatting issue of how many digits to display).

You can change the value of the tolerance by including definitions for TOL directly in your worksheet as shown. You can also change the tolerance by using the Built-In Variables tab when you choose **Options** from the **Math** menu. To see the effect of changing the tolerance, choose **Calculate Document** from the **Math** menu to recalculate all the equations in the worksheet.

If Mathcad's approximations to an integral fail to converge to an answer, Mathcad marks the integral with an appropriate error message.

When you change the tolerance, keep in mind the trade-off between accuracy and computation time. If you decrease (tighten) the tolerance, Mathcad will compute integrals more accurately. However, because this requires more work, Mathcad will take longer to return a result. Conversely, if you increase (loosen) the tolerance, Mathcad will compute more quickly, but the answers will be less accurate.

You can also use Mathcad to evaluate double or multiple integrals. To set up a double integral, press the ampersand key, [&], twice. Fill in the integrand, the limits, and the integrating variable for each integral. Keep in mind that double integrals take much longer to converge to an answer than single integrals. Wherever possible, use an equivalent single integral in place of a double integral.

Because certain numerical integration methods work best on certain kinds of integrals, Mathcad has an AutoSelect feature for integration. Depending on the kind of integral you are evaluating, Mathcad automatically chooses the most appropriate integration method to use. Using AutoSelect, Mathcad examines the integral and evaluates it using one of the following methods:

- Romberg (Romberg trapezoidal approximation with Richard extrapolation – equal intervals)
- Adaptive (if the values of $f(x)$ vary significantly over the interval – unequal intervals)
- Infinite Limit (if $a = -\infty$, $b = \infty$ or both)
- Singular Endpoint (if $f(a)$ and/or $f(b)$ is undefined)

If you want to evaluate an integral using a method other than the one chosen during the AutoSelect process, turn off AutoSelect and choose another method. To do so:

1. Type the integral and allow AutoSelect to return a result.
2. Right-click on the integral.
3. Click on the method you want to use.

The integral is automatically re-evaluated using the method you clicked and is re-evaluated that way from then on, unless you specify another method or AutoSelect later.

Algorithm   Romberg, Kahan transform, QAGS, Clenshaw-Curtis, Gauss-Kronrod formulas (Piessens 1983, Lorczak)

Indefinite integral $\int f(t)\,dt$

Keystroke   **[Ctrl]i**

Description   Returns the indefinite integral (that is, an antiderivative) of $f(t)$. Must be performed symbolically. The integrand, $f(t)$, cannot return an array.

Derivative $\dfrac{d}{dt}f(t)$

Keystroke   **?**

Description   Returns the derivative of $f(t)$ evaluated at t. All variables in the expression $f(t)$ must be defined. The variable t must be a scalar value. The function $f(t)$ must return a scalar.

Example

$$x := 2 \qquad y := 10 \qquad t := 0$$

$$g(t) := 5 \cdot t^4$$

Derivative	Actual result
$\dfrac{d}{dx}x^5 = 79.99999999999997$	$g(x) = 80$
$\dfrac{d}{dx}x^5 \cdot y = 799.9999999999998$	$g(x) \cdot y = 800$
$\dfrac{d}{dy}x^5 \cdot y = 31.99999999999998$	$x^5 = 32$
$\dfrac{d}{dt}x^5 \cdot y = 0$	**(Since expression does not involve t, derivative is zero)**

Comments   With Mathcad's derivative algorithm, you can expect the first derivative to be accurate to within 7 or 8 significant digits, provided that the value at which you evaluate the derivative is not too close to a singularity of the function. The accuracy of this algorithm tends to decrease by one significant digit for each increase in the order of the derivative (see nth derivative operator).

The result of differentiating is not a function, but a single number: the computed derivative at the indicated value of the differentiation variable. In the previous example, the derivative of x^3 is not the expression $3x^2$ but $3x^2$ evaluated at $x = 2$. If you want the expression $3x^2$, you will need to use either live or menu symbolics.

Although differentiation returns just one number, you can still define one function as the derivative of another. For example: $f(x) := \dfrac{d}{dx}g(x)$. Evaluating $f(x)$ will return the numerically computed derivative of $g(x)$ at x. You can use this technique to evaluate the derivative of a function at many points via range variables.

To change the appearance of the derivative symbol to a partial derivative symbol, choose **Options** from the **Math** menu, click the Display tab and use drop-down options to make the selection.

Algorithm   Modified Ridder's method (Press *et al.*, 1992; Lorczak)

*n*th derivative $\dfrac{d^n}{dt^n}f(t)$

Keystroke   **[Ctrl]?**

Description   Returns the *n*th derivative of $f(t)$ evaluated at t. All variables in $f(t)$ must be defined. The variable t must be a scalar value. The function $f(t)$ must return a scalar. n must be an integer between 0 and 5 for numerical evaluation or a positive integer for symbolic evaluation.

Comments   For $n = 1$, this operator gives the same answer as the Derivative operator. For $n = 0$, it simply returns the value of the function itself.

To change the appearance of the *n*th derivative symbol to an *n*th partial derivative symbol, choose **Options** from the **Math** menu, click the Display tab and use drop-down options to make the selection.

Algorithm   Modified Ridder's method (Press *et al.*, 1992; Lorczak)

Limit $\lim\limits_{t \to a} f(t)$

Keystroke   **[Ctrl]L**

Description   Returns the two-sided limit of $f(t)$. Must be evaluated symbolically.

Algorithm   Series expansion (Geddes and Gonnet, 1989)

Right-Hand Limit $\lim\limits_{t \to a^+} f(t)$

Keystroke   **[Ctrl][Shift]A**

Description   Returns the right-hand limit of $f(t)$. Must be evaluated symbolically.

Algorithm   Series expansion (Geddes and Gonnet, 1989)

Left-Hand Limit $\lim\limits_{t \to a^-} f(t)$

Keystroke   **[Ctrl][Shift]B**

Description   Returns the left-hand limit of $f(t)$. Must be evaluated symbolically.

Algorithm   Series expansion (Geddes and Gonnet, 1989)

Evaluation Operators

To access an Evaluation operator:

- type its keystroke, or

- choose the operator from the Evaluation toolbar:

Refer to "Accessing Operators" on page 447 for more information on how to access a toolbar.

Equals	$c =$	

Keystroke   =

Description Returns numerical value of c if c is: a variable previously defined in the worksheet; a built-in variable; a globally-defined variable; or a function of several such variables. Appears as an ordinary = on the screen. Not used for symbolic evaluation.

Definition $z := c$, $f(x,y,z,...) := expr$

Keystroke   :

Description Gives z the numerical value c from that point onward throughout the worksheet. Gives a function $f(x,y,z,...)$ the meaning prescribed by the expression $expr$ from that point onward throughout the worksheet. $expr$ need not involve x, y, z, ... but it usually does; it may involve other built-in or user-defined functions.

Examples

```
Computing distances between points      (DEFINITIONS)
   x1 := 0             y1 := 1.5
   x2 := 3             y2 := 4         dist(x, y) := √(x² + y²)
   x3 := -1            y3 := 1

Compute distance from origin:           (EVALUATIONS)
   dist(x1, y1) = 1.5
   dist(x2, y2) = 5
   dist(x3, y3) = 1.414

Compute distance between points
   dist(x2 - x1, y2 - y1) = 3.905
   dist(x3 - x1, y3 - y1) = 1.118
   dist(x3 - x2, y3 - y2) = 5
```

Figure 18-3: Example 1.

```
Simultaneous definition of three variables...
   x := 2

   ⎡ α ⎤     ⎡ atan(x) ⎤
   ⎢ β ⎥  := ⎢  ln(x)  ⎥      α = 1.1071487
   ⎣ γ ⎦     ⎣   √x    ⎦      β = 0.6931472
                              γ = 1.4142136

Swap two variables...
        A := 1      B := 2
        ⎡ A ⎤   ⎡ B ⎤
        ⎢ B ⎥ := ⎢ A ⎥
        ⎣   ⎦   ⎣   ⎦
        A = 2        B = 1
```

Figure 18-4: Example 2.

Comments	You can define arrays in the same way as scalars, with the array name **A** on the left side of a :=, and a corresponding array of values to the right.

You can likewise use arrays to define several variables at once, as the previous example shows. The left side of a simultaneous definition is an array whose elements are either names or subscripted variable names. The right side must be an array of values having the same number of rows and columns as the left side. Mathcad defines each variable on the left side with the value of the array in the corresponding position on the right side. Elements on the right side are all evaluated before assigning any of them to the left side. Because of this, nothing on the right side of an expression can depend on what is on the left side. You also cannot have a variable appear more than once on the left side.

When you define a function, Mathcad does not try to evaluate it until you use it later on in the worksheet. If there is an error, the use of the function is marked in error, even though the real problem may be in the definition of the function itself. For example, if $f(x) := 1/x$ and you attempt to evaluate $f(0)$, the error flag occurs not at the definition of $f(x)$ but when Mathcad encounters $f(0)$ for the first time.

Global Definition $\quad z \equiv c, \quad f(x, y, z, \dots) \equiv \text{expr}$

Keystroke	~
Description	Gives z the numerical value c and this holds throughout the worksheet (regardless of where the global definition is positioned). Likewise, gives a function $f(x,y,z,\dots)$ the meaning prescribed by the expression *expr* throughout the worksheet. *expr* need not involve $x, y, z, \dots$ but it usually does; it may involve other built-in or user-defined functions.
Comments	You can globally define arrays in the same way as scalars, with the array name **A** on the left side of a $\equiv$, and a corresponding array of values to the right.

This is the algorithm that Mathcad uses to evaluate all definitions, global and otherwise:

- First, Mathcad takes one pass through the entire worksheet from top to bottom. During this first pass, Mathcad evaluates global definitions only.

- Mathcad then makes a second pass through the worksheet from top to bottom. This time, Mathcad evaluates all definitions made with := as well as all equations containing $\equiv$.

Although global definitions are evaluated before any local definitions, Mathcad evaluates global definitions the same way it evaluates local definitions: top to bottom and left to right. This means that whenever you use a variable to the right of a $\equiv$:

- that variable must also have been defined with a $\equiv$, *and*

- the variable must have been defined *above* the place where you are trying to use it.

Otherwise, the variable is marked in red to indicate that it is undefined.

It is good practice to allow only one definition for each global variable. Although you can define a variable with two different global definitions or with one global and one local definition, this is never necessary and usually makes your worksheet difficult to understand.

Symbolic Equals $c \rightarrow$

Keystroke	**[Ctrl].**
Description	Returns live symbolic "value" of c if c is a variable previously defined in the worksheet, is a built-in variable, is a globally-defined variable, or is a function of several such variables.
Comments	The live symbolic equals sign is analogous to the numerical equals sign "=". You can use it to symbolically simplify or factor algebraic expressions, or to symbolically evaluate derivatives, integrals and limits. Note that "$\rightarrow$" applies only to an entire expression (unlike menu symbolics).

Prefix $f\ x$

Keystroke	**NONE**
Description	Using the prefix custom operator, $f\ x$ returns the value $f(x)$, where f is either a built-in or user-defined function and x is a real or complex number.
Examples	

Figure 18-5: Example 1: Defining your own operators.

$$\sin\left(\frac{\pi}{3}\right) = 0.866 \quad \longleftarrow \text{Displaying a function the usual way.}$$

$$\sin\frac{\pi}{3} = 0.866 \quad \longleftarrow \text{Displaying the same function as if it were an operator (using the xf button).}$$

Figure 18-6: Example 2: Displaying an operator as a function and a function as an operator.

Comments	In Figure 18-5, the symbol " $^{\circ}$ " comes from the Symbol font. First define a function "$^{\circ}(x)$" as illustrated, then click the Postfix button on the Evaluation toolbar to use postfix notation. For postfix notation, type the name of the operator in the right placeholder and the operand in the left placeholder.

Many publishers prefer to omit parentheses around the arguments to certain functions (*sin* x rather than $\sin(x)$). You can do the same thing by treating the *sin* function as an operator with one operand, as in Figure 18-6.

Postfix

$x\ f$

NONE

Description   Using the postfix custom operator, $x\ f$ returns the value $f(x)$, where f is either a built-in or user-defined function and x is a real or complex number.

Comments   In Figure 18-5, on page 465, the symbol "°" comes from the Symbol font. First define a function "°(x)" as illustrated, then click the postfix button on the Evaluation toolbar to use postfix notation. For postfix notation, type the name of the operator in the right placeholder and the operand in the left placeholder.

Infix

$x\ f\ y$

Keystroke

NONE

Description   Using the infix custom operator, $x\ f\ y$ returns the value $f(x,y)$, where f is either a built-in or user-defined function and $x,\ y$ are real or complex numbers.

Comments   In Figure 18-5, on page 465, the symbol "≈" comes from the Symbol font. First define a binary function "≈(x,y)" as illustrated, then click the infix button on the Evaluation toolbar to use infix notation. For infix notation, type the name of the operator in the middle placeholder and the operands in the left and right placeholders.

Likewise, in Figure 18-6, on page 465, the binary function "÷(x,y)" is defined and then displayed in the more conventional manner: "x÷y". Functions and operators are fundamentally the same. Although notation like "÷(x,y)" is unconventional, use it if you prefer.

Treefix

$x\ f\ y$

Keystroke   **NONE**

Description   Using the treefix custom operator, $_x f_y$ returns the value $f(x,y)$, where f is either a built-in or user-defined function and x and y are real or complex numbers.

Comments   In Figure 18-5, on page 465, the symbol "÷" comes from the Symbol font. First define a binary function "÷(x,y)" as illustrated, then click the treefix button on the Evaluation toolbar to use treefix notation. For treefix notation, type the name of the operator in the middle placeholder and the operands in the left and right placeholders.

Boolean Operators

To access a Boolean operator:

- type its keystroke, or

- choose the operator from the Boolean toolbar:

Refer to "Accessing Operators" on page 447 for more information on how to access a toolbar.

Greater than $x > y$, $S1 > S2$

Keystroke	>
Description	For real scalars x and y, returns 1 if $x > y$, 0 otherwise.
	For string expressions $S1$ and $S2$, returns 1 if $S1$ strictly follows $S2$ in ASCII order, 0 otherwise.

Less than $x < y$, $S1 < S2$

Keystroke	<
Description	For real scalars x and y, returns 1 if $x < y$, 0 otherwise.
	For string expressions $S1$ and $S2$, returns 1 if $S1$ strictly precedes $S2$ in ASCII order, 0 otherwise.

Greater than or equal to $x \geq y$, $S1 \geq S2$

Keystroke	[Ctrl])
Description	For real scalars x and y, returns 1 if $x \geq y$, 0 otherwise.
	For string expressions $S1$ and $S2$, returns 1 if $S1$ follows $S2$ in ASCII order, 0 otherwise.

Less than or equal to $x \leq y$, $S1 \leq S2$

Keystroke	[Ctrl](
Description	For real scalars x and y, returns 1 if $x \leq y$, 0 otherwise.
	For string expressions $S1$ and $S2$, returns 1 if $S1$ precedes $S2$ in ASCII order, 0 otherwise.

Not equal to $z \neq w$, $S1 \neq S2$

Keystroke	[Ctrl]3
Description	For scalars z and w, returns 1 if $z \neq w$, 0 otherwise.
	For string expressions $S1$ and $S2$, returns 1 if $S1$ is not character by character identical to $S2$, 0 otherwise.

Bold Equals $z = w$

Keystroke   `[Ctrl]=`

Description   Returns 1 if $z = w$, 0 otherwise (also known as Boolean equals). Appears as a bold = on the screen. Also used when typing constraint equations within solve blocks or when typing equations to be solved symbolically.

and $x \wedge y$

Keystroke   `[Ctrl][Shift]7`

Description $x \wedge y$ returns the value 1 if both x and y are nonzero, and 0 if at least one of x or y is zero.

Comments   The value 0 is regarded as FALSE; any nonzero value (including 1) is regarded as TRUE. The Boolean and operator evaluates the right argument if and only if the left argument is TRUE. $x \wedge y$ is also known as the logical conjunction of x and y.

or $x \vee y$

Keystroke   `[Ctrl][Shift]6`

Description $x \vee y$ returns the value 1 if at least one of x or y is nonzero, and 0 if both x and y are zero.

Comments   The value 0 is regarded as FALSE; any nonzero value (including 1) is regarded as TRUE. The Boolean or operator evaluates the right argument if and only if the left argument is FALSE. $x \vee y$ is also known as the logical (inclusive) disjunction of x and y.

xor $x \oplus y$

Keystroke   `[Ctrl][Shift]1`

Description $x \oplus y$ returns the value 1 if precisely one of x or y is nonzero, and 0 if both x and y are zero or both are nonzero.

Comments   The value 0 is regarded as FALSE; any nonzero value (including 1) is regarded as TRUE. $x \oplus y$ is the same as $(x \vee y) \wedge \neg (x \wedge y)$ and is also known as the logical exclusive disjunction of x and y.

not $\neg x$

Keystroke   `[Ctrl][Shift]5`

Description $\neg x$ returns the value 0 if x is nonzero and 0 if x is zero.

Comments   The value 0 is regarded as FALSE; any nonzero value (including 1) is regarded as TRUE. $\neg x$ is also known as the logical negation of x.

Programming Operators

To access a Programming operator:

- type its keystroke, or

- choose the operator from the Programming toolbar:

Refer to "Accessing Operators" on page 447 for more information on how to access a toolbar.

Special Note: these operators are valid only within a Mathcad programming structure.

Local Definition $\quad w \leftarrow f(a, b, c, \dots)$

Keystroke   **{**

Description   Gives w the numerical value of the function $f(a,b,c,...)$ within a program.
Outside the program, w remains undefined.

Add Line

Keystroke   **]**

Description   Inserts a line in a program. When you insert the Add Line operator the first time, a program is created (a vertical bar with two placeholders). If you select either of these placeholders and insert the Add Line operator again, more placeholders are created.

Conditional Statement ▪ if ▪

Keystroke   **}**

Description   Within a program, permits evaluation of a statement only when a specified condition is met. You must insert this operator using its toolbar button or equivalent keystroke. (Conditional if is not the same as the built-in if function (do not just type the word "if").

Otherwise Statement ■ otherwise

Keystroke   **[Ctrl][Shift]}**

Description   Within a program, used in conjunction with the if statement to exhaust possibilities not yet covered. You must insert this operator using its toolbar button or equivalent keystroke. (Do not just type the word "otherwise".)

For Loop   for ■ ∈ ■

■

Keystroke   **[Ctrl][Shift]"**

Description   Within a program, permits evaluation of a sequence of statements a specified number of times. The right hand placeholder usually contains a range variable. You must insert this operator using its toolbar button or equivalent keystroke. (Do not just type the word "for".)

While Loop   while ■

■

Keystroke   **[Ctrl]]**

Description   Within a program, permits evaluation of a sequence of statements until a specified condition is met. The right hand placeholder usually contains a Boolean expression. You must insert this operator using its toolbar button or equivalent keystroke. (Do not just type the word "while".)

Break Statement   break

Keystroke   **[Ctrl][Shift]{**

Description   Within a for or while loop, halts loop execution. Usually used in conjunction with an if statement, that is, halting occurs if a specified condition occurs. Execution moves to the next statement outside the loop. You must insert this operator using its toolbar button or equivalent keystroke. (Do not just type the word "break".)

See also   continue and return

Continue Statement   continue

Keystroke   **[Ctrl][**

Description   Within a for or while loop, halts loop execution, skips remaining steps, and continues at the beginning of the next iteration of the next loop. Usually used in conjunction with an if statement, that is, halting occurs if a specified condition occurs. You must insert this operator using its toolbar button or equivalent keystroke. (Do not just type the word "continue".)

See also   break and return

Return Statement   return ∎

Keystroke	**[Ctrl] [Shift] |**

`return`

Description   Within a program, halts program execution. Usually used in conjunction with an *if* statement, that is, halting occurs if a specified condition occurs. Also, within a for or while loop, halts loop execution; execution in this case moves to the next statement outside the loop. You must insert this operator using its toolbar button or equivalent keystroke. (Do not just type the word "return".)

See also   break and continue

Comments   The break function does the same as return, but gives the value only of the last expression evaluated before break is called. Therefore return is more flexible, because it allows you to interrupt the program and return particular values other than the default value last computed.

On Error Statement   ∎ on error ∎

Keystroke   **[Ctrl]'**

`on error`

Description   Within a program, permits computation of an alternative expression when an arbitrary numerical error flag is raised. You must insert this operator using its toolbar button or equivalent keystroke. (Do not just type the phrase "on error".)

Comments   on error executes the right-hand argument first. If no error occurs, it returns the result of the right argument. If an error occurs, then the error is cleared and the left argument is returned.

on error is a general purpose error trap. It is more powerful than using the return statement, coupled with some specific test, to deal with inputs that give rise to numerical error.

Chapter 19
Symbolic Keywords

This chapter lists and describes Mathcad's symbolic keywords. The keywords are listed alphabetically.

Accessing Symbolic Keywords

You can access symbolic keywords in two ways:

- Simply type in the keyword as shown for that keyword, or
- Select the keyword from the Symbolic toolbar.

    1. First, click the **Symbolic Toobar** button on the math menu:

    The Symbolic toolbar appears.

    2. Click the button of the keyword that you want to use.

The **Modifiers** keyword button corresponds to symbolic modifiers.

The modifier assume is discussed on page 475. The other three modifiers, real, RealRange and trig, are used in some cases with the simplify keyword; refer to simplify on page 481 to find out how to use these modifiers.

Most of the keywords have equivalent menu choices on the **Symbolics** menu.

However, these menu choices are not "live," which means they do not use any previous definitions in your worksheet and do not automatically update when you revise your worksheet.

Finding More Information

Refer to the Resource Center QuickSheets for examples involving keywords. Select **Resource Center** from the **Help** menu. Then click on the QuickSheets icon and select a specific topic.

Keywords

assume

<table>
<tr><td>Syntax</td><td>assume, constraint</td></tr>
<tr><td>Description</td><td>Imposes constraints on one or more variables according to the expression constraint. A typical constraint might be that var < 10.

assume can also constrain a variable to be real or to fall within a certain range of real values. Use the following modifiers:

    var=real evaluates the expression on the assumption that the variable var is real;

    var=RealRange(a,b) evaluates on the assumption that var is real and lies between a and b, where a and b are real numbers or infinity (type **[Ctrl][Shift]z** to display ∞).</td></tr>
<tr><td>Example</td><td></td></tr>
</table>

Symbolic evaluation   Complex evaluation

$$\int_0^{\infty} e^{-x^2} dx \rightarrow \frac{1}{2}\cdot\sqrt{\pi} \qquad e^{i\cdot n\cdot\theta}\ \text{complex} \rightarrow \cos(n\cdot\theta) + i\cdot\sin(n\cdot\theta)$$

Floating point evaluation

$$\int_0^{\infty} e^{-x^2} dx\ \text{float, 10} \rightarrow .8862269255$$

Constrained evaluation

$$x\cdot\int_0^{\infty} e^{-\alpha\cdot t} dt\ \text{assume},\alpha > 1, \alpha = \text{real} \rightarrow \frac{x}{\alpha}$$

(α is constrained to be greater than 1 and real)

coeffs

<table>
<tr><td>Syntax</td><td>coeffs, var</td></tr>
<tr><td>Description</td><td>Finds coefficients of a polynomial when it is written in terms of ascending powers of the variable or subexpression var. Mathcad returns a vector containing the coefficients. The first element of the vector is the constant term and the last element is the coefficient of the highest order term in the polynomial.</td></tr>
<tr><td>See also</td><td>convert, parfrac for example</td></tr>
<tr><td>Comments</td><td>Another way to find the coefficients of a polynomial is to enclose the variable or subexpression var between the two editing lines and choose **Polynomial Coefficients** from the **Symbolics** menu.</td></tr>
</table>

collect

<table>
<tr><td>Syntax</td><td>collect, var1, var2, ... , varn</td></tr>
<tr><td>Description</td><td>Collects terms containing like powers of the variables or subexpressions var1 through varn.</td></tr>
<tr><td>See also</td><td>expand for example</td></tr>
<tr><td>Comments</td><td>Another way to collect terms is to enclose the expression between the editing lines and choose **Collect** from the **Symbolics** menu</td></tr>
</table>

complex

Syntax	complex
Description	Carries out symbolic evaluation in the complex domain. Result is usually of the form $a+i\cdot b$.
See also	assume for example
Comments	Another way to evaluate an expression in the complex domain is to enclose the expression between the editing lines and choose **Evaluate⇒Complex** from the **Symbolics** menu.

convert, parfrac

Syntax	convert, parfrac, *var*
Description	Converts an expression to a partial fraction expansion in the variable *var*.
Example	

Expanding expressions to partial fractions

$$\frac{2 \cdot x^2 - 3 \cdot x + 1}{x^3 + 2 \cdot x^2 - 9 \cdot x - 18} \ \text{convert, parfrac, x} \rightarrow \frac{1}{[3 \cdot (x-3)]} + \frac{14}{[3 \cdot (x+3)]} - \frac{3}{(x+2)}$$

Use the "coeffs" keyword to treat an expression as a polynomial and write out the coefficients. Specify either a variable or a function as an argument to the keyword.

$$3 \cdot b \cdot x^4 - \pi \cdot x^2 + \frac{2}{3} \cdot x - .3 \cdot a \cdot b \ \text{coeffs, x} \rightarrow \begin{bmatrix} -.3 \cdot a \cdot b \\ \frac{2}{3} \\ -\pi \\ 0 \\ 3 \cdot b \end{bmatrix}$$

$$\sin(x) + 2 \cdot \sin(x)^2 \ \text{coeffs, } \sin(x) \rightarrow \begin{bmatrix} 0 \\ 1 \\ 2 \end{bmatrix}$$

Comments	The symbolic processor tries to factor the denominator of the expression into linear or quadratic factors having integer coefficients. If it succeeds, it expands the expression into a sum of fractions with these factors as denominators. All constants in the selected expression must be integers or fractions; Mathcad does not expand an expression that contains decimal points.
	Another way to convert an expression to a partial fraction is to click on the variable *var* anywhere in the expression. Then choose **Variable⇒Convert to Partial Fraction** from the **Symbolics** menu.

expand

Syntax	expand, *expr*
Description	Expands all powers and products of sums in an expression except for the subexpression *expr*. The argument *expr* is optional. The entire expression is expanded if the argument *expr* is omitted.

Expanding expressions

$$(x + y)^4 \text{ expand} \rightarrow x^4 + 4 \cdot x^3 \cdot y + 6 \cdot x^2 \cdot y^2 + 4 \cdot x \cdot y^3 + y^4$$

$$\cos(5 \cdot x) \text{ expand} \rightarrow 16 \cdot \cos(x)^5 - 20 \cdot \cos(x)^3 + 5 \cdot \cos(x)$$

$$(x + 1) \cdot (y + z) \text{ expand}, x + 1 \rightarrow (x + 1) \cdot y + (x + 1) \cdot z$$

Factoring expressions

$$8238913765711 \text{ factor} \rightarrow (73) \cdot (112861832407)$$

$$\frac{1}{x - 1} + \frac{x}{x + 3} - \frac{2 \cdot x}{x + 2} \text{ factor} \rightarrow \frac{-(2 \cdot x^2 - 9 \cdot x - 6 + x^3)}{[(x - 1) \cdot [(x + 3) \cdot (x + 2)]]}$$

$$x^2 - 2 \text{ factor}, \sqrt{2} \rightarrow (x + \sqrt{2}) \cdot (x - \sqrt{2})$$

Collecting terms

$$x^2 - a \cdot y \cdot x^2 + 2 \cdot y^2 \cdot x - x \text{ collect}, x \rightarrow (1 - a \cdot y) \cdot x^2 + (2 \cdot y^2 - 1) \cdot x$$

$$x^2 - a \cdot y \cdot x^2 + b \cdot y \cdot x - a \cdot x \cdot y \text{ collect}, x, y \rightarrow (1 - a \cdot y) \cdot x^2 + (b - a) \cdot y \cdot x$$

Comments   Another way to expand an expression is to enclose the expression between the editing lines and choose **Expand** from the **Symbolics** menu.

factor

Syntax   factor, *expr*

Description   Factors an expression into a product, if the entire expression can be written as a product.
If the expression is a single integer, Mathcad factors it into powers of primes.
If the expression is a polynomial or rational function, Mathcad factors it into powers of lower-order polynomials or rational functions. The argument *expr* is optional.

See also   expand for example

Comments   If you want to factor an expression over certain radicals, follow the factor keyword with a comma and the radicals.

You may be able to simplify an expression by factoring subexpressions, even if the expression taken as a whole can't be factored. To do so, enclose a subexpression between the editing lines and choose **Factor** from the **Symbolics** menu. You can also use the **Factor** menu command to factor an entire expression, but the **Symbolics** menu commands do not use any previous definitions in your worksheet and do not automatically update.

float

Syntax   float, *m*

Description   Displays a floating point value with *m* places of precision whenever possible. If the argument *m*, an integer, is omitted, the default precision is 20.

See also   assume for example

Comments   Another way to perform floating point evaluation on an expression is to enclose the expression between the editing lines and choose **Evaluate⇒Floating Point** from the **Symbolics** menu.
In the Floating Point dialog box, specify the number of digits to the right of the decimal point.

fourier

Syntax
: fourier, *var*

Description
: Evaluates the Fourier transform of an expression with respect to the variable *var*.

Example
:

```
Dirac (t) fourier, t   → 1          Press [Ctrl] [Shift] . to insert a transform keyword.


  3
───────  invfourier, x  →  3/2·exp(-t)·Φ(t)  +  3/2·exp(t)·Φ(-t)
      2
1 + x


exp(-a·t) laplace, t  →     1
                         ───────
                         (s + a)


   s
─────── invlaplace, s  →  -a·exp(-a·t) + Dirac (t)   ←— Dirac(t) is an impulse at t=0.
s + a                                                Although not numerically
                                                     defined, Mathcad's symbolic
                                                     processor recognizes this
sin( π/2 ·t )  ztrans, t  →      z                   function.
                             ─────────
                             (1 + z²)
                                                     (See Appendix A, "Other
   z                                                 Special Functions", for info
─────── invztrans, z  →  2ⁿ                          on the Dirac delta function.)
z - 2
```

Comments
: Mathcad returns a function of ω given by: $\int_{-\infty}^{+\infty} f(t)e^{-i\omega t}dt$ where $f(t)$ is the expression to be transformed.

  Mathcad returns a function in the variable ω when you perform a Fourier transform because this is a commonly used variable name in this context. If the expression you are transforming already contains an ω, Mathcad avoids ambiguity by returning a function of the variable $\omega\omega$ instead.

  Another way to evaluate the Fourier transform of an expression is to enter the expression and click on the transform variable. Then choose **Transform⇒Fourier** from the **Symbolics** menu.

invfourier

Syntax
: invfourier, *var*

Description
: Evaluates the inverse Fourier transform of an expression with respect to the variable *var*.

See also
: fourier for example

Comments
: Mathcad returns a function of t given by: $\frac{1}{2\pi}\int_{-\infty}^{+\infty} F(\omega)e^{i\omega t}d\omega$ where $F(\omega)$ is the expression to be transformed.

  Mathcad returns a function in the variable t when you perform an inverse Fourier transform because this is a commonly used variable name in this context. If the expression you are transforming already contains a t, Mathcad avoids ambiguity by returning a function of the variable tt instead.

  Another way to evaluate the inverse Fourier transform of an expression is to enter the expression and click on the transform variable. Then choose **Transform⇒Inverse Fourier** from the **Symbolics** menu.

invlaplace

Syntax   invlaplace, *var*

Description   Evaluates the inverse Laplace transform of an expression with respect to the variable *var*.

See also   fourier for example

Comments   Mathcad returns a function of t given by: $\dfrac{1}{2\pi i}\displaystyle\int_{\sigma-i\infty}^{\sigma+i\infty}F(s)e^{st}dt$ where $F(s)$ is the expression to be transformed and all singularities of $F(s)$ are to the left of the line $\mathrm{Re}(s) = \sigma$.

Mathcad returns a function in the variable t when you perform an inverse Laplace transform because this is a commonly used variable name in this context. If the expression you are transforming already contains a t, Mathcad avoids ambiguity by returning a function of the variable tt instead.

Another way to evaluate the inverse Laplace transform of an expression is to enter the expression and click on the transform variable. Then choose **Transform⇒Inverse Laplace** from the **Symbolics** menu.

invztrans

Syntax   invztrans, *var*

Description   Evaluates the inverse *z*-transform of an expression with respect to the variable *var*.

See also   fourier for example

Comments   Mathcad returns a function of n given by a contour integral around the origin: $\dfrac{1}{2\pi i}\displaystyle\int_{C}F(z)z^{n-1}dz$

where $F(z)$ is the expression to be transformed and C is a contour enclosing all singularities of the integrand.

Mathcad returns a function in the variable n when you perform an inverse *z*-transform since this is a commonly used variable name in this context. If the expression you are transforming already contains an n, Mathcad avoids ambiguity by returning a function of the variable nn instead.

Another way to evaluate the inverse *z*-transform of an expression is to enter the expression and click on the transform variable. Then choose **Transform⇒Inverse Z** from the **Symbolics** menu.

laplace

Syntax   laplace, *var*

Description   Evaluates the Laplace transform of an expression with respect to the variable *var*.

See also   fourier for example

Comments   Mathcad returns a function of s given by: $\displaystyle\int_{0}^{+\infty}f(t)e^{-st}dt$, where $f(t)$ is the expression to be transformed.

Mathcad returns a function in the variable s when you perform a Laplace transform since this is a commonly used variable name in this context. If the expression you are transforming already contains an s, Mathcad avoids ambiguity by returning a function of the variable ss instead.

Another way to evaluate the Laplace transform of an expression is to enter the expression and click on the transform variable. Then choose **Transform⇒Laplace** from the **Symbolics** menu.

series

Syntax   series, *var=z, m*

Description   Expands an expression in one or more variables, *var*, around the point *z*. The order of expansion is *m*. Arguments *z* and *m* are optional. By default, the expansion is taken around zero and is a polynomial of order six.

Example

Generating a series around the point x=0:

$$\ln(x + y) \text{ series}, x \;\to\; \ln(y) + \frac{x}{y} - \frac{1}{2}\cdot\frac{x^2}{y^2} + \frac{1}{3}\cdot\frac{x^3}{y^3} - \frac{1}{4}\cdot\frac{x^4}{y^4} + \frac{1}{5}\cdot\frac{x^5}{y^5}$$

Generating a series for sin(x) with order 6:

$$\sin(x) \text{ series}, x, 6 \;\to\; x - \frac{1}{6}\cdot x^3 + \frac{1}{120}\cdot x^5$$

Generating a series around the point x=1 and y=0 but show only those terms whose exponents sum to less than 3:

$$e^x + y \text{ series}, x = 1, y, 3 \to \exp(1) + \exp(1)\cdot(x - 1) + y + \frac{1}{2}\cdot\exp(1)\cdot(x - 1)^2$$

↑
Press [Ctrl] = for the equal sign.

Comments   Mathcad finds Taylor series (series in nonnegative powers of the variable) for functions that are analytic at 0, and Laurent series for functions that have a pole of finite order at 0. To develop a series with a center other than 0, the argument to the series keyword should be of the form *var=z*, where *z* is any real or complex number. For example, series, x=1 expands around the point *x*=1. Press **[Ctrl] =** for the equal sign.

To expand a series around more than one variable, separate the variables by commas. The last line in the example above shows an expression expanded around *x* and *y*.

Another way to generate a series expansion is to enter the expression and click on a variable for which you want to find a series expansion. Then choose **Variable⇒Expand to Series** from the **Symbolics** menu. A dialog box will prompt you for the order of the series. This command is limited to a series in a single variable; any other variables in the expression will be treated as constants. The results also contain the error term using the *O* notation. Before you use the series for further calculations, you will need to delete this error term.

When using the approximations you get from the symbolic processor, keep in mind that the Taylor series for a function may converge only in some small interval around the center. Furthermore, functions like sin or exp have series with infinitely many terms, while the polynomials returned by Mathcad have only a few terms (how many depends on the order you select). Thus, when you approximate a function by the polynomial returned by Mathcad, the approximation will be reasonably accurate close to the center, but may be quite inaccurate for values far from the center.

simplify

Syntax   simplify

Description   Simplifies an expression by performing arithmetic, canceling common factors, and using basic trigonometric and inverse function identities.
To control the simplification, use the following modifiers:

assume=real simplifies on the assumption that all the indeterminates in the expression are real;

assume=RealRange(a,b) simplifies on the assumption that all the indeterminates are real and are between a and b, where a and b are real numbers or infinity ([**Ctrl**]Z);

trig, simplifies a trigonometric expression by applying only the following identities:

$$\sin(x)^2 + \cos(x)^2 = 1 \qquad \cosh(x)^2 - \sinh(x)^2 = 1,$$

but does not simplify the expression by simplifying logarithms, powers, or radicals.

Example

$$\frac{x^2 - 3 \cdot x - 4}{x - 4} + 2 \cdot x - 5 \text{ simplify } \to 3 \cdot x - 4$$

$$e^{2 \ln(a)} \text{ simplify } \to a^2$$

$$\sin(\ln(a \cdot b))^2 \text{ simplify } \to 1 - \cos(\ln(a) + \ln(b))^2$$

$$\sin(\ln(a \cdot b))^2 \text{ simplify , trig } \to 1 - \cos(\ln(a \cdot b))^2$$

$$\left(2^b\right)^c \text{ simplify } \to \left(2^b\right)^c$$

$$\left(2^b\right)^c \text{ simplify , assume = real } \to 2^{b \cdot c} \quad \text{<-- Press [Ctrl] = for the equal sign.}$$

$$\sqrt{x^2} \text{ simplify } \to \text{csgn}(x) \cdot x$$

$$\sqrt{x^2} \text{ simplify , assume = RealRange}(-10, -5) \to -x \quad \text{<-- Press [Ctrl] = for the equal sign.}$$

Comments   You can also simplify an expression by placing it between the two editing lines and choosing **Simplify** from the **Symbolics** menu. This method is useful when you want to simplify parts of an expression. Mathcad may sometimes be able to simplify parts of an expression even when it cannot simplify the entire expression. If simplifying the entire expression doesn't give the answer you want, try selecting subexpressions and choosing **Simplify** from the **Symbolics** menu. If Mathcad can't simplify an expression any further, you'll just get the original expression back as the answer.

In general, when you simplify an expression, the simplified result will have the same numerical behavior as the original expression. However, when the expression includes functions with more than one branch, such as square root or the inverse trigonometric functions, the symbolic answer may differ from a numerical answer. For example, simplifying $\text{asin}(\sin(\theta))$ yields θ, but this equation holds true numerically in Mathcad only when θ is a number between $-\pi/2$ and $\pi/2$.

solve

Syntax   solve, *var*

Description   Solves an equation for the variable *var* or solves a system of equations for the variables in a vector *var*.

Examples

$$A1 = \frac{L}{r^2} + 2 \cdot C \text{ solve}, r \rightarrow \begin{bmatrix} \frac{1}{(A1 - 2 \cdot C)} \cdot \sqrt{(A1 - 2 \cdot C) \cdot L} \\ \frac{-1}{(A1 - 2 \cdot C)} \cdot \sqrt{(A1 - 2 \cdot C) \cdot L} \end{bmatrix}$$

$a := 34$

$$\frac{1}{2} \cdot x^2 + x = -2 + a \text{ solve}, x \rightarrow \begin{bmatrix} -1 + \sqrt{65} \\ -1 - \sqrt{65} \end{bmatrix} \quad \text{Use [Crtr] = for the equal sign.}$$

$$\frac{\alpha \cdot f + 1}{f - \beta} = e^{-\alpha} \text{ solve}, f \rightarrow \frac{-(1 + \exp(-\alpha) \cdot \beta)}{(\alpha - \exp(-\alpha))}$$

$$x^3 - 5 \cdot x^2 - 4 \cdot x + 20 > 0 \text{ solve}, x \rightarrow \begin{bmatrix} (-2 < x) \cdot (x < 2) \\ 5 < x \end{bmatrix}$$

$$e^t + 1 \text{ solve}, t \rightarrow i \cdot \pi \quad \text{You don't need =0 when finding roots.}$$

Figure 19-1: Solving equations, solving inequalities, and finding roots.

Using the "solve" keyword (press [Ctrl]+[Shift]+Period):

$$\begin{bmatrix} x + 2 \cdot \pi \cdot y = a \\ 4 \cdot x + y = b \end{bmatrix} \text{ solve}, \begin{bmatrix} x \\ y \end{bmatrix} \rightarrow \begin{bmatrix} \frac{1}{(-1 + 8 \cdot \pi)} \cdot (2 \cdot \pi \cdot b - a) \\ \frac{-(-4 \cdot a + b)}{(-1 + 8 \cdot \pi)} \end{bmatrix}$$

Using a solve block:

Given $x + 2 \cdot \pi \cdot y = a$ <- Use [Ctrl]= to type the equal sign.

         $4 \cdot x + y = b$

$$\text{Find}(x, y) \rightarrow \begin{bmatrix} \frac{1}{(-1 + 8 \cdot \pi)} \cdot (2 \cdot \pi \cdot b - a) \\ \frac{-(-4 \cdot a + b)}{(-1 + 8 \cdot \pi)} \end{bmatrix}$$

Figure 19-2: Solving a system of equations symbolically.

Comments   Solving equations symbolically is far more difficult than solving them numerically. The symbolic solver sometimes does not give a solution. Many problems can only be solved via numerical approach and many more yield symbolic solutions too lengthy to be useful.

Another way to solve for a variable is to enter the equation, click on the variable you want to solve for in an equation, and choose **Variable⇒Solve** from the **Symbolics** menu.

You can use either the symbolic solve keyword or a solve block, as illustrated above, to solve a system of equations symbolically. No initial guess values are necessary for symbolic schemes.

substitute

Syntax   substitute, *var1* = *var2*

Description   Replaces all occurrences of a variable *var1* with an expression or variable *var2*. Press [**Ctrl**] **=** for the equal sign.

Example

To substitute x for z in the expression below, use the "substitute" keyword and an argument indicating which variable to replace with which expression. Use [Ctrl] = for the equal sign in the argument.

$$z^2 + \frac{2}{z} \ \text{substitute}, \ z = x \quad \rightarrow \quad x^2 + \frac{2}{x}$$

Substituting f(sin(x)) for y:

$$\sqrt{1 + y^2} \ \text{substitute}, \ y = f(\sin(x)) \quad \rightarrow \quad \sqrt{1 + f(\sin(x))^2}$$

Comments   Mathcad does not substitute a variable for an entire vector or a matrix. You can, however, substitute a scalar expression for a variable that occurs in a matrix.
To do so, follow these steps:

1. Select the expression that will replace the variable and choose **Copy** from the **Edit** menu.

2. Click on an occurrence of the variable you want to replace and choose **Variable⇒Substitute** from the **Symbolics** menu. You can also use this menu command to perform a substitution in any expression.

ztrans

Syntax   ztrans, *var*

Description   Evaluates the *z*-transform of an expression with respect to the variable *var*.

See also   fourier for example

Comments   Mathcad returns a function of z given by: $\sum\limits_{n=0}^{+\infty} f(n)z^{-n}$, where $f(n)$ is the expression to be transformed.

Mathcad returns a function in the variable z when you perform a z-transform since this is a commonly used variable name in this context. If the expression you are transforming already contains a z, Mathcad avoids ambiguity by returning a function of the variable zz instead.

Another way to evaluate the z-transform of an expression is to enter the expression and click on the transform variable. Then choose **Transform$\Rightarrow$Z** from the **Symbolics** menu.

Appendices

- Special Functions
- SI Units
- CGS units
- U.S. Customary Units
- MKS Units
- Predefined Variables
- Suffixes for Numbers
- Greek Letters
- Arrow and Movement Keys
- Function Keys
- ASCII codes
- References

Special Functions

Mathcad sometimes returns a symbolic expression in terms of a function that isn't one of Mathcad's built-in functions.

You can define many of these functions in Mathcad. See the "Other Special Functions" topic in the QuickSheets of the Resource Center for examples.

The list below gives definitions for these functions. Except for Ei, erf, and Zeta, all of which involve infinite sums, and also W, you can use such definitions to calculate numerical values in Mathcad.

Function Definitions

Name	Definition

Euler's constant

$$\gamma = \lim_{n \to \infty} \left(\sum_{k=1}^{n} \frac{1}{k} - \ln(n) \right) = 0.57721566\ldots$$

Hyperbolic cosine integral

$$Chi(x) = \gamma + \ln(x) + \int_0^x \frac{\cosh(t) - 1}{t} dt$$

Cosine integral

$$Ci(x) = \gamma + \ln(x) + \int_0^x \frac{\cos(t) - 1}{t} dt$$

Dilogarithm function

$$dilog(x) = \int_1^x \frac{\ln(t)}{1 - t} dt$$

Dirac delta (unit impulse) function

$$Dirac(x) = 0 \text{ if } x \text{ is not zero.}$$

$$\int_{-\infty}^{\infty} Dirac(x) dx = 1$$

Exponential integral

$$Ei(x) = \gamma + \ln(x) + \sum_{n=1}^{\infty} \frac{x^n}{n \cdot n!} \quad (x > 0)$$

Complex error function

$$erf(z) = \frac{2}{\sqrt{\pi}} \sum_{n=0}^{\infty} \frac{(-1)^n z^{2n+1}}{n!(2n+1)} \quad \text{(for complex } z\text{)}$$

Fresnel cosine integral

$$FresnelC(x) = \int_0^x \cos\left(\frac{\pi}{2} t^2\right) dt$$

Fresnel sine integral

$$FresnelS(x) = \int_0^x \sin\left(\frac{\pi}{2} t^2\right) dt$$

Incomplete elliptic integral of the second kind

$$LegendreE(x, k) = \int_0^x \left(\frac{1 - k^2 \cdot t^2}{1 - t^2}\right)^{1/2} dt$$

Complete elliptic integral of the second kind

$$LegendreEc(k) = LegendreE(1, k)$$

Associated complete elliptic integral of the second kind

$$LegendreEc1(k) = LegendreEc(\sqrt{1 - k^2})$$

Incomplete elliptic integral of the first kind	$\displaystyle \mathrm{LegendreF}(x, k) = \int_0^x \frac{1}{\sqrt{(1 - t^2)(1 - k^2 \cdot t^2)}} dt$

Complete elliptic integral of the first kind

$$\mathrm{LegendreKc}(k) = \mathrm{LegendreF}(1, k)$$

Associated complete elliptic integral of the first kind

$$\mathrm{LegendreKc1}(k) = \mathrm{LegendreKc}(\sqrt{1 - k^2})$$

Incomplete elliptic integral of the third kind

$$\mathrm{LegendrePi}(x, n, k) = \int_0^x \frac{1}{\sqrt{(1 - n^2 \cdot t^2)}\sqrt{(1 - t^2)(1 - k^2 \cdot t^2)}} dt$$

Complete elliptic integral of the third kind

$$\mathrm{LegendrePic}(n, k) = \mathrm{LegendrePi}(1, n, k)$$

Associated complete elliptic integral of the third kind

$$\mathrm{LegendrePic1}(k) = \mathrm{LegendrePic}(n, \sqrt{1 - k^2})$$

Digamma function

$$\mathrm{Psi}(x) = \frac{d}{dx} \ln(\Gamma(x))$$

Polygamma function

$$\mathrm{Psi}(n, k) = \frac{d^n}{dx^n} \mathrm{Psi}(x)$$

Hyperbolic sine integral

$$\mathrm{Shi}(x) = \int_0^x \frac{\sinh(t)}{t} dt$$

Sine integral

$$\mathrm{Si}(x) = \int_0^x \frac{\sin(t)}{t} dt$$

Lambert W function

$\mathrm{W}(x)$ is the principal branch of a function satisfying $\mathrm{W}(x) \cdot \exp(\mathrm{W}(x)) = x$. $\mathrm{W}(n, x)$ is the nth branch of $\mathrm{W}(x)$.

Riemann Zeta function

$$\mathrm{Zeta}(x) = \sum_{n = 1}^{\infty} \frac{1}{n^x} \quad (x > 1)$$

Comments

The Psi function and Γ appear frequently in the results of *indefinite* sums and products. If you use a single variable name rather than a full range in the index placeholder of a summation or product, and you choose **Evaluate Symbolically** or another symbolic evaluation command, Mathcad will attempt to calculate an indefinite sum or product of the expression in the main placeholder. The indefinite sum of $f(i)$ is an expression $S(i)$ for which $S(i + 1) - S(i) = f(i)$.

The indefinite product of $f(i)$ is an expression $P(i)$ for which $\dfrac{P(i + 1)}{P(i)} = f(i)$.

SI Units

Base Units

m (meter), *length*   kg (kilogram), *mass*   s (second), *time*
A (ampere), *current*   K (kelvin), *temperature*   cd (candela), *luminosity*
mole or mol, *substance*

Angular Measure

$$rad = 1$$

$$deg = \frac{\pi}{180} \cdot rad$$

$$sr = 1 \cdot sr$$

Length

$$cm = 0.01 \cdot m$$
$$ft = 0.3048 \cdot m$$
$$mi = 5280 \cdot ft$$

$$km = 1000 \cdot m$$
$$in = 2.54 \cdot cm$$

$$mm = 0.001 \cdot m$$
$$yd = 3 \cdot ft$$

Mass

$$gm = 10^{-3} \cdot kg$$
$$mg = 10^{-3} \cdot gm$$
$$oz = \frac{lb}{16}$$

$$tonne = 1000 \cdot kg$$
$$ton = 2000 \cdot lb$$

$$lb = 453.59237 \cdot gm$$
$$slug = 32.174 \cdot lb$$

Time

$$min = 60 \cdot s$$
$$yr = 365.2422 \cdot day$$

$$hr = 3600 \cdot s$$

$$day = 24 \cdot hr$$

Area, Volume

$$hectare = 10^4 \cdot m^2$$
$$mL = 10^{-3} \cdot L$$

$$acre = 4840 \cdot yd^2$$
$$fl\_oz = 29.57353 \cdot cm^3$$

$$L = 0.001 \cdot m^3$$
$$gal = 128 \cdot fl\_oz$$

Velocity, Acceleration

$$mph = \frac{mi}{hr}$$

$$kph = \frac{km}{hr}$$

$$g = 9.80665 \cdot \frac{m}{s^2}$$

Force, Energy, Power

$$N = kg \cdot \frac{m}{s^2}$$
$$kgf = g \cdot kg$$
$$cal = 4.1868 \cdot J$$
$$W = \frac{J}{s}$$

$$dyne = 10^{-5} \cdot N$$
$$J = N \cdot m$$
$$kcal = 1000 \cdot cal$$
$$kW = 1000 \cdot W$$

$$lbf = g \cdot lb$$
$$erg = 10^{-7} \cdot J$$
$$BTU = 1.05506 \cdot 10^3 \cdot J$$
$$hp = 550 \cdot \frac{ft \cdot lbf}{s}$$

Pressure, Viscosity

$$Pa = \frac{N}{m^2} \qquad\qquad psi = \frac{lbf}{in^2} \qquad\qquad atm = 1.01325 \cdot 10^5 \cdot Pa$$

$$in\_Hg = 3.37686 \cdot 10^3 \cdot Pa \qquad torr = 1.33322 \cdot 10^2 \cdot Pa$$

$$stokes = 10^{-4} \cdot \frac{m^2}{s}$$

$$poise = 0.1 \cdot Pa \cdot s$$

Electrical

$$C = A \cdot s \qquad\qquad V = \frac{J}{C} \qquad\qquad mV = 10^{-3} \cdot V$$

$$kV = 10^3 \cdot V \qquad\qquad \Omega = \frac{V}{A} \qquad\qquad k\Omega = 10^3 \cdot \Omega$$

$$M\Omega = 10^6 \cdot \Omega \qquad\qquad S = \frac{1}{\Omega} \qquad\qquad mho = \frac{1}{\Omega}$$

$$H = \frac{V}{A} \cdot s \qquad\qquad \mu H = 10^{-6} \cdot H \qquad\qquad mH = 10^{-3} \cdot H$$

$$\mu A = 10^{-6} \cdot A \qquad\qquad mA = 10^{-3} \cdot A \qquad\qquad kA = 10^3 \cdot A$$

$$F = \frac{C}{V} \qquad\qquad pF = 10^{-12} \cdot F \qquad\qquad nF = 10^{-9} \cdot F$$

$$\mu F = 10^{-6} \cdot F \qquad\qquad Wb = V \cdot s$$

$$Oe = \frac{1000}{4 \cdot \pi} \cdot \frac{A}{m} \qquad\qquad T = \frac{Wb}{m^2} \qquad\qquad gauss = 10^{-4} \cdot T$$

Frequency, Activity

$$Hz = \frac{1}{s} \qquad\qquad kHz = 10^3 \cdot Hz \qquad\qquad MHz = 10^6 \cdot Hz$$

$$GHz = 10^9 \cdot Hz \qquad\qquad Bq = \frac{1}{s} \qquad\qquad Hza = 2 \cdot \pi \cdot Hz$$

Temperature

$$R = 0.556 \cdot K$$

Dose

$$Gy = \frac{J}{kg} \qquad\qquad Sv = \frac{J}{kg}$$

Luminous Flux, Illuminance

$$lm = cd \cdot sr \qquad\qquad lx = \frac{cd \cdot st}{m^2}$$

CGS units

Base Units

cm (centimeter), *length* gm (gram), *mass* sec (second), *time*
coul (coulomb), *charge* K (kelvin), *temperature*

Angular Measure

$\text{rad} = 1$

$\deg = \dfrac{\pi}{180} \cdot \text{rad}$

Length

$m = 100 \cdot cm$ $km = 1000 \cdot m$ $mm = 0.1 \cdot cm$
$ft = 30.48 \cdot cm$ $in = 2.54 \cdot cm$ $yd = 3 \cdot ft$
$mi = 5280 \cdot ft$

Mass

$kg = 1000 \cdot gm$ $tonne = 1000 \cdot kg$ $lb = 453.59237 \cdot gm$
$mg = 10^{-3} \cdot gm$ $ton = 2000 \cdot lb$ $slug = 32.174 \cdot lb$
$oz = \dfrac{lb}{16}$

Time

$\min = 60 \cdot \sec$ $hr = 3600 \cdot \sec$ $day = 24 \cdot hr$
$yr = 365.2422 \cdot day$

Area, Volume

$hectare = 10^8 \cdot cm^2$ $acre = 4840 \cdot yd^2$ $liter = 1000 \cdot cm^3$
$mL = cm^3$ $fl\_oz = 29.57353 \cdot cm^3$ $gal = 128 \cdot fl\_oz$

Velocity, Acceleration

$mph = \dfrac{mi}{hr}$ $kph = \dfrac{km}{hr}$ $g = 980.665 \cdot \dfrac{cm}{\sec^2}$

$c = 2.997925 \cdot 10^{10} \cdot \dfrac{cm}{\sec}$ $c\_ = c \cdot \dfrac{\sec}{m}$

Force, Energy, Power

$dyne = gm \cdot \dfrac{cm}{\sec^2}$ $newton = 10^5 \cdot dyne$ $lbf = g \cdot lb$

$kgf = g \cdot kg$ $erg = dyne \cdot cm$ $joule = 10^7 \cdot erg$

$cal = 4.1868 \cdot 10^7 \cdot erg$ $BTU = 1.05506 \cdot 10^{10} \cdot erg$ $kcal = 1000 \cdot cal$

$watt = \dfrac{joule}{\sec}$ $kW = 1000 \cdot watt$ $hp = 550 \cdot \dfrac{ft \cdot lbf}{\sec}$

Pressure, Viscosity

$$\text{Pa} = 10 \cdot \frac{\text{dyne}}{\text{cm}^2} \qquad \text{psi} = \frac{\text{lbf}}{\text{in}^2} \qquad \text{atm} = 1.01325 \cdot 10^5 \cdot \text{Pa}$$

$$\text{in\_Hg} = 3.38638 \cdot 10^3 \cdot \text{Pa} \qquad \text{torr} = 1.33322 \cdot 10^2 \cdot \text{Pa}$$

$$\text{stokes} = \frac{\text{cm}^2}{\text{sec}}$$

$$\text{poise} = 0.1 \cdot \text{Pa} \cdot \text{sec}$$

Electrical

These are CGS-esu units, based only on mass, length, and time. The "stat" units are defined in terms of dyne, cm, and sec.

$$\text{statamp} = \text{dyne}^{0.5} \cdot \text{cm} \cdot \text{sec}^{-1} \quad \text{statcoul} = \text{dyne}^{0.5} \cdot \text{cm} \qquad \text{statvolt} = \text{dyne}^{0.5}$$

$$\text{statohm} = \text{sec} \cdot \text{cm}^{-1} \qquad \text{statsiemens} = \text{cm} \cdot \text{sec}^{-1} \qquad \text{statfarad} = \text{cm}$$

$$\text{statweber} = \text{dyne}^{0.5} \cdot \text{cm} \qquad \text{stathenry} = \text{sec}^2 \cdot \text{cm}^{-1} \qquad \text{stattesla} = \text{dyne}^{0.5} \cdot \text{cm} \cdot \text{sec}^{-2}$$

Frequency

$$\text{Hz} = \frac{1}{\text{sec}} \qquad\qquad \text{kHz} = 10^3 \cdot \text{Hz} \qquad\qquad \text{MHz} = 10^6 \cdot \text{Hz}$$

$$\text{GHz} = 10^9 \cdot \text{Hz} \qquad\qquad \text{Hza} = 2 \cdot \pi \cdot \text{Hz}$$

Temperature

$$\text{R} = 0.556 \cdot \text{K}$$

Conversions to SI Units

$$\text{amp} = \frac{\text{c}}{10} \cdot \text{statamp} \qquad \text{volt} = \frac{\text{watt}}{\text{amp}} \qquad \text{ohm} = \frac{\text{volt}}{\text{amp}}$$

$$\text{coul} = \text{amp} \cdot \text{sec} \qquad\qquad \text{farad} = \frac{\text{coul}}{\text{volt}} \qquad\qquad \text{henry} = \text{volt} \cdot \frac{\text{sec}}{\text{amp}}$$

U.S. Customary Units

Base Units

ft (foot), *length*   lb (pound), *mass*   sec (second), *time*

coul (coulomb), *charge*   K (kelvin), *temperature*

Angular Measure

$$\text{rad} = 1 \qquad\qquad \text{deg} = \frac{\pi}{180} \cdot \text{rad}$$

Length

$$in = \frac{ft}{12}$$

$$m = \frac{ft}{0.3048}$$

$$yd = 3 \cdot ft$$

$$cm = 0.01 \cdot m$$

$$mi = 5280 \cdot ft$$

$$km = 1000 \cdot m$$

$$mm = 0.001 \cdot m$$

Mass

$$slug = 32.174 \cdot lb$$

$$oz = \frac{lb}{16}$$

$$ton = 2000 \cdot lb$$

$$kg = \frac{lb}{0.45359237}$$

$$tonne = 1000 \cdot kg$$

$$gm = 10^{-3} \cdot kg$$

$$mg = 10^{-3} \cdot gm$$

Time

$$min = 60 \cdot sec$$

$$hr = 3600 \cdot sec$$

$$day = 24 \cdot hr$$

$$yr = 365.2422 \cdot day$$

Area, Volume

$$acre = 4840 \cdot yd^2$$

$$hectare = 10^4 \cdot m^2$$

$$fl\_oz = 29.57353 \cdot cm^3$$

$$liter = 0.035 \cdot ft^3$$

$$mL = 10^{-3} \cdot liter$$

$$gal = 128 \cdot fl\_oz$$

Velocity, Acceleration

$$mph = \frac{mi}{hr}$$

$$kph = \frac{km}{hr}$$

$$g = 32.174 \cdot \frac{ft}{sec^2}$$

Force, Energy, Power

$$lbf = g \cdot lb$$

$$newton = kg \cdot \frac{m}{sec^2}$$

$$dyne = 10^{-5} \cdot newton$$

$$kgf = g \cdot kg$$

$$joule = newton \cdot m$$

$$erg = 10^{-7} \cdot joule$$

$$cal = 4.1868 \cdot joule$$

$$kcal = 1000 \cdot cal$$

$$BTU = 1.05506 \cdot 10^3 \cdot joule$$

$$watt = \frac{joule}{sec}$$

$$hp = 550 \cdot \frac{ft \cdot lbf}{sec}$$

$$kW = 1000 \cdot watt$$

Pressure, Viscosity

$$psi = \frac{lbf}{in^2}$$

$$Pa = \frac{newton}{m^2}$$

$$atm = 1.01325 \cdot 10^5 \cdot Pa$$

$$in\_Hg = 3.386 \cdot 10^3 \cdot Pa$$

$$torr = 1.333 \cdot 10^2 \cdot Pa$$

$$stokes = \frac{cm^2}{sec}$$

$$poise = 0.1 \cdot Pa \cdot sec$$

Electrical

$$\text{volt} = \frac{\text{watt}}{\text{amp}}$$

$$\text{mV} = 10^{-3} \cdot \text{volt}$$

$$\text{KV} = 10^3 \cdot \text{volt}$$

$$\text{ohm} = \frac{\text{volt}}{\text{amp}}$$

$$\text{mho} = \frac{1}{\text{ohm}}$$

$$\text{siemens} = \frac{1}{\text{ohm}}$$

$$\Omega = \text{ohm}$$

$$\text{K}\Omega = 10^3 \cdot \text{ohm}$$

$$\text{M}\Omega = 10^6 \cdot \text{ohm}$$

$$\text{henry} = \frac{\text{weber}}{\text{amp}}$$

$$\mu\text{H} = 10^{-6} \cdot \text{henry}$$

$$\text{mH} = 10^{-3} \cdot \text{henry}$$

$$\text{amp} = \frac{\text{coul}}{\text{sec}}$$

$$\mu\text{A} = 10^{-6} \cdot \text{amp}$$

$$\text{mA} = 10^{-3} \cdot \text{amp}$$

$$\text{KA} = 10^3 \cdot \text{amp}$$

$$\text{farad} = \frac{\text{coul}}{\text{volt}}$$

$$\text{pF} = 10^{-12} \cdot \text{farad}$$

$$\text{nF} = 10^{-9} \cdot \text{farad}$$

$$\mu\text{F} = 10^{-6} \cdot \text{farad}$$

$$\text{weber} = \text{volt} \cdot \text{sec}$$

$$\text{oersted} = \frac{1000}{4 \cdot \pi} \cdot \frac{\text{amp}}{\text{m}}$$

$$\text{tesla} = \frac{\text{weber}}{\text{m}^2}$$

$$\text{gauss} = 10^{-4} \cdot \text{tesla}$$

Frequency

$$\text{Hz} = \frac{1}{\text{sec}}$$

$$\text{kHz} = 10^3 \cdot \text{Hz}$$

$$\text{MHz} = 10^6 \cdot \text{Hz}$$

$$\text{GHz} = 10^9 \cdot \text{Hz}$$

$$\text{Hza} = 2 \cdot \pi \cdot \text{Hz}$$

Temperature

$$\text{R} = 0.556 \cdot \text{K}$$

MKS Units

Base Units

m (meter), *length*   kg (kilogram), *mass*   sec (second), *time*
coul (coulomb), *charge*   K (kelvin), *temperature*

Angular Measure

$$\text{rad} = 1$$

$$\text{deg} = \frac{\pi}{180} \cdot \text{rad}$$

Length

$$cm = 0.01 \cdot m \qquad\qquad km = 1000 \cdot m \qquad\qquad mm = 0.001 \cdot m$$

$$ft = 0.3048 \cdot m \qquad\qquad in = 2.54 \cdot cm \qquad\qquad yd = 3 \cdot ft$$

$$mi = 5280 \cdot ft$$

Mass

$$gm = 10^{-3} \cdot kg \qquad\qquad tonne = 1000 \cdot kg \qquad\qquad lb = 453.59237 \cdot gm$$

$$mg = 10^{-3} \cdot gm \qquad\qquad ton = 2000 \cdot lb \qquad\qquad slug = 32.174 \cdot lb$$

$$oz = \frac{lb}{16}$$

Time

$$min = 60 \cdot sec \qquad\qquad hr = 3600 \cdot sec \qquad\qquad day = 24 \cdot hr$$

$$yr = 365.2422 \cdot day$$

Area, Volume

$$hectare = 10^4 \cdot m^2 \qquad\qquad acre = 4840 \cdot yd^2 \qquad\qquad liter = (0.1 \cdot m)^3$$

$$mL = 10^{-3} \cdot liter \qquad\qquad fl\_oz = 29.57353 \cdot cm^3 \qquad\qquad gal = 128 \cdot fl\_oz$$

Velocity, Acceleration

$$mph = \frac{mi}{hr} \qquad\qquad kph = \frac{km}{hr} \qquad\qquad g = 9.80665 \cdot \frac{m}{sec^2}$$

Force, Energy, Power

$$newton = kg \cdot \frac{m}{sec^2} \qquad\qquad dyne = 10^{-5} \cdot newton \qquad\qquad lbf = g \cdot lb$$

$$kgf = g \cdot kg \qquad\qquad joule = newton \cdot m \qquad\qquad erg = 10^{-7} \cdot joule$$

$$cal = 4.1868 \cdot joule \qquad\qquad kcal = 1000 \cdot cal \qquad\qquad BTU = 1.05506 \cdot 10^3 \cdot joule$$

$$watt = \frac{joule}{sec} \qquad\qquad kW = 1000 \cdot watt \qquad\qquad hp = 550 \cdot \frac{ft \cdot lbf}{sec}$$

Pressure, Viscosity

$$\text{Pa} = \frac{\text{newton}}{\text{m}^2}$$

$$\text{psi} = \frac{\text{lbf}}{\text{in}^2}$$

$$\text{atm} = 1.01325 \cdot 10^5 \cdot \text{Pa}$$

$$\text{in\_Hg} = 3.38638 \cdot 10^3 \cdot \text{Pa}$$

$$\text{torr} = 1.33322 \cdot 10^2 \cdot \text{Pa}$$

$$\text{stokes} = 10^{-4} \cdot \frac{\text{m}^2}{\text{sec}}$$

$$\text{poise} = 0.1 \cdot \text{Pa} \cdot \text{sec}$$

Electrical

$$\text{volt} = \frac{\text{watt}}{\text{amp}}$$

$$\text{mV} = 10^{-3} \cdot \text{volt}$$

$$\text{kV} = 10^3 \cdot \text{volt}$$

$$\text{ohm} = \frac{\text{volt}}{\text{amp}}$$

$$\text{mho} = \frac{1}{\text{ohm}}$$

$$\text{siemens} = \frac{1}{\text{ohm}}$$

$$\Omega = \text{ohm}$$

$$\text{k}\Omega = 10^3 \cdot \text{ohm}$$

$$\text{M}\Omega = 10^6 \cdot \text{ohm}$$

$$\text{henry} = \frac{\text{weber}}{\text{amp}}$$

$$\mu\text{H} = 10^{-6} \cdot \text{henry}$$

$$\text{mH} = 10^{-3} \cdot \text{henry}$$

$$\text{amp} = \frac{\text{coul}}{\text{sec}}$$

$$\mu\text{A} = 10^{-6} \cdot \text{amp}$$

$$\text{mA} = 10^{-3} \cdot \text{amp}$$

$$\text{kA} = 10^3 \cdot \text{amp}$$

$$\text{farad} = \frac{\text{coul}}{\text{volt}}$$

$$\text{pF} = 10^{-12} \cdot \text{farad}$$

$$\text{nF} = 10^{-9} \cdot \text{farad}$$

$$\mu\text{F} = 10^{-6} \cdot \text{farad}$$

$$\text{weber} = \text{volt} \cdot \text{sec}$$

$$\text{oersted} = \frac{1000}{4 \cdot \pi} \cdot \frac{\text{amp}}{\text{m}}$$

$$\text{tesla} = \frac{\text{weber}}{\text{m}^2}$$

$$\text{gauss} = 10^{-4} \cdot \text{tesla}$$

Frequency

$$\text{Hz} = \frac{1}{\text{sec}}$$

$$\text{kHz} = 10^3 \cdot \text{Hz}$$

$$\text{MHz} = 10^6 \cdot \text{Hz}$$

$$\text{GHz} = 10^9 \cdot \text{Hz}$$

$$\text{Hza} = 2 \cdot \pi \cdot \text{Hz}$$

Temperature

$$\text{R} = 0.556 \cdot \text{K}$$

Predefined Variables

Mathcad's predefined variables are listed here with their default starting values.

Constant=Value	Meaning
$\pi = 3.14159...$	Pi. Mathcad uses the value of π to 15 digits. To type π, press [**Ctrl**][**Shift**]**p**.
$e = 2.71828...$	The base of natural logarithms. Mathcad uses the value of e to 15 digits.
$\infty = 10^{307}$	Infinity. This symbol represents values larger than the largest real number representable in Mathcad (about 10^{307}). To type ∞, press [**Ctrl**][**Shift**]**z**.
$\% = 0.01$	Percent. Use in expressions like **10*%** (appears as $10 \cdot \%$) or as a scaling unit at the end of an equation with an equal sign.
CTOL $= 10^{-3}$	Constraint tolerance used in solving and optimization functions: how closely a constraint must be met for a solution to be considered acceptable.
CWD = "[system path]"	String corresponding to the working folder of the worksheet.
FRAME = 0	Counter for creating animation clips.
in$n$ = 0	Input variables (**in0**, **in1**, etc.) in a Mathcad component in a MathConnex system. See the *MathConnex User's Guide* for details.
ORIGIN = 0	Array origin. Specifies the index of the first element in arrays.
PRNCOLWIDTH = 8	Column width used in writing files with *WRITEPRN* function.
PRNPRECISION = 4	Number of significant digits used when writing files with the *WRITEPRN* function.
TOL $= 10^{-3}$	Tolerance used in numerical approximation algorithms (integrals, equation solving, etc.): how close successive approximations must be for a solution to be returned. For more information, see the sections on the specific operation in question.

Suffixes for Numbers

The table below shows how Mathcad interprets numbers (sequences of alpha-numerics beginning with a number and ending with a letter).

Radix

Suffix	Example	Meaning
b, B	100001b	Binary
h, H	8BCh	Hexadecimal
o, O	1007o	Octal

Units and other

Suffix	Example	Meaning
i or j	4i, 1j, 3 + 1.5j	Imaginary
K	–273K	Standard absolute temperature unit
L	–2.54L	Standard length unit
M	2.2M	Standard mass unit
Q	–100Q	Standard charge unit
S	6.97S	Standard substance unit in SI unit system
T	3600T	Standard time unit
C	125C	Standard luminosity unit in SI unit system

Note Because Mathcad by default treats most expressions involving a number followed immediately by a letter to mean implied multiplication of a number by a variable name, you will need to backspace over the implied multiplication operator to create expressions like **4.5M**.

Greek Letters

To type a Greek letter into an equation or into text, press the Roman equivalent from the table below, followed by [**Ctrl**]**G**. Alternatively, use the Greek toolbar.

Name	Uppercase	Lowercase	Roman equivalent
alpha	A	α	A
beta	B	β	B
chi	X	χ	C
delta	Δ	δ	D
epsilon	E	ε	E
eta	H	η	H
gamma	Γ	γ	G
iota	I	ι	I
kappa	K	κ	K
lambda	Λ	λ	L
mu	M	μ	M
nu	N	ν	N
omega	Ω	w	W
omicron	O	o	O
phi	Φ	φ	F
phi (alternate)		φ	J
pi	Π	π	P
psi	Ψ	ψ	Y
rho	P	ρ	R
sigma	Σ	σ	S
tau	T	τ	T
theta	Θ	θ	Q
theta (alternate)	ϑ		J
upsilon	Y	υ	U
xi	Ξ	ξ	X
zeta	Z	ζ	Z

Note The Greek letter π is so commonly used that it has its own keyboard shortcut: [**Ctrl**][**Shift**]**P**.

Arrow and Movement Keys

Keys	Actions
[↑]	Move crosshair up. In math: move editing lines up. In text: move insertion point up to previous line.
[↓]	Move crosshair down. In math: move editing lines down. In text: move insertion point down to next line.
[←]	Move crosshair left. In math: select left operand. In text: move insertion point one character to the left.
[→]	Move crosshair right. In math: select right operand. In text: move insertion point one character to the right.
[PgUp]	Scroll up about one-fourth the height of the window.
[PgDn]	Scroll down about one-fourth the height of the window.
[Shift][↑]	In math: move crosshair outside and above expression. In text: highlight from insertion point up to previous line.
[Shift][↓]	In math: move crosshair outside and below expression. In text: highlight from insertion point down to next line.
[Shift][←]	In math: highlight parts of an expression to the left of the insertion point. In text: highlight to left of insertion point, character by character.
[Shift][→]	In math: highlight parts of an expression to the right. In text: highlight to right of insertion point, character by character.
[Ctrl][↑]	In text: move insertion point to the beginning of a line.
[Ctrl][↓]	In text: move insertion point to the end of a line.
[Ctrl][←]	In text: move insertion point left to the beginning of a word.
[Ctrl][→]	In text: move insertion point to the beginning of next word.
[Ctrl][↵]	Insert a hard page break. In math: insert addition with line break operator. In text: set the width of the text region.
[Ctrl][Shift][↑]	In text: highlight from insertion point up to the beginning of a line.
[Ctrl][Shift][↓]	In text: highlight from insertion point to end of the current line.
[Ctrl][Shift][←]	In text: highlight left from insertion point to the beginning of a word.
[Ctrl][Shift][→]	In text: highlight from insertion point to beginning of the next word.
[Space]	In math: cycles through different states of the editing lines.
[Tab]	In text: moves the insertion point to the next tab stop. In math or plot: move to next placeholder.
[Shift][Tab]	In math or plot: move to previous placeholder.
[Shift][PgUp]	Move up to previous pagebreak.
[Shift][PgDn]	Move down to next pagebreak.
[Home]	Move to beginning of previous region. In text, move to beginning of current line.
[End]	Move to next region. In text, move to end of current line.

[**Ctrl**][**Home**]	Scroll to beginning of worksheet. In text, move insertion point to beginning of text region or paragraph.
[**Ctrl**][**End**]	Scroll to end of worksheet. In text, move insertion point to end of text region or paragraph.
[↵]	In text: start new line. In equation or plot: move crosshair below region, even with left edge of region.

Function Keys

Keys	Actions
[**F1**]	Help.
[**Shift**][**F1**]	Context sensitive help.
[**F2**]	Copy selected region to clipboard.
[**F3**]	Cut selected region to clipboard.
[**F4**]	Paste contents of clipboard.
[**Ctrl**][**F4**]	Close worksheet or template.
[**Alt**][**F4**]	Close Mathcad.
[**F5**]	Open a worksheet or template.
[**Ctrl**][**F5**]	Search for text or math characters.
[**Shift**][**F5**]	Replace text or math characters.
[**F6**]	Save current worksheet.
[**Ctrl**][**F6**]	Make next window active.
[**Ctrl**][**F7**]	Inserts the prime symbol (').
[**F7**]	Open a new worksheet.
[**F9**]	Recalculate a selected region.
[**Ctrl**][**F9**]	Inserts blank lines.
[**Ctrl**][**F10**]	Deletes blank lines.

Note These function keys are provided mainly for compatibility with earlier Mathcad versions. Mathcad also supports standard Windows keystrokes for operations such as file opening, [**Ctrl**]O], and saving, [**Ctrl**]S], copying, [**Ctrl**]C], and pasting, [**Ctrl**]V]. Choose **Preferences** from the **View** menu and check "Use standard Windows shortcut keys" on the General tab to enable all Windows shortcuts.

ASCII codes

Decimal ASCII codes from 32 to 255. Nonprinting characters are indicated by "*npc*."

Code	Character	Code	Character	Code	Character	Code	Character	Code	Character
32	[space]	80	P	130	‚	182	¶	230	æ
33	!	81	Q	131	*f*	183	·	231	ç
34	"	82	R	132	„	184	¸	232	è
35	#	83	S	133	…	185	¹	233	é
36	$	84	T	134	†	186	º	234	ê
37	%	85	U	135	‡	187	»	235	ë
38	&	86	V	136	^	188	¼	236	ì
39	'	87	W	137	‰	189	½	237	í
40	(	88	X	138	Š	190	¾	238	î
41	)	89	Y	139	‹	191	¿	239	ï
42	*	90	Z	140	Œ	192	À	240	ð
43	+	91	[	141–4	*npc*	193	Á	241	ñ
44	,	92	\	145	'	194	Â	242	ò
45	-	93	]	146	'	195	Ã	243	ó
46	.	94	^	147	"	196	Ä	244	ô
47	/	95	_	148	"	197	Å	245	õ
48	0	96	`	149	•	198	Æ	246	ö
49	1	97	a	150	–	199	Ç	247	÷
50	2	98	b	151	—	200	È	248	ø
51	3	99	c	152	~	201	É	249	ù
52	4	100	d	153	™	202	Ê	250	ú
53	5	101	e	154	š	203	Ë	251	û
54	6	102	f	155	›	204	Ì	252	ü
55	7	103	g	156	œ	205	Í	253	ý
56	8	104	h	157–8	*npc*	206	Î	254	þ
57	9	105	i	159	Ÿ	207	Ï	255	ÿ
58	:	106	j	160	*npc*	208	Ð		
59	;	107	k	161	¡	209	Ñ		
60	<	108	l	162	¢	210	Ò		
61	=	109	m	163	£	211	Ó		
62	>	110	n	164	¤	212	Ô		
63	?	111	o	165	¥	213	Õ		
64	@	112	p	166	¦	214	Ö		
65	A	113	q	167	§	215	×		
66	B	114	r	168	¨	216	Ø		
67	C	115	s	169	©	217	Ù		
68	D	116	t	170	ª	218	Ú		
69	E	117	u	171	«	219	Û		
70	F	118	v	172	¬	220	Ü		
71	G	119	w	173	-	221	Ý		
72	H	120	x	174	®	222	Þ		
73	I	121	y	175	¯	223	ß		
74	J	122	z	176	°	224	à		
75	K	123	{	177	±	225	á		
76	L	124			178	²	226	â		
77	M	125	}	179	³	227	ã		
78	N	126	~	180	´	228	ä		
79	O	127–9	*npc*	181	µ	229	å		

References

Abramowitz, M., and I. Stegun. *Handbook of Mathematical Functions*. New York: Dover, 1972.

Devroye, L. *Non-uniform Random Variate Distribution*. New York: Springer-Verlag, 1986.

Friedman, J. H. "A Variable Span Smoother." *Tech Report No. 5*. Laboratory for Computational Statistics. Palo Alto: Stanford University.

Geddes, K. and G. Gonnet. "A New Algorithm for Computing Symbolic Limits Using Generalized Hierarchical Series." *Symbolic and Algebraic Computation (Proceedings of ISSAC '88)*. Edited by P. Gianni. From the series *Lecture Notes in Computer Science*. Berlin: Springer-Verlag, 1989.

Golub, G. and C. Van Loan. *Matrix Computations*. Baltimore: John Hopkins University Press, 1989.

Knuth, D. *The Art of Computer Programming: Seminumerical Algorithms*. Reading: Addison-Wesley, 1997.

Lorczak, P. *The Mathcad Treasury*. A MathSoft Electronic Book. Cambridge: MathSoft, Inc.

Nash, J.C. *Compact Numerical Methods For Computers*. Bristol: Adam Hilger Ltd., 1979.

Niven, I. and H. Zuckerman. *An Introduction to the Theory of Numbers*. New York: John Wiley & Sons, 1972.

Press, W.H., W.T. Flannery, S.A.Teukolsky, and B.P.Vetterling. *Numerical Recipes in C*. Cambridge University Press, New York, 1992.

Polak, E. *Optimization – Algorithms and Consistent Approximations*. New York: Springer-Verlag, 1997.

Singleton, R. *Communications of ACM*. Vol. 11, no. 11. November, 1986.

Wilkinson, J.H. and C. Reinsch. *Handbook for Automatic Computation*. Vol. II, *Linear Algebra*. New York: Springer-Verlag, 1971.

Winston, W. *Operations Research: Applications and Algorithms*. Belmont: Wadsworth, 1994.

Index

built-in variables 103
bulleted paragraphs 62
Bulstoer function 324
bulstoer function 324
business functions 183
bvalfit function 196, 325
CAD drawings 306
Calc on message line 123
calculation 14
    controlling 122
    disabling for individual equation 124
    equations 14, 103
    locking area 91–92
    order in worksheets 103
    result format 115
    units in 118
calculator, using Mathcad as 12
calculus operators
    definite integral 458
    derivative 460
    indefinite integral 460
    left-hand limit 462
    limit 462
    nth derivative 461
    product 457
    range product 458
    range sum 457
    right-hand limit 462
    summation 456
calling Mathcad from other applications 314
Cauchy distribution 334, 389, 398, 404
ceil function 326
Celsius 114, 120
CFFT function 327
cfft function 326
CGS units 119, 490
characters, deleting or inserting in math 46
Chebyshev polynomials 439
Chi function 486
chi-squared distribution 335, 390, 398, 404
cholesky function 328
Ci function 486
Clipboard 53, 270
closing a worksheet 20
closing Mathcad
    See exiting Mathcad
CMP (colormap) files 202
cnorm function 176
cnper function 328
coeffs keyword 263, 475
Collaboratory 22, 29

collapsing an area 92
collect keyword 263, 475
colon (:) as definition symbol 13, 101
color
    Electronic Book annotation 24
    equation highlight 89
    in equations 55
    in text 61
    of worksheet background 89
color images
    displaying 69
    reading 200
color palettes for bitmaps 73
colormap 367, 427
colormap files 202, 249
cols function 328
column vectors
    See vectors
combin function 329
combinatorics functions 155
    combin function 329
    permut function 390
combining matrices
    augment function 322
    stack function 432
common logarithm 369
complex conjugate 133, 451
complex keyword 262, 476
complex numbers
    arg function 321
    conjugate 133
    csgn function 332
    determining angle 133
    display of 117
    entering 36
    Im function 357
    imaginary unit symbol 117
    magnitude of 133
    operators and functions for 133, 156
    Re function 404
    real and imaginary parts 133
    signum function 429
    vector field plots 244
complex threshold 117
Component Wizard 298
components
    application-based 297
    customizing 310
    inserting 298
    overview of 297
    redistributing 310

series 263
series keyword 263, 480
Shi function 487
Show Border option 73
Si function 487
sigma (summation symbol) 136
    for vector 136
sign function 429
signum function 429
Simplify command 270
simplify keyword 262, 270, 481
simultaneous equations, solving 344, 387
simultaneous equations, solving numerically 164, 167
sin function 429
sine integral 487
sinfit function 429
singular matrix 370
singular value decomposition 437–438
sinh function 429
skew function 430
skewness 430
slope function 430
SmartSketch component 77, 306
smooth systems (differential equations) 193
smoothing functions
    ksmooth function 362
    medsmooth function 377
    supsmooth function 437
smoothing of data 183
soft page breaks 90
solve block 344, 387
solve blocks 167, 187
    constraints in 169
    definition of 168
    expressions allowed in 169
    finding multiple solutions 170
    Given in 168
    reports for 172
    tolerance 171
    using to solve differential equations 187
    using to solve numerically 168
    using to solve symbolically 277
Solve command 483
solve keyword 263, 275–276, 482
Solving and Optimization Extension Pack 168
solving equations 167
    AutoSelect of algorithm 171
    linear systems 171
    nonlinear systems 171
    See also solve blocks
    with *root* function 166

    with solve blocks 167, 277
    with Solve for Variable 275
    with solve keyword 275
solving functions
    Find 344
    Find function 387
    Maximize function 374
    Minerr function 379
    Minimize function 381
    polyroots function 393
    root function 422
sorting functions 165
    csort function 332
    reverse function 413
    rsort function 426
    sort function 165, 431
sorting vectors and matrices 165
space curves
    creating 239
    See also plots, 3D
spaces, inserting or deleting 87
special functions 156
    eff function 338
    erf function 339
    erfc function 339
    fhyper function 343
    Γ function 445
    Her function 352
    ibeta function 355
    Jac function 360
    Lag function 363
    Leg function 364
    mhyper function 379, 393
    other
        complete elliptic integral
            of the first kind 487
            of the second kind 486
            of the third kind 487
        complex error function 486
        cosine integral 486
        digamma 487
        dilogarithm 486
        Dirac delta 486
        Euler's constant 486
        exponential integral 486
        Fresnel cosine integral 486
        Fresnel sine integral 486
        hyperbolic cosine integral 486
        hyperbolic sine integral 487
        incomplete elliptic integral
            of the first kind 487